CHICKENS' LIB

CHICKENS' LIB

The story of a campaign

by Clare Druce

Bluemoose

Copyright © Clare Druce

First published in 2013 by
Bluemoose Books Ltd
25 Sackville Street
Hebden Bridge
West Yorkshire
HX7 7DJ

www.bluemoosebooks.com

British Library Cataloguing-in-Publication data
A catalogue record for this book is available from the British Library

Hardback   ISBN 13: 978 0 9575497 2 2

Printed and bound in the UK by Jellyfish Solutions Ltd

Every effort has been made to obtain the necessary permissions with
reference to copyright material, both illustrative and quoted. We apologise
for any omissions in this respect and will be pleased to make the appropriate
acknowledgements in any future edition.

Photographs courtesy of the author and Chickens' Lib, unless otherwise stated.

To Duncan,
With my love, and thanks for unfailing support.

CONTENTS

PROLOGUE

It's 1977, the year of the Queen's Silver Jubilee, and Great Britain celebrates. There's been nothing like it since the coronation. The *Sunday Times Magazine* (January 30th) publishes four pages of *Hellos* and *Goodbyes*, a selection of significant comings and goings since 1952.

There's 'Hello' to Dr Jonas Salk's polio vaccine, and 'Goodbye' to Ceylon (but 'Hello Sri Lanka'). 'Goodbye' to freedom, after Hungary's 1956 failed uprising, and 'Hello' to the world's first heart transplant. And it's 'Hello' to Chickens' Lib.

The caption below a photo of hens crammed into battery cages reads: *'Hens lost out and found themselves trapped in batteries. Chickens' Lib was founded in 1973.'*

In fact, this tiny pressure group, with no proper structure let alone a constitution, had emerged a few years earlier, but it wasn't until 1973 that we came up with a cracking good name.

Oh how the media *loved* Chickens' Lib!

LONDON DAYS

Parliament Square

June 27th 1971: Rain is falling, a steady, cold summer rain.

The Press Association's been alerted. We've told them about our protest, said the two of us would be here at 11 o'clock, next to the Canning statue in Parliament Square, with a mock battery cage complete with four live ex-battery hens.

I bend down and tweak the plastic shrouding the cage. The birds mustn't get wet. They're pathetic enough, without the rain adding to their troubles. Pale combs, scant feathers, the flesh around all four vents an angry red.

We desperately need the media's help, but a full hour has passed. We're losing hope.

"What if we're in the wrong place?" I say.

My mother fishes out our press release and checks. Thank God! We've not done anything stupid.

"They're just not interested," she says. "Nobody cares."

"Give it another half hour," I say.

*

Five minutes later two figures appear through the gloom and rain, one shouldering a serious-looking camera. Oh, thank goodness we didn't pack the hens back into the van and head for home.

If we had, we'd have missed the *Guardian*.

*

That same afternoon: The rain had cleared and London basked in hot sunshine. Still in Parliament Square, we'd erected our cage for people, six feet high and constructed of wood and wire netting. Placards on all four sides challenged Agriculture Minister Jim Prior to take action to end the birds' suffering.

Five human prisoners stood quietly inside. There was Dr Alan Long, tireless campaigner for a vegan diet, Yvonne Anderson from the Farm and Food Society, Violet and me – and our star guest the writer Ernest Raymond, whose 1920s novel *Tell England* had been a runaway best seller. Perhaps the most powerful among his later books is *We the Accused*, a dark compassionate story about capital punishment. Violet and I felt honoured to share a cage with Ernest Raymond.

Parliament Square was buzzing now and bemused Londoners and tourists stopped to stare, many of them supportive. On a fold-up table we gathered hundreds of signatures for our petition to Prime Minister Ted Heath. Best of all, a reporter and photographer from the Press Association turned up.

The next day we buy the *Guardian*, feverishly turn the pages. And we're in! Reporter Martin Adeney's article is excellent: '*A chicken with wings stripped of feathers gave powerful support in Parliament Square yesterday to the campaign against factory farming, which is demanding a meeting with Mr Heath to present its case for more humane treatment of farm animals. The chicken, its neck rubbed apparently by bars so that it looked like a victim of alopecia, was one of four bought the previous day from a battery farm and lodged together in a cage 20x17x18 inches...When* [the caged hens] *tried to change about, one at least got squashed and pecked... usually the one with wings without feathers...A leaflet handed out said:* "Many battery hens suffer from respiratory diseases or cancer. The eggs they lay in these fetid conditions probably come to you labelled 'farm fresh' or 'new laid'. After slaughter, the spent layers, so often diseased, still have their uses. They may become your baby's tinned dinner, chicken paste, or just a tin of soup."' There's a good big picture of the hens too, peering out through the cage bars.

Bars? In fact they're knitting needles, not even all of the same gauge, my father's inventive substitute for the real thing. Eccentric our homemade cage may be, but it's correct in all the important features, including floor slope. (Years later the *Guardian* ran a general article on factory farming, illustrated with a photo of caged hens. We studied it: something wasn't quite right with the bars. Ah! The knitting needles again.)

The Press Association has done its good work too. The image of five caged humans receives wide media coverage even, we discover later, in a German newspaper.

How it all began

So how did my mother and I come to be there, just the two of us standing beside the Canning statue, on that wet June morning in 1971?

It was like this:

Three or four years previously, I'd come upon Ruth Harrison's 1964 book *Animal Machines*, a disturbing exposé of how the post-war quest for cheap food had led to 'factory farming', that cocktail of cruelty to animals and danger to human health.

Shocked, I lent the book to my mother, Violet Spalding. She'd always had a gut feeling for sustainability, long before it was fashionable, lamenting the loss of topsoil, aware of the role of the earthworm. On reading *Animal Machines* she was as appalled as I'd been. We wondered what, if anything, we could do.

We contacted Ruth Harrison, who told us about The Farm and Food Society (FAFS), a small but influential organisation well known for valuable research into all aspects of farming, its moving force Joanne Bower.

At that time our two daughters were small and my husband was working as a BBC music producer. By now he was increasingly involved in the London contemporary music scene and it was hard for me to get out in the evenings. So Violet attended FAFS meetings on behalf of us both and was soon invited onto its committee, where she made long-lasting friendships, especially with Joanne.

But before long Violet's impatient nature got the better of her. I was feeling frustrated too, and we wondered about a change of tactics. Could we perhaps 'go it alone' in some way, and so add a new dimension to present-day campaigning? After some discussion, we decided on our way forward.

*

For fact finding, we'd already put our faith in the power of the pen. Here are two examples of responses to some of our early letters:

September 10th 1969: Ernest Shippam, Managing Director of Shippam's pastes, wrote to say he would have no problem in taking the Person of the Lord Jesus Christ round his factory, there to discuss the pros and cons of how the company obtained its raw materials.

September 29th 1969: A spokesman for H.J. Heinz Company Limited confirmed that 'spent' battery hens were included in its chicken baby foods, that the meat wasn't tested for residues of antibiotics and that no checks were made for the presence of Marek's disease, a form of cancer.

There's no proof that Marek's can be transferred to humans, but who'd want to risk feeding their baby chicken meat possibly contaminated with chicken cancer?

*

Already, we'd made an important decision: we'd limit our campaign to the plight of battery hens. Being obtainable and transportable, their extreme deprivation would be the easiest to highlight: hens trapped for life in metal cages, forced to stand on sloping wire, living in semi-darkness, unable to take a normal step *ever.* Surely these images would resonate with the public?

I dislike the term 'battery hen'. It seems to suggest a breed of hen ideally suited to imprisonment, while nothing could be further from the truth. But I'll use the term throughout as a form of shorthand.

*

When *Animal Machines* was published in 1964, around 80% of UK hens were incarcerated in cages, with their numbers increasing. By early 1969 our protest letters were landing on the desks of civil servants and Government officials, fired off from Violet's home in Croydon and mine in West London. Back came the replies, re-assuring, bland and misleading:

July 15th 1969: The Minister's Private Secretary wrote, in response to our complaints: *'I am sure that it would be true to say that this country holds a place second to none in the wealth of legislation to protect the welfare of animals.'* We reflected that fine words butter no parsnips, legislation being useless if millions of animals continued to suffer.

Worse was to follow: *'It is true that a valuable export trade in live poultry and hatching eggs has been developed in the last few years. The poultry and eggs that we export are valuable breeding stock and it is greatly in the interest of those who import them that they should be kept in excellent condition in the importing countries.'* No mention here of the likelihood of lower standards in those countries, or, worse still, a complete lack of welfare laws.

Months passed, merging into years. Names became depressingly familiar, as the same civil servants were instructed to fend us off. Eventually, our patience snapped. There was only one thing for it! We'd beard the pen pushers in their hitherto safe hide-out, the Department of Obfuscation aka the Ministry of Agriculture, Fisheries and Food (MAFF), Government Offices, Block E, Leatherhead Road, Chessington, in Surrey.

But first we needed the evidence.

To the East End

May 6th 1973: Violet and I, with my children in tow, set out for the Petticoat Lane area in London's East End. We'd been told that on pavements in certain streets we'd find filthy black plastic crates stacked high, crammed with skinny, often semi-naked end-of-lay battery hens, stinking of the sheds from which they'd recently been wrenched. Here they awaited ritual slaughter in the back rooms of butchers' premises.

It was Sunday and we'd expected the City to be quiet, but soon ran into crowds of football fans. Hanging on tight to the children we pressed on, following our noses. Soon we spotted the teetering crates and smelled the hens at close quarters. Alison, my elder daughter, turned pale and threatened to throw up in the gutter.

Feisty Violet offered to go into the shop alone. She hardly looked a typical customer but her presence could be commanding. If anyone was going to brazen this one out, it was my mother.

Five minutes later she emerged, lugging a bloodstained paper sack stuffed with four hens. We felt guilty. Would the hens be all right? Our overriding thought had been to act casually before making a quick getaway. Suitable containers would have aroused suspicion. But thank God the sack was sturdy, and somehow the hens found their own level. Once out of sight of the shop we made sure they had enough air.

The sack was surprisingly heavy, and we decided to take a taxi back to where we'd left the van, near the Bank of England.

Alison was worried. "But what will you say, Mamma, if the taxi driver asks what's that awful smell?"

"I shall say it is *me*," Violet replied regally.

In the event, the cabby took the situation in his stride, no questions asked.

*

Back in Barnes, the outside lavatory in Elm Bank Gardens awaited our four little hens. They ate hungrily (it's commonplace to starve poultry for twelve hours or more, prior to slaughter) and drank deeply. Then, with many peaceful clucking sounds, they sank down on a thick layer of straw to enjoy the most comfortable night's sleep they'd ever known.

The invasion

Early next morning I opened the door to the back garden full of trepidation. Would our hens have survived?

To my huge relief they seemed fine, bright-eyed and eager for breakfast. Just before Violet was due I packed them carefully into the mock cage, feeling again the warmth of their bodies, the roughness of exposed skin, the spikiness of broken feathers. Putting them back in the cage seemed like the worst betrayal. If only I could explain that it was in their own interest – or at least in the interest of millions of others like them.

Violet arrived and we set off under a forget-me-not blue sky. Once into rural Surrey, the hedges were snowy with blackthorn. We felt well prepared for our mission, excited even: we'd alerted the Press Association, and the twice-weekly *Surrey Comet* had shown interest, agreeing to send along a reporter and photographer. The arrangement was for us to meet them at the entrance to the Government Offices.

We parked the van near a range of dull red brick buildings, shared by the Ministry of Agriculture, Fisheries and Food's Animal Health HQ and the Ministry of Defence. Before lifting the cage out, we draped it with a clean white cloth (in fact an old sheet). If challenged, we'd say we were bringing specimens for – and here we'd mention a particular civil servant, her name by now all too familiar to us. The deception just might waft us past Reception.

The Surrey Comet Two were ready and waiting, a young female reporter and an older male photographer, his state-of-the-art camera surely shouting PRESS! Together, the four of us (eight, including the hens) entered the building, only to find the reception desk unmanned. In fact there was nobody in sight. Not a living soul.

We spotted notices pointing the way to MAFF, so we made our way briskly along corridors, past offices labelled Ministry of Defence, past open doors revealing unattended desks. Thoughts of abstracting one or two files marked *Top Secret* flitted through my mind as, with the Surrey Comet Two hot on our heels, Violet and I staggered on. A cage containing four hens weighs heavy.

Once sure we were well into MAFF territory we stopped the first person we saw, saying we had specimens to deliver to our civil servant.

"Just wait here," the young man said, and very soon the woman in question appeared. Now for our *coup de théâtre*. With a flourish we whipped away the cloth, revealing our four featherless 'specimens'.

Instantly, the woman tumbled to the horrible truth. A demonstration! Within MAFF itself! Actual *livestock* defiling Animal Health. Was nowhere safe? This was a situation calling for swift action!

Promising that someone would be sent to see us, our pen pusher beat a hasty retreat.

*

A few moments later Mr Foreman appeared and showed us into his office. We knew him to be a senior civil servant and Chair of the Farm Animal Welfare Advisory Committee (FAWAC). As backup, Mr Jackson, a Veterinary Officer, was quickly drafted in.

Since our numbers were so small, the Surrey Comet Two were assumed to be fellow demonstrators, a misunderstanding that suited us very well.

Carefully we lowered the hens' cage onto the floor, setting it down next to a tall grey filing cabinet. On Mr Foreman's spacious desk there was a coffee cup, suggestive of more relaxed times when no rude interruptions disturbed a serious morning's work.

Irritably, the hens pecked at each other, while Violet and I went over well-worn ground, the difference being that now we were here in person, with the degraded, living proof of our complaints before all our eyes. Surely, we argued, to keep hens, known for being busy from dawn to dusk, caged up, each allotted an area of floor space a good deal smaller than a sheet of A4 paper... surely this was cruel? And, if cruel, then illegal?

The Men from the Ministry wheeled out their predictable platitudes, though Violet and I agreed later that we'd detected a faint wave of sympathy from Mr Jackson. Perhaps he disliked the system as much as we did, but was hardly at liberty to speak his mind. Not if he wanted to keep his job.

Some way into the proceedings, the photographer prepared for action, squinting down his camera, struggling to get everything into the frame— the MAFF men, Violet and me *and* the hens – no easy feat.

Alarmed, Mr Foreman spoke sharply. "I insist that no photographs are taken in my office!"

With a vague, reassuring gesture the photographer indicated that he wouldn't dream of doing anything so underhand, yet he snapped away just the same. Mr Foreman's courage seemed to desert him and he let it all happen.

Suddenly, and without a word, our young reporter sidled out of the room. We all ignored this strange behaviour.

Desperate for something positive to say, Mr Foreman addressed Mr Jackson in low tones: would it perhaps be in order, we heard him mutter, to show us the prototype of an alternative to the battery cage, namely the Getaway Cage? Mr Jackson thought this a good idea and, once the proposal had been formally put to us, we said yes, we'd be interested to see it. Inwardly, we thought the name ridiculous and had low expectations of anything with the word 'cage' in its description.

The Getaway Cage turned out to be a larger version of the battery cage, but with a lot more height, and perches added at various levels. We studied it for a few moments.

"But what about birds on the lower levels?" I asked. "Surely those on the high perches would defecate on those below?"

An awkward pause followed my practical query, before it was admitted that this potential problem had yet to be addressed.

We began to weary, sensing it was time to say goodbye. We'd made our points, exhibited the hens and arrived at the usual *impasse.* We all shook hands (the remaining phoney demonstrator included), veiled the hens once more and were shown out into the corridor, there to be re-united with our young reporter

She explained that the sight of the semi-naked hens pecking at each other had made her feel sick and faint. MAFF staff had found her in the corridor, pale and trembling, and kindly plied her with hot sweet tea.

*

The next day we took the hens to the home of Vivienne Jenkins, a new and dedicated supporter of ours. Vivienne, a talented artist, lived in a charming cottage in Hampton Wick with a cream-coloured whippet and a pale and glamorous ferret named Marilyn Monroe.

So four lucky little birds were spared ritual slaughter in the back room of a reeking butcher's shop. Vivienne's pretty garden was mostly down to lawn and apple trees: now, for the very first time, the hens would feel grass under their feet, roam around at will, seeking out insects and herbs, and be able to lay their eggs in seclusion. Fortunately it was springtime, giving time for their feathers to re-grow before the weather turned cold.

*

May 9th 1973: Brilliant publicity in the *Surrey Comet.* Our demo had made the headlines, and billboards throughout Surrey proclaimed FACTORY FARM ROW. INVASION ON MINISTRY. Two photographs half-filled the front page, one a group scene, the other a close-up of the hens. *'Angry Ban Battery Farming protestors invaded the Ministry of Agriculture at Chessington on Monday – and dumped a crate of emaciated hens on startled civil servants. Their shock move came after demands for a probe into factory farming had been ignored,'* ran the story.

We felt hopeful. The battery system had been shown up for what it is, and in the very heart of Officialdom. Surely, change must be on its way.

*

June 18th 1973: This time a group of six activists, with Violet and me representing the hens, paid a second surprise visit to Chessington. We held up large photographs, one of caged hens, the other of crated veal calves. We'd come to deliver a letter demanding an inquiry into factory farming.

June 20th: *'Second Siege on Factory Farming'* reported the *Surrey Comet,* below a photograph taken outside the Government Offices, the six of us lined up in blazing June sunshine. Violet was quoted: *'An employee to whom we spoke at the gate agreed with us about factory farming methods and said "My God, they live in sheer agony. I've seen it." '*

Again, and with hindsight I would say naively, we felt we'd made real headway.

Update:

In Chickens' Lib's January 1988 fact sheet, fifteen years after our first shock visit to MAFF, we were able to report official confirmation of our fears for the Getaway Cage: *'Getaway Cages: Studies in Sweden on cages with perches at various levels, nests and sandbaths had shown disadvantages,*

particularly in terms of hygiene, inspection possibilities and egg quality.'
(Farmers Guardian, April 29th 1988)

Years later, *Poultry World* (April 2001) quoted poultry specialist Andrew Walker as deeming the Getaway Cage 'flawed' when put to the test. But loyal Mr Walker was at pains to forgive any lack of foresight for the invention's ultimate failure which *"in no way reflects badly on those scientists and advisers who put much intellectual effort into these designs."*

All that research, to prove what Basil Fawlty would have called the bleeding obvious. A pity nobody listened to us, back in 1973...

Blood running in the gutters

July 23rd 1973: Elizabeth Dunn, Editor of *Checkout,* the *Guardian's* consumer column, paid a visit to the East End: *'Cobb Street is not for the squeamish. It smells of old sawdust, entrails, rotting feathers, and worse. Checkout's intrepid reporter had never actually seen blood running in the gutters before and it came as something of a shock. Mrs Spalding and her ladies are familiar figures around Cobb Street...'*

Ms Dunn described her reception at the second shop she visited: *'At Wallers next door, they were a bit friendlier. They were unloading their chickens... Why were they all bald, we asked. And why, when they fell on the pavement, couldn't they get up? "They're seconds," Wallers' man said, cheerily.'*

Blood running in the gutters! Now something *must* be done! All those squalid shops would surely be closed down. We alerted Mr Foreman, able now to picture our letter resting in his in-tray. His reply, dated August 2nd, gave room for a little short-lived hope: *'...Finally, thank you for providing the information gained in the course of your visit to the Petticoat Lane area on 13th July. The local authority concerned is being informed of your complaint, in collaboration with the Department's local officers, to take appropriate action.'*

Sadly, it turned out that the local authority's idea of 'appropriate action' was to threaten to prosecute one of our supporters.

The criminal in question was Kathleen Graham, a forthright lady, then in her mid-sixties, described in a newspaper report as a travelling salesman. Kathleen was afraid of nothing when it came to the protection of animals. (Secretly, Violet and I had christened her 'The Bulldog.') Kathleen lived in rural Kent, and had a large garden. She would come with us on demos, taking hens home with her at the end of the day to restore them to health. She was also known to have given sanctuary to ex-battery hens bought from Sevenoaks market, and Kent County Council had Kathleen in its sights. Technically, such birds must be slaughtered within forty eight hours of purchase.

Never mind the blood running in East End gutters, never mind the callous attitudes on farms and in markets – it was Kathleen's blood the authorities were after.

*

August 1973: Kathleen's local paper reported: *'A knock on the door of Mrs Kathleen Graham of Broad Oak, Heathfield, on Friday confirmed her belief that she could be in trouble with the law by giving a new home to three battery hens which friends bought at a Kent market. Her visitors were a police officer and two officials of Kent County Council's Estate and Valuation Department (diseases of animals inspection)* [one official for each little hen?] *who explained that battery hens sold on the open market must be slaughtered within 48 hours of sale. A staunch opponent of battery farming, Mrs Graham is determined to keep the birds, thanked the men for their visit and is now waiting to hear if she is to be taken to court.'*

August 31st 1973: The *Sussex Express* made Kathleen front-page news. Under the heading *'Would rather go to court than have hens taken away'* Kathleen was quoted as saying: *'I am quite prepared to go on breaking the law. I don't give a hoot.'*

That's the spirit, Kathleen, we said when we read the cuttings she'd sent us. The battery hen needs people like you.

And Chickens' Lib is born

August 1973. Scene: the lofty vestibule of the *Daily Telegraph* offices in Fleet Street (Wapping and Canary Wharf not as yet dreamed of). Half a dozen women and one elderly disabled man cluster around the familiar cage, from which four semi-naked hens peer out, viewing their strange new world with interest. We're here to draw attention to what we've chosen to call Barnes Action Group, and we're tired out. For hours we've been carrying the cage around the streets of London, saying the same thing over and over again: *'These are battery hens. 80% of all UK laying hens live like this. Please don't buy battery eggs.'*

Despite our long day, Violet is in fighting form.

"We want to speak to a reporter about these hens," she explains in ringing tones to the woman on reception.

Noting the cage, the woman looks surprised, livestock not generally being a feature of life in Fleet Street.

"This is an important issue, a story of calculated cruelty," insists Violet.

The woman raises an eyebrow and puts through a call to Newsroom. Carefully we lower the cage, hoping the feed and water or, much worse, smelly wet droppings, won't spill out onto the gleaming floor. We prepare to wait.

A couple of minutes later a reporter appears. Neither bright-eyed nor seeming hopeful of a scoop he looks at us wearily, before listening half-heartedly to our complaints. When we admit to the name Barnes Action Group he's dismissive.

"You'll never get anywhere with a name like that."

Downcast, we shuffle our aching feet. Violet and I, suddenly aware that he's absolutely right, feel ashamed. What complete amateurs we are!

"What then?" Violet wonders aloud. "Chickens' Lib?"

"Spot on! Perfect!" our cynical reporter cries.

Suddenly he's seeing us in a new light.

*

No media coverage followed our visit to the *Daily Telegraph* but now we had a name to be proud of. Everyone knew what Women's Lib meant and, as we were about to find out, the media loved our new name. Catchy, with a light touch yet deadly serious, in just two words it said it all.

OXFORDSHIRE DAYS

To the country

January 1974: After eight years in Barnes, the last four or so busy with demonstrations on behalf of the battery hen, my family had tired of the racket of air traffic heading for Heathrow. A plane thundering overhead meant putting your phone conversation on hold until the worst of the noise had faded. We didn't get used to it, as some people do. And lovely though it was to have the river Thames just at the end of our road, and good as it had been for Duncan's work, with Barnes Bridge station a minute away, convenient for Waterloo and the South Bank, we took the rash decision to leave.

We found a cottage in a charming Cotswold village. For Alison there was a middle school nearby, a mile's walk over fields, knee-deep in buttercups in May, while Emily attended one of the smallest surviving schools in England, just a few doors from our home. When the school closed two years later, it numbered ten pupils and one teacher, the about-to-retire headmistress. With a single classroom and a cosy coke-fired stove in winter, Emily's early schooling had the air of a chapter from the past.

But there were downsides to this idyllic way of life. Duncan, by now a free-lance violinist, spent a lot of time travelling back to London, or abroad, touring with The Fires of London. And then – cruel irony! – Brize Norton, a military airport six miles or so from our village, became the base for pilots training to fly Concord. Lying in bed in the early mornings we could hear the hum of aircraft engines revving and, if you put your hand on a windowpane when the great beast was passing, the glass vibrated ominously. On one occasion a large chunk of a neighbour's ceiling came down.

Concord notwithstanding, for the next four years we did enjoy many aspects of country life. Our cat Chippy, London born and bred and one-time brave catcher of river rats, had come with us and settled down happily, and for the first time we had a dog, and then two. Our village had no street lighting, and the stars shone brightly at night. The sweet scent of wood smoke filled the air on winter evenings, and snowdrops grew in profusion under hedgerows.

Only a year after we'd moved out of London my parents followed us, having found a cottage some three miles from ours. So once again, Violet and I could get down to Chickens' Lib work properly, together.

Whitehall's had enough

April 3rd 1974: Before Violet left Croydon she took two featherless battery hens to Whitehall accompanied by Kathleen (Bulldog) Graham, Vivienne Jenkins and another woman supporter. Violet told me afterwards that things had turned ugly: they'd been pushed roughly down the steps by a strong-armed MAFF official.

Reported the Birmingham Post, of April 4th: 'MINISTRY RUFFLES "CHICKENS' LIB" FEATHERS *Four housewives and two tattered battery hens were forcibly removed from the Ministry of Agriculture in Whitehall Place, London, yesterday. The women, members of Chickens' Lib, had been trying to see Mr Fred Peart, the Minister, to persuade him to hold a public enquiry into factory farming, particularly as it affects hens which spend their lives in battery cages...As the women entered the Ministry, doormen and security officers rushed at them. Struggling fiercely, the women were forced into the street.'*

The *Daily Telegraph* of the same date told a subtly different tale: *'Four housewives carrying a cage with two tattered chickens in it were escorted from the Ministry of Agriculture's Whitehall headquarters yesterday after trying to confront Mr Peart...'*

Interesting, the way language can distort the emphasis. In DT-speak, the women were 'escorted' away (a charming word, suggestive of chivalry) while the women attempted to 'confront' Mr Peart, the word casting them in an aggressive light...

'Them ministers is a cunning lot'

Disgusted by the evasive letters coming from MAFF, one of our supporters (whose first language wasn't English) contacted us in a fit of exasperation: *'Them Ministers is a cunning lot!'* she wrote. And we were inclined to agree.

*

July 15th 1974: Miss Ann Evans, replying to Chickens' Lib on behalf of the Minister's Parliamentary Secretary, came up with a novel explanation for the pitiful nakedness of millions of 'spent' battery hens: *'The hardy breeds of bird usually kept on free range are normally more heavily feathered than the hybrids which have been evolved for intensive conditions of controlled environment. This may go some way towards explaining the difference in appearance between the two types...'*

So there we had it, on authority. Battery hens are semi-naked because they've no need for feathers in the battery sheds. Battery hens are of a special breed, designed to be free from those oppressively warm feathers.

*

August 14th 1974: Edward Bishop, Minister of State for MAFF gave Chickens' Lib the brush-off: *'Dear Mrs Spalding, Mr Moyle told me about his talk with you in June when you showed him some chickens. I am confident that I am entirely familiar with the detail of your representations and while I greatly respect your concern in this matter, I doubt that another meeting would be helpful...there is no evidence that intensive husbandry systems are necessarily detrimental to animal welfare, and we have adequate statutory powers to deal with offenders.'*

How these 'offenders' were to be identified was not made clear. We feared that most battery hens lived out their lives unobserved by anyone in authority.

*

March 19th 1976: Gavin Strang, Parliamentary Secretary to the Minister of Agriculture, wrote to John Stanley, MP, to mollify one of Mr Stanley's constituents, a supporter of Chickens' Lib: *'In one of her letters Mrs Spalding refers to the unorthodox methods used by her group to obtain hens for demonstration purposes. The group admitted that the hens which they produced to the ministry, as evidence of bad conditions in battery houses, had been purchased from premises in the Petticoat lane area of London and at other markets where birds are sold for immediate slaughter. Such birds have their tail feathers clipped back as required by law, and as they are often in a moult they present a bedraggled appearance. Moulting is a normal process in poultry which occurs under any system of management when birds reach the end of lay, and it does not reflect any ill-treatment.'*

Since those far-off days, I've observed many hens in a natural moult. Not one of them has made me think of an animal version of a concentration camp victim.

In fact, feather pecking in cages is the direct result of confinement, when hens can no longer forage for their own food. Dr Karen Davis, an American campaigner for respect for chickens, describes caged hens' frustrations thus: *'The hens' genetically-based foraging behaviour must have an outlet that in cages becomes misdirected against cage mates, because the bodies of the other hens is the only soft, flexible, biteable material in the metal, wire, or plastic prison.'* (1)

*

September 3rd 1976: More from Parliamentary Secretary Gavin Strang, to Anthony Grant, MP, this time, and yet another attempt to pull wool over the eyes of one of our supporters: *'...Normally it is not profitable for producers to keep battery hens after the age of 70-76 weeks when they cease to lay at an economic level, but most of the birds are in excellent bodily condition when they are sent for slaughter.'* Wrong, Mr Strang! Vast numbers of battery hens suffer from brittle bone disease, more properly known as osteoporosis, that dread disease of the elderly. As long ago as 1948 *Picture Post* ran an article by L.F. Easterbrook: *'...But can it really be true that birds kept under these unnatural conditions, without exercise, without exposure to the sun and the wind and rain...often with bones so brittle that they will snap like dry twigs...can it really be true that the eggs they produce for us are just as nourishing as eggs from birds kept very differently?'*

It's the almost total lack of ability to move, plus the huge demand on the hen's reserves of calcium (to form egg shell) that ruin her bones; the modern hen lays an egg most days – compare this with the 150 laid annually by pre-war hens. Thirteen years after Mr Strang's claim, research at Bristol's AFRC Institute of Food Research was to confirm that 24% of battery hens, sampled from eight separate battery farms, had broken bones by the time they were removed from cages prior to slaughter, while breaks occurring after transport and slaughter reached almost 100%. (2)

Mr Strang had probably asked advice before shooting his 'excellent bodily condition' line. It would be interesting to know the name of the poultry 'expert' who misinformed him. Or did Mr Strang simply pluck the notion out of the air, hoping thereby to keep us quiet?

Mercifully, the media were by now sitting up and taking notice, and offering our campaign much-needed support.

So what went wrong, down on the farm?

In Britain, the debasement of poultry farming started in earnest back in the late 1940s, in response to the post-war quest for cheap and plentiful food, following years of shortages. Suddenly, sustainable systems were no longer valued. Dazzled by the possibilities of genetic selection for fast growth in meat animals, and unnaturally high yields of eggs, agriculture experts turned their backs on traditional wisdom. At the same time, near-total automation was becoming a reality.

The concept of systems that suited the behavioural needs of the animals was cast aside. Maximum production in the shortest possible time became the order of the day, with the additional, and huge, economic benefits to the farmer of a drastically reduced workforce. At the same time manufacturers of veterinary drugs, and perhaps veterinarians themselves, were glimpsing a bright future – intensive systems would surely breed diseases calling for mass medication.

Not everyone, however, was fooled by post-war 'progress'. In 1948 an item appeared in *The Farmers Weekly* of April 2nd under the heading 'Science Gone Mad'.

'There was such strong criticism against a proposal for the poultry battery laying system at the Essex Institute of Agriculture's farms that Essex Education Committee last week decided to refer the matter back for further consideration.

Mr A L Shepherd said that this system of egg production condemned the hens to "permanent imprisonment in small cages."

Mr S S Wilson: "It is an example of science gone mad. It makes the bird a mere machine."

...Supporting the system, Mr S G Haskins said they had been assured by experts that they could not have a balanced course in poultry at the Institute without a battery system.'

I expect the 'experts' got their way, down in Essex. Certainly the battery system was taking off fast. Perhaps the most disastrous aspect of this sorry story has been the unwavering support intensive farming has received from government. Worse still, intensive systems and know-how have been enthusiastically exported worldwide.

In the early 1970s I attended a lecture by Fritz Schumacher, author of the influential book *Small is Beautiful.* Factory farming, he said, was the last thing needed by populations in developing countries. Factory farming drastically reduced the need for farm workers, with many now driven off the land and into the cities, there to suffer the miseries of unemployment, while farming lost all hope of sustainability.

*

Britain, famously a nation of animal lovers, naturally felt obliged to keep up appearances. Laws to protect animals must seem to be present and correct, and they continued to be passed.

As Violet and I delved ever deeper into the subject, we began to understand that the UK was guilty of enacting welfare legislation and codes of practice that *included* inherent suffering, thereby legalising it. This country, along with others, has indeed dug itself deep into a bottomless, merciless pit.

Bit by bit, Chickens' Lib realized that simply revealing the suffering for all to see was not enough. The need was for the basic legal framework to be challenged, a need that remains urgent to this day.

Over the last few decades, legislation relating to farmed animals has been updated many times. This book is not for those concerned with complicated points of law, past and present. My intention is to expose and simplify the crux of the problem.

I will merely highlight the fact that, while purporting to represent progress, even the updated animal welfare acts of the twenty-first century will, unless practices are radically changed, serve only to illustrate the same old double standards.

Cruelty enshrined in law

The campaign waged against the pathetic state of birds delivered to East End butchers' shops was ongoing, sustained by various animal rights' groups based in and around London. In March 1975 the *Evening Standard* highlighted the problem, accompanying the article with a photograph of those faeces-encrusted poultry crates stacked up on the pavement. An exhausted battery hen crouched nearby, on deformed feet. After a graphic description of local squalor, reporter Jillian Robertson told how the RSPCA had sent an inspector to Cobb Street and Leyden Street, all to no avail: *"The inspector found the chickens to be in bodily condition comparable to those of all hens kept in batteries" said a spokesman* [for the RSPCA] ***"Such conditions are not in breach of legislation currently in force*** [Chickens' Lib's emphasis] *and the society cannot prosecute. We are extremely concerned with certain aspects of intensive animal husbandry. We have set up the Farm Livestock Advisory Committee which is currently looking into the question of battery farming."*

So the RSPCA's hands were tied, apparently, by the very legislation drawn up to protect animals. How could it be that cruelty to farmed animals, obvious to any sensitive child, could yet be deemed 'not in breach of legislation currently in force'?

The above conundrum will be a recurring theme throughout this book.

A breakthrough

Summer 1975: We're in luck! Our application for a slot in BBC 2's *Open Door*, a make-your-own programme initiative, has been approved. We'll be 'lent' a television crew and producer, but the script and cast will be up to us. Allotted only ten minutes, we're to share the programme with two other groups (one of them dedicated to belief in UFOs).

*

Our producer Roger Brunskill turned out to be as helpful as could be. Gradually, Violet and I worked out a script, having decided we must have live hens in the studio: battery hens to illustrate the cage system, with a control group of healthy free range birds. We would describe the cruel frustration of a hen's natural behavioural patterns, the diseased state of millions of birds, antibiotic over-use, official lack of concern...

And, in good time, we must find our hens, ready for their star parts.

*

Thursday October 9th 1975: the two-hour long evening rehearsal at Television Centre in Wood Lane proved hellish. We (that's Violet, Vivienne, Reg Johnson, a good amateur actor friend, and me) were nervous. All except Reg fluffed our lines. We'd tried to learn our parts so we could do without scripts, but the evening proved how risky that might be on Saturday, when the programme would go out *live*.

For the rehearsal, some of the crew were trainees, and got things wrong. We'd provided photos of politicians past and present, with whom we had bones to pick, for example Mrs Thatcher, and Peggy Fenner, Parliamentary Secretary to the Agriculture Minister. The trainees managed to get several images upside down first time around, which added to the feeling that our programme was destined to be a shambles. The whole thing was shot in black and white and looked dreary in the extreme. We came away terrified.

Worse was in store. The following evening, transfixed with horror, I watched a trailer. In optimistic tones the announcer told viewers that three women from Chickens' Lib would be featured the following day, on Open Door. TV library pictures of the outside of huge battery sheds filled the screen, accompanied by excerpts from Beethoven's Pastoral Symphony (dramatic irony there). It all looked so smooth, so totally professional. But we'd not done it yet. There'd only been yesterday's ghastly rehearsal.

A friend rang and told me about a previous *Open Door*. Apparently a contributor had given up in despair, buried his head in his hands, and groaned 'Oh Christ!'

A pity she mentioned that.

*

Saturday October 11th 1975: Adrenalin must have flowed in bucketsful, for we all seemed on good form, hens included. We converged at the TV Centre lugging rolls of wire netting, with the 'good' and 'bad' hens in separate containers.

Once in the studio, we put the street-wise free rangers in one pen, hoping they wouldn't turn flighty, and the sad-looking ex battery ones in the other one. We'd just realized we'd be allowed to have scripts on our knees, so that was a huge comfort, though we hoped to do no more than glance at them.

Then it was time to begin.

*

Reg started off, playing a man about to enjoy his breakfast egg when he lit upon an article in the newspaper he was leafing through. It was telling it how it was. *'More like the dark ages. No natural daylight ever,'* Reg commented, reading on, with mounting disgust, that antibiotics were routinely given to battery hens. Finally, *'I think I'm going off the idea of this egg,'* he sighed. *'How do I know these antibiotics aren't part of my daily ration too?'* He pushed the egg away.

Next, Violet described Chickens' Lib's beginnings, and told viewers that 80% of all British eggs now came from battery farms. She described dishonest advertising, and the pathos of a battery hen's living conditions.

Now Vivienne took over. Gently she removed the battery hens from the cage, calmly placing them in one of the hastily constructed enclosures. They looked shocking, yet entirely typical of 'spent' battery hens. She spoke of Cage Layer Fatigue (a common cause of mortality), and of feather pecking by fellow prisoners, so severe as to cause death. She mentioned how we'd raised these subjects with Mr Moyle, then Parliamentary Secretary to Fred Peart. He'd asked *'How do we know it's cruel? I should want a scientific report before I make up my mind.'* She added: 'Incidentally, we invited Mr Peart the Minister of Agriculture and his henchman Mr Bishop to confront us in this studio today but unfortunately they both declined.'

Then it was over to me and I described some of our activities – our attempts to influence MAFF, our need to grab the attention of the media, how we were still demanding an impartial enquiry into factory farming.

After that, Reg read from two MAFF letters we'd received: *'This Department spent a whole year planning different flooring for battery cages,'* and: *'The Ministry has considered advising lighting in batteries being made mandatory, so that stockmen can see the hens.'*

I pointed out that our country's egg production was now in the hands of businessmen, not farmers, and claimed that the argument that this country could not provide enough farm land for free range egg production was a myth.

By way of a challenge to the Ministry of Agriculture, Violet concluded: *'We suggest that your refusal to sanction a public inquiry stems from the fear of what would be revealed. Monsieur Lardinois, the EEC Farm Minister, has publicly stated that he would like to see battery cages banned in all EEC countries. Chickens' Lib was heartened to read this and will continue to work for this ideal in this country.'*

She ended our programme with an appeal to the viewers: '*Will you help us to eradicate this crime against the animal kingdom?*'

And it all went wonderfully well! No fluffing of lines. No upside down Mrs Thatcher. We were in gorgeous colour and both lots of hens stayed within their little coops. Oh what a huge, what a *fantastic* relief! It was all over.

For the next week or two letters of support came flooding in, some enclosing donations.

Our *Open Door* marked the beginning of national support.

*

October 23rd 1975: '*Mrs Druce (and Mum) to the rescue*' ran the sarcastic heading in *Poultry World*. Disgust was expressed that we'd had: '*...ten minutes peak viewing time on the BBC2 programme for minority groups, Open Door.*' *PW* reported how an outraged Neville Wallace, Director General of the British Poultry Federation, had written to Sir Charles Curran, DG of the BBC, to complain about the programme, claiming that: '*... the corporation would never let the industry make such a programme without the opponents of intensive farming being allowed to state their case.*'

Well, tough, Mr Wallace. Just for once, we'd had it all our own way.

*

In the same volume of *Poultry World* we spotted an item headed '*The cost of chickens' lib*' (no capitals, please, we thought – we're generic). In the article, Dr David Wood-Gush of Edinburgh's Poultry Research Centre had told the industry: '*Animal welfare agitators are going to cost the industry money. They were also strengthening their lobby with scientific data on a ground swell of new research.*'

And that was all true. Scientists everywhere were embarking on careers in 'poultry welfare', much of it involving the study of cruel practices that a decent person could recognise as such, at a glance. Some ideas for projects were downright bizarre. Take this example: Professor Trevor Morris of Reading University yearned for a new kind of hen: '*Breeders should be working towards a "throwaway" hen that starts laying at around eleven weeks of age. Such early maturity would slash working capital requirement and please bank managers.'* (1)

In time we came to realise that the findings of much research would come in useful, if only to back up what we already knew, that a hen has retained every one of the instincts of her distant ancestor the junglefowl, and that intensive systems breed intractable problems all their own.

Our *Open Door* also sparked off criticism (kindly meant, I think) from the Director of the Enteric Reference Laboratory, part of the Central Public Health Laboratory. Violet had written to him with a query about antibiotic growth promoters, only to be told by Dr Anderson that, so far, there was no indication that they could cause harm to man. His letter dated September 9th 1975 ended: *'A word of warning! Please do not let fly on television unless you are sure of your facts!'* Future developments were to prove that Chickens' Lib was in sound command of the facts.

Man-made suffering

Despite several years of campaigning, neither Violet nor I had yet ventured inside a battery unit. All our knowledge of the system had been gleaned from literature, official advice to farmers, or hearsay. All the hens we'd known personally had been intercepted *en route* to slaughter.

We had at least chatted with one Oxfordshire battery farmer, glimpsing rows of caged hens as we stood on the threshold of one of his units, while he told us how he'd not had any kind of official inspection in seventeen years, nor did he expect one, ever.

Now that we were country dwellers, the time had come to face up to real life, as lived inside the sheds.

*

We'd recently heard of a large battery egg farm on the outskirts of Birmingham. Not too far, then, from our homes in Oxfordshire.

It was school holidays, and the children would have to come too. Perhaps not an ideal family day out, but they didn't complain. (At around that time, Alison had wondered aloud how it would be to live in a family that wasn't running a pressure group; I hadn't detected resentment, just idle curiosity.)

Most expeditions with me at the wheel involved getting seriously lost, and this one was no exception. Eventually, after several of what became known in my family as 'footling circles' we found the place: endless rows of dreary, windowless grey sheds stretching into the distance, holding captive many thousands of hens. Perhaps millions, for this was big business. Like a sick joke, the 'show' shed, the one nearest to the road, had pink climbing roses trained around its door.

We tracked down the boss, a cheery enough fellow, apparently doing very nicely out of all those hens. He wouldn't sell to us, his reason being that no flock was near enough to slaughter age; but it seemed this was a family business, with satellite farms in the area. Obligingly, he phoned through to one of these, telling a woman called Sheila to let us 'young ladies' have a few end-of-lay hens. With this introduction, we set off again, full of renewed optimism.

The August sun beat down, and the countryside just got better and better. Our destination turned out to be an old farmhouse built of mellow red brick, standing well back from the road, while in front of it crouched a range of low, forbidding battery sheds. We went up to the house, knocked on the door (rousing several dogs to frenzy) and waited nervously. Finally a woman opened the door and we said our piece, not forgetting to mention Sheila's name.

'Sheila? You'll find her over there,' said the woman, pointing to the sheds. 'Just give her a shout.'

We'd noticed two people working in the first one; probably the woman was our Sheila. Things were going well.

*

We expected a horrible scene, anticipated being outraged, but nothing had prepared us for this. A large open-topped tank stood near the door, full almost to overflowing with evil smelling slurry, around which clouds of flies swarmed. Tattered hens were crammed into their cages, some almost featherless, jostling for space, trying hopelessly to move around. The feeling of stress in the fetid air was tangible.

I experienced a powerful and quite unexpected reaction. I knew then that I'd have infinitely preferred witnessing a natural disaster, the aftermath of an earthquake, for example. I'd have rather been among victims of leprosy, even, because at least then I wouldn't have had to think that people had wilfully caused this terrible suffering. The misery we were seeing was man-made. It was unnecessary and despicable.

Despite our shock, we remembered to sound casual, to show no emotion. Could she spare us four hens, just for the garden?

"That's fine," said Sheila. "The boss phoned, said you were on your way."

We steeled ourselves not to look around too eagerly. If Sheila became suspicious she just might change her mind and show us the door.

But she didn't. She grabbed four of the pitiful, protesting hens from one of the cages, put them in our boxes, and took the money. In no time, we were outside once again, into the blessed daylight.

Afternoon sun was enhancing the beauty of the old house, and the fields and hedges. Back in the car, we remarked how ironic it was that this hellish 'farm' should be set amid such surroundings.

*

The children were bearing up well, and so were the hens, so, keen not to miss out on any publicity, we made our way to the offices of the local paper, the *Redditch Indicator*. Soon we were entering the newspaper's foyer, only to be quickly directed into an empty staff kitchen. I expect we looked a queer lot, and probably the hens still reeked of the battery. Maybe we did too, though Violet and I were too tired to notice, or to care.

A handsome young reporter soon appeared, to hear us out. Elegantly, he hoisted himself onto a draining board (chairs being in short supply) and began to take notes. Then, a good sign we thought, he arranged for a photographer to take pictures.

*

August 26th 1977: The *Redditch Indicator* ran an article, alongside a good sized photo of our hens, explaining that they were destined for a trip to Whitehall Place, to back up our argument about the cruelty of the cage system. The newspaper must have contacted MAFF, for the account concluded: *'However, a Ministry spokesman told the Indicator this would serve little purpose and he could not guarantee that anyone in London would even look at the hens...The group will not name the farm where they bought the birds. Mrs Druce says it is pointless victimising one establishment when the conditions there are duplicated all over the country.'*

27

Perhaps this reticence on my part had raised the editor's suspicions, for whenever the word 'rescued' appeared in the article, it was in speech marks. Perhaps he assumed we'd stolen the hens.

We didn't mind one way or the other what people thought, but did hope Sheila had spotted the article.

*

October 9ᵗʰ 1977: *The Times* newspaper featured our visit to Sheila's hens. The journalist got a few things wrong, but the spirit of the article was sympathetic. He reported my description of the hens' home-coming, how one little hen had straightaway pecked at the grass before falling on her side, yet continued to peck away, despite not having the strength to get back on her feet.

A visual aid for Parliament

In January 1978, just a few months after our first face-to-face encounter with caged hens, we produced sheets of paper measuring 19" x 15" (48 x 38 cms), representing the floor space in a typical battery cage for four hens. *'It is argued that batteries for hens are an economic necessity. The same was said of the slave trade,'* ran the wording on each sheet.

We suggested our supporters send letters of complaint to the Agriculture Minister, John Silkin, and to their own MPs, using our cage-sized sheets to write on. When folded into four, it became painfully clear that the floor area allotted to each hen was considerably smaller than a sheet of A4 paper.

What couldn't show up on paper was the slope of the cage floor, designed to ensure that eggs roll away as soon as laid. The birds must grip this sloping metal grid, day in, day out. With no exercise, claws get long (sometimes growing round the cage floor itself) and feet become deformed.

Neither could we indicate how the droppings fall through this grid, to obviate the need for manual cleaning. Often, moving belts between the tiers of cages carry the faeces away regularly, but sometimes the mechanism fails, and faeces build up under the hens' feet, making a mockery of the argument that battery cages are hygienic. In 'deep pit' systems, droppings accumulate below the bottom-most cages for a year. If birds escape (as sometimes they do) they can fall into these pits, gradually sinking into the semi-liquid slurry, there to drown.

We gave our supporters the option of writing to Mr Silkin's home address in London SW1, a pleasant area, well away from the stink of the battery shed.

*

It was depressing to see, a decade later, that farmers' attitudes hadn't changed. Ted Kirkwood, NFU spokesman on poultry matters, and a battery farmer himself, had this to say on Central Television when describing a typical day in the life of a battery hen, as he saw it : '*...once a hen has pecked about she'll walk to the back of the cage, settle down and have another rest. If she fancies an egg is in the offing she will stand up to lay... then she sits down again, and she can preen a little bit if she wants to do, but generally all they want to do is just sit back and watch the world go by. They've all the other hens in the cage, they're all talking, you can tell by the noise they're making if they're happy...*'. (1)

Compare Ted Kirkwood's 'observations' with the following, a doctor's eye-witness account of life on the slave ships, included in a report put before Parliament as part of the long struggle to ban one of the darkest times in British history: '*The only exercise of the men-slaves is their being made to jump in their chains; and this, by the friends of the trade, is called dancing.*' (2)

Chickens' Lib's next investigation was to involve us in one of the strangest chapters in the entire campaign.

The nuns' story

On February 1978, a stranger telephoned Violet. She'd been shocked to hear that an order of nuns was engaged in running a battery egg farm, just outside Daventry. Please investigate, she begged.

Violet contacted the Convent of Our Lady of the Passion, and spoke to a Sister Regina. An appointment was readily made for Chickens' Lib to visit, a week hence. Only when Violet had hung up did she realize she'd left no contact details for us. We decided this omission might be to our advantage. Should the Mother Superior object to the plan, as well she might, our visit could not easily be cancelled.

*

The appointed day dawned raw and cold – typical March weather. I picked Violet up, and we drove to Daventry full of wonder at the concept of battery-farming nuns.

The convent occupied a large Victorian house in a pleasant rural setting, the scene now marred by two low, windowless sheds, set near to the house. As we made our way up the drive we detected that musty, sickening smell.

Sister Regina herself welcomed us, leading us into a large, sparsely furnished room, for coffee and biscuits. Around the walls posters boasted the Apollo moon shot, the rocket thrusting upwards, ever upwards, symbol of America's limitless power... It soon emerged that most of these nuns were American.

We were told how they'd travelled to Britain from Kentucky fourteen years earlier, under the misapprehension that they'd be welcomed into a religious community (the finer points of the tale escaped us). Finding themselves mistaken, and consequently homeless, they had cast around for a *modus vivendi*. They eventually lit upon this large house with land, and a poultry feed company eager to set them up in the intensive egg business.

Sister Regina showed us some beautiful long-case clocks (she'd made the cases herself) and wooden toys she'd carved. We suggested that with such skills in evidence, she and her sister nuns might survive by means other than battery farming, but our suggestion fell on stony ground.

She seemed keen to talk, explaining that the nuns were Sisters of St Paul of the Cross, a contemplative order, founded in Italy over two hundred years ago. She told us how, when they first took up residence here, the nuns owned scarcely anything beyond what they stood up in. The room where we were having coffee had remained unfurnished for quite a while, save for the introduction of a few deck chairs and a gramophone. By good fortune, one of the nuns had a record of Tchaikovsky's Sixth Symphony, the Pathétique. Settled in the deck chairs, they'd whiled away many an evening, she said, to the strains of this music.

"That must have been a bit depressing," I ventured.

"Oh no!" she replied, misty eyed. "It was *just beautiful!*"

Time was passing, and we were no nearer to seeing the hens. We were beginning to suspect delaying tactics. Perhaps the nuns had done

30

their homework since our phone call and now knew a thing or two about Chickens' Lib. Clearly, we must assert ourselves. So we reminded Sister Regina we'd been promised a tour of the units, and (who knows how unwillingly?) she led us outside, and into the first shed.

By now we'd seen into battery units of different types, ranging from the 'small', holding around five thousand birds per shed, to the frighteningly large, housing sixty or seventy thousand, the tiers of cages stretching away into the gloomy distance. This one was of the modest kind – five or six thousand hens, at a guess, the narrow passages between cages lit by the usual low-watt, dusty light bulbs.

We'd not, of course, expected to find a good battery unit (for there's no such thing) but with women in charge – nuns, even – might there perhaps be just a hint of mercy? As it turned out, no, there was not. This was a business, with hens as raw material and eggs the finished product.

These birds' combs were exceptionally pale, even for battery hens, and we felt certain the cages were overstocked. The inevitable feeling of stress hit us, along with the appalling smell. Suddenly I was near to throwing up, and I thought afterwards how that would have served these women right. For the place was, literally, sickening.

We came away utterly dismayed, and angry with ourselves that we hadn't remembered to bring a measuring tape. We'd definitely counted six or seven birds in some cages.

But it's not the number of birds per cage that's relevant, it's the space allotted per bird, then suggested in MAFF Codes of Recommendations, and later dictated in law. Could these have been extra-large cages? We didn't think so, they seemed absolutely typical of the size recommended for four or five birds, but rough guesses wouldn't get us anywhere. It was positive proof we needed, in order to lodge our complaint. On the journey home, we vowed that somehow we would get this disgraceful battery farm shut down.

AND NOW TO YORKSHIRE

Violet caught red-handed

Shortly after Chickens' Lib's first visit to the nuns, the Druce family moved to Yorkshire; my husband Duncan was about to begin life as a music lecturer at Bretton Hall College, near Wakefield. Once settled in Yorkshire, personal visits or demonstrations in Daventry would be difficult for me, but we still needed those vital cage measurements, and Violet was up for another trip to the convent.

*

June 30th 1978: The *Oxford Times* reported *'Freedom fighter gets the bird'* (How the press loved these little chicken-related jokes!) The article told how Violet had returned to the convent, this time with a woman friend from Oxford, armed with that all-important measuring tape. *'They sneaked into the nuns' chicken hut,'* ran the story, *'and were promptly set on by a couple of irate nuns who ordered them out and called the police. Chief Inspector M.N. Cole of Daventry police said: 'It is most unlikely that any further action will be taken by the police. We do not anticipate any criminal charges.'*

Apparently Violet and friend were seen in a good light. Perhaps the Boys in Blue thought as badly of the nuns as we did.

*

July 19th 1978: *Punch* got in on the act, in jocular fashion. *'Help Free Battery Nuns'*, the article pleaded. *'Militant members of the Sisters of the Cross Liberation Front are urging massive support for Sunday's kneel-in and mass chant through the home counties in protest at the "inhumane" conditions inside Britain's "factory" convents...But one Mother Superior has hit back at the allegations: "Our ten thousand nuns are quite happy," she said. "They sit in their cages all day long and sing."'*

32

On August 3rd 1978 Mr C Llewellyn, Private Secretary to the Parliamentary Secretary wrote: *'Dear Mrs Spalding, ...As the Parliamentary Secretary stated in the House on 24 May last in reply to a question from Mr Robin Corbett MP, the Ministry Veterinary Officer who visited the battery units at the Convent of Our Lady of the Passion found no evidence that the birds were suffering unnecessary pain or distress in contravention of Section 1(1) of the Agriculture (Miscellaneous Provisions) Act 1968. In his reply the Parliamentary Secretary also made it clear that he would not wish to give details of a private business. I cannot therefore comment on the report in The Northampton Chronicle and Echo to which you refer...'*

Regarding cage space, Mr Llewellyn was at pains to protect the battery-farming nuns to the very best of his abilities, indeed almost to the point of desperation: *'...stocking density cannot be related to welfare in any simple manner, and...is only one aspect of a complex situation involving such things as breed, strain, type of bird, colony size, temperature, lighting and quality of housing...'* Surely Mr Llewellyn is running out of ideas here: breed, strain, type – aren't they the same thing?

We read his letter, and recognised our old brick wall, only this time with Holy Orders scrawled on it. To us, the situation was not 'complex' at all. It was simple. MAFF had an obligation to enact its own legislation, specifically drawn up to protect the welfare of farmed animals (1).

*

October 5th 1989: More than ten years later, and following many lively demonstrations by animal rights groups, the *Daventry Express* editorial column declared war on the nuns: *'It is about time the nuns of the Monastery of Our Lady of the Passion sorted out their livelihood – and stopped being a source of provocation to animal rights campaigners, and an embarrassment to the Roman Catholic Church... you don't have to be a farmer or a rights campaigner to understand the levels of cruelty in this type of egg production...how do the nuns reconcile their present activities with their commitment to the tenets of the church, of love, sanctity of life, and compassion – or does this only apply to humans? We weren't aware God made this definition.'*

Quite so. But there was yet more to come.

*

By now the nuns were under fire from MAFF too, but not on welfare grounds (no surprise there). Their birds were infected with *Salmonella enteritidis PT4*, the strain dangerous to people and, following Edwina Currie's outburst of honesty in Parliament, a mandatory national cull of infected birds was underway. However, this Holy Order wasn't taking orders from anyone.

The *Daventry Express* continued to keep its readers up to date with the feisty nuns. One way and another, it was a colourful tale, smacking of MAFF ineptitude, the nuns' devotion to the battery cage system, a pop concert, a 'love specialist', and Belgian chocolates – with the grim thread of cruelty running through it all.

*

Giving it front page status, the *Daventry Express* reported how on October 4th, and in defiance of MAFF's slaughter regime, twelve nuns, led by Mother Superior Sister Catherine, barricaded themselves into a 5,000 hen unit, telling MAFF inspectors they had no legal right of entry. Apparently they weren't bothered about the five or six thousand hens in the other shed, since they were about to go to slaughter anyway, having completed their first and most financially rewarding year of lay. MAFF could have those, no problem.

*

October 5th: The *Daventry Express* revealed that professional security guards were patrolling the convent's grounds day and night, protecting the nuns from '*any type of intruders including the Press and animal rights activists*,' as Sister Jane-Anne told the paper. She also touched on the nuns' fears, and plans for the future: '*If we lose our chickens our income is gone. We are waiting for conversion work to be finished before we can start producing Belgian chocolates but that could take months.*'

It seemed the years of tireless campaigning, plus a dangerous outbreak of salmonella, were at last paying off. The nuns were getting fed up, and casting around for alternative ways of remaining solvent.

*

October 11th 1989. The *Daventry Express* again: *Chaos Comes to Quiet Order*, ran the heading to the story, accompanied by two photos. We see the nuns leaving the battery unit after their sit-in. One is bowed down, apparently on the point of collapse. Well, they'd been in there for three hours solid, breathing in the foul air, perhaps experiencing something akin to the hens' stress. Under the photo of the nuns, there's one of animal rights protestors holding a huge banner aloft: *MORE LIES. MORE DEATH. SISTERS OF TORTURE*, it proclaims.

Further gaps in the nuns' history were filled in by Bridget Dunbabin of the *Daventry Express*: '*The nuns in the contemplative order, who take a vow of poverty, came from Kentucky in 1963 at the invitation of Cardinal Heenan,*' she writes. Could Cardinal Heenan have been the one who'd failed to make the situation clear? Had he inadvertently led the nuns to think they'd be taken care of?

Father Roger Edmunds, information officer for the Northampton Diocese, took up the story: '*When they first arrived they really had a lot of difficulties setting themselves up. They went into battery egg farming without much enthusiasm but it was a way of supporting themselves without interfering with a life of prayer. The Catholic Church has no particular stance on the issue of battery farming, and prefers to leave it to the individual.*'

Reading this, Violet and I saw red. This argument of individual 'choice' – we kept hearing it, usually from supermarkets unwilling to stop selling battery eggs. Nuns' choice...consumers' choice...what about the hens' choice? Barely able to move a step, incarcerated for a year, maybe two years, *they* have no choice.

And there was yet more bizarre stuff to come. The nuns had found support elsewhere. A 'love specialist', known only as Carloff, guitarist in Nottingham-based band 'Dr Egg' (named after a Dr Egg who posted packaged hard-boiled eggs anonymously to the public, explained the article) had sounded out the nuns. He'd like to put on a charity concert, on their behalf. '*The idea of a concert was floated around the Monastery,*' says Carloff, '*and apparently a couple of young Scottish nuns said it was a good idea.*' There was a snag though. The band had no transport (odd, that) and no 'KI PA' sound system, whatever that might be. But Carloff remained hopeful: '*The nuns are apparently ringing round to try to find a contact in the music world who can help them,*' he assured the Daventry paper.

*

October 12th 1989: Beneath the heading *STAY OF EXECUTION* the *Daventry Express* kept us up to date: '*Judgement Day for Daventry's nuns dawns tomorrow (Friday), when the battle to save their chickens from slaughter goes to the High Court...Mother Catherine, head of Our Lady of the Passion Monastery in Badby Road West, will be chauffeur-driven down to the court to witness what promises to be a bitter battle.'* Clearly, the nuns were being looked after well. Whether the industry was paying for *de luxe* transport to London, or the nuns themselves, was unclear. *'Consultant in Environmental Health and Safety, Richard North, who is acting as spokesman for the nuns, said: 'We expect it to be like David and Goliath. The Ministry will be armed with two or three lawyers. So far we have one. We have to get more guns...We're going straight for the jugular.'*

The article carried a picture of Miriam Warburton, Divisional Veterinary Officer for MAFF, leaving the monastery grounds. Clutching a bundle of paperwork, clearly battling against a stiff wind, she'd once again been sent packing.

In the event, the nuns lost their case and all the hens were slaughtered in a grossly cruel fashion. MAFF had no adequate plans in place to deal with the salmonella crisis, despite the fact that it had known for years that salmonella was rife in British laying flocks (2). Until Mrs Currie's unwelcome revelations, MAFF had simply kept its head down, praying, we assume, that the problem would never come to light.

MAFF certainly should have expected trouble – the Protein Processing Order 1981 had been up and running since 1982. The list of proteins allowed in livestock and poultry feed was startling, and included: *'... the whole or any part of any dead animal or bird, or of any fish, reptile, crustacean or other cold blooded creature or any product derived from them and includes blood, hatchery waste, eggs, egg shells, hair, horns, hides, hoofs, feathers and manure, any material which contains human effluent and any protein obtained from these materials by heat, sedimentation, precipitation, ensiling or other systems of treatment...'* We'd been surprised by human effluent, and so, it emerged, was MAFF. We interested Richard North in the matter (a different Richard North, this one the Environment Correspondent for *The Independent*) and he was able to report: *'Officials said yesterday that they did not know why such a provision* [human effluent] *that was noticed by an animal rights campaigner while reading the order, should have been included. The order has been criticised for allowing unsound design of works, and for containing very little regulatory control over plants which harbour harmful bacteria, such as salmonellae. At present about 13% of samples from plants reveal contamination by salmonellae, and about twice as high a percentage of imported animal feed is found to be contaminated. Because of a change in the practice of renderers, who supply animal protein to feed manufacturers, less heat is applied to feed than used to be the case.*(3) So expediency ruled in the matter of animal feed, putting a small saving in the rendering process above human and animal health: animals, even naturally vegetarian ones, were to be fed just about anything, as long as it was cheap.

Hindsight is reputed to be a wonderful thing but in this case, and others, a bit of foresight was what was needed. Although nobody could have foreseen the precise tragedy of Bovine Spongiform Encephalitis (BSE), the terrible cattle disease that caused CJD in humans, the precautionary theory should prevail. Because it did not, when BSE struck millions of animals were slaughtered, the countryside practically closed down for walkers and tourism, and all too many people paid the highest possible price.

But to return to salmonella. Given the scale of contamination in animal feed, nobody in the know should have been surprised when Salmonella *enteritidis PT4* was suddenly causing sickness and deaths in the British population. Now, with no time to rush through vaccination programmes for hens, there was nothing for it but a mass slaughter of infected flocks.

Totally inexperienced and unqualified men were involved in killing the birds. Teams of the unemployed could be taken on if 'supervised' by a MAFF inspector or vet. Rumours abounded of hens being killed by being swung round by the head, to break their necks. In the case of the Daventry nuns' hens, miners rendered redundant by Mrs Thatcher were called in to dispatch the birds. And so the nuns' story went from farce to tragedy, from black humour to a particularly ghastly end.

*

The salmonella crisis did bring about change. The current British Egg Information Council's 'Lion Egg' scheme claims that around 85% of UK hens are now vaccinated against *Salmonella enteritidis PT4,* the strain responsible for most salmonella food poisoning and deaths in humans. This leaves approximately 15% of UK hens unvaccinated, and the Chief Medical Officer's advice has remained unchanged since the 1980s – it's still risky to eat raw or lightly cooked eggs (unless in pasteurised form), especially for the very young, the elderly and anyone whose immune system is compromised.

Post script

The salmonella outbreak, and no doubt the unrelenting campaigning against the nuns' farming methods, hastened the manufacture of the 'Belgian' chocolates. But there was a snag. The hoped-for conversion of existing stables in the convent's grounds into a chocolate factory proved unexpectedly expensive.

From this point in the tale I have to be a little vague. Recently, I tried to establish the precise facts. I visited the Daventry Express offices and looked through relevant past editions but, just at a crucial stage in the saga, some front pages were missing. I did read that the Pope had given his approval (or was it a blessing?) to the chocolates idea, but after that I'm relying on memory. I'd heard that, in gratitude for papal approval/blessing, the nuns had sent the Pope a box of chocolates, perhaps the very first one they'd produced, and that when the gift was acknowledged it was pointed out that the chocolates tasted odd.

My belief is that the nuns, unable to afford the stable conversion, decided to use the redundant battery sheds for their 'factory' and, fearful that traces of deadly salmonella might yet linger in the woodwork, had been over-zealous with the creosote.

*

But now I must zoom back to those early years of Chickens' Lib. Again, my parents had upped sticks and followed us, a move that made perfect sense, both for the sake of Chickens' Lib and because by a lucky chance my sister Helen and her family were now living not too far away, in North Yorkshire.

The Halifax Four

Violet quickly set up her Chickens' Lib office in a small outbuilding at her home, while mine was now a study measuring roughly six feet square. In one respect I liked it – I could reach everything without moving from my desk. An old-fashioned photocopier loomed in our hallway, while the dining room table served for some tasks and the living room for others. When, four years on, we came to sell the house the estate agent who came to value it took a dim view of our somewhat unconventional set-up; trying to remain courteous, he warned us that our home appeared 'cluttered'. Well, what did he expect? The house was never intended to accommodate a pressure group.

Fortunately for our self-esteem, a neighbour had spotted the frontage being measured, and guessed we were moving. He had a friend looking for just such a house...Later that same day, we were able to phone the agent, telling him we'd virtually sold, and so we had.

But to return to 1978: Violet and I now felt ready for action. It was high time to get down to the serious business of finding some Yorkshire battery hens.

*

November 22nd 1978: A quick trawl through 'poultry' in Yellow Pages pointed us to a battery unit just outside Halifax, safely out of our immediate area. With two cat baskets on the back seat we set off on the first bitterly cold and frosty morning of the season, to find ourselves blessed with immediate success. The battery owner told us he had thirty thousand hens, and the birds in one shed were going to slaughter in two weeks' time. So yes, he was willing to sell us a few 'spent' hens.

He took us inside the shed and dragged four pitiful looking birds from their cage. Hastily we stowed them away in the baskets, paid, and made a quick getaway.

So what exactly are 'spent' hens? Old, spent, end-of-lay – they're all industry terms, usually describing hens of just 76 weeks of age.

Of course a hen of this age is not old, nor should she be spent, and she certainly won't have given up laying eggs. It's just that the most prolific, and therefore the most profitable, egg production occurs in the first year of lay. Profits aside, she should have five or six years of life ahead of her, maybe more. I remember Peter Roberts, founder of Compassion in World Farming, boasting a hen aged ten. "She's still laying," he told me. "At least once a year, usually around mid-summer's day."

But in the world of commercial egg production, most hens are off to slaughter at eighteen months.

*

Our cluttered Yorkshire home had a double garage accessible from the house. I'd already fenced off one corner of it in readiness for the hoped-for hens, suspending a heat lamp over the enclosure to mimic the warm environment battery hens are used to.

Carefully we removed our newcomers from the two baskets, feeling again that warm, rough skin of battery hens against our hands. Only one hen still had plumage. We noticed her beak was intact. Clearly she'd missed the red-hot blade of the de-beaking machine and been left with the perfect tool for relentless pecking of the other three, in a doomed attempt to fulfil a hen's instincts to use her beak to good purpose.

Nearly a year of laying 'farm fresh' eggs had taken its familiar toll and the featherless hens certainly looked spent. We'd name them all soon, but there and then we decided on Minny for the smallest and perhaps most vulnerable of the group.

For a few minutes we watched spellbound as the birds took their first tentative steps. They looked uncanny, almost grotesque, yet immediately behaved like true farmyard hens, pecking around in the straw for grain. The only giveaway was their mode of walking: cautiously they would pick up one foot then doubtfully place it down, experimenting, finding that by putting one foot in front of the other they could actually make progress.

We wanted to linger there, observing our new hens, but there was work to do. MAFF (Leeds division) must be contacted, and the RSPCA. Though we held out little hope of support, we knew we must report this unit.

*

The next day, a local RSPCA inspector visited our hens, complete with camera. He explained that in the past he'd been a professional photographer, and we were encouraged. Even if nothing else came from yesterday's expedition, we'd saved four little hens from transport and slaughter and just might end up with some good photographs.

*

A week later, the RSPCA inspector's photographs arrived in the post and they stunned us. The naked birds look weird, almost graceful, yet at the same time truly shocking.

No action followed our complaints but we now had the material for a devastating and unique leaflet.

*

The winter of 1978-9: The Halifax Four stayed in the garage until late March. The feathers of the three most damaged ones took an unusually long time to re-grow, and the winter had been hard. Conker, the one with the intact beak, was splendid, her feathers a rich brown. But there was no more harmful feather pecking now. Happily occupied hens rarely damage each other.

The heat lamp glowed warmly night and day, and, despite their pitiable condition, all four went on producing eggs. Watching them indulging in their age-old behavioural patterns, frustrated until so recently, was infinitely rewarding. Their feet and legs grew strong as they kicked them back in search of grain buried in the straw.

*

Spring 1979: At last it was time to let the birds outside. We'd bought a hen house and run, and they soon settled in, perching at night like proper hens. One day I became seriously worried – two were contorting their bodies in a patch of dry, dusty soil. They looked grotesque, and for a moment I thought they were having fits (both at once? surely not!). Then I tumbled to it – they were dustbathing.

Hens, as I came to realise, are enthusiastic about their dustbathing. Given a patch of dry earth or similar, they writhe around in it, preferably in groups. And how they flick it about!

Dr Marian Stamp Dawkins, lecturer in Animal Behaviour at Oxford University, has described how battery hens will go through the motions of dustbathing, even on the bare wire of the cage floor. In scientific circles this fruitless attempt to clean the feathers is known as 'vacuum dustbathing'. This pathetic activity demonstrates the strength of ancestral memory. Born and bred in barren captivity, living on harsh wire, still battery hens will attempt to keep their feathers in good condition, using purely imaginary dust. Dawkins also observes how, if released from the cage environment and supplied with suitable dustbathing material, hens carry out what she calls 'an orgy' of dustbathing (1).

On one occasion we put food for a group of newly acquired battery hens in a nine-pint iron cooking pot, chosen because they wouldn't easily knock it over. They soon found a good double use for it, treating the dry mealy contents as the perfect medium for a thorough dust bath. Food in battery units is in a trough outside the cage, only reached through the bars. It's possible that battery hens look longingly at this substitute for dustbathing material.

But to return to the Halifax Four. Sometimes they would stay up until dusk, and we sensed they were making the most of every bit of daylight. Over the years we've often enough been accused of anthropomorphism, but maybe research to prove the obvious will one day be carried out into how much deprived hens long for natural light, grass and fresh air. Certainly we got the impression that the Halifax Four couldn't get enough of it.

*

Summer 1982: The Animal Liberation Movement, Queensland (QUALM) issued a battery hen leaflet. The photo on the front was of the Halifax Four, and the credit below read *BATTERY HENS FROM 'FARM' IN YORKSHIRE, UK. Photo courtesy of Chickens' Lib, UK.* The text inside was ours, with the relevant statistics changed and QUALM's contact details replacing ours. The battery system had already spread like wildfire in that vast country of open spaces; to our delight our leaflet was helping in what was fast becoming a worldwide campaign.

*

Twenty-two years on: August 14th 2004. Scene: Borders bookshop in Leeds. My children's book *Minny's Dream* had recently been published. The story tells how Paula moves to the country and finds her way into the battery farm next door. Secretly she befriends one of the hens, Minny, who tells Paula all about her misery.

That August afternoon was to be a book-signing event, and I was ready and waiting, complete with a good pen. Nervously I hung about, while the tannoy boomed out my name through the store. I'd prepared a short talk, and decided to show the QUALM leaflet and tell the children how far little Minny had travelled. All the way to Australia, from Yorkshire!

Only there were no children to tell, not a single one. Eventually, a middle-aged woman did wander over and we had a chat. Realizing from her accent that she was Australian, and on the off-chance she'd be interested, I dug out the QUALM leaflet.

And she *was* interested. In fact she was the lawyer responsible for drawing up QUALM's constitution, some quarter of a century previously. And she remembered the leaflet well.

We agreed it was quite a coincidence, and she took the evidence away with her, to tell the story on her return home.

*

With all our rescued birds, we wondered if they ever thought back to their incarceration. Recent research suggests it would be arrogant to assume that those dark days are forgotten. No longer is it necessary to listen helplessly to the taunt that it's anthropomorphic to award feelings and judgements to animals – at last the expression 'bird brain' has lost its sting. Consider the following facts...

Brainy birds

Dr Joy Mench, Professor of Animal Science at the University of California at Davis, has stated: *'Chickens show sophisticated social behaviour...that's what a pecking order is about. They seem to recognise, and remember, particular characteristics of other flock members, and that helps them figure out their position in the social hierarchy. In addition, they have more than thirty types of vocalization.'* (1)

Dr Lesley Rogers, Professor of Zoology at the University of New England, Australia, has stated: *'It is now clear that birds have cognitive capacities equivalent to those of mammals, even primates.'* (2)

Dr K-lynn Smith, Associate Lecturer in the Department of Biological Sciences at Macquarie University, Australia, has this to say about a chicken's intelligence: *'Chickens are remarkable animals. They live in long-term stable social groups consisting of a dominant male and a dominant female and several subordinates of each sex. Their communication is quite sophisticated, on a par with many primates. They produce over 24 distinct signals, two specifically in the context of food and two in the context of predators. These sounds are as specific as a word. For example, females that hear a male 'food calling' will approach him and begin to look for food. However, if the female has previously found food, she will ignore the signal. This suggests that the sound creates a mental representation of food and that the female compares her knowledge about the presence of food with that provided by the male. If the information is not useful, she will discount it.*

In these groups, females also eavesdrop on the food calling behaviour of males and remember their reputation for providing food. Occasionally males call in the absence of food, which may be a form of deception to lure the female closer to the male. Females will begin to ignore males that use this tactic too often.

Chickens can perform transitive inference, have numeracy, exhibit empathy and social learning. If you were to describe this list of abilities most people would assume you were talking about chimpanzees or some other 'higher' primate. They are truly surprised when told that this is a description of the humble chicken.' (3)

Professor John Webster of Bristol University set up an experiment in which corn was dyed, some yellow, some blue. Both were harmless to the chickens but the blue corn made them feel sick, and they soon left it alone. When the hens in the study came to hatch out *their* chicks, a similar mix of coloured corn was spread around. Straightaway the mothers taught their young to avoid the blue. Professor Webster commented: *'What this tells us is that the mother hen has learnt what food is good, and what is bad for her, that she cares so much for her chicks she will not let them eat the bad food, and she is passing on to her young what she has learnt. To me, that is pretty close to culture – and an advanced one at that. Chickens are sentient creatures and have feelings of their own.'* (4)

*

The considerable intelligence of birds is now widely recognised, which serves to highlight the tragic plight of factory-farmed poultry. Many a time we've seen ex-battery hens take their first proper steps, experience for the first time the rustle of straw underfoot, enjoy a first-ever dust bath. Having scientific confirmation of chickens' intelligence makes the history of our rescued birds all the more poignant.

Governments have sanctioned the cruel battery system, plenty of farmers (though not all) have been happy to go along with it, but what about the country's supposed 'moral compass'?

Where did, and does, the Church of England stand in this particular moral dilemma – the treatment of so-called food animals?

The Church

Chickens' Lib was never a religion-based organisation but our policy had always been to approach those in a position of influence. Believing our campaign to be a moral one, we naturally went straight to the established top, to the Archbishop of Canterbury. Perhaps he could be persuaded to put ending the suffering of the battery hen onto his list of Things To Do.

In 1977, Violet had written to the Archbishop, at that time Dr Coggan, and received the following reply from Lambeth Palace. Hilda Whitworth who wrote on the Archbishop's behalf (or was it Hugh? the signature wasn't clear) certainly knew how to set homework.

'Dear Mrs Spalding,' (she/he wrote) *'Thank you for your letter of the 22*nd *July about Chickens' Lib. I respect your deep anxiety, but there is no easy way to assuage it. In this matter I find myself going back to what St Paul said in the eighth chapter of his letter to the Romans, verse 18 and following. The same thought is perhaps differently expressed once again in his second letter to the Corinthians at the beginning of chapter five. The Archbishop receives every second week requests that he should lead some kind of campaign. The plea advanced is nearly always what can rightly be called a good cause. It is physically impossible, even if it were desirable, for the Archbishop to sponsor all these. He has rather to address himself to a much broader front.'*

We considered the degradation of billions of animals a very broad front indeed, and not one impossible to address, given the will. We didn't seek sponsorship, just outright condemnation of the battery system from those claiming a certain moral authority. We puzzled over that first reference. Can she/he really be pointing us to: *'For I reckon that the sufferings of this present time are not worthy to be compared with the glory which shall be revealed to us... For we know that the whole creation groaneth and travaileth in pain together until now.'*

We puzzled even more over the second reference: *'For we know that if our earthly house of this tabernacle were dissolved, we have a building of God, an house not made with hands, eternal in the heavens. For in this we groan, earnestly desiring to be clothed upon with our house which is from heaven: if so that being clothed we shall not be found naked.'*

No help then, from the Archbishop.

*

Autumn 1980: Polite letters from Chickens' Lib to the Provost of Wakefield cathedral, outlining the suffering of battery hens, had met with what we took to be disdain. Perhaps a personal visit would change his mind? We'd recently bought five 'spent' hens from a local battery unit. One had been near to collapse, but a couple of B12 injections worked wonders, and she was now fit to join in our next demo.

On a Sunday in mid-October, Violet and I met up with a small group of our supporters outside the cathedral. Violet ventured in and respectfully asked an official if we might have a few words with the Provost, the Rev John Lister. Back came a message that no, we could not. We hung about, uncertain what to do next.

Initially, we'd had no intention of taking the hens *into* the cathedral, and most certainly not during a service. But suddenly our blood was up. Why could not the Provost see us? Christians *should* see these abused creatures, and why not while the congregation was gathering for a service?

Holding our cage proudly, Violet and I climbed the flight of steps and entered the cathedral. The organ was playing softly, and already some worshippers were seated, or kneeling in prayer. We took a short cut along a row of empty pews, just making it to the central aisle before the Provost bore down on us.

"This is most improper. You are interrupting a service. Please leave the cathedral!" he thundered. One of our supporters took exception to the Provost's choice of words.

"Battery farms are most improper too," we yelled.

Feeling we'd made our point but were getting nowhere, we left with the Provost in hot pursuit. Cast us out of the temple, you might say.

*

October 13th 1980: The *Yorkshire Post* reports the incident beneath an interesting photo of Violet and me, clutching the cage of hens between us. I'm looking defiant, while Violet glances anxiously over her shoulder, as well she might, for just behind her is the Provost, a tall man resplendent in gorgeous brocade robes, towering above us and absolutely livid.

We didn't regret taking the hens into the cathedral. After all, many churches make time for animal blessing services, when members of the congregation take in their pets. Cats, dogs, rabbits, hamsters, tortoises if they're still awake – you name it. Only don't mention the battery hen, she who truly needs a blessing...

*

We 'took on' several Archbishops over the years, and at times thought we detected glimmerings of progress. In January 1981, possibly as a result of pressure from Chickens' Lib, the then Archbishop of Canterbury, Dr Robert Runcie, issued a two-page document entitled Statement on Animal Welfare Matters. Here's an extract from it: '*As a practical pig farmer I have found it possible to keep my pigs in conditions which respect their natural sphere of existence. I derive pleasure from seeing their response to this more humane treatment and am sure other stockmen feel the same towards their animals in similar circumstances...History has repeatedly shown that when man exploits his fellow creatures for immediate gain it rebounds on him eventually and leads to spiritual poverty. In the end lack of regard for the life and well-being of an animal must bring with it a lowering of man's own self-respect: "in as much as ye do it to these the least of my little ones ye do it unto me!"* ' (The exclamation mark is the Archbishop's, not ours, and probably not the gospel writer's either.)

We'd always assumed Jesus meant children when he spoke of 'little ones' but we weren't going to quibble. This was excellent stuff! We had the last sentence printed onto a colourful postcard, and distributed it widely.

Earlier on in the Statement, Dr Runcie had revealed that he'd received 'numerous letters' on the subject of animal welfare. Well, we'd been urging our many supporters to write in, and clearly they had. But we'd hoped for more than this. We were after a resounding cry for compassion from pulpits up and down the land. We doubted whether the man on the Clapham omnibus, or many others, had heard about the Archbishop's 1981 Statement.

*

That same year, still denied a meeting with the Archbishop, we decided to present him with a wreath. There were now around fifty million battery hens in the UK so we'd have it made from fifty flowers, each flower representing one million battery hens. Perhaps we could jog the Archbishop's memory about this massive insult to living creatures – or God's creatures, as he might feel duty bound to call them.

We wondered about sharing the gesture with Compassion in World Farming, and put the idea to Peter Roberts. He liked it, and we agreed to make it a joint venture. Violet arranged for her local florist to make up the wreath (spring flowers, mainly pale yellows and whites) and on January 8th we boarded a train for London, along with our fragrant luggage.

Mark Gold, newly appointed to CIWF's staff, was deputed to accompany us, and we'd be meeting him for the first time. The *rendezvous* was for noon at Waterloo station and thence to Lambeth Palace. So we'd be looking out for the unknown Mark, and he'd be scanning the crowds for two unknown ladies, one of them carrying a wreath.

And now a young man was heading our way, wearing a woolly hat and, I thought, a slightly disenchanted expression. Maybe he was dreading this mission, feeling he'd be better employed back in the office. And who could blame him? Still, he greeted us warmly.

Once inside the ancient walls of Lambeth Palace we handed the wreath to a gloomy official. Our message read as follows: '*The fifty flowers in this wreath represent the fifty million battery hens who will suffer and die in Great Britain in 1981. Chickens' Lib and Compassion in World Farming beg your Grace actively to encourage compassion towards these suffering creatures through the medium of the Church.*'

I don't recall any good coming from the occasion. Our gesture became just another of those endless drips on the stone, wearing away a rock-hard surface, or so we hoped. We came away with an impression of endless corridors, old-world stuffiness, an abundance of secretaries wearing twin sets and pearls, and a general air of suspicion of our good selves. And no hope whatsoever of seeing the Archbishop.

*

The expedition did end most pleasantly. Mission accomplished, we discovered that we had longish waits before our trains, Mark's to Petersfield, and ours back to Yorkshire. Though not generally *au fait* with London events, this time I rose to the occasion, remembering a small exhibition about George Eliot, one of my very favourite authors, and loved by Violet too. It turned out that Mark had read English at York University and shared our enthusiasm so, all of one mind, we hurried to the British Museum and spent an interesting hour there before going our separate ways.

It had been quite a relaxing day, and a pleasure to meet Mark, who was soon to become a good friend. Violet and I arrived back in Yorkshire in better-than-usual form. A wreath of spring flowers had been a lot simpler to transport to London than a cage of live hens, and returning home completely empty-handed was a breeze.

*

Seventeen years later Dr Runcie, by then Lord Runcie, underwent a change of heart, though not the one we'd hoped for. In January 1998 the *Daily Telegraph* reported: *'Runcie Stymies Bill to Tighten Pig Farm Rules – A move to improve the lives of pigs...was defeated in the Lords with the help of senior clergymen. Lord Runcie was among those who spoke against a backbench Bill designed to tighten the standards of pig farms. He told peers: "I do not believe this legislation is urgent for the well-being of the pig. It is certainly not timely for the morale of those who look after them"... He opposed the Bill because of the "severe problems bearing down on farmers." Lord Runcie, a pig keeper for twenty five years, was backed by the bishop of Hereford, the Rt Rev John Oliver.'*

It seemed commercial pressures had wiped out morals, at least in regard to some of God's little ones. Pigs were now outsiders, respect for their 'natural sphere of existence' no longer on the cards. Farmers were going through a bad time, so pigs must stay put in their grim buildings, with nothing but filthy bare concrete under their trotters.

Mercifully, they did have the proposer of the Bill, Lord Beaumont of Whitley, to speak up for them. In the House of Lords he described the 'intelligent and lovely' nature of pigs, adding: *'Today, the vast majority of pigs are forced to spend their lives in barren, overcrowded sheds.'*

*

2006: I had admired the Archbishop of York, Dr John Sentamu, when he appeared on television, fasting and praying for peace in the Middle East. Encouraged, I wrote to him outlining our work and wondering if he could spare a few minutes of his time for a discussion on the suffering of factory farmed animals. He replied only to say his diary was full for 2006, with very few spaces apparent throughout 2007.

I wrote again, expressing disappointment, this time mentioning the wider picture – the destruction of rain forests to grow crops for animal feed, the excessive use of water for intensively farmed animals in countries where the poor must daily walk miles to collect water for their own scant needs. I pointed out that people were starving, while imprisoned animals ate the soya and cereals that humans could well survive on. I even suggested the year 2008 as a possible date for a meeting, and ended my letter: *'Animals are now accepted, for the first time ever, as "sentient". Their present suffering, in the name of food production, is intolerable.'*

Dr Sentamu then proposed that I contact the Bishop of Monmouth whom, he told me, had especial and informed interest in the subject.

I did as suggested, and the Bishop wished us well, and explained his support for various organisations, mentioning the importance of the different animal welfare people working together (a principle we've always believed in, as it happens).

While understanding the considerable demands on Archbishops' time, we remain convinced that their remit should include non-human animals. Despite its avowed support for the RSPCA, the Church of England appeared unwilling to get down to grass roots. Surely C of E clergy need to alert parishioners to the atrocities perpetrated on sentient animals in the name of food production? Wrongly perhaps, Chickens' Lib limited its considerable efforts to the C of E, failing to spread our net wider.

Eventually, we all but stopped dreaming of the day when church congregations discuss what's going on inside those windowless sheds with their closed doors, and decide to do something about it. Still, an age of enlightenment just may dawn.

Harvest Festival would be a good time to start the good work, should a particular date in the church calendar be needed.

*

2010: Tragically, millions of British pigs continue to live in squalor. Secret filming by Hillside Animal Sanctuary, shot in East Anglia in 2010, revealed pigs living in filth, shivering with cold in sub-zero temperatures, pigs and piglets huddled together, hopelessly seeking warmth. Following cruelty charges, the farmer concerned had previously been prohibited from keeping other farmed animals for ten years but, because he'd once won an industry award for his pigs, the magistrate had exempted that species from the prohibition.

Hillside has filmed on several pig farms, finding evidence of almost unimaginable squalor: pigs struggling through two feet of excrement to reach food, pigs driven to cannibalism, decomposing pigs (1). Let nobody be complacent about British pig farms. Many are bad beyond belief. Over the Christmas period 2011-2012, Hillside Animal Sanctuary filmed in yet another disgraceful pig farm. This same unit had been exposed previously by Hillside, yet conditions for the pigs had not improved, and May Farm continued to operate under the British Quality Pig (BQP) logo and, worse, that of Freedom Food (the latter accreditation applying at least into 2011). The meat from these pigs, who'd spent their last few (cold) weeks of life living on a wet layer of their own excreta, were destined for the shelves of 'upmarket' supermarket Waitrose. Complaints from Hillside were, in time-honoured fashion, brushed aside.

In 2010, Compassion in World Farming reported on secret filming of seventy-four pig farms in six EU countries, including the UK: 'An undercover investigation, alongside the European Coalition for Farm Animals (ECFA) suggests that the vast majority of the 250 million pigs reared each year in the EU are being farmed in illegal conditions...CIWF chief policy advisor Peter Stevenson said: "It's a scandal that, seven years after the new laws came into force, they are still being ignored by most of Europe's pig farmers. Pigs are inquisitive intelligent animals, with a real zest for life – it is both illegal and inhumane to keep them in barren factory farms where there is simply nothing for them to do. We call on Member States to enforce the law that requires pigs to be given enrichment materials, such as straw and that bans routine tail-docking." ' (2)

The good old days?

I've just come upon an old newspaper cutting with *District Chronicle* scrawled on it, the district in question unspecified. But the date is clear – June 15th 1979:

'Mrs Violet Matilda Spalding and Mrs Clare Druce are names that mean nothing to most people. But in the corridors of Whitehall they are names that can cause shudders of fear. Mrs Spalding and Mrs Druce have been known to halt a whole morning's work at the Ministry of Agriculture; they have demonstrated in Whitehall addressing ministry officials by loud-speaker; they have appeared on television in their own programme; they have been threatened with prosecution by the police; and they have had to be forcibly ejected from a Roman Catholic convent...Chickens' Lib may sound like a joke but it isn't.'

It's a longish article, mainly hinging on the nuns.

Loud speakers blaring out challenges to MAFF, in Whitehall Place? No chance of this sort of bad behaviour now, it would be down to the police station with the adults, the children perhaps whisked into care. How different in the 1970s, when indulgent MAFF secretaries let my daughters loose on their typewriters and plied them with refreshments, glorying in an interrupted morning's work, while we'd be busy bullying whomsoever we could get hold of, refusing to leave the building until we'd had our say.

*

One of these occasions stands out as being especially long-winded. We'd taken our trademark into MAFF's Whitehall Place HQ: four abused ex-battery hens in the cage.

As usual, we'd demanded an interview, explaining that we'd brought positive proof of the shameful end result of the battery system. We must have a comment, we insisted ('we' being a handful of women – Violet, Vivienne, one or two other supporters, and myself). A doorman showed us into a small pressroom, and there we waited. And waited. We had one packet of sweets between us, which helped a little to keep our spirits up, along with blood sugar levels.

At one point I left the room, to seek out the Ladies. A notice in there caught my eye, informing staff that sanitary towels could be obtained from Room X (actually I think it was room 18, but should hate to misinform anyone on that score). I felt sorry for the female staff, having to make their way down long corridors, before retracing their steps to the loo. I only hoped that once in Room 18 (?) employees were allowed to help themselves, and not obliged to fill in forms before their pitiful requests were granted. But I digress...

After a good hour and a half with no sign of action, Violet snatched up an internal phone, only to find herself on a direct line to Peggy Fenner, Parliamentary Secretary to the Agriculture Minister, who personally answered the call. At the very moment that Violet embarked on our demand for an interview, *now*, the hens broke into a cacophony of clucking, true farmyard noises.

'And where are you phoning from, Mrs Spalding?' asked Mrs Fenner, coldly. That wretched woman again! Thank God she must be at a safe distance, down some muddy lane with her flaming hens. And yet... The *internal* telephone?

'I'm phoning from the Press Room!' replied Violet. 'And our patience is exhausted.'

But Mrs Fenner wasn't giving in, not that easily. Another long wait ensued, no doubt calculated to break our spirit, before a civil servant was sent down, a Mr Sparks. He was not the first official to claim the need for specific expertise before he could risk a comment on the condition of our hens.

Once out of the building, Vivienne insisted on taking Mr Sparks lightly, claiming that he blushed every time he set eyes on Violet. We liked Vivienne's interpretation of his red face but it's just as likely it was fury that brought the roses to his cheeks.

Sadly, MAFF couldn't afford to be seen as a permanent sitting target for lunatic-fringe invasions. Simply trying to wear us down by leaving us in the Press Room for hours on end was no longer enough. All too soon the barricades went up; no more could we get past the reception desk uninvited, let alone into the very bosom of MAFF.

Those were the good old days, at least in some respects. Visit Ministry of Agriculture's premises in London now, and you'll need a pass to get inside the building, while a colour coded warning in the foyer will let you know which degree of alert from a terrorist attack is in operation on that particular day.

In Yorkshire, MAFF was, initially at least, blissfully unprepared for our attentions. Soon, though, we were attracting the media with sit-ins and demonstrations all around that county and beyond.

At the same time, our workload was threatening to overwhelm us.

THE CAMPAIGN ESCALATES

By the late 1970s, Chickens' Lib had hundreds of members, and we contacted them all at least three times a year. Between us, Violet and I still addressed the envelopes for mail-outs by hand, always managing to get into an alarming muddle.

'Have we done the Ns?' Violet might ask.

'God! *I* don't know! They'll be here somewhere. Behind the sofa, maybe?'

And one of us would hunt through a collapsing pile of envelopes behind the sofa. Neither of us was made of the right stuff for the 'office' side of things, yet somehow, miraculously almost, things did get done, and properly.

But with the campaign expanding by the week, we desperately needed help. Just where to look for it was the problem. The spectre of the *wrong* help hung over us. We'd far prefer to go on dithering around forever, just the two of us, than link up with someone we couldn't work happily with. And there was no question of offering payment: everything connected with Chickens' Lib was done on a voluntary basis.

*

Not long after we'd all settled in Yorkshire, word reached us of a woman living in South Yorkshire. Apparently Irene Williams was *the* person to contact if we wanted to meet someone totally dedicated to the cause. We phoned Irene and an arrangement was made to go to her house one afternoon. Just to say hello, you understand...

*

Irene lived in a neat bungalow with her husband Eric, two dogs and three cats. Much later, she told us she and Eric had met while they were children. Romance flourished in their teens, when, as members of Barnsley's RSPCA Committee, they would cycle round the countryside, authorized to empty the all-important collecting boxes.

An air of orderliness struck us the moment we walked through Irene's door; here was a competent lady, with a bookcase packed with important books on animal rights. Over a cup of tea Irene revealed that she'd recently addressed six thousand delegates in London's Albert Hall, those six thousand representing the quarter of a million members of the Townswomen's Guild. Irene's theme had been the evils of factory farming, and the support she'd received had been overwhelming.

Through Irene, we were introduced to a network of people in Yorkshire and beyond, many of them CIWF supporters (later, Irene was to become a trustee of CIWF). In all weathers they'd be out on the streets manning stalls, spreading the word about abused factory farmed animals.

By the time we moved house yet again we knew Irene well and were nearer to her, separated now only by a beautiful twenty-minute drive over the moors. It was a red-letter day when Irene made her suggestion: would we like her to help Chickens' Lib in the office, on a regular basis? With absolutely no doubt that she was the person we most wanted to work with, we took up her generous offer.

For the next sixteen years Irene would spend two long working days every week at my house, her sole reward the knowledge that she was helping in the fight against factory farming. My only problem was in persuading her to take a break for lunch: Irene would willingly have survived all day on cups of coffee. When mail-outs were under way she recruited friends to help, often half a dozen at a time.

On those occasions our spacious Victorian house came into its own as office, packing room and staff canteen. Quite early on we'd given the large dining room over to office use, reasoning that we used it only a few times a year for family get-togethers. Almost overnight, its former elegance was camouflaged by a miscellany of second-hand office furniture, soon to be submerged beneath signs of frantic activity. In 1994 our home suffered a serious burglary, with many musical instruments stolen, and an antique grandfather clock. When the police officers put their heads round the office door one of them let out a low whistle, commenting that the burglars had done this room over in a big way. I can't now remember whether I admitted that I didn't think the burglars had set foot in there. The chaos was all mine.

Without our many helpers we'd have foundered. Not content with more than a thousand members, we'd taken to sending our detailed fact sheets to around two thousand non-supporters. These recipients (many no doubt more annoyed than grateful) ranged from poultry researchers, poultry industry chiefs, environmental health officers, schools and colleges, to MPs and MEPs. Mail-out days were long and exhausting, accompanied by the thud of the franking machine and ending with trips to the post office, two or three of us staggering under bulging mail bags, a significant proportion of the contents going overseas.

We'd established Penny Perkins as a perfect person for re-homing needy ex-battery hens. Deeply concerned about the welfare of animals, she lived in a former farmhouse set amongst acres of fields, perfect for two horses and a donkey, as well as ducks and assorted rescued hens. Her husband Ken, a Manchester solicitor, was as dedicated as Penny to all their animals.

For a while we knew Penny only in the capacity of a trusted re-homer: she would arrive to collect the latest consignment of sad specimens or we'd take them to her home. One day, just as Penny was leaving our house, complete with her latest batch of hens, she asked if we'd like help in the office.

Gladly, we accepted her offer, and from then on Penny, always the best of company, was part of the team.

*

Some years ago Philip Lymbery, who'd recently joined the staff at Compassion in World Farming, was on a fact-finding tour. His quest was to get acquainted with experts in the field of farm animal welfare research. At Roslin, the Scottish research institute (of Dolly the Sheep fame), he was feeling overwhelmed by the amount of information flying at him and asked a well-known poultry researcher if he could recommend a good way of keeping up to date with that side of things. The researcher paused for a moment and then came out with his advice:

"Well, Chickens' Lib's fact sheets are very good."

Philip had been astounded and amused, in about equal proportions. We were too, when told about it, but it set us thinking – for whom were we working so hard, producing detailed fact sheets? Though confident that some of our members read them, many might have found them daunting in their detail. Were we in fact spoon-feeding the wrong people, those researchers making a living out of the suffering of poultry, spending their time studying problems that only needed compassion and common sense to solve?

I do know one eminent poultry scientist, but only one, who gave up working in that area. No longer could he stomach carrying out research into what was essentially factory-farming-induced suffering, and which earned him his pay cheque,

Ethics, as we were to realize more and more, were in short supply in many places, some of them surprising.

Take the shelves of the Co-op supermarkets...

Customer choice

Few of our battles were easily won, and ours with the Co-op wasn't one of them. In 1979 we began a campaign aimed at persuading the Cooperative Wholesale Society (CWS) to stop stocking battery eggs in its Co-op stores. Despite its claim to be ethically driven, the CWS was slow to respond. And I'm talking in decades. Customers must be given 'choice', came the repeated cry. Year after year we pointed out that the hens have no choice.

Letters from Customer Services painted emotional pictures of shoppers driven by poverty to set morals aside and buy eggs from caged hens. We responded by telling them we'd seen many a Co-op customer drive out of the car park, their cruelly produced eggs stowed away in smart cars, 4x4s even. To strengthen our case further, we worked out that the price difference between a dozen free range eggs and the same number of battery eggs equated to the cost of a packet and a half of crisps or less than two and a half cigarettes, and we suggested that the average family probably bought no more than one dozen eggs a week. We urged our supporters to write to the CWS headquarters in Manchester. But for years, the Co-op was to stand firm, its 'ethics' in tatters, as far as Chickens' Lib was concerned.

*

In 2003 we'd asked supporters to send postcards (yes, twenty-four years after we'd first accused the Co-op of hypocrisy in its ethics). Now we mocked their current slogan, "IT'S HOW IT SHOULD BE", boldly displayed in their supermarkets. We had the slogan printed on a postcard, applying the words to a hen's life on free range, as opposed to the miseries of caged existence.

*

But to return to the late 1970s: anxiety was brewing within the battery egg industry, especially, it seemed, in Scotland. Who, or what, producers were asking themselves, lay behind these welfarists' most unwelcome progress?

Who is Mr Big?

1979: At the AGM of the Scottish Egg Producer Retailers Association it was reported in *Poultry World* that *'...the threat of a ban on battery cages dominated the evening. "Producers have been sitting back, while welfare groups have been lobbying MPs – now we must fight,"* said Denis Surgenor, SEPRA's secretary. *"The welfare groups have been too successful for my liking,"* he warned. *"Now the industry must present a unified front."* ' (1)

Mr Surgenor said egg producers were suspicious about welfare groups with sufficient funds to support the publicity material they were distributing. *'Many believe there is a "Mr Big" in the background, perhaps a foreign country intending to market eggs in the UK.'*

Immodestly perhaps, we thought that maybe, just maybe, Mr Big was none other than Chickens' Lib.

Granny agents

December 1979: Peter Roberts telephoned from Compassion in World Farming. Could Chickens' Lib get hold of a few ex-battery hens, for an important event in London? CIWF's petition for the abolition of the battery cage, signed by 191,000 people, was to be handed in at Number 10 Downing Street on December 11th. Afterwards, there'd be a press conference in an upstairs room at The Clarence, a pub in Whitehall. Celebrities including Spike Milligan would be supporting the event, and live ex-battery hens were a must.

Our reputation for 'getting hens' was now well established; how could we let CIWF down?

*

Generally, we operated at a safe distance from home, to avoid possible recriminations from local farmers. Since the problem was a national one, it seemed foolish to stir up trouble on our own doorsteps. But on this occasion there wasn't time to meander around the countryside hoping for a lucky break – CIWF needed the hens in a few days' time. We knew of a likely place just outside Wakefield, far too close for comfort. Still, just this once, we'd risk it.

And, we agreed, there'd be no reporting of this farm to MAFF or the RSPCA. This time, Chickens' Lib would definitely keep its head down.

*

The egg production side of things turned out to be small, with around thirty thousand hens in all, divided between three sheds; near the farmhouse, in an old stone barn, was a farm shop.

The woman serving in the shop had a substantial bunch of keys hanging from her belt; perhaps she was the farmer's wife, with authority to sell hens. Posing as normal customers, we bought one or two items from a selection of vegetables, taking particular note of the 'Farm Fresh' eggs nestling in hay-lined baskets. Then, as if an afterthought, we trotted out our piece. Would it be possible to buy a few old hens, just four or so, for the garden? To our relief she was happy to oblige.

I rushed to the car and grabbed the cat baskets. A minute later the door to the nearest unit was unlocked and Violet and I were following the woman into the shed's gloomy depths.

*

Many of the cages at the end nearest the door were empty of live hens. We were told the shed was being gradually de-populated, and guessed that smallish numbers of birds were being bought for local restaurants. But why had nobody bothered to remove the dead ones? In many a cage lay a corpse and most of the hens, dead or alive, were almost featherless. Appalled, we followed the woman along the dusty, dimly lit central aisle between the banks of cages.

And now we were at the far end, peering into a cage on the bottom tier. We'll have those, we said, and the woman yanked the hens out. We stowed them away, paid, and were soon backing out of the yard, realising that in no way could we *not* report this 'farm'.

*

Back at my house, we settled the four in the garage, aware now that one little hen was badly crippled. With one leg sticking out at an unnatural angle, she crouched awkwardly. We spent a minute or two watching the others move around gingerly in the straw, then went indoors to phone a vet. We had to know what was wrong with the crippled bird, and stressed to the receptionist that we'd need a written report. An appointment was made for the following day.

*

The vet issued a certificate: '*This hen has arthritic changes of right hock joint, possibly caused by previous dislocation.*' Clearly, her suffering had lasted for weeks, months maybe, her 'farm fresh' eggs laid with painful difficulty in the discomfort of the cage. We imagined her trying vainly to grip the wire floor with the dislocated leg.

Gullible 'farm shop' customers had been buying her eggs, prettily displayed in hay-lined baskets. We wondered once more why so many people fail to put two and two together: the absence of visible hens, those windowless buildings, silent except for the hum of extractor fans, the sickening musty smell.

*

We phoned MAFF and the RSPCA. RSPCA inspectors attempted to investigate but, having no powers of entry, were turned away. MAFF visited a day or two later, by appointment.

Yet again, we pointed out to MAFF the uselessness of their inspections. Police raids of suspected criminals aren't made by prior appointment: '*We're just phoning to say we've had a report of illegal firearms on your premises, would it be convenient if we called round, perhaps somewhere around the beginning of next week?*' That doesn't happen, we reminded MAFF.

It was obvious to us: MAFF, with its policy of giving prior warnings, wasn't motivated to catch anyone out. Clearly the bother and expense, and the embarrassment of convictions (remember, MAFF actively encouraged farmers to set up in intensive systems), these were the last things the Ministry of Agriculture wanted.

No doubt all dead hens in this unit had been removed and incinerated before this latest 'inspection'. But there's no way the remaining inmates could have been 'upgraded'. So MAFF saw most of what *we* saw, but through very different eyes.

Eventually, there came more irritable twaddle from the pen of MAFF's Divisional Veterinary Officer at Leeds, claiming he would investigate any 'genuine' case of cruelty brought to his notice. (This from the same official who'd insisted that the almost naked hens in photos we'd sent him previously were in a natural moult.)

Apparently this latest case didn't rank as 'genuine'.

*

The day of the press conference: We met up with Peter Roberts and CIWF staff in Whitehall, where Vivienne was waiting, ready to help with the hens.

Spike Milligan arrived, and we proceeded along Downing Street to Number 10 where, under the scrutiny of two duty police officers, the petition was handed in. This offered a good photo opportunity, with Spike and we three Chickens' Libbers each supporting one corner of the cage.

Then it was on to the press conference, where speeches were made and more photos taken, including ones of Spike, author Brigid Brophy and other celebrity 'prisoners' staring out despondently between the bars of a cage for humans. The little crippled hen was photographed too; later CIWF produced a post card featuring her.

At one point I said something (heaven knows what) that raised a laugh. Quick as a flash, Spike came back: "Hey, I'm meant to be the funny one round here!" So, a little light relief and something to remember.

It had been an interesting day, if tiring, but at least we could return to Yorkshire with an empty cage. Vivienne took the three uninjured hens home with her, and the little crippled one went off with animal rights campaigner and author John Bryant, to be lovingly cared for at his sanctuary in the West Country.

*

January 3rd 1980: *Poultry World* panics: '*Under cover "rescuers" of old hens. Farm gate egg producers have been warned to beware of old ladies pleading poverty and who want to eke out their pensions by buying a few old hens for their garden. They could be undercover animal welfare agents seeking birds for anti-battery propaganda purposes, it is claimed... Two ladies persuaded the producer's wife that they could not afford point-of-lay birds but wanted some cut-price end of term birds that they could take on for a second year. A bargain was struck, and they went away with the birds. Within 24 hours the birds had been photographed and prints* *rushed round to the nearest RSPCA office, which then sent an inspector to the farm. Permission to inspect the birds immediately was refused, and the RSPCA called in ADAS* who made an appointment before coming to see how the unit complied with the welfare codes. The Ministry found that stocking densities, feed, water and general management were well within the requirements of the codes and went away satisfied.'*

*   Agricultural Development and Advisory Service, an arm of MAFF. Originally, ADAS gave free advice to farmers, but now there is a charge.

*

February 18th 1980: *The Times* picks up the story, with colourful references to 'little old ladies' and 'swarms' of RSPCA inspectors. The secretary of the National Egg Producers' Association, Mr D Parnell, is quoted as warning poultry farmers up and down the land to beware of anyone wanting to buy live hens after one was approached in Yorkshire by 'a pair of granny agents'. It could well be, wrote Mr Parnell in the Association's magazine, that such old ladies are spies, secretly working for animal welfare organisations.

Well, there were a good few inaccuracies in both stories (for example two RSPCA inspectors hardly constituted a swarm) and we weren't too pleased by all this talk of little old ladies. I was forty, and though Violet was seventy-one she looked years younger. Our convenient theory was that the farmer's wife didn't pay much attention to us at the time; later, casting her mind back, she remembered us as wanting a few old hens, cheap, for the garden (surely a sign of poverty and old age) and simply embroidered the rest.

Still, there was no getting away from it – she just might have remembered us quite clearly, and in a most unflattering light. We comforted ourselves that she was of the bold and brassy type, so perhaps anyone casually dressed and minus jewellery and heavy make-up at eleven o'clock in the morning was, in her eyes, well over the hill.

*

The incident showed up the complacency of battery farmers. The woman hadn't thought twice about the dead birds left in their cages. She'd had no need to take us into the shed with her, and clearly had felt no anxiety that we'd report the terrible conditions. Her hens were just typical of a perfectly legal system, their shocking state of no account.

For decades, battery farmers had been encouraged by government agriculture departments to set up systems tailor-made to promote serious welfare problems. Even now, thousands of farmers in charge of livestock rarely undergo a welfare inspection of any kind, much less an unscheduled one.

In 1988, **Andrew Smith** (MP for Oxford East) put this Parliamentary Question:

To ask the Minister of Agriculture, Fisheries and Food, what was the number of: (a) prosecutions and (b) convictions in respect of unnecessary pain or distress caused to broiler and battery chickens in each of the last five years.

Mr Donald Thompson: *The number of prosecutions undertaken and convictions obtained by the ministry of Agriculture, Fisheries and Food in respect of causing unnecessary pain or unnecessary distress to poultry in England within the last five years is as follows:*

Year	Prosecutions	Convictions
1987	1	1
1986	1	1
1985	Nil	Nil
1984	Nil	Nil
1983	1	1

Taking into account the thousands upon thousands of farms holding laying hens and broiler chickens, the above numbers are staggeringly low.

*

Fast-forward twenty-two years: The following Parliamentary Question was tabled:

Norman Baker (Lewes, Liberal Democrat): *To ask the Secretary of State for Environment, Food and Rural Affairs how many (a) prosecutions and (b) convictions there were for offences relating to unnecessary pain and distress caused to broiler and battery chickens in each of the last five years.*

Jim Fitzpatrick (Minister of State) Minister for Food, Farming and Environment, Department for Environment, Food and Rural Affairs; Poplar and Canning Town, Labour. Holding answer 4th March 2010: *The information requested cannot be provided because records are not held centrally.*

It seems systems were more sophisticated, back in the 1980s.

Crossing the Pond

September 11th 1980: *The Wall Street Journal* ran a front-page item drawing attention to a new move in Britain to return hens to the 'barnyard', and describing Chickens' Lib in colourful terms. According to the Wall Street journal, we employed 'hard-boiled' tactics, making 'commando-style' raids on battery barns.

Well, not quite. Bursting in, all guns blazing, was hardly our style. But we were gathering evidence, steadily, and our next venture was an important one, destined to convince us of the downright illegality of the battery system.

Illegal systems

The National Farmers' Union had found a battery farmer willing to open his units to supporters of Compassion in World Farming, for just one afternoon. The NFU's stance was that farmers had nothing to hide, nothing of which to be ashamed. Their hope was that once people could see for themselves what went on down on the farm their fears would melt away, like snow in summer.

Sunday February 1st 1981: by mid-morning, on an unusually warm February day, Violet, Duncan and I, along with our daughters, were heading northwards under a clear blue sky. *En route* we stopped to eat sandwiches in the car and then carried on to the farm to join the CIWF group, which numbered around thirty.

After cups of tea in the farmhouse we were shown into the first unit. Selected areas had been roped off, but a few of the more bold amongst the party ducked under the ropes, later claiming that the out of bounds cages were seriously overstocked. On the 'official' tour, we were shown pullets of only thirteen weeks of age and already showing signs of feather loss, and we wondered about the condition this farmer's 'old' hens, the ones nobody saw that day – unsurprisingly perhaps, they'd all gone for slaughter shortly before our visit.

The in-lay hens we did see were poorly feathered, and after only a minute or two our throats felt dry and scratchy. I urged our daughters to wrap scarves around their mouths and noses. Surely it wasn't good to breathe in this dust and pollution?

We walked slowly along the aisles, stopping now and again to peer into a cage, hardly liking to look the hens in the eye, for we could do nothing to help them. One pecked at a button on my coat; anything must be of interest in this barren environment, I thought. And did battery hens ever quite give up hope that some day they would find a way out? They see there's another world; even the rows of dim lights overhead and the hens in the opposite cages proved there's something beyond their prison bars. But for these hens the only change of scenery would be the journey to slaughter. We left the farm deeply depressed.

On the way home, we stopped off at a smart hotel for a cup of tea. Why were people looking oddly at us, we wondered? Then we tumbled to it – the terrible smell from the batteries must be clinging to our clothing.

It's the stink of 'farm fresh' eggs, we should have told them.

*

Eight years on, and I knew I'd been right to urge my daughters to wrap scarves around their faces. In Chickens' Lib's Fact Sheet 22 we were able to quote part of a letter to us, dated January 5th 1989, from Professor John Webster, at the Department of Animal Husbandry, University of Bristol: *'Thank you for your letter concerning the airborne transmission of salmonella and other potentially harmful matter from intensive poultry houses. Poultry house dust contains a wide range of material which may provoke asthma and other allergies...Workers in poultry and pig houses can suffer from severe respiratory problems and its is probable that some living downwind of intensive poultry units may be affected to a lesser degree.'*

Then, much later, *Poultry World* of June 2009 reported on new Health and Safety Executive guidelines, for the poultry industry. (1-3) Referring to all types of poultry, the article reminded readers: *'Workers on poultry farms are exposed to an airborne cocktail of particles, including feathers from the birds and dust from dry bedding and droppings. In addition there are mites, bacteria, fungal spores, endotoxins (toxic chemicals released from dead bacteria) and even pesticide and fertiliser residues.'*

The PW article detailed the various symptoms suffered by workers, including irritation of breathing passages, and ended on an ominous note: *'Workers may become allergic or sensitised to specific agents and suffer severe reactions if then exposed to even low levels for short periods. Severe asthmatic attacks can be fatal.'*

*

But to return to that NFU trip, back in February 1981: For a day or two we felt helpless. To us, the battery system was so obviously cruel. Hens need to be busy from dawn to dusk, foraging for food, enjoying sunshine, walking, running, nest-building, dustbathing, not incarcerated behind bars. Surely there had to be something in existing law, *something* we could use to prove the battery system illegal. I decided to go through all the relevant legislation we'd collected.

Eventually I lit upon *The Welfare of Livestock (Intensive Units) Regulations 1978*. These regulations demanded that the hens should be thoroughly inspected not less than once a day, to check they were in a state of well-being.

Laboriously, I did some sums.

*

Rather grandly, we called the result of our calculations *Chickens' Lib's February the 4th 1981 Statement*. Our conclusion was that if each hen were to be inspected adequately, the battery system for egg production, as now practised, would be rendered instantly uneconomic.

We took a forty-thousand-bird unit as our example, and worked out that, allowing just one second's glance per bird, one member of staff would have to work seven days a week, putting in a twelve-hour day. Then we added in the time needed for all the miscellaneous events that would crop up on a daily basis – the removal of dead hens, the mending of a broken cage, shoe laces to tie, toilet and meal breaks, the blowing of noses – and the fact that nobody in normal employment works a twelve hour day, or a seven day week, with no holidays.

Then we considered the logistics of the inspection itself. Cages on the bottom tier, being almost at floor level, are notoriously difficult to see into. Lighting is at its dimmest in these cages, and anyone inspecting the hens properly would need to squat down, kneel, or bend almost double, and proceed in one of those positions along the concrete shed floor. We pointed out that in a four-tier forty-thousand-hen unit ten thousand of the hens would be caged at ground level. Imagine the discomfort of peering into these low cages! No wonder dead birds linger, unnoticed, sometimes for weeks.

In the 1980s most battery cages were stacked three or four tiers high. (Later, we were to see systems of eight tiers, on display at the Royal Show at Stoneleigh.) Even in three or four-tier cages, hens in the topmost cages are impossible to see into without the stock man or woman being elevated, as is now required by law, but wasn't then. From ground level, only the feet and heads of hens in top cages are readily visible. Anything could be going on in *those* cages.

From our calculations it became clear that, for the law to be adhered to, the workforce in any typical battery farm would have to be multiplied several times over, thereby forcing the price of eggs up dramatically. In addition, spending whole days in the stifling and unhealthy atmosphere that prevails in battery units would routinely endanger workers' health.

The battery system exists on the premise that it can keep going on the absolute minimum of labour, yet the authorities have chosen to turn a blind eye on the fact that effective inspection is demanded by law, while being impossible to achieve.

The Welfare of Livestock (Intensive Units) Regulations 1978 seemed the ideal vehicle for proving what Chickens' Lib believed: that just about every battery farmer in the land was operating illegally. Here was the chance for a wealthy organisation, able to risk a potentially costly court case, to take action. Surely the fact that the battery system was inherently illegal could be exposed, in court? Naturally, we sent our February 4th Statement to the RSPCA, the only animal protection organisation in a position to take on the task of challenging the legality of the battery system.

Not long after we'd drawn up our February 4th statement and distributed it far and wide, a senior RSPCA investigative officer generously admitted to me that it was our calculations that had drawn the Society's attention to the potential of the 1978 legislation.

Then, in what seemed no time at all, the Society swung into action.

The RSPCA and the scapegoat

The summer of 1981: for just over a twenty-four hour period, Superintendent Donald Balfour and Inspector Mike Butcher of the RSPCA's Special

Investigations Unit kept watch on a battery egg farm in Newdigate, Surrey. As a result of their observation, a prosecution of the owner was launched, and on January 28th 1982 *Poultry World* covered the story in detail.

It seems the RSPCA officers had taken precautions to ensure no errors were made, using an army-issue image intensifier to enable them to see what was going on around the farm, even in complete darkness. They also laid concealed traps at the rear of each of the three sheds, putting gravel on the door catches, to make sure nobody could enter the units unnoticed.

Philip Brown, Chief Veterinary Officer of the RSPCA, told the court that the law required a thorough inspection of each bird individually to check its overall bodily condition, adding: *'In my view, the very minimum time required to undertake such a thorough inspection in the best battery houses would be one second per bird.'*

Cecil Schwartz, a private vet acting for the RSPCA, considered that the inspection guidelines in the codes of practice should be observed, and this meant that inspection must be in *addition* to normal management tasks. (This all seemed uncannily reminiscent of Chickens' Lib's February 4th Statement.)

Over the 24-hour plus period, the farmer spent nine and a half minutes in the three battery houses and two teenagers had taken just under three hours collecting eggs. The court ruled that the regulations called for a 'thorough inspection, not a cursory glance' and the farmer was fined £150 with a £250 contribution toward the Society's costs. In his defence, the farmer claimed that, as an experienced poultry man, he would know instinctively when anything was wrong with his birds. Chickens' Lib had heard similar claims before and has heard them since – tales of farmers happily blessed with a 'sixth sense' about the health of their flocks.

During the proceedings Humphrey Malin, prosecuting, explained that the case had been brought to test the definition of the law, and not as an allegation of cruelty. Later, a spokesman for the RSPCA expressed the hope that MAFF and the livestock industry would respond in a positive manner: *'We are not getting at the individual farmer. The 1978 Regulations specifically state that all livestock, and that includes battery hens, must be thoroughly inspected at least once in a 24-hour period. We felt that the regulations were not being complied with by the vast majority of intensive livestock farmers.'*

Sadly, neither the livestock industry nor MAFF responded in the hoped-for spirit. Peter Jones, head of the NFU's intensive livestock division, said the court decision would worry many poultry farmers, and spoke of the union's concern that the RSPCA was prepared to trespass to gain evidence, warning poultry farmers to look out for any suspicious activity around their units. Predictably, MAFF carried on as before, unperturbed.

*

February 4th 1982: Precisely one year after our February 4th Statement, the editor of *Poultry World* was fuming: *'To make their point about inspection of poultry in intensive units RSPCA men have suffered considerable discomfort, trespassed on a Surrey farmer's land and made the whole process of looking after the well-being of stock utterly ridiculous. There can be few better examples of the law being an ass through man's attempts to define legislation that is beyond him. It seems safe to assume Mr Constable's layers were kept at a comfortable temperature and ventilation rate and that they had adequate feed and water, since he was not accused of cruelty... So I am wondering what he did wrong in a mass management system that depends on catering for flocks not individual birds. Quite rightly he was concerned about flock health and maintaining the best environment for the flock. When we fail to do that we deserve all the RSPCA can throw at us, but not for failing to look every bird in the eye every day.'*

It's clear from the above that the industry interprets laws at its convenience. The legislation specified 'thorough' inspection, not a quick glance around the thousands of hens, including those living in semi-darkness on the bottom tiers, or largely hidden from sight in topmost cages.

*

The failure of the RSPCA to take further, similar, cases has been of lasting regret to Chickens' Lib. The spokesman quoted above emphasised that the Society wasn't looking for a scapegoat. He also said the RSPCA suspected 'the vast majority' of battery farmers of breaking the law. And even the NFU wasn't arguing. *'The NFU said that following this test case at Dorking, brought by the Royal Society for the Prevention of Cruelty to Animals, most poultry farmers in Britain were breaking the law.'* (1) Yet in effect this Surrey farmer became just that – a scapegoat. He must often have pondered on his bad luck.

Surely, our contention that the battery system would crumble if staffed at an appropriate ratio of hens to stock men and women should have been used to hit intensive systems hard, and not only the battery system. The RSPCA could have taken case after case, and maybe won them all on the maths alone, exposing the inherent cruelty and illegality of intensive poultry systems in courts up and down the land.

We believed that RSPCA supporters would have been glad to know their donations were helping to stamp out widespread cruelty. We felt certain there would have been no question of a serious loss of revenue for the Society, following such a progressive course of action.

Charities are not allowed to attempt to change laws. We were not asking for laws to be changed, but for existing legislation to be adhered to.

*

We felt bitter that the case of the Surrey battery farmer was a one-off. We've come across so many cases of neglect, including hens dead (sometimes long-dead) in their cages. Once, in a bleak place with the even bleaker name of Scapegoat Hill, Violet and I noticed some half demolished battery sheds. The roof of one had already been removed, and there, for any passer-by to see, were dead hens in several of the abandoned cages. I'm sure we must have reported it – and even more sure that no good resulted from our complaint. We did reflect at the time that if those corpses had been of dogs or cats, it just might have been a different story.

*

We were bitter about other things too – the blatantly dishonest advertising of battery eggs. In particular, a company going by the gross misnomer of Goldenlay had caught our eye. Having taken note of Goldenlay's marketing tactics, flagged up in the pages of *Poultry World*, and knowing the company to be based in Yorkshire, we decided action was called for.

So here began a series of happenings that took in the sustained hounding of a leading name in the world of battery eggs, much dressing up, a visit to the police, a visit *from* the police, and contact, of sorts, with the Royal Family.

71

THE QUEEN AND GOLDENLAY

In December 1970, Egg Farms Limited had been formed. Just a year later the company was to become Goldenlay Eggs (UK) Ltd., the result of a merger between Thames Valley Eggs, Yorkshire Egg Producers, West Cumberland Farmers, and giant battery egg producer Jack Eastwood. Goldenlay set up in Carlton House in Wakefield, and dreamed up its slogan *The Taste of the Country*, so epitomising the misleading marketing of battery eggs.

*

Back in 1976 we'd read in *Poultry World* of an art competition: '*Latest national promotion by Goldenlay is a joint effort with The Observer newspaper*' ran the heading. Prizes for the winners in the children's competitions (to feature Goldenlay eggs – what else?) included trips to the USA for nine children, with ten days on a ranch in Arizona, three days in Los Angeles, plus visits to Disneyland and a film studio. Judging the sculpture entries was the renowned sculptor Elizabeth Frink, while Laurie Lee, that champion of all things romantically rural, was to select the winning poems. Could either of these celebrities have known anything about Goldenlay's hens, every one of them caged? We could only hope not.

In 1981 Goldenlay celebrated its tenth anniversary. The occasion was marked by the publication of a shiny (golden) brochure, complete with a message of congratulation from the then Minister of Agriculture, Fisheries and Food, the Rt Hon Peter Walker, MP.

As well as enlisting the support of the Minister, the brochure featured celebrities of the day... Larry Grayson, Sir Roger Bannister, Lance Percival – all pictured presenting prizes or cheques to charitable causes. Surely none of them could have been aware of the animal suffering they were helping to promote?

*

Goldenlay was notoriously devious in its advertising, and the industry made no bones about it. On October 2nd 1980 *Poultry World* ran an item about the company's marketing tactics: '*Goldenlay are to spend £225,000*

on TV commercials...Britain's biggest egg marketer has spent some consid-
erable time researching consumers' attitudes and this confirmed that the
average shopper likes to link eggs to a farm background...With most of
Goldenlay's 100,000 cases a week being sold through multiple grocers, this
was an important factor in the new marketing programme. The need to
promote Goldenlay eggs as local, farm fresh eggs was apparent, distracting
the housewife from her vision of the factory-farmed eggs associated with
supermarkets...The commercials feature three farming characters, linking
in with the housewife's wish for farm fresh eggs...Both commercials are
amusing, ending with the Goldenlay image-builder "The taste of the
country"...'

In the same issue *PW* revealed that: *'...two major parts of* [Goldenlay's]
£750,000 expenditure on egg promotion this year – just under a half p
a dozen – follows this autumn. With the £225,000 TV campaign, some
£40,000 is also being spent on a "Nest-Egg Competition" run in conjunction
with Family Circle and the Leicester Building society.'

Perhaps if representatives from Family Circle and the Leicester Building
Society had been with Chickens' Lib when we'd watched an amazing and
touching sight, they might not have been so keen to support Goldenlay's
cynical 'nest-egg' competition.

*

Violet and I had purchased four hens with an especially harrowing history.
We'd called at a small poultry slaughterhouse in North Yorkshire and,
though the owner had refused to sell, he was helpful. Apparently only
that week some 'spent' battery hens had been brought in, but been spared
immediate slaughter when a battery farmer had called by and spotted an
opportunity of some dirt-cheap replacement birds. No doubt he'd reasoned
that they'd lay fairly well for another year, with the advantage of costing
him next to nothing.

So, instead of being slaughtered that day, the hens suffered the trauma
of transport to another farm, to be re-installed in *that* farmer's set of cages.
The slaughterhouse owner cheerfully directed us to the nearby farm, and the
farmer proved willing to part with a few birds from his second-hand purchase.

One of them we immediately called Denise – her facial feathers gave
the impression of heavy eyebrows, reminding us of Denis Healey, MP (later
to become Lord Healey). As soon as we got home we transferred our new
arrivals to a straw-filled enclosure, complete with feed and water, then

paused for a minute or two to watch them – our usual indulgence after a tiring day out.

Immediately, and to our wonderment, one hen began to build herself a nest. Carefully, she selected strands of straw, picking them up in her beak one by one, placing them to one side of her body, then the other, weaving a perfect structure around her. On and on she went with her task until she was almost hidden from sight.

To us this was a spectacular example of how, despite thousands of years of domestication and generations of incarcerated ancestors, every one of a hen's primeval instincts remains intact. Inside each hen's brain, and maybe in her conscious mind too, those instincts remain locked up, awaiting a chance to be enacted. Only most battery hens never do get their chance.

How dare Goldenlay promote their battery eggs with cruel puns on 'Nest-Eggs'!

*

*June 11*th *1981*: Incensed by Goldenlay's deceptions, Chickens' Lib took up their theme of the three jolly farmers. A group of us met up outside Goldenlay's HQ at Carlton House in Wakefield, some of us dressed as farmers and carrying baskets of 'farm fresh' battery eggs. The event went well, though the management declined to accept our offering of cruelly produced eggs.

Good publicity followed, with a photo in the *Guardian* the following day of the three 'farmers' (Violet, Irene and me), complete with battered hats and straw in our hair, alongside one of our number in a hired hen costume. The article concluded: *'The "farmers" of Chickens' Lib were not allowed into the Goldenlay offices to put their case.'*

The *Yorkshire Post* reported the demo too, quoting a company spokesman as saying: *'Our egg production is carried out within regulations, and our advertisements have been approved by the relevant authorities.'*

Apparently the Advertising Standards Authority was happy to turn a blind eye on advertisements clearly calculated to mislead.

*

Derek Gee, a regular contributor to *Poultry World*, had doubtless been reading about our exploits, and on July 20th 1981 he sounded off in its pages: *'With no wars to fight, Empire to rule or natives to save, the militant missionaries who want to turn the clock back seem well on their way to winning, at least the battle of words. If I refer to them as a sort of pseudo-intellectual middle–class National Front it is not in order to insult, but to underline their approach, their attitude and background.'*

Don't worry Mr Gee, we don't feel insulted. It's just good to know you're so rattled.

*

September 23rd 1981: *Punch* magazine took an interest in Chickens' Lib's 'militant' exploits, likening us to the Provisionals of the environmental movement.

*

December 9th 1981: Accompanied by a walking Christmas tree, Father Christmas attempted to deliver a parcel of dishonest advertising to Goldenlay's Managing Director. I'd recently discovered a talent for writing corny verse and we handed out copies of *The First Goldenlay Song* to our assembled supporters, to be sung to the tune of Jingle Bells:

> Goldenlay, Goldenlay, we would like to know
> Why you keep your hens caged up
> And make them suffer so-oh.
> Goldenlay, Goldenlay,
> Give us no more guff,
> We have come from far and wide
> To call your awful bluff.
>
> Goldenlay, Goldenlay,
> Where are your eggs laid?
> In stinking sheds, on wire floors,
> That's where the profit's made.
> Goldenlay, Goldenlay,
> Tell us why the hens
> Are prone to stress and fatty liver syndrome
> And die from cage fatigue. (Two more verses followed.)

Mike Maas, a stalwart supporter on our demos, played Father Christmas, cutting an imposing figure as he pulled a glittering sledge on which was poised a gold-wrapped box containing our gift – a large scroll of dishonest advertising slogans. Goldenlay's management proved not to be in party mood. A spokesperson for the MD refused to accept our gift and, after we'd laid it at his feet, kicked it vigorously back in our direction. As the *Yorkshire Post* put it: *'Santa was shown the door and asked by police to leave an egg firm's office after he and ten helpers tried to deliver a special message yesterday.'*

Never mind that our gesture went to waste, it was the publicity we were after. And we got this in plenty, in local radio, in newspapers and on BBC TV's *Look North,* the programme giving us a full five minutes. Our impromptu choir sounded a bit weak but the words came over clearly enough, on radio and on TV.

*

At the time of our Goldenlay demos, I was the visiting clarinet teacher at Wakefield High School for Girls, then a rather stiff institution (I thought) and uncannily like the school I'd once attended. Twice a week I would turn up, soberly dressed, to give my lessons and seeming, I trust, quite normal.

Although there was no way that Chickens' Lib's demos could have escaped the notice of teachers or girls, no mention was ever made of them, at least not in my presence. Such behaviour was obviously beyond the pale. And so I led a double life, although, due to our excellent publicity, my exploits were certainly no secret.

One day I received a letter from the headmistress. Seeing the heading, I read on with trepidation, fully expecting the sack. But no, the letter was to say that she admired our campaign, and wished us luck.

*

Spring 1982. We tell our supporters: *'Perhaps the most bizarre thing to have happened since we last wrote to you has been the conferring of the Queen's Royal Warrant of Appointment on Goldenlay Eggs (UK) Ltd! It appears that Goldenlay has been supplying the Royal Household with eggs for several years and the firm has exercised its right to apply for a Royal Warrant, and been successful.'*

We wrote to the Queen, pointing out the typical size of a battery cage for four or five hens. We said: *'We feel that in giving Goldenlay Eggs (UK) Ltd. this Royal Warrant your Majesty is expressing approval of the battery system.'* Several well-known and well-respected people endorsed our letter with their signatures.

We approached the Lord Chamberlain, whose office dealt with Royal Warrants. *'However,'* [wrote the Secretary of the Royal Household

Tradesmen's Warrants Committee, replying on the Lord Chamberlain's behalf], *the firm assures me that the Code of Practice for Intensive Farming and other regulations governing standards of hygiene and hen welfare laid down by the responsible authorities, are strictly adhered to...*' etc. etc.

Rather than investigate our complaint, it was the 'flying to the defence of factory farmers' syndrome, the familiar brick wall. 'Hen welfare' did the Lord Chamberlain's Secretary say? Less than the area of a sheet of A4, constructed of harsh sloping metal, for each hen *for life*? Whatever was the Queen thinking of?

We conferred with CIWF and agreed on a plan. We'd send the Queen two free-range eggs daily (not to leave the Duke of Edinburgh high and dry, with nothing but a battery egg for breakfast). We each managed three postings, before being asked politely to desist. Good publicity followed this initiative.

*

April 6th 1982: We presented Goldenlay with the *Chickens' Lib 1982 Award for Cruelly Produced Eggs*, on this occasion adopting a patriotic theme. A dozen or so of us met up near the company's HQ decked out in red, white and blue, along with Sir Walter Raleigh (Mike Maas, in splendid hired costume). The image of Mike struggling to force his long legs into tights in a chilly Wakefield car park would stay with us forever. The Award, in the form of a huge certificate, was eye-catching. Margaret Skinner, a tireless supporter of CIWF and Chickens' Lib, had designed and painted it, and it looked splendid.

We had two new Goldenlay songs prepared. This is verse one of the first song, set to the tune of The British Grenadiers:

> We think the Queen's mistaken
> To approve of Goldenlay.
> The hens who lay the Royal eggs
> Never see the light of day.
> No sun for them, no daylight
> No space to move about,
> They live their lives in misery
> Of that we have no doubt.

Our second song was sung to the tune of Sing a Song of Sixpence. It went like this:

Eleven million battery hens
Shut up in the gloom,
Wishing they could wander,
Longing for more room.
Gripping with their feet, a-
Round the wire floor,
Oh isn't there, some-where,
An anti-cruelty law.

So we have come to Wakefield
To plead with Goldenlay
To listen to our message
This chilly April day.
We hope you will consider
A basic change of scene
And give your hens their freedom
And eggs fit for a Queen!

The *Wakefield Express* reported: '*Chickens' Lib protestors and the management of Wakefield-based company Goldenlay were involved in yet another confrontation on Tuesday when the group tried to deliver an award for "cruelly produced eggs"... But the management at the Sandy Walk headquarters refused to accept the award, telling the protestors to leave it and a letter of explanation in the doorway. The protestors, all wearing red, white and blue were complaining about Goldenlay being granted a Royal Warrant by the Queen...Co-founder of Chickens' Lib, Mrs Violet Spalding, said the group was very concerned that the Queen had given Goldenlay her patronage. "Goldenlay have been granted a Royal Warrant and we want the Queen to rescind it," she said.*'

'Bystander' of *The Tatler* ran a piece about us too, alongside photographs of smart people getting wet at Henley Regatta. '*Anyone passing the Yorkshire eggquarters* [sic] *of Goldenlay Ltd. one day in May would have seen the Chickens' Lib 1982 Award for Cruelly Produced Eggs being unceremoniously kicked down the steps by a ruffled director. The Chickens' Lib representative, quixotically dressed as Sir Walter Raleigh, had presented the award after The Queen conferred a Royal Warrant on Britain's biggest battery egg producer earlier this year.*'

Bystander did rather muddle our demos, one with another, but ended: '*They also produce fact-filled news sheets which convince that no fowl ought to spend its brief life suffering in a space the size of this page.'* So this last bit was crystal clear.

*

June 5th–12th 1982 CIWF organised a Don't Eat a Battery Egg Week and to support it we held yet another demo outside Goldenlay's HQ. By now, the company must surely have come to dread our dedication.

We'd asked supporters to make cages from cardboard boxes, cutting slits on one side so they could peer out from between rudimentary bars. We sang a new Goldenlay song, this time to the stirring tune of 'Jerusalem'. The first verse went like this:

> And were those eggs for Goldenlay
> Laid midst a pleasant country scene?
> Where are the hens who laid your eggs?
> What does your silly slogan* mean?
> And do you really think you should
> Deceive the public as you do?
> When all the hens who lay your eggs
> Live in conditions most obscene.

(* 'The Taste of the Country')

After delivering our letter to Peter Kemp, Goldenlay's MD, we proceeded in a flock to Trading Standards, where we handed in our letter of complaint about dishonest advertising. We had a special song for TS, set to 'You are my Sunshine':

> We fear the standards
> Of Trading Standards
> Have really sunk to
> An all-time low.
> Who shall we turn to
> If Trading Standards
> Won't help us out
> Oh where shall we go? (Etc.)

Once again, publicity was excellent, with the first demo featured on local TV and in several newspapers.

We understood all too well why Goldenlay was hell-bent on defending the battery system. But the police? Now *that* was to come as quite a surprise.

79

Police support battery system

We must have been feeling energetic for, after one of our Goldenlay demonstrations, Violet and I decided the day was yet young. Furious about the battery system in general and Goldenlay in particular, we decided to visit one of their farms. We knew of a large one, set in a remote location up on the moors above Sowerby Bridge. We just might strike lucky...

*

And there it was, a huge blot on the grand landscape, row upon row of long low battery sheds dropping down the hillside. Not for the first time, we were reminded of concentration camps.

As we drew nearer, any hope of buying hens faded. This was no small-time enterprise with a farmer keen to pocket a fiver. We noticed a hut, probably somewhere for workers to brew up tea. A man hurried out to waylay us, possibly the manager. We put our request, only to be asked, none too gently, to leave the premises.

On principle, we didn't hurry. By now we'd found we could pick up information just by keeping our eyes wide open, and maybe passing the time of day with one of the workers. We'd thought at first that all the sheds were closed but we noticed one with its sliding door fully open, so we sidled over, getting as near to it as we dared. The cages near the open door seemed to be empty, though in the gloom we couldn't see far into the shed.

But now we were listening, appalled. Usually, the only sound from a battery unit is the dull hum of extractor fans, and, if the doors are open, the low and continuous complaining sound of thousands of hens. But this was different. A ghastly screaming was coming from the open shed. What could be happening in there? We returned to the car feeling shaky, determined to investigate further.

*

We drove down into Sowerby Bridge to the police station, to report the sounds of distress. The police officer on duty was courteous, taking notes in the long-winded way of police officers. Eventually we left, satisfied with the promise that someone would report back to us in a day or two.

By now, we'd had enough of campaigning, and returned with relief to our respective homes. It had been a long day.

*

When the police did contact us it was the usual well-worn story: the officers visiting the farm had found everything in order, though they'd not been allowed inside the sheds 'because of the disease risk'.

By now we'd come to realise that the catchers must have been emptying the open shed and the screaming we'd heard was of terror and pain, as the hens were dragged from their cages.

Usually catching goes on at night, so the birds can be ready and waiting at the slaughterhouse first thing in the morning. This daytime catching probably meant the birds were in for a long journey. Or a long wait on the transport wagons. There are fewer than half a dozen slaughterhouses for laying hens in the UK, so many 'spent' hens, often almost devoid of feathers, must travel a hundred, perhaps two hundred miles, crammed into crates, frequently suffering the pain of shattered bones.

We wrote to the police superintendent for the area, putting before him the whole question of the suffering of battery hens and the ineffectual animal protection laws, taking the Goldenlay farm on his patch as an example.

*

Early in August we had a family holiday in Scotland, and on our return Violet had a tale to tell.

A few days after our departure, she'd been at home on her own when, with no warning, the police superintendent from Sowerby Bridge had called on her, along with a young constable (the Super's Little Henchman, as she described him). By the end of the visit, she wished she'd had someone with her, simply to witness that extraordinary hour.

The 'Super' had ordered Chickens' Lib not to cause any more trouble. He'd said that since we'd wanted the hens for propaganda, we had in fact been trespassing. And now his 'little henchman' took over. The battery system was the very best one for egg production! The hens were warm and dry and cosseted, etc. He went on to assure Violet that, despite not being allowed into the sheds, he'd looked through the windows and it had all looked fine – a remark which gave his little game away, since purpose-built battery sheds (as these were) have no windows.

Then the Super warned Violet that if we committed a breach of the peace we could be in for violence (from the farmer, he hinted), threatening that if we returned to the farm we'd be told to bugger off. (We didn't mind the buggering off bit, but the mention of violence didn't appeal.) His parting words, Violet told me, had been 'Don't let me see you in the Calder Valley again!'

Now the Calder Valley encompasses a large area, and would be hard to avoid. The prohibition became a standing joke – 'My God! We're in the Calder Valley! – but the threat had been disturbing as well as ludicrous, because of what it told us about the attitude of some police officers.

I was as outraged as Violet by all this, though at least I knew she'd not been intimidated. Her calm manner must have been deeply disappointing to her surprise visitors. Violet described the police visit to Richard Wainwright, our ever-supportive MP, hoping he might advise us on how to take the matter further. But he explained that without a witness our case was hopeless from the start.

*

Following a hunch, in 2010 I wrote to the West Yorkshire Police, outlining the police visit to Violet (though omitting some details) and asking for the name of Sowerby Bridge's Police Superintendent at that time. The reply I received stated that although there were no records available of the visit I described, it having occurred so many years ago, the Superintendent (or sub Divisional Commander) at that time had been Superintendent Dick Holland (1).

Now Dick Holland had been second in command in the hunt for the 'Yorkshire Ripper', part of the team that delayed Sutcliffe's arrest while the enquiry focused on the hoaxer, 'Wearside Jack'. And before this, Dick Holland had been prominent in the team investigating the brutal murder in 1975 of a child, Lesley Molseed. This hopelessly flawed investigation had resulted in a tragic miscarriage of justice. A vulnerable and totally innocent man, Stefan Kiszko, was wrongfully imprisoned for sixteen years, only to die two years after his release from a mental ward, having developed schizophrenia while in jail. An in-depth account in the *Guardian* of the botched case of Stefan Kiszko stated: '*The treatment of Kiszko by a team including Supt Dick Holland, who was later involved in the bungled hunt for the Yorkshire Ripper Peter Sutcliffe, was a disgrace. Kiszko was not told he was entitled to a solicitor, was denied the company of his mother and a confession was obtained as he sat alone and dazed with detectives.*'

The author of the article, written to mark the eventual arrest of Lesley's real killer, Ronald Castree, was Martin Wainwright, son of our late MP (2).

A year or two after our visit to the unit in the Calder Valley, an ex-poultry industry worker wrote to us describing the catching process. Had we received that letter earlier, we'd have immediately guessed the significance of those Goldenlay hens' cries. Here is part of his letter:

'Birds were dragged from the cages by their leg. Four birds were carried in each hand end down, down the shed to the door. The noise was deafening, the smell was putrid. Legs, wings and necks were snapped without concern. As I now look back, the whole system is incredibly cruel. After saying all this, this particular farm was good as far as battery farms go. The floors were swept daily and precautions taken against disease and pests...I gave up work in the poultry industry after bad dreams at night.'

Five Freedoms and a Convention

In 1965 the Brambell inquiry into the welfare of intensively kept animals concluded that the protection of animals should go further than simply prohibiting cruel treatment. Henceforth, positive welfare was to be considered. Fourteen years later, in 1979, as a direct though much delayed result of Brambell the concept of the Five Freedoms emerged. They are:

- Freedom from hunger and thirst
- Freedom from discomfort
- Freedom from pain, injury or disease
- Freedom to express normal behaviour
- Freedom from fear and distress

These aspired-for freedoms are frequently quoted in official quarters, not least in the various codes of recommendations for farmed animals, and in publications of the Farm Animal Welfare Council (FAWC). Codes do not carry the weight of law but, in the event of a prosecution, failure to have followed the advice contained in a relevant code tends to establish guilt.

Logically, and given the conditions in battery cages or a conventional broiler, duck or turkey unit, any farmer charged with cruelty should have his or her guilt established pretty quickly, for how could the fourth freedom, 'freedom to express normal behaviour' ever be ensured within such barren and restrictive environments?

Somehow, MAFF (now DEFRA) has managed, with a barrage of meaningless words, to obscure the fact that illegal practices are the norm, down on the factory farm. The odd thing is, they've got away with it.

*

Established in 1949, the Council of Europe (COE) now embraces forty-seven European countries. The COE's primary goal is to guarantee the dignity of the nations and citizens of Europe by enforcing 'respect for our fundamental values' including the rule of law (1). Human rights are high on the agenda but farmed animals have not been forgotten. In 1976 the UK ratified the *Council of Europe Convention for the Protection of Animals Kept for Farming Purposes.*

In May 1983 the then Minister of Agriculture, Peter Walker, wrote to his colleague Sir Keith Joseph MP. Peter Walker's letter must have stemmed from one of mine to Sir Keith, but the mists of time prevent me from remembering exactly why I'd written to him. Here are extracts from Peter Walker's letter to Sir Keith: *'Mrs Druce is in regular correspondence with my Department...she and her mother, Mrs Spalding, are the founders of and motive force behind Chickens' Lib, a pressure group which strongly opposes the battery cage system ...she has expressed the view that British livestock farming is (also) contrary to the European Convention for the Protection of Animals Kept for Farming Purposes, which the UK has ratified. The Government does not accept any of these contentions.'* (The other contention involved accusations of Government failure to adhere to UK legislation.)

Let's look at specifics, by taking a few examples from this Convention's 'Recommendations for Domestic Fowl – *gallus gallus* [chickens]'. In line with recommendations for other species, there's a section at the beginning called General Provisions. This consists of a description of the natural behaviour of chickens, and informs us that the domestic fowl is descended from the red junglefowl of south-east Asia, a species domesticated for the last six to eight thousand years: *'Although there is variation between strains of domestic fowl, all retain certain biological characteristics of their wild ancestors. Junglefowl show complex patterns of courtship, nesting, laying, incubation, brooding behaviour and defence against predators...Domestic fowl have retained the typical feeding pattern of junglefowl, which consists of pecking and ground-scratching, followed by ingestion...if frustrated these behaviours may be re-directed towards injury to or even cannibalism of flock-mates...The motivation to dust-bathe remains particularly strong, even in birds reared on wire floors.'* (2) Then we learn that: *'The design, construction and maintenance of enclosures, buildings and equipment for poultry shall be such that they allow the fulfilment of essential biological needs and the maintenance of good health.'* (3)

Sometimes 'should' is used, and sometimes 'shall', as in *'...and equipment for poultry shall be such that they allow the fulfilment of essential biological needs...'* This variation in terms was puzzling, so eventually I wrote to the COE, querying the difference, if any, between 'should' and 'shall'.

On September 20th 1999 I received a reply from the COE's Directorate of Legal Affairs, Laurence Lwoff, who wrote: *'The articles contained in these Recommendations, as you rightly pointed out, contained provisions with "shall". These provisions have to be applied by the Parties* [i.e. member states which have ratified the Convention]. *The provisions containing the word "should" are to be considered as guidelines and duly taken into consideration as indicating the way forward.'*

So that was clear enough. Any member state that ratifies a COE Convention is under a legal obligation to carry out certain of its provisions – its 'shalls', so to speak.

I queried this state of affairs with the RSPCA and in a letter dated May 4th 2007, the then Director General of the RSPCA, Jackie Ballard assured Chickens' Lib that the Society had often been present on working parties and drafting groups, and had raised with our government the issue of the UK's duties following ratification of the Convention, as had Ruth Harrison. (I was already well aware that Ruth – author of the 1964 book *Animal Machines* – had bravely carried on travelling to Strasbourg, fighting the animals' cause at meetings even when seriously, indeed terminally, ill).

Over the years we drew attention in relevant places to the UK's failure to take heed of the demands of the Convention, but to no effect.

A touch of arson

One summer's evening, two be-suited men appeared on our doorstep, discreetly holding out proof of identification.

I took them into the living room, curious as to why they'd come but not worried. Chickens' Lib's conscience was clear: we didn't steal our hens, we bought them, and we disapproved of violence. What could the CID want with me?

It transpired that I was suspected of a crime. There'd been an arson attack at a nearby Goldenlay depot. Two thousand pounds' worth of damage had been caused, to vehicles. This was news to me, and I said so.

One of the detectives fixed me with a steady gaze. "What if I were to tell you that someone of your appearance was seen leaving the scene of the crime?" he asked.

I'm afraid I laughed. I repeated that I didn't even know the crime had been committed (though would read about it later, in *Poultry World*).

The officers seemed to accept that they'd drawn a blank, and soon we were shaking hands, and I was seeing them to the door.

*

At that time we had a small and highly unsuccessful vegetable plot. When the door-bell had sounded I'd failed to switch off the cooker before leaving the kitchen.

The outcome? Our entire runner bean crop, along with those Goldenlay trucks, burnt to a cinder.

*

Early in 1983 we received a letter from an ex-Goldenlay site-manager. He'd read about the dim view we took of the company and wanted to dish the dirt. This was interesting!

Violet and I made an appointment to visit our whistleblower (we'll call him Mr X) wondering what we might learn straight from the horse's mouth. We decided we'd record the interview, and perhaps come up with something worth sending to the Queen.

Inside information

On a raw March day, more like winter than spring, we set off to visit our whistle-blower, complete with tape recorder. We found his first floor flat, reached via an outside staircase and above a row of small shops, part of a 1960s development.

Mr X welcomed us warmly and we chatted for a few minutes over a cup of coffee before getting down to the serious business. He'd already agreed to allow us to record his reminiscences and soon we had the tape running.

Mr X told us that one of his legacies was a recurring respiratory disorder brought on, he claimed, by the nature of the work. Since asthma and bronchitis are acknowledged as occupational hazards in the pig and poultry industries worldwide, we had no reason to think he was exaggerating (1).

We heard how common prolapses are among battery hens, and remembered the words of Nobel Prize winner Konrad Lorenz: 'For a person who knows something about animals it is truly heart-rending to watch how a chicken tries again and again to crawl beneath her fellow-cagemates, to search there in vain for cover. Under these circumstances hens will undoubtedly hold back their eggs for as long as possible. Their instinctive reluctance to lay eggs amidst the crowd of her cagemates is certainly as great as the one of civilized people to defecate in an analogous situation.'

Maybe this holding back of eggs accounts for the prolapses? It could be due to all manner of other things too – poor muscle tone from lack of exercise, or the unnatural number of eggs now expected from the laying hen (double that of pre-war hens) to name just two. Whatever the reason, we knew that when part of the oviduct protrudes, red and glistening, other hens will peck at it, the taste of blood often marking the start of injuries leading to death. Mr X explained that prolapses aren't readily noticed in the congested cages, amid the general gloom.

We asked him about veterinary care and he stressed that only if a whole flock were threatened, as when infectious bronchitis strikes, would the (expensive) poultry vet be called in. Then, antibiotics as mass medication in the feed or water would be prescribed. Non-contagious diseases and injuries were routinely ignored.

Mr X told us that however well the extractor fans worked, still the air in the sheds was heavily contaminated with particles of feathers, grain, mites and general dust. When alarmed, hens attempted to flap their wings, hitting each other and the sides of the cages, raising clouds of contaminants. All this convinced us that our 'February 4th Statement' was accurate. Even if the will to inspect battery hens properly were present, no worker could endure being in the polluted environment of a battery shed for more than short spells.

Mr X claimed the stocking density recommended in MAFF Codes was frequently exceeded on Goldenlay farms, and that water was sometimes withheld for periods exceeding 24 hours. The Code states: *'When birds are induced to moult it may be necessary to withhold food and water for short periods; but in no case should food or water be withheld for more than 24 hours.'*

Back in the car we wondered why, as site manager, Mr X hadn't insisted on better conditions for the hens. But maybe he had tried his best, while knowing his job would be on the line if he rocked the boat. In any event, we were convinced of the authenticity of his account. Everything he'd told us tied up with what we already knew.

*

Mr X was happy to have his identity revealed to the Queen, so he was named in our letter that accompanied the tape. On April 18th we posted the recording, thinking what a far cry was Buckingham Palace from our informant's bleak little flat. Again, we begged the Queen to rescind her Royal Warrant to Goldenlay, stressing the illegality, as we saw it, of the system. And we issued a Press Release, to coincide with the posting of the letter.

*

On January 20th 1983 *The Yorkshire Post* reported our 'partial victory': *'A pressure group opposed to battery farming claimed partial victory over one of Britain's biggest battery-egg producers yesterday. Chickens' Lib has been told by the Lord Chamberlain's office that the Royal Household is to buy more free-range eggs – and so fewer battery eggs supplied by the Wakefield-based Goldenlay company. The group learned of the decision from the Secretary of the Royal Household's Warrants Committee, Mr John Titman...Mrs Clare Druce, of Wakefield, a co-founder of Chickens' Lib, said last night: "We are very pleased with this decision and regard it as a partial victory, though it's a pity that it has not been decided to stop buying battery eggs for the Queen's Household."'* In other words, battery eggs were still on the menu for those outside the royal circle.

The following year there was more to come. On September 16th 1984 the Sunday Express Magazine ran a feature entitled *'Life Inside the Royal Nursery'* and apparently Chickens' Lib had a foot in the door there, too: *'Farmyard hens lay the nursery eggs. Since the Queen cut the royal order for battery-laid eggs following a protest from Chickens' Lib (an organisation of housewives campaigning to ban battery eggs), all the royal households have followed her example.'*

Well, that was excellent news, and good publicity for Chickens' Lib too.

FUNDING THE CAMPAIGN

Scottish battery egg producers were still worrying away about that Mr Big, the shadowy figure plotting their downfall from some 'foreign country'. Three years after the Scottish Egg Producers' Retail Association had first voiced its fears, it finally got down to an investigation, but what it revealed was to leave them bemused.

*

Poultry World, July 1st 1982: *'Where do these welfare fanatics get the money to mount their campaigns, chairman of the Scottish Egg Producer Retailers Association [SEPRA] Jim Steel asked his secretary Denis Surgenor? First to be investigated was Chickens' Lib and to their surprise they found that the organisation spent only about £2,000 a year. Mr Surgenor reported that their balance sheet for the two years ending 31st December 1981 showed an income of £4,279 and expenditure of £4,058. Among the costs were £36.50 for maintenance of hens and £17.90 for demonstration effects. He concluded that they got a lot of attention for very little money. In fact a lot of their expenditure must go on postage, writing letters for publication, like that on page 23. As long as we have a free press this will remain a cost effective way of being heard.'*

We were flattered by this attention, though a little concerned to realize we had a spy in the camp; our financial reports, duly audited, were for the eyes of supporters only – or so we'd believed.

*

Around the time of SEPRA's investigation into our finances something wonderful happened. In his capacity of Chairman of the RSPCA Council, our friend and patron Richard Ryder arranged for a short feature about Chickens' Lib to appear in the Society's magazine. In it was included an appeal for donations toward our work.

The publication went out to the many thousands of RSPCA members, and secretly Violet and I calculated that if a decent proportion of them sent just £1 each, our present dire financial problems would be solved at a stroke. We'd be able to forget the looming prospect of jumble sales and street collections, and the need to find people to help run them. Many of our local supporters were already committed to other organisations; it would be wrong to ask them to give up more of their precious time.

The keenly anticipated magazine appeared. Eagerly we awaited the arrival of those thousands of donations.

And nothing happened. Nothing at all, until...

There was one response, and one only, but it made a dramatic and lasting difference to the scope of our campaign. A letter arrived written in pale blue ink in beautiful copper-plate handwriting, and inside it was folded a cheque for £3,000. This gentleman (let us call him James) had read about our work in the RSPCA magazine and he wanted to help.

I remember bursting into tears when I opened James' letter. I was so moved by his generosity, so relieved at this sudden release from mounting anxieties and frustrations about finances. While he was there to help, James said, we must never lack for funds. He considered the battery system an abomination.

For the next two decades, James continued to send us very generous donations, insisting we must let him know if ever we were in difficulties (only once did we appeal to him, not wishing to take advantage of his kindness). When his work moved him from London to the North, we arranged for him to visit us. Duncan and I collected Irene, then met James at a nearby station, and took him to our house for tea, where Violet and my father joined us. It was a beautiful summer's day and we sat out on the lawn against a backdrop of our rescued hens wandering contentedly in the orchard.

Our benefactor was just as we'd imagined him – charmingly old-fashioned, and a little reserved. His handwriting, by then so familiar to us, seemed to mirror his personality to perfection.

*

Another delightful gentleman stands out in my memory. I'll call him Albert. By the time Albert made contact with us he was a widower in his eighties, and living in sheltered housing in the Lake District. He began to send us regular donations, accompanied by long letters detailing his concerns about animals. While on holiday Duncan and I decided to visit him, so I could thank him personally for his support.

He seemed delighted to see us. Over a cup of tea he described how he economised at every turn, saving whatever money he could to help animals in distress. The little flat was attractive and comfortable enough, but Albert told us he lived very frugally, eating the simplest of vegan food and buying all his clothes, shoes included, from charity shops.

When we left, Albert came outside to see us off and it was then that another side of him came to light. A sudden glint came into his eye, as with clenched fist he thumped the roof of our very ordinary car. "I'm *wild* with envy!" he exclaimed. Apparently he'd been a rep in his working life and still hankered after life on the open road.

For years we kept up a correspondence, and Albert remembered us generously in his Will.

*

A happy arrangement began when I received a phone call from Tony Thrush. He introduced himself as one of the directors of the National Society Against Factory Farming (NSAFF). This society had been founded and run by Lucy Newman, who had continued to campaign tirelessly into her nineties.

After Lucy Newman's death, NSAFF still had funds in reserve and wanted to put the money to good use, while keeping NSAFF's name alive. The directors were seeking another organisation to produce and distribute their material, to do the work, in effect, and that's where we came in. I was invited to meet all four directors in a London hotel, near Buckingham Palace. Tony didn't approve of spending NSAFF money on lunches in plush hotels, so he and I met up outside, before joining the others inside for coffee. The purpose of the meeting seemed to be to vet me, and apparently I passed the test.

After that first meeting, Tony became our main link with NSAFF. He would phone me, and, with me holding the receiver at a safe distance (Tony did shout down the phone), we'd arrange to produce leaflets, booklets, and eventually videos, the deal being that assuming NSAFF approved of the texts, and as long as its name was prominently on all the shared materials, we'd go halves with the costs, including postage.

Thanks to this arrangement, we were able to mail booklets, leaflets and videos out to hundreds of secondary schools throughout the UK, and to meet the expense of translating our booklet *Today's Poultry Industry*, and some of our videos, into French and Spanish. ADDA, a Spanish organisation, then produced a booklet based on ours but adapted to that country's needs.

Tony was probably in his sixties when we first met, and very active. He swam regularly and went on walking holidays – once he called in on us at the end of one of these, so Violet and he could meet. He and his wife were great dog lovers too, and rescued many. Often, there was a spectacular cacophony of barking in the background when I phoned him, once accompanied by a deafening crash of breaking china.

Sadly, Tony suffered from a rare disease that meant he could die at any moment with no warning. In the time that we knew him he did collapse when in the swimming baths, but he was resuscitated. We all knew his life was on a knife-edge, a fact he seemed to face philosophically, even cheerfully.

In February 1999 I was staying in Harrogate, where my mother now lived in a residential home near to my sister, Helen. Violet was very ill and the feeling of gloom deepened when I received a call from Tony's daughter. Tony had died, suddenly.

With his death, our mutually beneficial arrangement came to an end. For a long time I missed hearing his voice, missed holding the telephone receiver at arm's length while planning our next activities. Tony was totally committed to the cause and it had been a pleasure to co-operate with him.

*

The St Andrew's Fund in Edinburgh was supportive of our work, too, and we were grateful for their help.

*

I've listed just a few of the striking ways in which we got by without funding worries. In addition to the grand sums, a steady stream of donations continued to come in, ranging from the substantial to the odd coin Sellotaped to a scrappy piece of card. And once in a while a very welcome legacy would come our way.

Every single donation was received with real gratitude. People cared deeply about animals on factory farms and we were touched that they trusted us to spend their money wisely.

No worse than any other battery...

May 1983: We wrote to Chief Superintendent Frank Milner, head of the RSPCA's Special Investigations and Operations Department, describing a dump of a battery unit I passed on my way to work. I'd noticed that the only source of lighting in the daytime seemed to be via one open door per shed, and a few dusty windows. Lights were on after dark, to make up the seventeen hours of dim 'daylight' that battery hens must have to induce egg laying. We were worried too by the presence of windows in this ramshackle set-up. Battery sheds are designed to be windowless for a good reason – shafts of bright light encourage aggressive pecking, and, to make matters worse, the hens may suffer from extremes of temperature.

While Violet distracted a member of staff, I wandered over to one of the sheds and witnessed a disturbing sight: a hen repeatedly and frantically attempting to escape from her cage. From her well-feathered condition, I guessed her to be newly caged. On this farm, pullets (young birds not yet in lay) could be seen in outdoor coops, destined to be incarcerated in cages at point-of-lay, when around eighteen weeks. Little could the bird I saw have guessed that this harsh rectangle of metal, its floor sloping uncomfortably, with four other hens crammed into it, was to be her 'home' for life.

Writing about this has reminded me how the driver of a vehicle loaded with point-of-lay hens once stopped to ask me directions to a nearby battery farm. With the heaviest heart I told him where to go – for what else could I have done?

*

A local RSPCA inspector did visit the shabby premises with windows, but there was no good outcome. Dissatisfied, we then wrote again to the RSPCA's HQ, urging the Society to consider a prosecution. I ended my letter: *'You will find from your records that this unit was entered at the instruction of Superintendent Marshall after we alerted him. He stated that nothing was more wrong there than in any other battery, so no action was possible. We are not prepared to accept this, since if domestic animals were treated in this way their owners would be prosecuted for cruelty.'*

No action followed our complaint and the only visible change was a motley selection of old plastic sheeting nailed over the windows.

*

The RSPCA's Superintendent Marshall's response highlighted once again the problem of cruelty enshrined in law. As usual, what we longed for was a bold leap of the imagination from RSPCA Headquarters. We wanted the law to be taken at face value – for what other value does it have?

Goldenlay hens make the Guardian

One day an animal rights activist sent us a range of photographs featuring a farm in Essex, one of Goldenlay's suppliers. One photo showed escaped hens surviving in the deep pit area beneath the cages. In another, the photographer had somehow managed to snap hens from beneath their cages. A weird pattern emerged of the underside of many feet, claws gripped around the grid of the sloping cage floors.

Later, in March 1985, author and food writer Colin Spencer wrote a full page article for the Guardian, illustrating it with this remarkable photograph. His opening read: *'Easter may seem the best time to look at the egg. But I don't mean the chocolate one. That innocent looking breakfast egg, if it is not free range, hides a tumult of unnecessary suffering for the hen that laid it. If it needs a day in the calendar, Passion Sunday might suit it.'* The article itself was passionate, and at the end Colin included Chickens' Lib's address for further information. Over five hundred readers wrote to us, many of them becoming dedicated and long-term supporters.

We produced a postcard showing three hens from the Essex farm, staring out between the cage bars. We added a question mark to Goldenlay's by now (in)famous slogan *The Taste of the Country*. The photo was in black and white, its impact bleak, and our question mark neatly transformed the sense of the slogan.

Our next venture provided proof, if any were needed, that the battery system is better suited to nuts and bolts, or to any other inanimate object you care to name, rather than to living, feeling beings.

A strange incident

On May 6th 1983, Violet and I paid a return visit to a battery we'd come upon, on the outskirts of Leeds. A few days previously a lad working there had been happy to show us around but, being an honest lad, or at least a cautious one, he'd refused to sell hens in the absence of his boss. On our next visit, we managed to track down the owner.

We said our standard piece and he agreed to sell, so we followed him into one of the units, not mentioning that we'd been there before, so knew our way around pretty well.

The hens were just as we'd remembered them, very thin, with what looked like small tumours the length of their near-featherless necks. We knew we'd want to report this place, and desperately tried to take everything in: the condition of the birds, the state of the cages, the number of hens to a cage... Then, from among the many thousands, I noticed one particular hen, caged on the uppermost tier.

She was poking her head and neck through the bars and I could sense her anxiety: although her comb was a healthy red and she seemed well feathered, I knew there was something terribly wrong. Pointing her out, I suggested she'd be a nice hen to have. The farmer, a stocky little man, looked irritated. Only by treading on the feed trough of the lowest tier could he reach her cage, but he made the attempt. Having taken a closer look, he changed his mind.

"You'll not be wanting that one," he said, stepping back down to floor level.

And now I wanted that particular hen even more. We *had* to have her. Desperate, I resorted to absurd behaviour, nudging him in the ribs. "Oh, go on," I urged.

"There's summat wrong with it," he snapped. "You'll *not* be wanting it!"

"Oh, but I like her face!" I pleaded.

And at that he gave in. Probably *he* was feeling desperate now, desperate to get rid of these nutty women.

He clambered up again, dragged the hen out of her cage and threw her to the floor. She looked abnormal but in the dimly lit surroundings we weren't sure why. We said we'll have three more please, and in no time had paid our money and were away.

At a safe distance, we stopped the car to check on the hens. And oh my God! I hadn't mistaken the distress in the eyes of the one from the topmost tier – her abdominal area was grossly distended.

Instinctively we realized there was no hope for her, and drove straight to the MAFF Veterinary Investigation Centre in Leeds where, in those days, for just £10 it was possible to have a bird euthanased and examined *post mortem*. A PM certificate would tell us exactly what was wrong.

While the vet prepared the lethal injection I held her gently, glad she could know a few moments of kindness before her grim life was over. I wondered if she'd been reared on deep litter before being caged for egg production, or if she'd known nothing but a 'Day-old to Death' cage, as the other popular rearing system is officially called.

And what would be worse? To enjoy a degree of freedom, only to have it snatched away at eighteen weeks of age, or to be a prisoner from the very start?

*

That night I lay in bed feeling gutted. Amazingly, this was the first battery hen we'd ever bought and not been able to rehabilitate ourselves, or pass on to a trusted carer. I was thinking how infinitely sad are the lives of battery hens. I longed to believe they would all have a second chance, a time to walk on cool grass, to search for their own food, to follow their instincts. In my mind's eye I saw a vast sunlit meadow, where hundreds, no, *thousands* of hens roamed contentedly on the greenest grass... and, although I was lost in a kind of dream world, I was wide awake. A fanlight in the bedroom was open, and suddenly I heard a flapping of wings, as of a large bird alighting on the window ledge.

That I heard the sound of wings, there is no doubt. And yes, it could have been an owl. Yet I'd never been aware of an owl near the window before, nor did anything similar ever occur again. Posthumously, we named our hen Angela.

*

A few days later, the post-mortem certificate arrived in the mail: *'The chief abnormality noted was in the body cavity which contained a massive quantity of egg material in various stages of inspissation*. There was a solid formed egg in the oviduct and some normal eggs developing in the ovary... At some later date this would almost certainly have developed into an egg peritonitis.'*

(*Inspissation : The plugging, in this case of the oviduct, with a thickened viscid material having a decreased fluid content.)

So our hen was suffering, probably acutely, her blocked oviduct preventing the passage of other eggs. Nothing of her distress had been apparent to our farmer, glancing casually up at the top tier. Nothing had seemed amiss to him until he'd climbed up at our request. The distension must have been getting worse for days, weeks maybe, and who knows for how much longer Angela would have survived?

So much for the cage system.

*

With no delay, we alerted the RSPCA to Angela's farm, and this time a prosecution did get underway. Violet and I were called as witnesses; Frank Milner, who I believe was head of the Society's Special Investigations Unit at that time, was well pleased with us. As he put it, the lawyer for the defence 'took a step back' when Violet and I entered the witness box.

Incredibly, Angela's condition was not considered proof of neglect. The post mortem report had included the fatal phrase: '*The bird was in bright condition*.' This short sentence was apparently enough to dismiss the suffering Angela endured unnoticed while her body became increasingly blocked with rotting eggs, egg peritonitis only a step away.

However, the farmer was found guilty of failing to inspect his hens properly, since at the time of the RSPCA's visit several birds had been found dead in their cages, some displaying evidence of starvation.

*

March 13th 1984: ' *David Kemp, 49, of Springfield Farm, Horsforth, Leeds was fined £100 on March 13th, for causing unnecessary suffering and for failing to inspect his hens...Mr Kemp's farm had been the target for investigators from a group called "Chickens' Lib", which campaigns against battery farming, the court was told*.' *Poultry World*, March 22nd 1984.

*

Of course we welcomed this case, but with serious reservations. At the RSPCA's 1982 AGM a Chickens' Lib's motion that a battery farmer be prosecuted on the grounds of the cruelty of the battery system *per se* had received wide support. Yet nearly two years later, the Society was still no nearer to achieving this goal. As with the Surrey case, the Springfield Farm prosecution was taken under the *Welfare of Livestock (Intensive Units) 1978 Regulations*, and limited to inadequate daily inspection.

So we remained frustrated. We wanted it proved in a court of law that the battery system, however well or badly run, is illegal. We'd continue with our efforts to expose the cruelties *inherent* in the system.

Our next foray into the dark world of factory farming was to be one of our most interesting ones, though dangerous, especially for Violet.

But before that, some good news: 'Top people' are happy to support Chickens' Lib!

Starry patronage for Chickens' Lib

In October 1983 we wrote to our supporters: '*We are very pleased to be able to announce that Chickens' Lib now has four patrons – the Bishop of Salisbury, the Rt Rev John Austin Baker, the writers Brigid Brophy and Margaret Lane (Miss Lane is the Countess of Huntingdon), and Richard Ryder, author of "Victims of Science" and a former Chairman of the RSPCA Council. We are most grateful to them all for the confidence they have shown in us by agreeing to help us – and thereby all battery hens – in this way.*'

Later, peace campaigner Bruce Kent was to become a much-valued patron too.

*

In the mid-1980s we issued a battery hen leaflet, its front and back covers decorated with the signatures of around thirty VIPs – a selection of authors, philosophers, politicians and others. Among them were Richard Adams, Catherine Cookson, Ken Livingstone, Joanna Lumley, Lord Peter Melchett, Mary Midgely, Patrick Moore, Desmond Morris, Iris Murdoch, Jonathon Porritt, the Bishop of Southwark and Colin Spencer.

On another occasion we invited well-known people to write to Prime Minister Margaret Thatcher, and/or to sign our petition. Again, many supported us, including Julie Christie, Dawn French, Nigel Hawthorne, Cleo Laine and Johnny Dankworth, Bryan Forbes, Clare Francis, Miles Kington, Twiggy Lawson, Michael Mayne (the Dean of Westminster,) Linda McCartney, Spike Milligan, Hayley Mills and Indajit Singh (now Lord Singh), broadcaster and at that time editor of The Sikh Messenger.

I'm sure that the late Sir John Gielgud wouldn't have minded me telling readers that he too was a keen supporter of Chickens' Lib.

We were so grateful to them all.

Bitten but unbowed

October 24th 1983: Violet, Irene, Emily (it's half-term) and I set out on a new battery hen quest, this time heading for Derbyshire. The manager of our chosen farm turned out not to be the type to sell off a few old hens to strangers, but obligingly he told us of a smaller place a mile or two down the road.

We soon found the range of shabby battery sheds alongside some old stone farm buildings, near to the farmhouse itself. All was quiet, so in the yard we practised our 'Is anybody there?' technique. If someone did appear, we'd trot out our piece about wanting a few old hens. If not, we'd have a little look around. We noticed a large Alsatian, but he was securely chained up, so we wandered towards the sheds.

The door of the first one stood open; a mask hung near the doorway, the kind people wear when engaged in hazardous work. We ventured a little nearer, until we could make out the cages, stacked high and crammed with hens, many almost featherless. The stench was overpowering. On the floor lay the remains of past inmates, mostly skulls and a few bones picked clean, probably by rats. We hung back, afraid to pass the threshold. Then, in a nearby stone barn we discovered thousands more caged hens, surviving in semi darkness.

We drove away, found a phone box and phoned the police. The police suggested we contact the RSPCA, whose phone was permanently engaged. We phoned MAFF at their Derby office, where a woman vet showed a deep level of unconcern. Having met our usual solid brick walls, we had a snack in the car and discussed what to do next. Simply going home was not an option.

We decided to return to this nightmare of a 'farm' in the afternoon.

*

At two o'clock we went through our routine once more.

'Hello! Anyone there?'

Suddenly the Alsatian, no longer chained, charged across the yard. Snarling, he headed straight for Violet, sank his teeth into the back of her leg then, almost as suddenly, was gone. Had he been set on us and then called off? Never had a Chickens' Lib team moved so fast. Within seconds, we were slamming car doors and backing out of the yard.

I remembered some homeopathic 'shock' tablets in my bag, and at a safe distance we stopped to dose Violet before making for Chesterfield hospital's A&E department, where we spent a couple of hours hanging around for the necessary tetanus jab and stitches.

Though literally scarred for life, Violet weathered the incident remarkably well, especially for someone who'd always feared being bitten by an Alsatian.

*

Following our complaint, MAFF did visit the farm the next day. On November 24th MAFF wrote to Chickens' Lib insisting that no warning was given to the farmer, when it came to investigating our complaint. Apparently, we were told, a woman vet accompanied by an RSPCA inspector had carried out the inspection. Interestingly, this same RSPCA Inspector later let slip to us that the MAFF vet hadn't ventured more than a few feet into any of the units. Had she, like us, felt afraid?

In emphasising the absence of forewarning for the farmer, MAFF had tacitly admitted that the vet and the RSPCA inspector almost certainly saw precisely what *we* had seen, yet MAFF had found no evidence of unnecessary pain or unnecessary distress. A recurring phrase, this unnecessary pain or unnecessary distress.

*

Things were soon to take an encouraging turn. The local RSPCA inspector was, according to the Society's Assistant Executive Director (Designate), not fully satisfied with his visit. The Assistant ED(D) explained, in a letter dated November 11th, that he awaited the MAFF veterinary report before possibly taking things further.

*

Two weeks later, and still determined to make headway, we asked friends in the animal rights movement to try *their* luck at the farm, having duly warned them about the dog. Regardless of danger, they agreed to help.

They'd go the following Sunday morning with a trailer, spinning a tale about an uncle with an allotment wanting a few hens.

They must have looked the part, for they came away with an impressive twenty-four hens.

*

Sunday afternoon: We'd arranged temporary accommodation for our expected guests in the basement of our house, in an old wardrobe sporting several small partitions. With the wardrobe laid on its side, these cubby-holes had rather the look of open-plan battery cages, from which the hens could emerge and enjoy a straw-filled area.

We saw a car draw up, a shabby tarpaulin-covered trailer attached, and rushed out to congratulate our helpers. As we began the task of transferring twenty-four hens to the basement we realised these were no ordinary victims of the cage system. Panic-stricken, they were also remarkably strong and unusually vocal. In the midst of the frantic operation, our ears ringing with their desperate squawks, something unfortunate occurred.

Our nearest neighbours lived in a converted barn, the front door of which was only yards from our basement door. Suddenly, bizarrely, a large family group plus friends began filing past us. Then I remembered. Their younger child's christening! No wonder everyone was dressed so formally, so respectably, so very smartly... Mercifully, they were all too polite to stop and stare – or at least I think they were. Actually, I couldn't bring myself to look in their direction, let alone ask how the christening had gone. Just ignore the awfulness of this situation I told myself, just go on trying to get a grip around each hen's flailing wings. Pretend none of this is happening...

We kept up the pretence, on both sides. Nothing was ever said. Well, not to our faces. Once the procession was safely indoors and the champagne flowing, the topic of neighbours lowering the tone of the neighbourhood may well have come under discussion.

*

Monday: the RSPCA sent a local veterinary surgeon, employed to act on the Society's behalf, to examine our hens *in situ*. Pleasant in manner, if unforthcoming, he briskly examined each one with the help of a young veterinary nurse. We'd assumed the vet to be in sympathy with our cause, so when HQ contacted us again, quoting from his report, we were taken aback.

In his letter, the Assistant Executive Director Designate informed us that the Society had found no contravention of the law. He then invited us to 'reflect' on part of the examining vet's statement, which claimed he'd found no signs of suffering. Indeed the vet had gone one (giant) step further, noting that the birds he'd examined seemed to him 'more than happy' and were strong and healthy; his final thrust was to suggest that we'd caused the hens more stress than they had ever previously endured, by transporting them to a completely new environment. Away, in fact, from a rat-infested hell hole (my comment, not the vet's).

And reflect we did. Both on the anthropomorphic and illogical veterinary 'report' and on the odd, schoolmasterly tone from RSPCA headquarters.

Dave Clegg, professional photographer and good friend to Chickens' Lib, called round; a photographic record of the hens was essential. We'd already named the most pitiful and naked among them Felicity, bearing in mind that she'd been deemed 'more than happy'.

The season of goodwill was approaching. So we mounted Felicity's photo on colourful card, added a decorative design of holly leaves and a festive greeting, and sent it to our visiting vet's Huddersfield surgery.

*

April 25th 1984: Having gained no satisfaction from MAFF, we gathered a large group of protestors (around one hundred of them, plus a few dogs for good measure) and visited the MAFF offices in Derby, where the vet who'd inspected Felicity's farm worked. Or didn't work.

Unchallenged, we made our way upstairs to a spacious office on the first floor where, to the surprise of assorted staff, our sit-in took place, lasting two and a half hours. Eventually we were told a small number of us could have an official meeting at a pre-arranged date, if we all left immediately.

Three weeks later, three of us met with the Divisional Veterinary Officer and two other non-veterinary officials. The DVO confirmed his whole-hearted support of the battery system and his belief that the hens we'd bought were moulting. The sop he offered us was that a (woman) vet would inspect all the thirteen battery farms in Derbyshire housing more than five thousand hens. This didn't thrill us, since she too appeared totally dedicated to the battery system, and in the end the plan was abandoned anyway due to an outbreak of Fowl Pest.

To round off the sorry story, here's an extract from our newsletter dated June 1984: *'Derby MAFF expressed its gratitude for our good behaviour during the sit-in but asked us not to come again, giving as a reason the fact that there are drugs and shotguns on the premises.'* (Optimistically, we assumed these to be for veterinary use, rather than to subdue protestors.)

*

We re-homed most of the hens easily, keeping half a dozen for ourselves and, after a period of sheltered rehabilitation to allow for re-growing of feathers, they thrived in our little orchard. A mere six months after she'd arrived at our house, terrified and nearly naked, Felicity was on her way to stardom.

Dave Clegg had come in the spring and once again taken Felicity's picture. This time she was striding across the lawn, friendly, confident, and fully feathered. More than happy, one could say! Soon, Dave's photos, featuring Felicity 'before and after', were to become the subject of a poster, possibly the best battery hen poster ever produced, and one that was to go all over the world.

'This is the same hen – True or False?' ran our heading above photos of Felicity as we'd first known her, and six months later. *'TRUE! The battery system routinely reduces hens to this pitiful state. This little hen was lucky – the photo on the right shows her just six months after her release from a dimly-lit, stinking shed. REMEMBER! Eggs described as "Farm Fresh" etc. are often laid by cruelly-imprisoned hens – and for them it's a life sentence. Their only change of scenery will be the terrifying journey to slaughter.*
SAY NO TO BATTERY EGGS.'

And there was more. In April 1985 issue of *Harpers and Queen* ran an article on Chickens' Lib, written by Violet and myself (and representing virtually our only financial gain during the entire campaign). Under the heading *'Free as a Bird'* was a photo of Violet and me with – who else? – Felicity.

*

Post script: Felicity lived with us for two more years, in comfort and contentment, the friendliest of hens, a special hen. She died peacefully, and we buried her under a flowering cherry tree.

*

Post post script

Eight years on, a headline in the local paper caught my eye: *Vet guilty of disgraceful conduct*. And goodness! The vet turned out to be *our* vet of the 'more than happy' diagnosis. His surgery had been deemed by a former president of the Royal College of Veterinary Surgeons to be: '...*filthy and blood-spattered with bird droppings and cigarette ends on the floor and the body of a dog in a warm chest freezer...in the room there were syringes full of blood and a blood-stained drape. Medicine bottles were covered in horse dung and encrusted with dust...*' and so the charges went on. (1)

Nor was it the first time the RCVS had had cause to check on this vet. There'd been an earlier occasion, in 1988, when his registration had been suspended. Then, he'd been found guilty of illicitly selling EC certificates to a meat company (2).

It seemed the RSPCA had sent along the wrong person if they wanted an honest and professional opinion on our abused battery hens. To be fair, we knew that vets willing to stand out against intensive farming were truly hard to find. Indeed they could probably have been numbered on the fingers of one hand. But should not the Society have questioned that strange report instead of allowing Chickens' Lib to be vilified? Should they not have enquired into their chosen vet's history, so avoiding wasting an opportunity, along with RSPCA funds?

*

It would be hard to imagine a worse example of a battery farm than Felicity's. Face masks to protect workers, rat-eaten hen remains littering the shed floors, thousands of near-featherless hens crammed into a dimly-lit barn, an RSPCA inspector 'not fully satisfied' with what he'd seen.

And yet no pressure was exerted by the Society to challenge MAFF's protection of an establishment where the law was being broken at every turn. Surely this was a golden opportunity to prosecute, not merely on the grounds of lack of inspection, but on the system *per se*. On many occasions the Society was to point out that there was nothing to stop *us*, or any other organisation, from mounting a prosecution.

But of course there was. In the past, certainly, the RSPCA alone had the funds and the necessary legal know-how at their disposal.

A CRUEL 'SOLUTION'

The practice of de-beaking poultry has developed hand in hand with intensive systems. It's a mutilation intended to minimise injury and death due to birds pecking at each other in their frustration. The industry freely uses the terms 'aggression', 'cannibalism' and even 'vice' to cover abnormal behaviour induced by the severe deprivations imposed on most commercially kept poultry. Battery hens were the first to suffer from widespread de-beaking but now un-caged poultry endure the mutilation too, when severe overcrowding can lead to outbreaks of feather pecking that can end in high mortality.

Once seen as a handy method for the control of 'aggression', the practice of de-beaking is now widely regarded as unacceptable, in terms of animal welfare. Yet the mutilation of de-beaking seems destined to hang like a millstone around the necks of ministers attempting to take heed of welfarists, for the solution to feather-pecking remains elusive. Small flocks could be the answer – an unpopular one in today's harsh commercial climate – while selecting birds of a different, more docile, strain is under consideration.

*

Following the House of Commons' Agriculture Committee's scrutiny of intensive agriculture, its 1980-81 Report was published. Despite serious reservations put forward by welfarists, the Ministry of Agriculture, Fisheries and Food (MAFF) remained stoutly in favour of de-beaking, stating: *'It is considered that the provisions of the Veterinary Surgeons (Exemptions) Order 1962 and the guidelines on beak-trimming laid down in the welfare code for domestic fowls are, taken together, adequate to safeguard the welfare of all domestic fowls, including those kept in battery cages. FAWC may make recommendations on this subject as part of its review of the welfare codes.'* (1)

*

MAFF's 1987 Welfare Code for Domestic Fowls stated (in paragraph 47): *'Beak trimming should be carried out only as a last resort, that is, when it is clear that more suffering would be caused in the flock if it were not done.'* A last resort? This advice didn't sit well with what was and still is happening on a vast scale, day in day out, in the poultry industry: the routine partial beak amputation (PBA) of very young chicks. The updated Code (2) tactfully displays less outright enthusiasm for the mutilation, but the message is in essence the same – that it's still acceptable as long as no more than one third of the beak is removed before chicks reach ten days of age. Under the telling heading *Mutilations*, the Code instructs: *'Beak trimming should be carried out to the highest possible standards by trained operators. Operators should be continually re-evaluated for efficiency of their beak trimming skills.'*

DEFRA's new *Guidance on The Mutilations (Permitted Procedures) (England) (Amendment) Regulations 2010: Beak Trimming of laying hens* gives the same advice, but with the provision that, in the case of chicks of under ten days, only the infra-red beak treatment may be used. The 'hot blade technique' is recommended for older birds, should a serious outbreak of aggression occur.

*

The 1980s: Poultry scientists Breward and Gentle carried out exhaustive research into the sensitivity of chickens' beaks (3), and we welcomed their published paper warmly. Here was the scientific evidence everyone in the welfare movement had been waiting for! We read that not only is the avian beak a complex sensory organ but, as most people know, essential to a bird for food finding, grooming, nest building and more. It's also richly endowed with nerves. Having observed the de-beaked objects of their research, the team concluded that chickens endure chronic pain in their shortened beaks, comparable to the phantom limb pain suffered by human amputees.

We referred in some detail to this research in our 1993 booklet *Hidden Suffering*, and issued a fact sheet on the subject.

*

At one point in our investigations we purchased an Agricultural Training Board video about the mutilation, and it made difficult watching. Day-old chicks' heads were rammed into a cone-shaped device, allowing just their tiny beaks to poke through, the tips to be pressed against a heated blade, a procedure known to result in possible severe blood loss, shock and even death.

The operation could be performed at any age, should aggression get out of hand. When older birds' beaks were cut and cauterised with a red-hot blade, explained a MAFF leaflet (4) : *The legs and wings are held firmly in one hand whilst the other is employed in holding the bird's head and at the same time keeping the beak open with thumb and finger.*

It doesn't take much imagination to picture the scene – thousands of birds, terrified, dragged from their cages (most were caged then), the unpleasant and difficult task to be performed by a stressed and soon exhausted man (or woman)...

Yet MAFF's optimism knew no bounds, expressing itself confident that its guidance would be *'adequate to safeguard the welfare of all domestic fowl.'*

*

De-beaking, beak-trimming, conditioning, re-conditioning if the operation needs doing twice (the last two euphemisms are American) and the scientific term – partial beak amputation (PBA) – all amount to the same thing – a mutilation intended to limit damage caused by aggressive pecking. Not only are there several ways of describing the operation, some sounding less brutal than others, but different ways of spelling it too – debeaking comes with or without the hyphen. For simplicity, as well as accuracy, I'll opt for PBA.

Poultry forced to live in unnaturally large groups or in the constraints of battery cages are under sustained stress, and so behave abnormally. Rather than providing a suitable environment where birds can live peaceably, the industry has resorted to PBA to solve its problems.

*

1991, and the situation looked more hopeful when a FAWC Report called for a ban on routine PBA by 1996 (5). However a Dissenting Minority Report drawn up by several members on the FAWC working party, including Ruth Harrison, called for prohibition within two years. (6)

In the same year, 1991, Chickens' Lib circulated a four-page questionnaire to around one hundred farmers of free range hens. The form contained sixty-two questions, the intention being to find out how environment and breed of bird affected welfare, and in particular the need to de-beak the hens. Our initiative enjoyed good publicity, being reported in several industry publications including *Poultry World, Farmers Guardian*, the National Farmers Union's *Poultry Forum*, and was reproduced in full within the pages of *UKEPRA News*. The response was good, with several farmers claiming that they never had to resort to de-beaking.

However, the informative responses met with no interest from MAFF. Ah well, it seems we were ahead of our time – in fact, twenty-one years in advance of official thinking. For in 2012, researchers at the University of Bristol, headed by professor of animal welfare Christine Nicol, are, at DEFRA's behest, appealing to free range egg producers for help. The aim is to discover how free range flocks can be managed without beak trimming, and the hope is to introduce a ban on the abuse – this time in 2016.

*

In 1995 we were shocked when FAWC published its Report on the Welfare of Turkeys. In paragraph 55 the Council noted that previous studies on PBA of poultry were limited to chickens. However, some FAWC members had developed doubts, expressed in paragraph 55. No longer did they believe that the Breward and Gentle findings should be *'...automatically assumed to apply to turkeys. We discussed the lack of information with the British Turkey Federation who agreed to fund work at an independent research institute to determine the relative merits of different methods of beak trimming turkeys at different ages.'* This struck us as odd – surely a beak is a beak?

In 1995 *Veterinary Record* published the results of this independent research, carried out by some of those same poultry researchers at Roslin who'd concluded that chickens suffered chronic pain. (7) The account of the research is complicated, describing three common methods used to achieve PBA. FAWC concluded that beak-trimming (FAWC's preferred name for the procedure) *'...influenced behaviour* [in turkeys] *only to a minor extent and yet had beneficial effects in reducing feather damage and mortality.'* However, since FAWC considered the study to have been carried out in insufficient depth, it believed there was room for *'more research'*.

We were left puzzled again that a turkey's beak should be so different from a chicken's, as regards its endowment with nerves, resulting in post-operative pain. A new method, described as being less invasive, was now an option, namely electronic infra-red trimming. However, ominously, the researchers described the procedure as *'hazardous in unskilled hands'*.

*

Only two years later, in paragraph 62 of its 1997 Report on the Welfare of Laying Hens, FAWC was to describe PBA as a *'major welfare insult'*. It would seem the species difference was alive and well. Chickens feeling chronic pain, turkeys less bothered. And I've now been informed that the further research, for which there was room, was never carried out.

*

In 2002 DEFRA decided to listen to the anti-PBA lobby and optimistically decreed a total ban on the mutilation, scheduled for 2011. DEFRA was thereby allowing the poultry industry nine years in which to set up new systems, or to demand that the breeding companies select for a strain of more docile birds.

*

In 2008 the *Poultry Science Association* published a paper entitled *Comparative Effects of Infrared and One-Third Hot-Blade Trimming and Beak Topography, Behaviour and Growth.* In summing up, this American research concluded that the initial pain impact was greater in the infra-red treated birds, than in beaks cut with a red-hot blade, but the difference disappeared 'relatively quickly'.

However, the treated birds may have considered that the pain experienced made time seem to go by exceptionally slowly. They were observed to feed at a slower rate for three or four weeks after treatment by infrared heat *'which likely reflects the increased feeding difficulty that these birds experienced because of the differences in tissue erosion rate in the upper and lower mandibles'.* The fact that birds minus part of their beaks eat less, suggests, at best, an inability to pick up food easily. But not to worry! *'Reduced feed wastage may be an important factor from the producers' perspective because feed represents a large proportion of the costs associated with egg production.'* (8)

On page 1476 of this paper there are photos, two illustrating the different methods used in the experiment. Photo B shows an infra-red-treated

110

chick, eyes closed, apparently in pain. That's odd, because according to the literature *'Following treatment, the corneum-generating layer remains intact until 7 to 10 days post-trimming, after which the tip of the beak begins to slough off and is subsequently eroded away with use.'* The inference (to me at least) is that the photo of the bird in pain was taken several days after treatment, since both upper and lower beaks are already truncated. Closed eyes in a chicken, such as seen in photo B, indicates either pain or impending death. It seems likely that long-term pain may follow any type of PBA.

*

In 2010 FAWC underwent a change of heart. The Council advised DEFRA to defer the ban and the Government listened, issuing new regulations (9). The 2011 ban was now under threat of an unspecified delay, but with instructions that from that year only infra-red technology would be legal for chicks of up to ten days old, though older birds could still be treated with the 'hot blade technique'.

*

Still in 2010, and the poultry industry appears happy with the *status quo*, indeed blissfully unaware of the harsh impression it gives. *Poultry World's* February edition ran a feature on salmonella in turkeys; included was a photo of four on free range. The beak of the one on the right showed all the signs of serious damage, the result of bungled PBA. How could the editor have allowed this dubious image to be used?

Then, in June 2010, the cover picture of *Poultry World* featured five turkeys, also ranging freely, the beak of the one nearest the camera clearly and severely mutilated. Stressed turkeys are notorious for attacking each other, and even free range flocks must be crowded together in sheds at night, and may be kept in during the daytime in the worst winter weather. So, off with their beaks too, partially at least!

Reassuringly, the Soil Association's superior standards prohibit PBA. I'm informed by the RSPCA's Farm Animals Department that the society is actively looking for solutions to the problems of feather-pecking in laying hens but, meanwhile, Freedom Food* accepts the need for the operation

---

* Freedom Food is the RSPCA logo applied to food animals reared according to higher welfare standards than average commercial ones.

to be carried out on day-olds using the cold-cut method. Should serious feather-pecking break out in older birds, though, PBA with a heated blade, followed by cauterising to stem bleeding, is permitted.

Stonegate Farms have, in recent years, proved that a more docile breed of hen, if combined with a genuinely appropriate environment, can be kept without the need to de-beak. The Black Columbian hen is such a bird.

In the minds of DEFRA, FAWC and poultry industrialists in general, PBA presumably remains that old enemy 'necessary pain', representing yet another example of a cruel practice enshrined in law.

*

In fact, there's no easy way out of the problem. While birds are kept caged, or together in huge flocks, without sufficient environmental enrichment, they *will* feather peck and vent peck, often causing cage mates an excruciating death. PBA effectively highlights what's wrong with today's farming systems – rather than being built around the needs of animals, the combined aims of low staffing levels and maximum profits generally rule supreme. Unless such systems are changed, this painful mutilation, now officially termed a major welfare insult, is likely to continue.

Ironically, it's often the birds in gloomy, controlled-environment battery sheds who may escape the mutilation. In these, lights may be dimmed at will to quieten the birds and achieve 'acceptable' levels of mortality, while those kept in natural light or on free range may well have to endure the pain of PBA.

In her richly referenced book *Prisoned Chickens Poisoned Eggs* (10) Dr Karen Davis explains in detail the multitude of frustrations that lead intensively-kept birds to resort to injurious feather-pecking. Based on practices in the USA, her book is relevant to the worldwide abuse of poultry.

Sadly, from many a farmer's point of view PBA makes sense. For where are the farmers who will risk potentially massive losses while partial beak amputation remains legal?

*

But to return to the mid-1980s: we were even busier in Chickens' Lib – certainly there were enough problems associated with the battery hen to keep us fully occupied. But then, quite by chance, we discovered an additional area of abuse.

And this one, in terms of sheer numbers, was vastly greater.

A can of worms

August 1984: I'm driving with my younger daughter through our local town. It's a particularly oppressive, airless sort of day. We notice something white lying in the gutter. Could it be a chicken? It's very still... I draw into the side of the road and we hurry to investigate. It *is* a chicken, and alive, just about.

We start for home, the bird crouching on Emily's lap, when we become aware of a terrible smell; we'll definitely need to clean this bird up! I stop outside the chemist's shop to buy Dettol, leaving my daughter cradling the chicken.

*

When I returned, Emily was pale.

'It's horrible,' she said. 'It keeps reaching round to its rear end, and coming back with maggots in its beak.'

Maggots! Now it was straight to the local vet, only to be told he wasn't due back for at least an hour. So we took our chicken home, ran warm water into the deep old-fashioned sink in our basement, added a liberal slosh of Dettol, and gently washed her tail end. And thank God for that sink, well away from our living quarters, for before long its porcelain sides were crawling with maggots, dozens of them.

By now, we'd decided that our chance find was a broiler chicken, the kind reared for meat, not eggs, and probably female. She had delicate feet and a dove-like look about her. While my daughter held the little bird, damp and smelling now of Dettol, she rested her head on Emily's arm, exhausted, but seeming grateful for some comfort.

We knew there was something horribly wrong, probably she was terminally sick, and soon we were back at the vet's surgery, our chicken on the examination table. She sank down (there was no question of her attempting to escape) while the vet explained that her rear end was by now dead flesh. Clearly, she would have to be put down.

'Is this sort of thing unusual, in chicken farms?' I asked, knowing that this vet treated farmed animals as well as small animals; would he give me an honest answer?

'There'll be plenty like this one, in the hot weather we're having,' he replied, and I sensed he knew exactly what went on inside chicken farms. Then he gave the lethal injection, to put the patient out of her misery.

We took our dead broiler chicken home and buried her respectfully, vowing that her life would not have been in vain. And it wasn't, for she had, almost literally in this case, opened a whole new can of worms. From that moment, our campaign, exclusively dedicated until now to the battery hen, must expand.

We had no hard proof of where she'd come from, but felt certain we knew. Since moving house, we'd been puzzled by wagons thundering past in the dead of night. A couple of hours later the same vehicles would be back, their brakes protesting as they manoeuvred slowly round an awkward bend in the road.

Following our roadside find, we put two and two together. Those returning vehicles were groaning under the weight of thousands of chickens, stacked high, on their way to slaughter. Our little bird must have fallen onto the road, perhaps through a gap in a broken transport crate.

*

That evening I cast my mind back to the House of Commons' Agriculture Report. What exactly did the MPs on that committee have to say about the broiler industry? I found the report and re-read the relevant section: *'Paragraph 168: As we said at the start of this chapter, the battery cage system of housing laying hens, and possible alternatives, constitute the main feature of poultry farming which has claimed our attention. The raising of broiler chickens, turkey and ducks does not pose comparable problems and was little mentioned in evidence.*

169: Broilers are raised on deep litter in large undivided houses...There are fewer behavioural problems with these younger birds, and the main potential risk to welfare lies in the possibility of a too high stocking density. We received no evidence that this was prevalent or that the recommendations in the code are inadequate.' (1)

So why the silence? It was not as if nobody was aware of the grim facts. I took another look at Ruth Harrison's *Animal Machines*, published sixteen years before the House of Commons report. It was no secret that broilers were crammed in their thousands into windowless sheds. Ruth had written about the attitude of one broiler farmer: an electrician had been brought in to do a repair in the broiler shed, and nearly vomited when he could not walk around without injuring the birds. When he'd complained about this, the owner had told him not to worry, but just to go ahead and tread on them. (2)

And MAFF certainly knew. In one of its pre-1964 booklets entitled 'The Broiler House', MAFF had described the atmosphere in a typical broiler unit as 'dusty, humid, and charged with ammonia' and a MAFF spokesman is on record (March 8th 1962) as describing broiler units as: 'The biggest single risk of (Fowl Pest) spreading...So many poultry were in a confined space, and extractor fans in broiler houses carried the virus out and into the wind, causing a great risk to all poultry in the vicinity.' (3)

So despite a wealth of information out there, much of it recorded by MAFF itself, the House of Commons report made only a passing reference to broilers, all but omitting that massive industry from its enquiry. And the failure had been ours – all of us in the welfare movement. For the whistle-blowing was *our* job.

So what exactly had gone wrong? I believe it was a matter of priorities, and too heavy a workload. The battery system and the conditions for pigs and crated veal calves were so cruel; those horrors had claimed almost all the attention.

Chickens' Lib, having vowed to campaign exclusively for the battery hen, had turned a completely blind eye on broiler chickens. It took just one little bird by the roadside to kick-start us into action.

Bungled slaughter

Though an increasing proportion of poultry is now killed by the contro-versial Halal method, the majority of chicken slaughter is achieved as follows: the birds' feet are slotted into metal shackles, a procedure described by researchers as likely to be very painful (1). Hanging upside down, they pass along the killing line until their heads enter an electrically charged water bath. At this point all birds should be rendered unconscious until death is caused either by the initial strength of the electric shock, or from blood loss following neck cutting. The scalding tank, a container of very hot water to loosen feathers, is the final stage of the operation.

*

During that same month of our roadside broiler find, August 1984, an important article entitled *Slaughter of Broilers* appeared in *Veterinary Record* (2). Its author was an Official Veterinary Surgeon (OVS) of many years standing, Mr Bryan Heath.

Many chicken processors believed that the bleeding out process must take place *before* death, the assumption being that a stronger electrical charge in the water bath, designed to kill the birds outright, could occasion unsightly marks on the carcase, known in the trade as 'red-skin'.

The nub of Mr Heath's article was that, in his experience, meat from birds killed outright by the electrical charge in the water bath should be as acceptable to retailers and consumers as that from birds merely stunned, then later bled to death. Stunning to kill was, Mr Heath claimed, a good deal better in welfare terms. The birds' hearts, he claimed, need not still be pumping at or after the neck-cutting stage in order to achieve an acceptable carcase.

So Mr Heath wanted all poultry to be killed at the first stage of slaughter, by the use of a stronger, more efficient electric shock. The conclusion to his *Veterinary Record* article made clear his reason for urging a stun-kill system in all poultry slaughterhouses. He believed the present stunning method was hit-and-miss, leading to cruel deaths for huge numbers of chickens. He concluded: '*The consensus is that about one third of all broilers are not stunned so this means that, every day in the UK, more than half a million are sentient when they go to the knife. Surely, this is a problem which OVSs* [official veterinary surgeons] *should tackle?*'

In short, Mr Heath believed that much chicken slaughter was a shambles: he claimed that huge numbers were reaching the scalding tank alive, many of them still conscious.

*

Following the publication of this disturbing article I contacted Mr Heath, who seemed glad to talk. Soon I was to discover he was a man of wit, and passionate about his cause. Like us, he was used to brick walls and the idiocy of officialdom, both of which drove him nearly to distraction. I've kept my first letter from Mr Heath – in it he addressed me as Ms Druce, admitting that he was using the modern term 'Ms' for the very first time, and consequently rather tentatively. For some while, he was to send me copies of letters between himself and researchers, MAFF and others, all relevant to his desperate attempts to change the climate of opinion.

He sent me a draft of a proposed lecture to an institution called The Research Club, which I believe was attached to the then Silsoe Agricultural Centre in Bedfordshire. Here's a flavour of Mr Heath's proposed talk, starting with a description of 'red-skin': '*When production plants began to handle poultry, they found that, instead of being white all over, some dressed carcases have patches of coloured skin. The colour varies from pale knicker-pink to deep red and it is confined mainly to the pimply bits of skin from which hackles grow...Literature about the need for bleeding is a bit unusual. Some authors, without producing any evidence to back up their statements, wrote something like: "Complete bleeding is essential"... The other lot of authors were a bit more conventional; they wrote: "Proper bleeding is essential (Smith, 1970)". Smith wrote the same thing, followed by Jones (1960). And Jones kept the thing going by referring to Robinson (1950). I managed to get back to the early 1900s and they were still playing this game. When I went to talk about killing to the Ostertag people in Berlin, they told me they had got hold of a paper dated 1856 and they were still referring to earlier work. I think you can be pretty sure that Moses was the original culprit but his reprints are no longer available. The sad thing is that, although this belief is based on no work – and is wrong – it has achieved the status of Holy Writ in the factories. There is one other sacrosanct belief on which the killing of poultry is based. They think an animal will not bleed properly unless its heart keeps beating for as long as possible after venesection* [neck cutting]. *This, also, is wrong, but it was fostered by a great deal of literature. The authors, though, rather overplayed their hand by claiming that proper stunning causes almost everything that could go wrong- and a lot that couldn't. Hans Anderson and Lewis Carroll would have been proud to be associated with some of these papers. Although a few days' simple research or even a few hours' clear thinking would have shown the absurdity of most of these beliefs, the Industry, and, sadly, UFAW* [University Federation of Animal Welfare] *swallowed all this rubbish unquestioningly. UFAW recommended 50V for stunning broilers. In the average stunner, 50V would deliver less than 40 mA through each bird- and 120 mA are needed.... The author of the textbook which is looked on as being the Vade Mecum for PMIs [Poultry Meat Inspectors] and is approved by all in authority wrote: "...cutting of the blood vessels should be delayed after stunning for a period of thirty seconds to ensure good bleeding and death." As stunners are normally set, this allows ample time for the bird to recover before it goes to the knife. The same author, though, shows that, really, he's quite a kind sort of fellow: he wrote that, if birds are scalded alive, it is "not entirely satisfactory". (Canadian Department of Agriculture)... As a result of all this muddled thinking, the vets found a pretty gruesome situation when they took over inspection of the factories [slaughterhouses] in 1979. Most of the birds were fully sentient when they had their throats cut (or the backs of their skulls crushed, depending on how the machine was set) and many were alive and almost normal when they were dragged head-first into the scalding tank. Any expressions of resentment by these unfortunate birds were dismissed as being "reflex actions".*

Remember that all this cruelty was an attempt to stop red skin from occurring.

By now you may have guessed why I am bothering you with a potty little problem, which must be intolerably boring to brains as big as those in the Research Club. We* have shown that lack of bleeding does not cause red skin, but, until we can show what does cause it, most of the factories are likely to continue looking for bizarre ways of keeping the heart beating for as long as possible...'

Mr Heath concluded: *'I feel a bit of a fool for giving such a prosy paper but please realize that I am just a front man for an awful lot of poultry. Since you got up this morning, about two million broilers have been killed and at least 600,000 of them were not stunned properly. Anybody who helps us, even with advice, will earn a lot of gratitude from a very old man, and about 400 million broilers and a lot of other poultry each year.'*

(September 27ᵗʰ 1984)

I've quoted extensively from Mr Heath because who could better express the awfulness of broiler slaughter, especially in and before the 1980s? His

---

*   'We' being colleagues at Faccenda's chicken slaughter premises where Mr Heath, recalled from retirement as an Official Veterinary Surgeon, observed chicken slaughter and clarified his theories.

August 1984 article in *Veterinary Record* (this one expressed in suitably scientific language) did, I believe, force a re-think about poultry slaughter, and not before time.

In our January 1986 fact sheet, we were able to report that Webb's Poultry Products in West Yorkshire (previously visited by Violet, Irene and myself) was adopting the stun-kill system, so ensuring that few if any of the chickens killed there would reach the knife or, worse, the scalding tank, still conscious.

*

Officialdom would have us believe that slaughterhouses are strictly monitored. However, rumours abound of would-be whistleblowers threatened into silence by the companies for which they work. There's no doubt that the potential for abuse of animals at the time of slaughter is vast.

Anyone interested in getting a true picture of traditional British slaughter of farmed animals other than poultry, should turn to Animal Aid's website (5). To describe the images and information available therein as disturbing would be to understate the case a thousand times over.

An ugly picture

While leafing through some old copies of *Poultry World*, I've just come across an article from a copy dated January 14th 1982. The author (whose name I can't tell you, as I'd only saved part of it) described the worries of a 'large company' concerned that a 'disturbingly large' proportion of its chicken leg portions were being rejected because of muscle haemorrhages. The same article lists ten of the 'commoner forms' of leg weakness found in meat chickens – all in birds destined for slaughter at around 49 days of age.

In the same year, *Poultry World*'s July 1st issue contained a grim indictment of the broiler industry as it was then, nearly thirty years ago – and yet again I'm aware of the depressing fact that nothing much has changed, except that broilers are now slaughtered at an even earlier age. In 1982, leading broiler producer Metford Jeans (OBE and chairman of Quantock Poultry Packers) had commented: *'In chasing weight-for-age above all else, we have just not appreciated what we are doing to the bird. One of the biggest restrictions to supplying the market for larger birds is damaged hocks and breast blisters.'* I hadn't even marked the 1982 articles as being of interest, for it pre-dated by just two years the start of our broiler chicken campaign.

I've also kept a MAFF/ADAS booklet from 1986 (1). Its Introduction stated that broiler leg weakness in all its forms caused considerable economic losses and suffering, sometimes, it seems, from the start. Day-old chicks with red hocks, bruising below the hocks, and twisted legs were to be found, arousing suspicions that diseases had been passed through the parent flock (2).

Unfortunately there's no reason to be optimistic that great changes for the better have taken place, despite industry warnings and MAFF/ADAS investigations going back nearly a quarter of a century: the thrust towards fast weight gain and bigger profits still appears to rule supreme.

*

By the mid-1980s, around four hundred and fifty million meat-type chickens were slaughtered annually in the UK. Chicken, no longer reserved for high days and holidays, was fast becoming the new junk food: half eaten chicken legs could be seen lying around on pavements on Saturday nights; what had been an occasional luxury was now the cheapest of the cheap.

Few people looking at the plump birds neatly ranged on butchers' slabs or supermarket shelves would have guessed these were seven weeks old, mere babies. Under natural conditions chickens can live for as many years, or longer, and a seven week old chick will follow its mother everywhere, still just about small enough to shelter under the maternal wings.

*

September 1984: Our latest fact sheet set out the basic facts for our supporters. We explained how the modern chicken has been divided into two distinct types, the one destined for egg production, the other for meat: the first light-weight, the broiler chicken genetically selected for fast growth, a factor encouraged by 'lifestyle' and diet.

And the mother hen, that dedicated fowl, inspiration for the expression 'fussing like a mother hen'? She's past history. All intensively reared birds are hatched out in huge metal cabinets under strictly controlled conditions, orphans every one.

Once hatched, the day-olds are delivered to farms where they're tipped *en masse* from boxes onto the shed floor. For these defenceless baby birds, golden symbols of Easter, spring and new life, there's no maternal figure to follow, no comforting pattern in their lives. They must huddle for warmth under the brooders and attempt to find feed and water points for themselves. Those who fail to cope on their own, who never grasp the basics for survival, are known as starve-outs in the trade. These chicks simply give up the fight for life, almost from the start.

*

Genetic selection in the chicken industry has wrought astonishing changes. Ever impatient for greater profits, poultry scientists have ensured that seven weeks (now down to forty days or fewer) is all the 'lifetime' today's birds are allowed. Geneticists have ensured that, by this stage, they've put on their most profitable burst of growth. When well under two months of age, they're ready for slaughter, their eyes still baby-blue and vocalisation high-pitched.

Broiler chickens live loose on the floor, in windowless sheds, while each flock (known, significantly, as a crop) may number up to fifty thousand chickens, or more. In the 1980s, the dim lighting was kept on for at least twenty-three hours out of the twenty-four, broken only by half an hour or so of darkness to simulate a power cut (a blackout could create panic, ending in mass suffocation). This near-continuous lighting, just sufficient for birds to make out their surroundings, encouraged maximum eating time, so maximum growth.

The accepted stocking density was 0.55 of a square foot per bird (less than a sheet of A4 paper), multiplied by the number of birds in the shed. Tiny chicks of a few days old roaming around on clean litter might look fine. But, as slaughter age approaches, conditions become more and more squalid, for sheds are never cleaned out during the growing cycle. (In America, the same broiler litter may be used many times over.) (3)

By week six, chickens virtually cover the floor wall-to-wall, squatting on legs that can barely carry their weight, or struggling through the crowds to the food and water points, on a build-up of faeces. Poor ventilation, the time of year and the state of the birds' droppings can all result in damp litter, and you can be sure there'll be a smattering of chicken corpses amongst the living, pecked at by fellow birds or half eaten by rats. Filthy litter and 'deads' must account for the increasingly objectionable smell coming from broiler sheds near the end of the growing cycle.

Having studied the broiler system on paper, our next job was to gather first-hand information. In December 1984 we identified a broiler farm in South Yorkshire and Irene and I set off on our quest, aware that we were venturing into unknown territory.

Down in the quarry

The farm's location, down a steep path leading to a disused quarry, made us uneasy, but it was a bright sunny day and the two men who came out to see what we wanted were friendly enough. And our luck was in! That very morning one of the sheds was being cleared. No, it would be no trouble at all to sell us half a dozen live birds.

Having placed our order, we stood around, patiently at first, pleased with the way things were turning out. Although it was cold, a December sun was shining, flattering the dismal scene. But after some minutes we became restive. What was going on? Why the delay? We wandered round the corner of the shed, following the sound of men's voices.

To our dismay our six birds were hanging in shackles from a machine designed to record their weight. So honest were the owners, they didn't want to overcharge us, little knowing we'd have happily paid double their market value or more.

It was then, as they hung there, that we noticed the colour of the birds' frightened eyes, pale blue in the sunshine; baby birds' eyes, dazzled by the first natural light they'd ever seen. Trying not to appear anxious, we waited for the men to unhook them, handed over our money, and bundled the ungainly creatures into boxes.

At that stage we were unsure what they would prove, if anything. We were only glad to have spared six chickens the journey to slaughter.

*

Once back at my house, we unloaded our purchase. Here's how we described the chickens in our January 1985 newsletter: *'The birds we bought were filthy and, for several days, hardly able to stand. This leg weakness was due to lack of exercise and the totally unnatural weight of their bodies (the result of forced growth). The feet of several of them were severely deformed; one had feet resembling a swastika. They stumbled over each other (despite being housed by us in a roomy pen), a clear sign that they'd been used to doing this in the terrible congested conditions they had endured. During the time they were in Chickens' Lib's care, they changed from being filthy, bemused creatures who could hardly walk, to clean, bright looking birds who moved around confidently, if clumsily. Nevertheless, they suffered a 66% mortality rate...'*

Our garage was eccentric, and certainly not purpose-built. A long, low stone building, vaguely industrial, it dated back to the nineteenth century, and was too narrow for two cars to be parked side by side. It did house a rather grand inspection pit but, as neither Duncan nor I knew what to look for underneath a car, that was wasted on us. More often than not our cars were left outside, braving the elements. The garage had no electricity, but neighbours who owned the other section of the building kindly allowed us to tap into their supply, at a roughly estimated cost. Warmth was essential – however much our rescued birds had suffered, they were at least used to feeling warm.

That Christmas the garage was already giving shelter to six ex-battery hens, and now our broilers joined them, in an adjacent pen. Later, we wrote to our supporters: *'Over Christmas a straw-filled outbuilding gave shelter to a strange collection of poultry – the six broiler birds, huge and ungainly and off-white, next to six battery hens, some scraggy and featherless, some brown – people coming in to view them said it looked like the setting for a rather bizarre nativity scene, with the soft lamplight falling on the livestock.'*

After a while, the broiler with the swastika feet was euthanased – our vet could see no good future for him, and neither could we. Yet without our intervention his future had been predictable enough – the feet discarded, as likely as not he would have entered the food chain, appearing on a restaurant menu, or maybe in a tin of soup, or even in baby food.

By law, chickens are supposed to be inspected on the slaughter line for health defects, but they go by at lightning speed. Our crippled chicken could easily have made it to the electrified water bath and thence to the knife – at a glance he'd have just looked like any other filthy broiler. Or he might have been destined for religious slaughter, in which case the knife alone would have dispatched him.

Some twenty-five years later, while accessing an Australian website, I found myself looking at a familiar photo. It was of *our* chickens, the one with the swastika feet.

The five surviving broilers enjoyed a short convalescence in our garage, before Violet and I took them to a nearby RSPCA sanctuary. A few weeks later we were told that one apparently healthy bird had dropped dead before the new owner's eyes. We arranged to collect the bird for a *post mortem* examination, and received this veterinary report: '*...general poor condition, pale breast muscle, arthritis in the left hock, slightly blotchy kidneys (though the liver was firm) and an engorged heart.*' All these signs of sickness, in a chicken not yet four months old!

I believe most people who rescue broiler chickens choose to feed them to appetite. We always did, feeling it would be cruel to deny them *ad lib* food, since they'd been specifically bred to eat almost continuously.

And therein lies the problem. By failing to restrict their rations, one ensures an early death in all but unusually robust birds. But, given an existing cruel dilemma, a short life and a happy one would seem the best option.

*

Six months later, and only two of the five sanctuary broilers were surviving, for the modern broiler chicken was never intended to last. By the time broiler chicks exchange fluffy yellow down for feathers (at around four weeks) they are, by industry design, more than half way through their short lives.

By slaughtering the birds at around forty days of age, the chicken industry manages to catch their 'crops' in the nick of time, just days before the real rot sets in.

*

In 2010 a depressing article appeared in *World Poultry* by Frans Fransen, General Manager of IFT-Poultry in Belgium. In it he extols the virtues (all economy-driven ones) of battery cages for broilers. These have been considered for several decades, but the idea has not made much headway. Mr Fransen admits that 'public perception' and cages are not compatible in the EU, but predicts that countries outside the EU '*...will move step by step toward broiler cages in an unstoppable move for efficiency, lower costs and reduction of their ecological footprint.*' (1) Fortunately, recent EU legislation has curbed moves in Europe to cage broilers (2).

*

As if the massive broiler chicken industry were not enough to satisfy what's often called 'consumer demand', we were about to light upon another such industry, though one much smaller in every respect.

Did I say 'consumer demand'? In fact this newly emerging industry knew no such thing, but was to grow out of an official plan to create that demand where none had existed.

Factory farming's smallest victim

1985: When driving home after a day's teaching in Wakefield, a roadside notice advertising chicken feed caught my eye; this could be a convenient place to pick up supplies for our poultry. I parked the car and followed the sign up a narrow alley, between terrace houses.

Suddenly, unexpectedly, I was in familiar territory. Could this be some kind of backyard battery hen enterprise? I peered into a shed, and there, incarcerated in tiers of mini-battery cages, were thousands of quail.

Until that moment, I'd had no idea that this shy little wild bird might be a victim of factory farming.

*

By chance, MAFF's Agricultural Development and Advisory Service (ADAS), ever on the look out for ways of encouraging farmers to intensify, had just produced a document on quail meat and eggs. The author was a M.P.S. Haywood and his *Quail Production* is dated 1985.

Mr Haywood was surprisingly frank about the way ADAS goes about things.

The section on marketing ended with the warning that no *'ready market'* was in place for quail products: this *'has to be created and developed'*, he stressed.

Under the heading *The Future* he advised that the way forward was in marketing. Advertising would be the key, as *'probably 90% of the population have never heard of quail'*. He saw it as 'quite conceivable' that quail products could find their way into ordinary market outlets, including supermarkets, and followed this advice up with hints on how to improve 'the production side', which included the possibility of 'improved' growth rate. Mr Haywood suggested quail producers should employ feed restriction and day-length control.

So quail were to be dragged onto the factory-farming scene, but this time with no pretence of filling a need – no hint of the cheap food argument, the urgency to feed the nation. Times had changed, but not, apparently, official enthusiasm for factory farming.

How often have we heard that a new product is on the supermarket shelves because the consumer (it used to be 'the housewife') has demanded it? But here was ADAS, advising farmers to create the demand for something hitherto virtually unheard of, let alone desired.

*

The type of quail farmed for their meat and eggs is the Japanese Quail. The ADAS document told us these birds would once have weighed 150g (5oz) when adult, but genetic selection had by then almost doubled their natural weight. Chicks weighing 8-10g on hatching would achieve twice this figure at five days.

A fraction ahead of chickens genetically selected for fast growth, these tiny birds reach between 160g and 260g in weight at five weeks, by which time they've achieved about 90% of their mature weight *'and as food conversion deteriorates markedly after this age it is not worth growing the birds on longer.'* (2) Like broiler chickens, meat-type quail are killed years in advance of their natural lifespan.

Females kept for what ADAS terms 'eating egg production' were to endure months of incarceration in mini battery cages, kept twelve to a cage measuring 415mm x 600mm (approximately 16" x 24"), the average height being 200mm (8"), on a wire mesh floor with a 7 degree slope to allow eggs to roll away (3).

*

Breeding quail: ADAS advised putting nine females and three males together, to be kept in cages measuring the same as those for the miniature battery egg producers. The 'useful breeding period' (in 1985) apparently ranged widely, from 8 to 30 weeks.

*

Quail are timid, and easily frightened. Their characteristic escape response is to crouch *'...and then make a sudden and strong vertical take-off leap which, in cages, results in them striking the ceiling'* (4). This take-off leap is known in the industry as head-banging, and often results in severe injury.

Breeding females suffer head wounds from the vertical leaps, while uterine prolapse is a common cause of death (5). Skin lesions, eyelid injuries, eye-loss and the head injuries from head-banging and feather-pecking result in infections (6).

Intensive conditions deny quail any normal courtship behaviour, resulting in mating which is *'brutal, rapid and unrelated to the receptivity of the female* (7), and the frequent mounting of the female results in back wounds, and even in death (8).

*

Some free-range meat-type quail are on sale. Most, though, are reared in broiler chicken conditions in 'barns' (for which read crowded, windowless sheds).

*

ADAS must have known of the suffering inherent in keeping quail in captivity. There's been plenty of research detailing the eye-loss, the lethal head injuries, the infected wounds. Perhaps Mr Haywood was only doing his job, doing as MAFF and ADAS expected of him. Whatever his motivation, his keenness lead entrepreneurs down the slippery slope to large-scale quail farming, already widespread in many European countries as well as in the Far East, but hitherto virtually unknown in Britain. So the year 1985 marked Britain's official launch of yet another form of food production fit only for abolition.

*

The September 1993 issue of *Poultry World* ran an article about *Fayre Game*. Apparently, the company had been set up in 1980 by Michael Kaye, a Lancashire entrepreneur seeking an opening in poultry. *'ADAS adviser Martin Haywood put him on to quail, recommending that he start with just 40 birds on a one acre site at Lytham-St-Anne's'* PW told its readers. Thirteen years on, and Mr Kaye owned a company with a 13,500 breeding bird operation, producing broiler and layer hatching eggs, with rearing space for 125,000 meat birds and a 20,000-bird egg flock. A far cry, then, from those 40 'starter birds' back in 1980.

Heading the article was a photograph of a row of tiny quail hung in miniature shackles, awaiting slaughter. Alongside it we see the same birds, still hanging in shackles but dead now and plucked naked of their feathers. The caption read: *'The Orty plucker has come from France and FEOGA cash has come from Brussels to help build the £400,000 EC licensed plant'.*

*

We produced a fact sheet on quail meat and quail egg production, and distributed it widely. We accused Sainsbury's of misleading consumers, when we found they'd included *Fayre Game* quail in a list headed 'Wild Game'. With our letter of complaint, we enclosed a copy of the *Poultry World* article.

Sainsbury's modified the listing, but remained defensive. In a letter to Violet, dated November 13th 1995, the supermarket claimed to have always been concerned about the welfare of animals. They had dealt with the same supplier of quail meat for more than eight years, they said, and for two years for quail eggs, and considered *Fayre Game 'a well established supplier who has staff with considerable experience of quail production'.*

In her wisdom, the lady from Customer Services went on to describe how the caged layers *'...are grown in cages which have a good supply of feed and water. The system has been inspected by our own Technologists, by MAFF and by ADAS. No reason has been found to raise concerns with the supplier's current practices'.* In view of the MAFF/ADAS connection, it would have been surprising indeed if either were to be anything but supportive of the company.

She then claimed that Sainsbury's stocking quail meat *'reflects consumer demand for the product'.* And we remembered Mr Haywood's advice, urging farmers to *create* that demand.

The letter was typical of those written by just about all Customer Service Departments in those days, the writers totally ignorant of the facts, the letters' sole aim a cover-up.

*

Fast-forward twelve years, to December 22nd 2007: There's bad news for anyone who'd hoped for welfare improvements on the quail front. *The Guardian* reported on secret filming by the League Against Cruel Sports (LACS) of *Fayre Game's* operation: *'Footage recorded in the poultry farms of Britain's biggest quail and quail egg producer, Fayre Game, and seen by the*

Guardian, shows hundreds of birds packed in filthy, multi-level wire cages in dim lighting. Many have virtually no feathers left on their bodies. Dead birds lie among the living and dying birds, with eggs falling onto trays below.'

The article described *Fayre Game* as producing pheasants, partridges, guinea fowl, quail and other game birds, as well as exotic meats including ostrich, to supply UK supermarkets, food halls, London's Smithfield, the catering industry and many top restaurants too. Harrods and Selfridges had been among *Fayre Game's* customers, but after LACS' revelations they immediately removed the company's produce from their shelves.

Fayre Game's commercial director, Mike Haines, was reported as saying: *'I don't know if the footage is of our farm or not...The League Against Cruel Sports hasn't shown anything to me.'* He did however confirm that about 20% of FG's quail production was confined in battery conditions. Any dead birds would routinely be removed, he said. Feathers coming off during mating did, he felt, explain the birds' near-nakedness. FG maintained 'the highest welfare standards' and the presence of heavy rain had forced him to divert his staff, to attend to other birds. *'It was unfortunate that dead birds were there in the cages but we had to take the decision to use our staff to help save the birds outdoors',* he concluded, managing somehow to cast FG workers in an almost noble light.

Mr Haines told the Guardian that *Fayre Game* took animal welfare 'extremely seriously' and was working towards gaining formal recognition of its efforts through the RSPCA's farm assurance and food labelling scheme, Freedom Food.

*

Fast-forward once more, to March 18th 2010: Having received no reply to an email, I telephoned Alan Jervis at *Fayre Game*. Our conversation went something like this:

CD: What percentage of your egg-producing quail is caged?

AJ: Around 20%.

CD: Is FG registered with Freedom Food?

AJ: Not yet, but the idea is ongoing. Our parent company, Tom Barron, is with Freedom Food for various things, so we hope to join the scheme.

CD: Are *Fayre Game* meat-type quail free range?

AJ: No, they're in barns.

CD: Are your quail still slaughtered in the conventional way – hung in shackles etc?

AJ: Yes, that's how all poultry is killed.

CD: No, gassing poultry is a method that's getting used more and more.

AJ: That wouldn't be commercially viable for *Fayre Game*. Anyway, a vet from the Meat Hygiene Service is always on duty – and the MHS is about to become part of the Food Standards Agency.

CD: Birds go by very fast though, on the slaughter line.

What is the speed of your line?

AJ: I can't tell you that.

CD: And how many quail does *Fayre Game* slaughter daily?

AJ: I can't tell you that.

*

When we first tried to raise awareness about farmed quail I'd hoped to photograph some myself, to feature on a leaflet. We occasionally visit a park where quail are kept in a spacious Victorian conservatory. The vegetation is rich in there, with plenty of shelter for small creatures, and it's warm – probably an environment not unlike the quail's natural one.

But the little birds were so timid, and so good at hiding away among the plants on the soft, moist earth floor of the conservatory floor, that I never did manage my picture.

*

A recent feature in *Poultry World* reported that *Fayre Game* quail for egg production now spend their 35-40 weeks of lay under a 'Free to Fly' system.

Kept on litter, with access to verandas, the birds lay their eggs on the floor, in one area. And the group size for these shy birds? Apparently it's five thousand. So, vastly better than cages, but no life for a quail.

Russell Holdsworth, the company's sales manager, views the pretty mottling on quail eggs as 'a useful marketing tool'. And he tells readers that quail meat and eggs are gaining in popularity as TV chefs and cookery programmes 'continue to fire the imagination of consumers'(9).

Grey Girl

There once was a small auction hall near Huddersfield, now mercifully closed down. On a Saturday, you'd see all sorts of items for sale, from small species of livestock to old lawn mowers. And you could pick up information of all sorts too. One morning Violet and I stood near to a brash sort of punter, listening in to his conversation. He was boasting to a friend how one night he'd outwitted the police when they'd opened his car boot, revealing a spade. Badger digging...I can picture him now, full of himself, a heavy gold chain around his neck. Beside him stood his young son, about ten years old, drinking in his father's every word. I had a sinking feeling the child could be a badger digger of the future.

It was that same morning that Grey Girl came our way. We'd come hoping to bid for a few battery hens, but could only see cockerels, rabbits and a goose or two. And then we noticed this most beautiful grey hen. Chickens' eyes are often described as beady but hers were soft and appealing. Now and again she'd shake her head, a sure sign of stress.

A fat, red-faced man came up and poked at her breast through the cage bars, checking for meatiness. I looked into her eyes, and felt for her. I overheard the man who'd brought the grey hen in to be sold to the highest bidder tell the fat man she was ten months old.

One more trawl round the cages, and I knew I couldn't go home without her. Violet and I agreed we were prepared to outbid anyone, and an hour later Grey Girl was ours.

*

At that time we had three fully-grown broilers. We kept them separately from the ex-battery hens, since they were slower in their ways, indeed they seemed almost like another species. I decided to introduce Grey Girl to them, as she too was of a heavy build. There was no aggression, as can occur when introducing a new member to a flock – but for a week or two Grey Girl just stood around on her own, like a new girl at school whom nobody wants to play with.

Then one morning, just for a few moments, I carelessly left the gate between the two groups open. When I turned round, Grey Girl had slipped through to join the 'proper' hens, and she never looked back. Had she sensed she didn't belong in amongst those genetically altered, clinically obese birds? We shall never know, but she lived happily with her new, slimmer, friends for some years and gave us much pleasure.

A secretarial blunder

In 1986 we received a letter from a confused supporter.

'Can't think what this is all about,' she wrote. 'I thought *you'd* be able to make more of it.'

Enclosed was an official MAFF document, several pages long. And what glorious luck, there'd been a mix up! Our supporter had been sent *Animal Health Circular 85/83*, an internal MAFF memo destined for all regional Divisional Veterinary Officers, giving instructions how to deal with letters on animal welfare, and demonstrations by the likes of Chickens' Lib.

Under the heading *Correspondence on Welfare Matters* Point 59 urges staff to deal 'promptly and sympathetically' with letters from individuals.

Point 61 instructs that even postcards must be acknowledged, adding: '*Because it is useful for Headquarters to be aware of the extent of such campaigns, postcards should, after acknowledgement, be sent to Headquarters – if necessary in batches!*' We liked the jaunty exclamation mark. We also liked picturing our postcards being parcelled up for Headquarters. We'd produced thousands of cards, asking our supporters to send them to MAFF, and clearly many were reaching their destination.

Point 63 was headed: '*Involvement by Welfare Organisations.*' Here, we learned: '*Veterinary staff should be alert to the activities of the more militant of the welfare groups such as "Compassion in World Farming", "Chickens' Lib", "National Society Against Factory Farming" and "Animal Liberation Front".*'

Point 67 warned: *'Demonstrations by welfare organisations need to be handled with care. In the case of extreme welfare groups, immediate police assistance must be requested. Other groups should be treated with tact, so as not to destroy goodwill and credibility.'* We assumed Chickens' Lib fell into the category of 'other groups', but whose goodwill and credibility must not be destroyed, we wondered – MAFF's or ours?

Under *Demonstrations by Welfare Organisations* instructions were given to guard against making MAFF a laughing stock: For example: *c) 'At demonstrations, small local TV company video cameras are unobtrusive and staff should be instructed to stay away from office windows, even if the demonstrators invite this by wearing fancy dress.'* Well, we took full credit for that bit. Chickens' Lib's trademark was fancy dress. *'A film of laughing faces at a window could make "good" media film for a news report'* concluded the warning.

The advice went on:

f) 'While representatives are within the office, 2 or 3 staff should be nominated to monitor all of the Group movements ensuring that they do not disperse around the site.'

g) 'Whilst the interview is in progress, all staff should be instructed to be quiet in the area of the interview room. Laughter may be interpreted as a comment on the demonstrators' cause and can undermine goodwill.' (Goodwill cropping up again.)

The final point was brisk and down to earth:

h) 'A full record of the points discussed should be made immediately the interview is completed.'

Early on in Circular 85/83 came a mysterious item. *'UPUD Cases: In future Regions will deal entirely with such cases without notification to or input from HQ, except in cases of a politically sensitive nature.'* We suspected the battery system was listed as politically sensitive, but what on earth were UPUD cases?

*

I telephoned the Divisional Veterinary Officer at Leeds MAFF. Though not exactly old friends, we were well known to each other by now, and I guessed it was he who'd drafted the Circular, having suffered more than most DVOs from lightening demos on his premises.

Archly, I confessed to a query about Circular 85/83, indicating that I had the document before me.

There was a longish silence.

'You *have* it?' he managed at last, in a strangled little voice.

'Yes, here, on my desk,' I replied cheerfully, quoting the name of the senior Whitehall official who'd obligingly signed the attached compliment slip.

'*He* sent it to you?' This was the stuff of nightmares! Had someone at MAFF HQ gone stark raving mad? Defected, even?

I let him sweat for a moment or two before adding, 'In error.'

The upshot was, I discovered that UPUD stood for unnecessary pain and unnecessary distress. Well, we should have guessed...

*

So, exactly how had Chickens' Lib harassed MAFF Departments of Animal Welfare in Leeds, and elsewhere? A few demos stand out in my memory, and perhaps in the memories of some of the erstwhile staff, too.

Pity Leeds' MAFF

It's fair to say that Chickens' Lib did sorely try the patience of the staff housed in Government Buildings, Lawnswood, Leeds, and at Quarry Dene too. On June 1st, 1979 the Divisional Poultry Adviser had been obliged to cancel an appointment with us, by telegram. Apparently she'd informed Headquarters of our impending visit, only to be instructed to put it off. ADVICE FROM HQ TOLWORTH. PLEASE CANCEL OUR APPOINTMENT ON 4TH JUNE AT MAFF LAWNSWOOD, LEEDS. LETTER FOLLOWING, read the desperate text. The letter, which did follow, requested that we should submit the questions we wished to have answered before any meeting was 're-convened'. Did MAFF need time in which to prepare its ground?

But appointments were the exception rather than the rule. One morning we turned up in force at Quarry Dene, the Leeds centre for MAFF's Animal Health Department. Over thirty of us had gathered nearby, ready to descend on the unsuspecting staff, armed to the teeth with a very long banner, made from an old roll of unused PVC-coated wallpaper, dating back to London days. Originally, our slogan was to have read *WHY CONDEMN OUR HENS TO HELL, WHEN HUMANE ALTERNATIVES EXIST?*

I'd volunteered to do the lettering, and must have left the task to the last minute. I remember working on it the night before the demo, using a large chopping board as a guide. As midnight approached I despaired – I'd never make it beyond HELL. Leave it at that, I decided wearily, comforting myself that the first part of the slogan was the vital one.

Originally, Quarry Dene had been a grand Victorian dwelling; perhaps a mill owner had lived there, certainly someone prosperous. It was to be found at the end of a long downward sloping drive, edged with dark, sprawling evergreens. Held firmly aloft by strategically placed demonstrators, our wallpaper banner stretched a good way along the drive. On these occasions we always insisted on speaking to the Divisional Veterinary Officer (they're now known as 'managers' – a sure sign of the times). Rarely refused a hearing, a handful of us would be invited into the building, generally Violet, myself, and two or three others. Possibly the motive for obliging us was to avoid escalating aggro, with the media out there eager to record every embarrassing moment. So, not for the first time, down we trooped *en masse*, brandishing our message, while later the chosen few were allowed into the office of a disenchanted DVO, to complain about the suffering of the battery hen.

*

On another occasion we'd decided to present a wreath to MAFF, this time a cheap, homemade version – shabby compared with the one for the Archbishop, which he probably never set eyes on. We'd alerted our usual loyal supporters, and were pleased when the local BBC TV 'Look North' team turned up to film us processing solemnly down the path and handing in the wreath to a reluctant official.

We were about to disband when ITV appeared.

"Sorry to be late!" gasped a cameraman.

"We've given the wreath in," we explained. "What a shame. The demo's over."

"Well, could you get it back? So we can film you?"

Of course, publicity was all. We mustn't miss a moment of it. So we rang the bell once more, and explained the situation to a surprised official. No doubt in the interests of avoiding an ugly scene, thereby providing even more damaging TV footage, the wreath was promptly returned.

Our wreath once more ours, we plodded up to the main gate and (on camera again) marched in lively fashion down the slope for the second time.

Another ring on the doorbell. This time the hands of the official who took the wreath were visibly shaking. We felt sorry for him – just a little.

*

Some while later, we joined forces with Compassion in World Farming to produce a new broiler chicken leaflet. CIWF had supplied the photograph for the front, showing an elderly woman – facing away from the camera – selecting a chicken from a supermarket chill cabinet. Soon after we had distributed this leaflet I had reason to phone the Divisional Veterinary Officer at Leeds – the one I suspected of having drafted the internal circular that came our way so conveniently. Our conversation went as usual, rather formal, verging on the chilly, with me asking awkward questions and refusing to be satisfied with the answers I received. We were about to ring off, when he brought up the subject of the new leaflet.

"By the way," he said, studiedly casual. "Where was the photograph on the front taken? Was it in a Yorkshire supermarket?"

"I've no idea," I said. "But it would have been somewhere in the south, nowhere round here."

"Right!" he said, apparently hugely relieved. "I thought it was my mother!"

It made a refreshing change to be ending one of our 'chats' in gales of laughter, on both sides.

Poor man, he was becoming quite paranoid.

Sleuthing with Irene

By the mid-1980s Violet was less physically active in the campaign. She still wrote and responded to many letters, helping to run Chickens' Lib from her office at home, but from now on it was often just Irene and me on fact-finding excursions

Determined to uncover further incriminating evidence about the broiler industry, we began to skulk around small slaughterhouses in the Bradford area. Peering into skips piled high with evil-smelling chicken parts, we discovered severely ulcerated feet, blackened hocks (hocks are the chicken's equivalent to the human ankle joint) and whole birds too, presumably those rejected as too badly injured or diseased to enter the human food chain. Flies swarmed around these skips and the smell was sickening. On one occasion we pushed our way through strips of plastic curtaining at the entrance to a small slaughter plant, only to be seen off by the management.

But soon we found there was no need to haunt these grim places – the proof of on-farm suffering was there for all to see, right there on the supermarket shelves. The average consumer had no idea what the ugly dark marks on chickens' hocks implied. To us, the wounds spoke of heavy, inactive birds forced to squat down on filthy, damp litter high in ammonia content. Until Chickens' Lib exposed the pain endured by the birds (1) and the dangers posed to consumers (2), the ugly truth had been kept from the public. And that's just how the industry would have liked things to stay.

Soon, Chickens' Lib was publishing leaflets displaying photographs of hock burns and ulcerated feet, along with a richly illustrated booklet, 'Today's Poultry Industry'. To help consumers recognise hock burns we'd purchased a supermarket chicken, polythene wrapped and resting on its moulded tray, severe hock burns plain to see. The backdrop for the photos illustrating ulcerated feet was the boot of my car. We'd bought birds complete with feet from a small butcher's shop in Bradford, photographing them the moment we were safely round a corner and out of sight. In both examples, harmful bacteria were surely thriving in the wounds (3).

These days, severe hock burns are seen much less often on whole birds and, if given to reading *Poultry World*, you might be lulled into thinking that problems in the broiler industry are fading fast: *'In the 1980s, leg problems were more commonplace among broilers, compared with today... Leg issues were largely bred out through genetic selection and by the late 1990s, birds had become more mobile',* stated a cheerful Ms Short, in a Health Special (*Poultry World*, February 2010). She went on to say that, as a consequence of better legs, breast blisters and hock burns were fewer. However '*...these were replaced by an increased number of birds suffering from irritation on the soles of the feet. During the 2000s, a degree of gut* *instability was noticed, resulting in the production of wetter faeces that exacerbated the problem in some cases.'*

In the same article, ADAS poultry specialist Justin Emery backed up the theory that footpad dermatitis is usually associated with gut problems leading to wet droppings, often combined with housing conditions.

All this was confusing. Could broilers' legs really be so much stronger these days? And why should 21st century chickens' guts be failing to cope? Had broiler shed conditions actually *worsened*? Explanations were called for.

I tried to contact Ms Short, and finally discovered, via *Poultry World*, that she was unavailable, and anyway had gleaned all her information from Justin Emery. So next I emailed him.

ADAS was set up as an advisory service to farmers, its advice free in the old days. Not so now! Mr Emery could tell me nothing at all, unless I requested a formal reply, the fee unspecified since Mr Emery had no way of knowing how long it would take him to come up with the answers to my queries.

So I turned to Bristol's School of Veterinary Science, and straight away was told what I should read: a paper by Toby Knowles *et al.* about leg disorders in broiler chickens, published in February 2008 and funded by DEFRA itself (4). The abstract at the beginning succinctly exposes what poultry scientists have achieved in their quest for fast-growing chicken: *'Broiler (meat) chickens have been subjected to intense genetic selection. In the past 50 years, broiler growth rates have increased by over 300% (from 25 g per day to 100 g per day). There is growing societal concern that many broiler chickens have impaired locomotion or are even unable to walk...We assessed the walking ability of 51,000 birds, representing 4.8 million birds within 176 flocks. We also obtained information on approximately 150 different management factors associated with each flock.'* From this substantial number of birds tested, the researchers discovered the following: *'At a mean age of 40 days, over 27% of birds in our study showed poor locomotion and 3.3% were almost unable to walk.'*

Those birds culled, due to suffering extreme lameness before reaching 40 days, were excluded from the figures. Had they been allowed to live and been included in the statistics, the incidence of leg problems would have been even greater. The lameness was put down mainly to the birds' unnatural growth rate. So nothing much has changed – it seems there's no reason to believe Ms Short. Or should I say ADAS.

To add to this depressing picture, *Poultry World's* November 2010 issue reported that Dr Dave Watts, Regional Technical Manager for Aviagen* (Western Europe) took time at a 'broiler roadshow' in Bradford-on-Avon to draw attention to the 'significant issue' of foot pad pododermatitis. (In our experience, this painful condition goes together with hock burns.) Dr Watts warns against false economies such as tinkering with ventilation, and buying cheap litter.

Certainly, supermarkets now want clean-looking birds on their shelves. They've had enough of petitions and complaints from inconveniently well-informed customers. Back in the 1990s, the industry began to impose financial penalties should more than 2% of a consignment of birds arriving for slaughter show signs of hock burns. However, there's no way of knowing how many of those ugly dark marks are simply cut off at the processing stage, so allowing the rest of the bird to enter the food chain. And how many scarred birds still end up in 'disguised' form, in products such as soups, pastes and stock cubes, or feature in packs of breasts?

And the feet? Of no value to the meat trade here, most are exported to China, Jamaica and South America. Nowadays chicken feet are worth something to the tune of £700 a tonne to the export trade, this figure enhanced when the saving of rendering them in the UK, some £55/t, is taken into consideration (5).

*

The Bristol scientists described the implications of their findings as 'profound', pointing out that, worldwide, billions of broilers are reared within similar husbandry systems, and that any of their suggestions for reducing leg problems would be *'likely to reduce growth rate and production.'*

And what breeding company wants to reduce growth rates when faster growth equals bigger profits? The major global broiler chicken breeding companies can be numbered on the fingers of one hand, with all of them very, very interested in profits.

---

* Aviagen claims to be the market leader in poultry genetics.

Poultry litter claims victims

January 1989: One morning Irene and I were busy in the office when we heard a tractor rattle past the window. Looking up from my desk, I saw its trailer was piled high with what appeared to be spent chicken litter. We were pretty sure whose tractor it was, but where was the farmer taking the stuff?

Grabbing a camera, we hurried out to the car and followed at a safe distance, noticing how every now and again chunks of impacted litter were dropping onto the roadway. After a couple of miles, we guessed where the tractor was heading, and when it shuddered to a halt, we parked by the roadside. We watched as the farmer opened a five bar gate into a field, got back into the tractor then began to mechanically fling the load over the pasture.

We waited until the job was done and the tractor well on its way back to the farm, then went to take a closer look.

*

The litter was distributed thinly over the now not-so-green grass. And there, among a scattering of soiled white feathers, we found the body parts, along with a couple of whole chickens, the ones who'd died and not yet been partly eaten by fellow birds, or rats. From the remnants we could guess the ages of some of the victims. A delicate beak here, once belonging to a chick of about two weeks, a smallish foot there, from a four-week old bird maybe? Before us was a record of week-by-week deaths of the sick birds, ignored and left to die and rot on the shed floor.

I took photos, quite a lot of them, before we left and they turned out well (we wondered what the technicians who developed them thought when the morbid images emerged). Here was proof, if any were needed, that birds of all ages die in the sheds, remaining there until turn-out time.

We found a company that reproduced photos in strips on self-adhesive backing and ordered hundreds of the one of the whole chicken, sprawled on the grass. We sent them to supporters, to use on the outside of letters to MAFF etc. We stuck them onto a statement informing the public that a MAFF official had admitted to Chickens' Lib that small chicks *inevitably* die and disappear in the litter. We also drew attention to the danger of sick birds infecting other farmed animals and spreading disease via wild animals and birds.

Poultry litter (composed mostly of faeces by the end of a growing cycle) was at that time not only used for cattle bedding but, once ensiled, actually fed to cattle. In 1988 an outbreak of botulism in cattle was reported in *Veterinary Record*. Out of 150 housed cattle, 68 had died as a result of being fed ensiled poultry litter (1).

*

Since following that tractor, we now knew for certain that dead chickens accounted in part for the vile smell coming from our least-favourite broiler farm. So we tried to interest Kirklees' Environmental Health Department in the issue, urging them to use their powers. We could assess the precise age of the latest batch of birds because we'd often notice a little white van, its logo proclaiming day-old chicks, passing my office window.

'Please,' I urged a female Environmental Health Officer. 'Make an inspection on day thirty nine or forty of the growing cycle – that's when you'll get the true picture, and see for yourself the dead birds among the living. That stench can only be from decomposing birds, and if you don't believe us, we have photos to prove it!' I said (or words to that effect).

Eventually she reported back to us. And when did she go? On day three, she said, and it had all looked fine! No need for any action. And of course it would have looked fine, those charming three-day old yellow balls of fluff, cheep cheeping their way around the shed, on whistle-clean litter.

I remember having an overwhelming urge to shake this woman from Environmental Health. How could I *force* her to understand the simple mathematics of the broiler chicken cycle? Had she applied intelligence to the problem, it's possible that cases of botulism wouldn't have continued to crop up, and far fewer animals today would be picking up a potentially fatal disease as they innocently graze their pastures. Our authority could and should have warned other local authorities against the practice of spreading contaminated poultry litter on fields.

Was Kirklees simply too proud to listen to a pressure group? It's really not easy to understand that particular brick wall.

*

Contaminated spent chicken litter spread as 'fertilizer' attracted our attention over the years, as cases of botulism in cattle continued to be reported in *Veterinary Record*.

*

When Unigate set up a huge complex of broiler units in Humberside, with each farm holding nearly half a million chickens, a serious environmental problem emerged. Residents in the area attended planning meetings and complained bitterly, pointing out the likelihood of environmental degradation (animal suffering counting for nothing in planning decisions) but their representations were over-ruled. Soon, all ten Unigate farms were up and running, with used poultry litter from nearly five million chickens to be disposed of, somehow, every few weeks.

One of our supporters, directly affected by the sudden massive influx of chickens and associated traffic, took photos of the huge mounds of litter stacked on agricultural land, some right beside a well-used footpath. Rats scavenging on chicken corpses were plain to see. We visited the area too, and took similar photographs.

A local farmer, opposed to yet another 'farm' with its 450 million chickens complained in his local paper (November 28th 1987): '... *environmental health officers say there will be no problems and that Unigate's site in Spalding has had only one complaint in 10 years...But I do business with people in Spalding. I was told that the stench from the units is absolutely terrible and there are complaints about the additional traffic.*'

*

It's clear from a 2005 letter to *Veterinary Record* (2) signed by scientists working at three UK Veterinary Laboratory Agencies that it's an accepted fact that dead chickens are routinely left behind in poultry litter. Their first piece of advice, from a list of eight Dos and Don'ts, was: '*Poultry carcases and carcase material must be collected and disposed of by rendering or incineration in accordance with the Animal By-Products Regulation 2003.*' Presumably 'carcase material' means the half-eaten bits of chickens, rather than the whole bird; more than a hint there, then, that dead birds are not collected on a daily basis.

*

Botulism in farmed animals caused by contaminated poultry litter seems to be on the increase, with two reports from the Veterinary Laboratories Agency appearing on its September 2009 web page (3). Here I read of the death of ten ewes from a group of sixty. The pasture they'd just been moved from '*...had recently received a dressing of poultry manure from the owner's own layer and broiler flocks...a diagnosis of botulism in the affected* *animals was made on clinical grounds. The Food Standards Agency was notified.'* The involvement of the Food Standards Agency, plus the lack of any specific information as to the type of botulism was worrying. Could it be that this outbreak was of a kind dangerous to humans?

Another case, this time among fattening cattle, was identified as type D botulinum toxin. Four animals died, no doubt painfully and miserably. *'The pasture had been spread with poultry and bovine manure while the animals were still grazing.'*

The outbreak among the ewes, also listed under the Veterinary Laboratory Agency's (VLA) 2009 list of 'highlights' for September, ended with the plaintive statement that there was now: *'...further evidence of lack of awareness of the risk for cattle and sheep of contact with poultry litter. In this case it was the flock owner's own manure* [not very well put, that] *causing the problem. Specific targeting of producers who have both poultry units and cattle or sheep enterprises with information could have a beneficial effect. Greater awareness by cattle and sheep farmers is still needed.'*

Not much good had come, then, of the VLA's own News Release, dated December 7th 2006: *'The Veterinary Laboratory Agency (VLA) today announced new guidelines to help farmers protect their stock from botulism. Incidence of suspect botulism has increased substantially since 2003...The use of poultry litter containing carcasses or any carcass material as fertiliser to spread on agricultural land is contrary to the Animal By-Products Regulations 2005 in England, with equivalent legislation in Wales, Scotland and NI.'*

Chickens' Lib did its best to spread the word, way back in the 1980s. We tried our best to create 'awareness', sending our information sheet, complete with photograph, to MPs, MAFF, bacteriologists, Environmental Health Departments... At that time we were contacting hundreds of officials in addition to our own supporters.

It's just another example of legislation that means next to nothing. How often have farmers been prosecuted under the 2005 Regulations? I thought I'd like to know for sure.

After reading about the two new cases reported in September 2009 I emailed DEFRA, asking if I could have a list of prosecutions of anyone causing death to cattle via the spreading of infected litter and was surprised to learn that my query would be a case for Freedom of Information; I would hear back from the appropriate department in due course.

Eventually, I was asked if I could 'narrow the search'. This was impossible and, since I had a strong hunch that the answer would be nil, I decided not to pursue the matter.

*

In 2009, *World Poultry* reported research carried out at Johns Hopkins University in the USA. The study's researchers looked for two different types of antibiotic-resistant bacteria, namely staphylococci and enterococci, in stored poultry litter. These bacteria are found in the digestive systems of both chickens and humans, and apparently were present, over a period of four months, in poultry litter too. During this time both types of antibiotic-resistant bacteria survived and even increased.

The researchers concluded by querying whether further studies were needed to determine whether these resistant strains of bacteria found in chicken manure could end up in people, or if better manure/litter storage was needed. This same article put the annual size of the USA's used poultry litter problem at an estimated 13 to 26 million metric tonnes. Better storage of all those contaminated litter mountains sounded a tall order indeed (4).

Not so clever ...

Irene and I worked out a technique: when approaching a farmer with our most usual request – four or five end-of-lay hens, for the garden – Irene did the talking. A local accent would surely arouse fewer suspicions.

While out driving one day we'd noticed a shocking old battery unit, really a big shed, or possibly disused garages, smelling terrible and complete with severely de-feathered birds standing on collapsing wire flooring – all easily seen through broken windows. We'd earmarked the place for a return visit, and also reported it to Leeds MAFF, telling them we estimated that thousands of hens were incarcerated there under worse than usual conditions.

When we drove by a few days later we spotted the farmer coming out of the shed, so we drew to a halt and approached him. Irene, the picture of innocence, engaged him in conversation while I stood by, keeping quiet.

He let her ramble on for quite a while. This is promising, I thought. But suddenly his manner changed. With arms akimbo, he fixed us both with a steely glare.

"*You* know more about this than *I* do," he snarled. "Be off with you!"

We'd been rumbled. Word had *really* got around in battery farming circles, even as far as this outpost. Our plans thwarted, we made our exit, the farmer still standing by the roadside staring truculently after us, doubtless making a note of my number plate.

CHICKENS AND FOOD-BORNE ILLS

Botulism isn't the only danger lurking in used poultry litter and all that it contains – salmonella too can hang around in it. Regarding salmonellosis, my Concise Veterinary Dictionary says: *'The application of contaminated manure on pasture can be an important method of spreading the disease'* (and this includes to humans). As most people know, the Salmonella bacterium can contaminate meat, and handling raw or undercooked meat poses dangers. Eggs too may harbour the bacteria and if eaten raw or lightly cooked can cause food poisoning, especially in the very young and old. In 1988 a Food Hygiene Laboratory's estimate (1) was that around four fifths of chickens on sale were contaminated with salmonella. It was later that year that Junior Health Minister Edwina Currie spoke out in Parliament about contamination in eggs, whereupon panic broke out throughout the egg industry and Edwina lost her job.

Salmonella can persist in surprising places, even on furniture. I remember the tragic case of a toddler who died from salmonellosis. His mother's work had been associated with Unigate's broiler farm development on Humberside. It was revealed at the child's inquest that the fatal *Salmonella enteritidis* bacteria had been identified on upholstery, in all likelihood brought home on the mother's clothes and deposited on a chair.

*

Scandalously, MAFF only reacted to the public health danger from salmonella food poisoning once the situation hit the headlines. But the threat was not new. It had simply been ignored by officialdom. Fifteen years previously an article in *The Times,* dated August 6th 1973, had pointed the finger at MAFF. Journalist Philippa Pullar told how the Ministry of Agriculture had set up a computer programme with the avowed intention of clarifying patterns of salmonella infections. But it seems the plan came to nothing.

Perhaps the computer didn't work or, if it did, nobody at MAFF understood it. Or could the reason have been darker? Was it because hens often show no symptoms, being merely carriers of the disease, simply soldiering on, laying their secretly infected eggs? Certainly nothing was done to protect the public from an illness that could, and sometimes did, prove fatal. Broiler chickens too were infected, to the extent that irradiation of poultry meat was under consideration (2).

Encouragingly, a Food Standards Agency survey found that by 2009 only 0.5% of chickens tested positive for Salmonella *enteritidis* and Salmonella *typhimurium* (3). This improvement is due to vaccination programmes. Yet despite vaccination, one in every two hundred chickens remains contaminated. In addition, vaccination programmes have greatly decreased the incidence of salmonella food poisoning from eggs.

I'd considered putting this huge reduction in chicken meat and eggs infected by salmonella in the 'progress' chapter near the end of this book. But this book has been written on behalf of the chickens; it was animal cruelty that sparked off the founding of Chickens' Lib. Vaccination programmes may protect consumers from illness but often do nothing to help the birds. Indeed, the success rate accorded to vaccination programmes could be seen as a means of helping the poultry industry to continue with its practice of keeping animals in cruel and squalid conditions.

In 2010, turkeys were deemed responsible for most cases of S *enteritidis* and S *typhimurium*, the two strains of salmonella that commonly threaten human health (4).

*

Now the search is on for a vaccine against the most common causes of food-borne illness – *Campylobacter jejuni* and *Campylobacter coli*. Campylobacter has been endemic in poultry for years, down on the factory farm. In 1982, Dr Martin Skirrow of Worcester's Royal Infirmary warned that campylobacter could be cultured from chicken and turkey carcases sold in retail outlets right across the world (5). In November 1985 *Farmers Weekly* described broiler chicken sheds as 'the most potent breeding ground for campylobacter organisms'. It reported Dr Keith Lander, head of work on campylobacter at MAFF's Central Veterinary Laboratory at New Haw, as saying: '*It now seems beyond dispute that most human campylobacter infections are derived directly or indirectly from animals. This is a matter that greatly concerns the veterinary profession and the livestock industry.*' In 1992 the two forms of campylobacter dangerous to humans were described as the bacteria most frequently reported as causing acute enteritis in the

UK and most developed countries (6). In the intervening years, the dangers from eating contaminated poultry have not diminished.

A bout of illness after eating food contaminated with the campylobacter organism might mean a few days off work, or something far more serious: *'In severe cases grossly bloody stools are common, and many patients have at least one day with eight or more bowel movements. Most patients recover in less than a week, but 20% may have a relapse or a prolonged or severe illness'* (7). While animals may act simply as carriers of the campylobacter organism, the infection in humans can cause pains so severe as to mimic acute appendicitis. Infected children may suffer *grand-mal* seizures. In extreme cases, an attack of campylobacter food poisoning can leave a legacy of reactive arthritis, or it can even prove fatal (8).

*

Fast-forward to January 2010: Rob Newbery, the NFU's chief poultry advisor, told *Poultry World* that he believes: *'...the figures* [for campylobacter food poisoning] *reflect the fact that little is known about the organism... The industry does take it seriously, but we need science to help us out, and, therefore, find ways of preventing it infecting flocks'.*

It's almost touching, this faith in science. Apparently it hasn't yet sunk into the consciousness of industry people that filthy conditions breed disease like nothing else.

Then in May 2010 *Poultry World* ran an article entitled *Getting to Grips with Campylobacter.* This revealed that a recent report by the European Food Safety authority declared 75% of UK flocks to be infected, while the UK's Food Standards Agency (FSA) found contamination in 65% of chickens on sale in 2009.

Suggested solutions, based on lower figures in Scandinavian countries, included biosecurity measures involving 'minimum contact with the birds'. I was left wondering how minimum contact would sit with the new legal EU obligation to inspect broilers at least twice daily, and about the morality of minimising human contact with farmed animals.

Another idea put forward in the article was to abandon 'thinning' of flocks, which is the periodic removal of selected birds to provide the market with chickens of specified weights. If thinning in any way accounts for the prevalence of a potentially fatal form of food-borne illness, why is the practice not outlawed in the UK?

To *Poultry World's* Philip Clarke's query: *'How extensive is the problem in humans?'* Food Standards Agency's Gael O'Neil responded: *'Campylobacter is a number-one cause of food-borne disease in the UK. Just in England and Wales we estimate that there are about 300,000 cases a year...Of these, about 15,000 result in hospitalisation, and there are even about 80 deaths. It is estimated that 60-80% of campylobacter food poisoning is related to chicken. If we can get on top of this, we will be making a major contribution to improving human health.'*

From time to time Chickens' Lib attempted to promote joined-up thinking between government departments (namely Agriculture and Health) but it seems there's not been much progress.

Recently, major scams that surely put the public at risk have been hitting the headlines. In the next chapter you will read tales of corruption bold enough to take your breath away.

A word of warning

Over the years, meat classed as unfit for human consumption has been entering the food chain, doubtless far more of it than is ever detected. Here are just a few examples of cases that did come to court:

In 2002 Michael Bloomfield, Norfolk farmer and owner of the 'Fresh and Frozen' company in Tibenham was found to have been supplying, for human consumption, chicken and other meat condemned as fit only for pet food. For years Bloomfield had collected the condemned meat from an abattoir near Ipswich, cleaned it up, packed it in trays, and sold it on to butchers, markets, restaurants, shops and wholesalers in Norfolk, Suffolk, Luton, Hitchin and, it was thought, London too. When his premises were raided by environmental health officers, trays sufficient to wrap 200,000 chickens were found, along with nine tonnes of decomposing meat, as well as poultry carcasses covered in rat droppings and maggots. In addition, evidence was found that pigs had been illegally fed putrescent poultry carcasses. Commenting on the six-month prison sentence handed out to Bloomfield, Sue Nixon, the EH officer who had led the case said: *'This put public health in serious jeopardy. The case was moved to the Crown Court because of the crime's severity, and yet the final sentence seems not to reflect how serious this was.'* (1)

Then there was the case of the fraudulent eggs: On March 11th 2010 Keith Owen, owner of *Heart of England Eggs Unlimited* of Bromsgrove in Worcestershire was jailed for three years for passing off 100 million battery eggs as free range, organic and Freedom Food eggs (though I understand from FF that no phoney FF eggs actually reached retail outlets). During his two-year-long fraud, Mr Owen made himself a profit of £3 million. The operation knew no bounds: eggs classed as 'industrial' (typically those with cracked or broken shells, suitable only for non-food purposes) were being packed into boxes labelled 'free range', as were imported battery eggs, subsequently marked with the Lion Eggs logo, only applicable to British eggs from vaccinated hens (2). How he managed to pull wool over supermarket managers' eyes on such a massive scale remains a mystery. It seems the fraudster was finally unmasked when lorry drivers became suspicious of the long time they had to wait before they could load up with eggs – time in which, it turned out, Owen was busy re-labelling the boxes.

A frightening example of the lengths some butchers will go to was reported just before Christmas 2010. Food Safety Officers, acting for local authorities in the north east of England, took samples of marinated meat from thirty-three shops across the region, targeting premises that had already given reason for food safety concerns. The officers were following up anecdotal evidence that meat going 'off' was being disguised in marinades then sold for barbecues and for stir-frying. Their suspicions were more than justified – more than half of the samples they took were showing the first signs of putrefaction (3).

Not all scams are quite on the scale of the above. Recently, small-scale crooks have been exposed. There was the case of a farming couple from East Yorkshire, Colin and Katherine Chambers, who were fined £21,000 and banned from keeping farm animals for five years for subjecting animals to 'appalling medieval conditions.' They were well known locally as organisers of the monthly Humber Bridge Farmers' Market, which attracted thousands of visitors. The couple had also sold their meat and poultry on stalls in Hull city centre and in Beverley (4).

Then there were two men I read about, complete amateurs when it came to farming. Dressed as true jolly farmers-cum-butchers, in stylish hats and aprons, they'd been doing the rounds at farmers' markets, selling meat from animals found to be living in filthy conditions, and dying in misery.

At the start of 2013 a new scandal hit the headlines. Revelations of animal suffering, official inertia, risks to human health and the widespread duping of consumers combined to paint a hideous picture of an illegal trade in horses and donkeys for meat. Nobody likes to be cheated, but fraud involving living, feeling animals must surely be of the worst kind.

I've heard of a 'butcher's' shop in the Netherlands selling nothing but vegetables and meat-replacement products made from protein-rich lupins. And apparently a nearby *bona fide* butcher is now stocking the lupin-based products too, so maybe that's a glimpse into a better, safer future.

The following chapter takes us back to the late 1980s, when Chickens' Lib was intent on exposing the true scale of abuse involved in chicken meat production. We were now ready to reveal a situation sometimes described as a 'welfare dilemma', a term that scarcely hints at the seriousness of the abuse involved.

Half-starved (by design)

In May 1987 Chickens' Lib revealed an especially ugly aspect of chicken production: that the millions of birds producing the billions of eggs for the worldwide broiler chicken industry are forced to go hungry, and sometimes very hungry indeed. Poultry scientists and industrialists were, of course, well aware of the plight of broiler breeders, but in general the subject was hidden from the public.

In a fact sheet, we referred to the Royal College of Veterinary Surgeons' evidence to the 1980-81 Session of the House of Commons *First Report from the Agriculture Committee on Animal Welfare in Poultry, Pig and Veal Calf Production* (1). The RCVS had commented on the *'heavily restricted'* rations given to female breeders, describing how these birds drank excessively in an attempt to assuage their hunger and how this unnatural intake of water resulted in damp litter in the breeding sheds, whereupon the producers *'responded by reducing the availability of water...'* The RCVS concluded that this reduction in the water supply *'may exacerbate their distress'*. You bet it did.

I've described how intensively reared chicken meat now comes from obese birds killed when only six weeks old, or even younger. The parent stock reach sexual maturity at around twenty weeks, and, somehow, these adult birds must remain slim and healthy enough to breed for around one year. The problem is that the parent birds share the identical genetic make-up to their obese offspring, being the result of the same selection for abnormally fast growth and 'meatiness'. Even the brains of broilers have been tampered with, to encourage abnormally large appetites (2). So how exactly does the industry deal with this problem of its very own making?

Dr Joy Mench of the Department of Poultry Science, University of Maryland, USA outlined the issues in her paper *'Problems Associated with Broiler Breeder Management'*. Here's a taste of what she had to say at the Fourth European Symposium on Poultry Welfare in Edinburgh in 1993 (3): *'Broiler breeders are truly caught in a welfare dilemma, because the management practices that are necessary to ensure health and reproductive competence may also result in a reduction in other aspects of welfare...The selection of broilers for increased growth rate has resulted in an increase in appetite* (Siegel and Wisman,1966) *by modulating both central and peripheral mechanisms of hunger regulation* (Lacey et al., Denbow,1989). *The increased food intake causes obesity, which must be controlled in broiler parent stock in order to maintain reproductive competence. This is typically accomplished by limiting the quantity of food provided. Food restriction is initiated when birds are between 1-3 weeks of age, and results in a reduction in the body weight of approximately 45-50% of that of ad-libitum-fed birds* (Katanbaf et al.'*1989a) (2)*.

Irene and I attended this symposium (3), and in the discussion time that followed her lecture Dr Mench memorably elaborated on conditions in America, where skip-a-day feeding of broiler breeders was, and still is, legal (though outlawed in the UK).

Dr Mench described how not only one day's rations might be skipped, but two: *'You could hear their beaks tap-tapping on the shed walls, as they searched around for food'*, she told the assembled delegates.

As so often happens when one delves into the hidden world of factory farming, the reality proves much worse than had been feared.

*

In 1996 we produced a detailed fact sheet on broiler breeders, and the project involved collating many complicated facts. I sent the final draft to both Cobb Breeders and Ross Breeders, two leading producers of breeding stock, asking them to check the information and to let me know if it was accurate before we went to press.

Ross Breeders declined to reply but, rather to our surprise, Cobb confirmed that the facts *were* correct but the company didn't support our conclusions. So with that endorsement we went ahead.

*

The wording on the fact sheet's front cover read as follows:

BROILER BREEDERS

A FARM ANIMAL WELFARE NETWORK FACT SHEET

- *Bred to be 'good eaters' yet kept on severely restricted rations.*
- *'Skip-a-day' feeding practised in some countries.*
- *'Baby giants' on supermarket shelves the offspring of desperately hungry birds!*

We included information on feed restriction, the stress of hunger and a run-down of the typical diseases and injuries in breeders. In a spirit of irony, we quoted from a letter to us from the then Director General of the British Poultry Meat Federation, Peel Holroyd: *'We cannot support your suggestion that parent stock birds are badly exploited; rather, to the contrary, they are reared carefully and sensitively and thereafter live long and healthy lives.'*

*

Among the many distressing facts to emerge was the extraordinarily stress the parent birds are subjected to at feeding time. The sexes are of course together, in order to breed, but they must eat separate, meticulously calculated rations. Fed in the morning, the birds would take no more than 10-15 minutes to finish their meagre food supply (4), and this for a species that likes to feed little and often throughout the day. *'Fowls normally spend a considerable portion of their day in activities associated with foraging, and when given the choice prefer to work for at least part of their daily intake of food rather than eating it all from a free supply* (Duncan and Hughes, 1972).

Desperately hungry, at feeding time the birds rush to the feeders, sometimes incurring injuries to their feet, a recognised cause of Staphylococcal arthritis (5). Grids on the females' ration troughs, purposely narrow to exclude the larger males, must have caused intolerable stress to hungry cockerels, while in one study 15% of females were found to have severely swollen heads, the result of forcing their heads through badly designed feeders (6).

*

Eventually, following recommendations by Chickens' Lib, the Farm Animal Welfare Council decided to study conditions endured by the parent stock (its April 1992 report on broiler chickens had made no reference to the breeding stock). We'd complained to FAWC about this serious omission, and six years later, in August 1998 (two years after we'd issued our fact sheet on the subject) the Council brought out its Report on Broiler Breeders. While meekly accepting the necessity of feed restriction, FAWC did draw attention to some of the worst aspects of the cruel regime.

Under the heading *Pedigree (Elite) Stock* (that's the valuable 1% or so of birds selected to form the basis of the national/international breeding stock) paragraph 66 states: '*The process* [of selecting suitable birds at an early age] *creates a welfare dilemma because, having been fed ad libitum, the weights achieved by the birds at about 8 weeks of age will be above those required at point-of-lay. It is therefore necessary to restrict feed intake severely during the next 2 or 3 weeks to return the bird to physical fitness. The level of restriction which is imposed may limit intake to as little as 25% of previous feed over this period and this would imply a potentially serious welfare problem.*'

A potential problem? More than potential, surely, to those chickens genetically programmed to be big eaters and suddenly denied 75% of their previous rations. Even after this severe and sudden restriction, more moderate restriction must continue throughout their lives, as is the case with the non-elite breeders too.

*

Research dating back to the 1970s left us in no doubt that broiler breeders, elite or otherwise, are truly hungry: *Food restricted broilers, however, consume their food ration in a very brief period of time.* (Kostal et al., 1992) *Restricted males are more aggressive than fully-fed males* (Mench,1988; Shea et al., 1990; Mench et al.,1991) *while restricted hens and pullets are more fearful and active and also display high levels of pecking stereotypes* (van Niekerk et al., 1988; Savory et al., 1992). And so on....and on...The quest for morbidly obese chickens for a chicken-besotted public has led to sustained cruelty, assumed to be 'necessary' by the industry, by MAFF/

154

DEFRA, and now by FAWC. But what solution could there be to this 'dilemma'?

*

Professor Ian Duncan, a leading poultry welfare researcher, was present at the 1993 Edinburgh symposium that Irene and I attended. Workshops were arranged to take place between lectures and I was drafted into Professor Duncan's. Representatives from true animal welfare interest groups were few and far between at the symposium and I felt a little like Daniel entering the lion's den. Indeed, when I went through the door into the room where the workshop was held, I swear I sensed waves of antagonism coming my way from what appeared to be a collection of international poultry industrialists.

The topic of Professor Duncan's workshop was welfare problems within the broiler industry. Some way into the proceedings he threw out a question for all of us to ponder: what solution might there be to the serious health and welfare problems afflicting broiler chickens?

When the time came, and risking a metaphorical knife in my back, I ventured the thought that the only way out of the dilemma was to select backwards, in the direction of slower growing and therefore slimmer, healthier birds. (Selecting backwards? I may even have used that most unscientific term).

At the end of the workshop I enjoyed a moment of quiet satisfaction when Professor Duncan returned to his challenge.

"I think I agree with Clare Druce," he said.

*

February 2011: There is little progress to report, if secret filming of broiler breeders by investigators for Hillside Animal Sanctuary is anything like typical. In the unit they entered, thousands of hens, along with the 'approved' number of cockerels (roughly nine hens to every cockerel) were recorded. It was night-time, but no comfortable perches were to be seen. Instead, the birds crouched on the floor, or roosted on the harsh metal edges of feed and water equipment. One had settled down on the corpse of another, possibly taking some comfort from the soft surface.

Most of the hens' backs were denuded of almost every feather and many showed scratch marks, the result of unnaturally frequent mating. Cockerels in such an environment, hungry and bored out of their minds, have little else to do but subject the females to what must increasingly feel like painful assaults as their damaged backs become more and more raw. One hen had a swelling the size of an orange on the upper part of one leg, with blood beginning to seep from it. Anxiously, she kept turning around, trying to remove this terrible burden. The presence of such an advanced swelling proved the total inadequacy of the daily inspections (the ones demanded by law).

Concentrations of ammonia were found to be well over recommended limits. The suggested 'safe' upper limit for young broilers throughout the EU is 20 parts per million, but the reading in this unit went as high as 38 ppm, suggesting an air quality damaging to lungs and respiratory tracts, and possibly eyes too. Research indicates that ammonia levels lower than 20 ppm can be dangerous too, especially if the exposure is prolonged.

While the young broilers may be hatched and slaughtered within a space of six weeks, the breeders must live for roughly a year after reaching sexual maturity. In the unit described above, it's unlikely that the litter on the shed floor was ever changed over the course of that year, its quality worsening steadily as time went by. DEFRA tells me that litter may be topped up as and when required and some patches of especially solid or damp litter exchanged. No past activity of that nature was apparent in the unit described above.

Although there is no specific legislation for ppm of ammonia gas for broiler breeders, EU law states that: *'Air circulation, dust levels, temperature, relative air humidity and gas concentration must be kept to limits which are not harmful to the animals.'* (7) Certainly, the birds were exposed to harm.

Litter high in ammonia leads to foot problems and many of the birds were found to be suffering from an advanced form of pododermatitis, a condition that results in lameness and abscesses caused by the bacterium *Staphyloccocus aureus* entering wounds, most often caused by injuries and prolonged contact with ammonia-soaked litter. And this breeding unit was no small-time operation but attached to a well-known company.

Readers may be glad to know that a successful operation was carried out on the chicken with the orange-sized swelling. Who knows if she remembers her terrible days in the broiler breeding unit as she wanders on grass under sheltering trees, her leg now totally healed?

*

But now I've been getting ahead of myself, by decades. It had taken us a long while to produce our broiler breeder fact sheet, and meanwhile much work had been going on to publicise the plight of those over-sized baby broilers, bred to satisfy an ever-increasing demand for chicken.

By 1987 the plight of broiler chickens formed a major part of our campaign. The suffering caused by hock burns and pododermatitis, frequently found in chickens of less than seven weeks of age, was of especial concern. Then suddenly, quite unexpectedly, we had an ally.

*

Geoff Ord was Area Manager for Meat and Poultry Inspection for Bradford, and something of a rarity among officials. He knew that millions of broiler chickens routinely endured pain and, what was more, he cared. In fact he cared so much that he wanted MAFF to admit that Chickens' Lib didn't indulge in exaggeration.

In June 1987 we were due to meet with MAFF in London, and we'd be taking the evidence of suffering with us. For Geoff had offered to bring us off-cuts from a Bradford poultry slaughterhouse. Practical support like this from an official employee was pure gold dust.

But in the event, our plans were to go just a little awry...

The saga of the feet

Wednesday June 17th: A fine summer's evening and I'm at home, expecting the visit from Geoff. Ah! Here he comes, hurrying up the path.

I'd pictured the amputated feet discreetly packed in a container smacking of the laboratory – stainless steel maybe, with a tight fitting lid. Instead, he has them rattling around in a shallow open box marked *Mars Bars*. Never mind, they are well and truly frozen. Once Geoff has gone I wrap them in a plastic bag, then a second one, and put the grim bundle in our freezer.

An hour later the phone rings. It's the London friend in whose house Irene and I were to stay. She is *so* sorry: a domestic crisis! Beds for the night are now out of the question.

Our carefully laid plans, in disarray!

*

Mark Gold, by then Director of Animal Aid, the animal rights organisation based in Tonbridge, was the moving force behind the annual *Living Without Cruelty* exhibitions. For one weekend every June, from 1987 to 1994, the whole of the Kensington Town Hall was given over to hundreds of stands representing the major UK animal welfare, animal rights and environmental organisations, and attracting many thousands of visitors. Chickens' Lib had a stand booked, and to save on train fares we'd tacked the meeting with MAFF onto the end of this event. And now we desperately needed an alternative place to stay, with shelf space in someone's freezer an absolute priority.

I rang around and eventually struck lucky, though it turned out that our visual aid would have to remain with us throughout Thursday while we set up for the exhibition: a dangerous swathe of de-frosting time.

I couldn't face explaining about the parcel to our new hostess. I'd just allow her to put it trustingly into her freezer, believing us to be normal people anxious to preserve some delicacy.

*

Thursday June 18th 1987: Irene and I took the train to London. Boxes of leaflets, posters and much else had been sent on in advance, courtesy of a kind supporter willing to drive the load down to London. Our meeting with MAFF was scheduled for Monday afternoon at 2pm.

*

Monday June 22nd: We met up with Violet for a coffee in the Army and Navy Stores in Victoria Street, a *rendezvous* convenient for MAFF's Horseferry Road offices. We'd stowed our parcel well out of sight under a bench and, on leaving, were half way across the restaurant before we remembered it. We thanked our lucky stars that we had. That parcel was no average item of lost property...

*

The meeting had been convened to discuss welfare problems within the battery and broiler industries, and it turned out to be lengthy, lasting nearly three hours. The five MAFF officials agreed to watch extracts from our new video, *Sentenced for Life*, though cynically we suspected it was the seductive tones of Joanna Lumley, who'd generously supplied the voice-over, rather than the message of the video that appealed. Among the MAFF men present was Roy Moss, Chief Veterinary Officer, and Henry Brown, a rising star, we sensed, in Animal Welfare Division. After the video we had our 'discussion'. Round and round went the arguments, the denials, while all the time on the floor beside me, in a zipped up shopping bag, lurked The Feet.

Our frustration was nearing boiling point, when Henry Brown allowed his imagination to run away with him.

"But how can we be *certain* the hens suffer?" he queried, apparently in all seriousness. "Surely we can't know, without further research?"

Then, unwisely, he began to muse as to whether *people* would actually suffer, if they were shut away in, say, a broom cupboard, so long as they had food and water brought to them. Perhaps Henry was more cut out for some university's Department of Philosophy, or an obscure Think Tank. Something more abstract than farming systems, certainly.

By now we were at the end of our tethers, and beyond. Enough was enough. Ignoring the fact that the present item on the agenda was the battery hen, I reached down and unzipped the bag.

"I have here," I said, lifting out the package, "*official* proof of the suffering of broiler chickens."

*

And then, as I began to open the plastic bag, it hit us: the putrid stench of rotting flesh. Clouds of the dreadful smell engulfed the spacious room, wafting around the gleaming boardroom table, a truly shocking smell, though familiar enough to anyone who's been near a skip full of 'deads' outside a poultry slaughterhouse.

I realised that this time we had Gone Too Far. No way could I fully unwrap our valuable official proof. I turned to MAFF's Chief Veterinary Officer and asked him if he could *very kindly* dispose of The Feet, in view of their unforeseen deterioration. Meekly, obediently, Mr Moss took the packet from me and disappeared – for a very long time. We pictured him making repeated attempts to flush the sad amputated bits and pieces down a ministerial lavatory, or searching around outside for the nearest dustbin.

And now Irene rode to the rescue. Ever resourceful, always well supplied with the essentials of life, she took a perfume bottle from her handbag and liberally sprayed the air. Gradually, Lily of the Valley began to mask the ghastly odour, or at least mix with it, roughly fifty-fifty.

We didn't chalk the meeting up as a success, just another drip on the stone, though Roy Moss did let drop a hint of sympathy. But then he *was* about to retire.

*

June 29th 1987: I wrote to thank Henry Brown for arranging the meeting, concluding : *'We apologise again for the unpleasant state of the samples, but can assure you that many almost equally unpleasant smells exist on factory farms, both in batteries and broiler houses, where live birds are suffering. Had we been able to refrigerate the samples adequately we are sure you would have found them enlightening and horrifying, even without the smell.'*

Post script: Henry Brown sent Chickens' Lib a Christmas card after this event, repeating the gesture for two or three years, until he moved to another department – Economics, I seem to remember. Could it be that Henry harboured a secret admiration for our derring-do?

The shortest of lives

Approximately half of all chickens hatched are male. In the broiler industry both sexes are reared, but egg production-type males are deemed worthless; if reared, they'd be skinny, by comparison to the modern, clinically obese broiler.

As mentioned earlier, ruthless genetic selection over the last five or six decades has ensured that breeds of chickens now fall into two distinct types – those destined for egg production, the rest – the vast majority – for meat. And it makes no difference whether commercially produced eggs come from intensive systems or the best of free range: day-old male chicks, the brothers of the future laying hens, have no future.

*

One of the saddest purchases ever made by Chickens' Lib was of a dozen dead male day-old chicks. We'd found a nearby hatchery willing to sell to us – destroyed chicks are routinely bought as food for captive animals, so our request wasn't considered strange.

We wanted them so the image of these beautiful little birds could be shown on our latest video, to highlight the waste of life in the poultry industry – around forty million male chicks would have been destroyed that year, when the national flock of laying hens was estimated to be around that same number. We arranged to have hundreds of small sticky-backed photos made of the little heap of fluffy day-olds, for our supporters to distribute.

*

As soon as chicks of the egg-laying strain have struggled out of their shells and their down has dried, they are sexed. Sexing is a high-speed operation and doubtless skilful. All female chicks are added to the mass on a passing conveyor belt, all males tossed aside.

The approved methods of killing male and other chicks regarded as surplus are threefold: 'mechanical apparatus producing immediate death', 'exposure to gas mixtures', or dislocation of the neck (the last not used in large-scale operations)(1) .

Maceration is used for unhatched embryos, but is not popular in the larger hatcheries, since, according to FAWC, '*the rate of delivery of chicks exceeds the capacity of the* [macerating] *machine*' (2). Because of this, gassing is still the favoured method. We used to hear of supposedly gassed chicks reviving, while large numbers, especially those near the bottom of the bins, suffocated before the gas overcame them. FAWC in its report mentions the 'highly aversive' nature of 100% carbon dioxide, in that it causes a distressing and relatively prolonged death. While recognising that the use of 100% carbon dioxide is legal, FAWC recommends alternative gas mixtures as being more humane (3).

This cruel mass destruction of life is a direct result of having divided chickens into two distinct types and has nothing whatsoever to commend it. What is more, the manipulation of nature, if you like, has had a direct effect on human health, and in more ways than one.

Let's take a look at the most obvious connection – the rise in obesity in humans.

Clinically obese humans

When only a few weeks old, broiler chickens are so heavy their legs cannot comfortably carry their own weight. More and more people are fat too. Clinical obesity is taking a huge slice out of the National Health Service budget as cases of Type 2 diabetes increase, even in children. 10% of UK citizens are currently being treated for obesity, one in twenty of them for diabetes, mostly those of Type 2, the kind linked to diet and lifestyle. Worldwide, 80% of people with Type 2 diabetes are found to be obese when diagnosed (1).

The fat-chicken trap has caught people from all walks of life. Poultry meat has been foisted on the public as the healthy alternative, part of 'lean cuisine', while at the same time reduced to junk food. Not so long ago, you could pick up a leaflet in any doctor's surgery and find chicken recommended as a healthy option, though I fancy that this advice is not seen so frequently now. However, if you consider when the dangers from modern chicken meat were first logged, it's taking a remarkably long time for the penny to drop.

*

Towards the end of 1986 an interesting letter had appeared in *The Times*. Above it was a cartoon showing a very fat man consulting his doctor. The caption read: '*As I see it your main problem is that you've been intensively reared*'. The letter was from Professor Michael Crawford, then Head of the Department of Biochemistry and Nutrition at London's Institute of Zoology, and a consultant for diverse organisations including the World Health Organisation and Action for Research into Multiple Sclerosis. He now heads the Institute of Brain Chemistry and Human Nutrition at London Metropolitan University.

The letter, published nearly a quarter of a century ago, described how he and his wife were planning a dinner party and had bought several packs of frozen chicken thighs from a well-known supermarket. The recipe they'd chosen called for the chicken pieces to be first boiled, and they were amazed at the amount of fat that rose to the surface. After some kitchen-based experiments, Professor Crawford concluded that the calories obtained from the chicken pieces were largely from fat. In his words: *'Clearly such 1986 chickens as we purchased need to be crossed off the list of low-fat foods.'*

I wrote to Professor Crawford, enclosing our fact sheet on broilers and our recently produced video *Chicken for Dinner?* He replied saying that he had found the contents disturbing. *'Quite apart from the importance such a distortion would have on the health of the bird itself,'* Professor Crawford wrote, *'it is a colossal waste of energy* [energy in the dietary sense] *and directly contrary to the current recommendations which are being made by the DHSS and NACNE and specifically against the recommendation of the FAO/WHO expert committee of 1978, who specified the need to produce leaner livestock'* (2).*

In 1987 *Poultry World* reported on a conference at which Professor Crawford told delegates that the UK was 'top of the league' in the highest death rate from heart disease in the Western world and this could be directly linked with the amount of saturated fat consumed. He'd gone on to explain the harm done by saturated fats in meats, saying that meat was part of a normal diet – but meat fat was a killer, so far as heart disease was concerned. While the body needed unsaturated fat for structural and brain development, he said, saturated fat was stored in the body. Modern meat was low in polyunsaturates and harmful to health (3). Since the rise of factory farming and changes in animal feed contents, the fat in meat is found throughout the animal's body, so cannot simply be cut off. This infiltration of muscle with saturated fat is known as 'marbling.'

Some years previously, Professor Crawford and colleagues had pointed to the difference in the fat quality to be found in traditionally reared livestock in Africa. The fat in such meat was found to be polyunsaturated, similar to that found in wild animals, while for intensively reared animals it's a very different story: *'This fact is simply explained by the large amounts of adipose fat (energy store as opposed to structural lipid) which infiltrates*

---

* DHSS Department of Health and Social Services
  NACNE National Committee on Nutrition Education (UK)
  FAO Food and Agriculture Organization (United Nations)
  WHO World Health Organisation

the muscle tissue of intensively reared animals fed high energy, fattening foods without exercise.' (4)

In 1991, *World Health*, the magazine of the World Health Organization, (July-August issue) published an article by Professor Crawford, at that time Director of The Institute of Brain Chemistry and Human Nutrition at Hackney Hospital in London. The opening paragraph to *'Fat Animals – Fat Humans'* was startling: *'The accepted wisdom on animal agriculture is that it is there to produce protein. So it may come as a surprise to learn that beef, lamb, poultry and pork provide consumers in northern Europe and America with more fat than protein. Not just more, but several times more!'* Later on in the article he commented: *'Sadly, developing countries are already copying this unhealthy type of animal husbandry.'* Sad indeed, that ruthless multinationals continue to foist potentially lethal food onto largely unsuspecting populations. Though why the people in China and India should choose to adopt diets proven to be harmful is not easy to understand. Nor is Africa immune to the temptations of fast and fatty food. According to a report in *The Lancet* obesity is occurring in sub-Saharan Africa, a region more often associated with famine (5).

Having taken a trip through the development of modern farming methods, Professor Crawford then explained how the recent mania for fat has been profit-led, starting with high energy diets, so allowing more animals per field – a development emerging well before factory farming got going: *'This high–energy diet plus low exercise regime led to a third development. When the animals were sold in the market, the heavier they were the better the price. So the ones that put on weight fastest were chosen for breeding. Farmers fell into the trap of selecting for the fat animal. This at first seemed not a bad idea, since people liked a bit of fat and it was useful for many purposes from boot polish to soap. At the same time they were selecting animals that would tolerate the kind of food man gave them to eat,'*– in that case more 'managed' but less appropriate natural grassland, as well as (relatively speaking) restricted space. Turning to factory farming, he went on to describe one of its worst examples, the imprisonment of breeding sows *'...sows tied down so their nipples were constantly available to the ravenous piglets.'* He gave Chickens' Lib a mention too: *'Chickens' Lib has also highlighted the plight of battery hens and broiler chickens. Genetics, environment and food have been designed for fat gain.'*

Now for a leap forward, in time if not in terms of progress: In 2005 the Observer Food Monthly published details of Professor Crawford and colleagues' on-going research. They'd found that chicken meat in 2004 contained more than twice as much fat as in 1940, a third more calories and a third *less* protein – despite the fact that protein is what the consumer generally assumes he or she is paying for. As Professor Crawford commented: *'We now need a new definition of what we mean by a healthy food.'* He revealed too that even organic chickens had not been found to be much healthier as food, since they too are bred for rapid weight gain. It seems the 'slower growing' chicken, introduced in recent years, is only very slightly behind the worst of an average broiler, in the fat stakes. Most of the slow growers are slaughtered at around 80 days rather than the 40 or so common to intensively reared birds. It seems the race is still well and truly on to get chickens off the farm and into the supermarket, whether factory-farmed, free range, or organic.

The 2005 Observer Food Monthly article proved to be the precursor of research published in 2009 (6). The conclusions in the paper's Abstract are as follows: *'Traditional poultry and eggs were one of the few land-based sources of long-chain n-3 fatty acids, especially DHA, which is synthesised from its parent precursor in the green food chain. In view of the obesity epidemic, chickens that provide several times the fat energy compared with protein seem illogical. This type of chicken husbandry needs to be reviewed with regard to its implications for animal welfare and human nutrition.'*

For the layperson like me it's a complicated paper, but the nub of it is that the researchers believe that both physical and mental health problems, including behavioural problems in children, may be the result of poor nutrition: *'Explanations for the tripling of obesity since 1980 include a lack of exercise, fast food, social factors, television, schoolchildren's snacks, sugary drinks, genes and ethnic backgrounds. The National Institute for Health and Clinical Excellence, the Food Standards Agency and the National Collaborating Centre for Primary Care have published recommendations to deal with the "obesity epidemic". Yet there is no reference to the changing composition of food...The increase in brain disorders this century has catapulted mental ill health to cost £77 billion in the UK during 2008, greater by far than all other burdens of ill health. Although the intensification of chickens alone cannot be responsible for this rise in disorders, it is part of a package in the changing food system that has ignored the nutrient requirements of people and, specifically in this case, for the brain. It would be helpful if human food production was again linked to human nutritional requirements as its first priority, as was achieved during World War 11 by Professor Sir Jack Drummond.'*

So far Chickens' Lib's campaign hadn't strayed far from chickens, as befitted its name. Soon though, we were to speak up for another kind of bird, when we turned our attention to a whole new world of darkness and disease.

But before going there, I'll mention just a few of the valuable contacts we were now making.

Overseas links

Contacts with activists all over the world brought home to us the enormity of the damage that's been done in the name of cheap food and 'efficiency'. Sometimes, the wide world seems to cry out with the distress of cruelly exploited animals, yet conversely one small scene can encapsulate the whole rotten story.

We were in the process of making *Sentenced for Life*, our video about the battery hen, and had just released a batch of newly rescued hens into our orchard. A few seconds of the filming still haunt me.

In among a patch of summer weeds, a semi-naked little hen cautiously takes a few steps. It's the lack of confidence, the obvious strangeness of experiencing a sense of purpose that reveals her history. After a year of so spent on the harsh metal cage floor, never once able to take a meaningful step, pecked relentlessly by the other hens in her cage, suddenly she has options. And, best of all perhaps, nobody is bothering her. So she makes her little bit of progress, slowly, hesitantly, wondering at her new surroundings.

So many of the images we received from overseas have told and continue to tell the same stories of abuse. A battery hen, it seems, is a battery hen the world over, and the same can be said for other factory-farmed animals.

*

South Africa

In 1989 we'd received a letter from a certain Louise van der Merwe in South Africa. She wanted to start her own campaign and had written to Bristol University's School of Veterinary Medicine requesting information, and wondering if she might be given an introduction to organisations in Britain. Contact details for several organisations including Chickens' Lib were supplied, and we responded eagerly.

Clearly, Louise cared deeply about farmed animals, and poultry especially. Keen to get her campaign established, she suggested she might become 'Chickens' Lib South Africa'. Cautious as ever, fearful of taking a step we'd regret, Violet and I decided to decline her offer, but said we'd be delighted to send her as much information as we could. And there began a great and mutually beneficial friendship. Soon Louise had formed her own organisation, 'Humanity for Hens' and before long was making remarkably fast progress.

Over the years, Humanity for Hens was transformed into The Humane Education Trust, and its magazine Animal Voice, edited by Louise, is now the official mouthpiece of Compassion in World Farming South Africa (1). Here follows no more than a tiny snapshot of what Louise and her colleagues have achieved. For simplicity, I'll (inaccurately) refer to the organisation in all its stages as CIWF (SA).

By 1991, following two years' hard lobbying, Pick'n Pay and Woolworths were stocking free range eggs and a mere decade later CIWF (SA)'s Humane Education programme was introduced into eleven schools as part of the Western Cape Education Department's *Safe Schools* programme, while a related video was shown in Brussels, to international acclaim.

By 2003 CIWF (SA) was participating in the process of integrating Humane Education into South Africa's Curriculum, and in the same year it hosted the All-African Humane Education Summit in Cape Town, attended by educators from eighteen African countries.

In 2010, following a presentation from CIWF (SA), Cape Town's Health Committee unanimously voted for one meat-free day a week.

*

Since that first letter in 1989, Louise and I have met, just once. In 2005 CIWF held a two-day international conference in London on animal sentiency, *'From Darwin to Dawkins'*. Initially I'd thought I'd be unable to attend, and Louise had sounded unsure of her plans, but at the last minute I did book in, just for one day. Half way through the morning session, I was in the ladies cloakroom, when I heard an unmistakably South African accent. Whirling around, I immediately recognised Louise from photographs in Animal Voice. We literally fell into each other's arms and spent as much time as possible together for the rest of the day. It was such a pleasure to meet at last.

I'm proud to be a friend of someone whose influence has spread throughout South Africa and beyond, and rewarded to think that in the early days of Louise's campaign Chickens' Lib was able to be of help and encouragement.

America

We've kept in touch with several animal rights/welfare organisations in the USA, but most closely with United Poultry Concerns (UPC). UPC's founder and President is author and tireless campaigner Karen Davis, and her passion is poultry. On her website (2) Karen describes how, by chance, she'd found and cared for an abandoned and very sick chicken. Soon, she came to realize that this one little bird was a typical victim of America's massive broiler industry. In 1990, as a result of all that this one chicken represented, she founded United Poultry Concerns.

At around that time someone mentioned Chickens' Lib to Karen and recommended my book *Chicken and Egg: Who Pays the Price?* Karen read it, and got in touch. She tells me the book influenced her campaign; soon she had no doubt that the poultry meat and egg industries in both our countries were based on the same mindset – the profit motive above all. Karen has said that our videos *Chicken for Dinner?* and *Sentenced for Life* affected her deeply when first she saw them and was planning her campaign strategy.

All UPC's information is admirably detailed and Karen lectures widely, informing the public, teachers and academics about the terrible abuses meted out to farmed birds. An updated version of her book *Prisoned Chickens, Poisoned Eggs* (3) covers all aspects of domesticated poultry. As well as detailing the cruel abuse of poultry, she highlights the effect on humans of the filthy practices within the poultry industry, via antibiotic resistance. (4)

Then there are the toxins ingested directly: Karen quotes the U.S. Department of Agriculture's figures relating to the arsenic content in an average intake of chicken meat: *'Arsenic concentrations in young chickens are three times greater than in other meat and poultry products... people ingest 3.6 to 5.2 micrograms of inorganic arsenic, the most toxic form of the element,'* and she warns that: *'People who eat more chicken may ingest 10 times that amount of arsenic, which can cause bladder, respiratory, and skin cancers from a daily intake of 10 – 40 micrograms of arsenic.'* (5)

In its magazine *Choice*, the Association of Colleges and Research Libraries of the American Library Association reviewed *Prisoned Chickens, Poisoned Eggs*. Describing it as 'riveting and brilliant' their reviewer commented: '[Karen Davis] *illuminates the ugly, the brutal, and the robotically efficient, the greed of heartless owners, and the callousness of workers in this machinery of exploitation and extermination.'* (6)

An on-going campaign with UPC involves opposition to a custom sometimes still carried out in the days leading up to Yom Kippur, the Jewish Day of Atonement. Live sacrificial chickens are swung around the perpetrators' heads before slaughter, a custom hardly likely to atone for anything, one would think. On September 25th 2009 Rob Eshman, Editor-in-Chief of the *Jewish Journal of Greater Los Angeles* had this to say about the practice: *'You'll recognise places to swing a chicken by the stench, the shrieks of the birds, the stealthy, guilt-clouded atmosphere in which men (mostly it's men) carry out a duty they know most people find cruel, and which inflicts a measure of absolutely superfluous cruelty on animals destined to die. A Kapparot area represents nothing so much as the seediest strip club, where men slink in and out, compelled by a force they can scarcely understand.'* For more on this, visit www.upc-online.org and key the word 'Kapparot' into 'search'.

In an attempt to wake American consumers up to the facts of chickens' lives and deaths, United Poultry Concerns has lately taken to displaying huge posters on buses in both Washington and New York, and on hoardings in Times Square.

*

169

Australia

Another courageous woman, and a contact of Chickens' Lib, is Patty Mark, President of Animal Liberation Victoria (ALV). Patty founded ALV in 1978, and in 1993 her Open Rescue Division began its work. Fearlessly, Patty and her colleagues infiltrated some of the biggest and worst intensive poultry farms in her region, filming and rescuing injured and dying hens and broilers. Her website (7) testifies to the terrible conditions on intensive farms in that country of vast open spaces.

On February 25th 2007, the *Herald Sun* reported on a visit by ALV to Happy Hens farm, Victoria's biggest battery farm, situated in Meredith (already investigated by Patty Mark and fellow activists over a period of many years). The newspaper told how on this occasion they broke in and stole eighteen chickens, vowing later to increase their 'guerrilla strikes'.

Despite electric fencing, guard dogs and security lights, the protestors had entered the units undetected. They had found illegal overcrowding, filthy conditions, birds stuck in manure pits, hungry birds eating the rotting bodies of dead ones... all the old familiar horrors. Patty Mark, described in the report as a 'serial activist', commented that the sheds were being converted to hold 80,000 battery hens in a space that once held a quarter of that number.

The egg industry threatened to hit back with prosecutions (no new experience for Patty). Danny Colla, manager of Happy Hens told the *Herald Sun* that it was in the hens' best interests to be treated well, adding that the RSPCA had been to the farm and found nothing amiss.

The report did end on a happier note, stating that the 'pilfered' hens had been given to homes around Melbourne, as pets, and that the RSPCA was about to investigate ALV's complaint against Happy Hens.

Make no mistake about it, this is a tale of persistence. I've just come across a fax from Patty dated August 1996, and it concerns ALV's *thirteenth* undercover inspection of Happy Hens Egg World in Meredith. By that date, ALV member Diana Simpson had compiled over fourteen hours of damning video evidence, which had been shown around the world on numerous TV news reports.

A court case was then looming, the charge being trespass, and not for the first time. Patty had been fined on previous occasions; Pam Clarke, another serial rescuer, had already been arrested many times in Tasmania and seen the inside of a prison following her refusal to pay fines. This history of sustained complaints against a major battery farm, backed up with hours of video evidence, points to the power of industry and the gross failure of those whose job it should be to protect the animals.

*

A recent and horrific four minutes of film on the ALV website shows Patty in a laying hens' breeding unit – a building holding thousands of hens, many with backs rubbed raw from unnaturally frequent mounting by the cockerels, along with enough of those to ensure the maximum number of fertile eggs. Patty describes the frantic noise in the shed as of chickens 'gone mad': cocks crowing non-stop, and a sort of screaming coming from the hens as they're relentlessly mounted by the males. My guess is it's the sound of hungry birds too – feed restriction for egg-type chickens, though not as severe as with broilers, is practised. The filmed hens are mostly near-featherless, their backs scabby and raw, testament to never-ending attention from the cockerels. Above the racket within the shed, Patty explains that part-way through this year of torture, the initial males are replaced by younger, fitter and keener ones, to ensure the number of fertile eggs doesn't decline (to view this footage go to *Patty Mark's Diary*, on the ALV website www.alv.org.au).

Chickens' Lib's contact with Patty has been specific to poultry, but ALV campaigns on all animal-related issues, for example the tragic long-distance export of livestock from Australia's shores.

I've been forced to be selective, when writing about our overseas contacts. It would take too long to include every group or individual we've exchanged material with, learning from their experiences and eager to send them any information that might help with their campaigns. But I must mention Charles Notin who, on behalf of *Protection Mondiale des Animaux de Ferme*, CIWF's branch in France, kindly helped me translate our booklet *Today's Poultry Industry* into French.

While writing this, I've been thinking back to that 1969 letter from MAFF, when the Minister's Private Secretary boasted of Britain's thriving export trade in breeding stock and farming know-how, and find myself reflecting on the immense suffering caused (8).

But now for that other grim world, new then to Chickens' Lib – the abuse of turkeys, right here in Britain.

171

ENTER TURKEYS

1989 found Chickens' Lib extra busy. In the run-up to Christmas, we'd arranged to have 70,000 new leaflets condemning the intensive turkey industry delivered with local papers in selected areas throughout the UK. Our January 1990 newsletter to supporters enclosed a fact sheet in which we laid bare the reality of how modern farmed turkeys lived. Under an etching of a pair of slim and elegant wild turkeys (probably dating back a century) we described their enforced fall from grace at the hands of a ruthless industry: *'The widespread factory farming of turkeys is relatively new. Until the 1960s turkeys were mainly reared for the Christmas market, but now they are the raw material of a fast-growing industry, supplying birds all the year round, plus many 'value added' convenience foods such as turkey breast roll, sausages etc. Turkeys still run wild in America, and are more closely related to the pheasant and partridge than the chicken. Their semi-wild nature ill befits them for life in intensive units, where, even when debeaked or kept in semi-darkness, they resort to cannibalism. Chickens' Lib believes that not enough is known about the cruel turkey industry, and has prepared this fact sheet to alert the public.'*

We set out some of our major concerns:
- Slaughter age for commercially reared turkeys ranging from 12-26 weeks. (A turkey's natural lifespan is around 10 years.)
- 33 million turkeys slaughtered in the UK (during 1988).
- Mortality running at around 7% with a wide range of causes, one being cannibalism, to which stressed turkeys are prone.

We included a detailed description of how the modern turkey procreates. As a result of selective breeding, the male is now too heavy and broad-breasted to mate with the smaller female. Consequently, his semen must be artificially extracted, two or three times a week, by teams of artificial insemination (AI) operators.

A 1983 reference book (number 242 – Crown copyright) produced by the Agricultural Development and Advisory Service (ADAS) described the recommended procedure in detail: teams of two or possibly three AI operators were needed, one to restrain the turkey by the legs, in readiness for the semen to be collected, the other to massage the male bird around the vent area, using the palms and fingers of both hands until the vent opens and the phallus protrudes. Now, the vent must be kept open, with the phallus protruded, using finger and thumb. This allows semen to be 'milked' and set aside, at a carefully controlled temperature, for subsequent insemination.

The next stage, the insemination of semen into the female, would be achieved via a hypodermic syringe, or by more basic means, namely a length of rubber or plastic tubing, through which the operator must blow. Apparently, the latter method was convenient, though with one drawback. If the number of females to be inseminated was large, the operator might well end up with a dry mouth.

Artificial insemination, preceded by the 'massaging' of the male until he ejects semen, is now 100% throughout the intensive turkey industry. Surely 'the bird', centre stage at millions of Christmas and Thanksgiving celebrations, represents animal abuse of a particularly distasteful kind.

*

In the same January 1990 newsletter we wrote about a shocking competition, then in its thirtieth year, run for charity by the British Turkey Federation (BTF). *'Well done,'* enthused poultry feed firm BOCM Silcock Ltd, in one of its advertisements. *'Champion Tyson weighed in at a magnificent 86 lbs to win the British Turkey Federation Heavy Turkey competition, smashing all previous records.'*

86 lbs – that's around six stone, or almost 40 kilos. No details were offered as to how Tyson reached this gross weight, but the temptation may have been to administer growth promoters in abundance. Clearly, Chickens' Lib must do all in its power to stop this disgraceful competition.

We urged all our supporters to write to the BTF, demanding that the competition be abandoned. I don't know how one of them – let's call him Mr G – had expressed his disgust, but Neville Wallace, Director-General of the BTF, hadn't liked his style, sternly suggesting that he should check his facts before sending 'threatening letters'. However, he did promise to take Mr G's views into account when the time came for the British Turkey Federation to decide on the future of the Heavy Turkey competition, admitting that some members of the public clearly found the whole thing 'distressing or repugnant'.

And take such views into account they did, for on June 25th 1990 Raymond Twiddle, Chairman of the BTF, wrote to Chickens' Lib telling us that in spite of the fact that in all the thirty years of the competition the turkeys did not suffer in the way we and our supporters 'suggested', the Federation was 'constantly reviewing' its charitable activities. It had just been decided to change the format and to omit the heavy turkey competition. Mr Twiddle didn't state that the competition was over for good and all. That would have seemed like admitting defeat. But that was indeed the outcome.

In his opening paragraph, Mr Twiddle revealed that over the previous two years the BTF had, as a result of the competition, been able to provide fifteen motorised wheelchairs for disabled children. While not wishing to denigrate the motives behind this generosity, the irony was not lost on us. In a roundabout way, severely disabled children were benefiting from the sufferings of grossly deformed turkeys.

It was good to wave goodbye to the infamous Heavy Turkey Competition. Sadly, few battles were to be won so easily.

*

In 2003 one of our supporters failed to be reassured by the letter she received from a leading turkey producer in which he explained that AI 'pays handsomely' by increasing fertility, and while it represents a chore for staff, 'both hens and stags enjoy it', a claim that rang exceedingly hollow.

I'm not aware of any undercover filming of artificial insemination of turkeys in the UK but the principles of AI are the same worldwide, though the scale of the operation will differ. While trawling the net recently I came across Farm Sanctuary's website (1) and there viewed undercover filming shot inside an American turkey breeding establishment. The process undergone by the birds is even more savage than I'd imagined. This is how it goes in the States: first we see the male turkeys (known as toms in America, stags in the UK). With their feet clamped together, forced onto their backs, the operator arouses his trapped turkey to ejaculation, roughly and fast. It's all happening in a huge hangar-like building, the rows of pens packed with toms. There must be hundreds, maybe thousands of them, waiting their turn.

Separately, the females are inseminated at breakneck speed, despite the fact that vaginas can be bruised and damaged unless the procedure is undertaken with care (2). This process is accomplished with savage haste, each operator aiming at inseminating several hundred females an hour. An employee there told Farm Sanctuary that for the first couple of visits from the AI team the birds showed friendly curiosity, but by the third one only fear.

I noticed one of the inseminators was wearing a wedding ring, and wondered about *his* sex life. Did he ever stop to think what he was doing to these defenceless birds?

All the while, loud pop music mingled with the sounds made by the terrified birds.

*

It's by no means easy to obtain turkeys – each bird is far more valuable than the almost worthless battery hen or a cheap-as-chips broiler. Nobody half-way normal is likely to stop by an intensive turkey farm and ask to buy a couple of birds, and if he or she did, alarm bells would ring (and possibly security alarms too).

But in the April of 1990 Chickens' Lib managed to acquire four turkeys, with no forethought whatsoever.

Introducing Boyo

On the last Monday before Easter, Irene and I travelled to a livestock market in Chelford, Cheshire. We'd gone in the hope of buying a few 'spent' battery hens, and to look around. As well as auctioning cattle, this market dealt in anything from chicks and baby rabbits to turkeys. We were sure to find something of interest.

And we did. We found Boyo.

*

For several minutes we'd wandered about, horrified by the lack of concern for the animals about to be auctioned. Regardless of the occupants, all the metal cages had openings of the same dimension, a fact soon to be forcefully brought home to us. As each lot was sold, the auctioneer routinely brought his hammer crashing down on the top of the nearest cage, the noise and its reverberations terrifying animals and birds all along the line.

We noticed a large number of turkeys, mostly looking sickly – perhaps Easter was a good time to turn out unwanted birds. In fact we could

175

see poultry of all kinds, but no 'spent' hens. Miserably, we walked back and forth, peering into the cages, stopping for the second time by two in particular, both containing turkeys. Two females, labelled as weighing 12 lbs (5.44 kilos) each, were next to two male birds crammed into a cage of the same size, each of these, according to the label, weighing 25 lbs (11.34 kilos).

Irene and I sometimes agree that our minds work alike, and they did on that occasion. We looked at each other. Could we possibly buy these four? How would we get them home? Finally, how could we bear to leave them here?

So we bid for all four, successfully. The next trauma to hit the turkeys, and us, was when the market staff came to yank them through cage openings suited to an average hen or rabbit, but hopelessly inadequate for turkeys, especially the males. A horrific struggle took place, while we stood by, helpless. We felt guilty, but the turkeys had to be got out somehow. It would have been the same nightmare operation for whoever had bought them.

Finally, with all four stowed safely in boxes in the boot of the car, we were heading back to my house wondering just how foolhardy we'd been. Turkeys? What did we know about turkeys, in the flesh?

These four turned out to be an education for us, though with a very different slant from the 'education' at the same time being aimed at an unsuspecting public by the Health Education Authority (HEA). In September of that year, a supporter received a letter from the HEA – she'd written (at our suggestion) complaining about the Authority's link with the British Turkey Information Service (BTIS). In the letter the manager of the HEA's Nutrition and Dental Health Programme explained that the HEA had issued a leaflet, in association with the BTIS, promoting 'dietary messages' for the prevention of heart disease, including the role played by 'low fat poultry meat'. Finally, our supporter was informed that the leaflet was entirely funded by the turkey industry (1). No surprises there, then.

But to return to our Chelford market turkeys. Hastily we erected a pen in the (car-free) garage, and unloaded our new acquisitions. The sight of the birds, now out of close confinement, shocked us anew. One of the males was especially filthy and dejected, and obviously crippled. We held out little hope for him and called our vet, who came straight away.

176

He confirmed our fears. This turkey, perhaps destined for the catering trade and clearly deemed suitable for auction at a market where MAFF and RSPCA inspectors were regularly on duty, was a very sick bird. The vet's diagnosis included synovitis (a viral or staphylococcal infection resulting in swollen legs), a long-standing dislocation of one wing and a broken wing, the injury possibly sustained when being stuffed into or dragged from the market cage.

While the vet waited for the lethal injection to take effect, the other male turkey began to preen himself – a hopeful sign. Then we heard a 'clonk'. A rock-hard and filthy chunk of dead flesh (necrotic tissue, in the vet's words) had become dislodged. The vet wouldn't commit himself as to its origin – it could have come from another turkey altogether and merely been stuck to one of ours. A dreadful picture was emerging of cruelty and of danger to public health.

*

Soon we could write to our supporters: *'The three remaining turkeys are now outside, near CL's little collection of seven hens and a cockerel. Boyo has matured with dramatic speed, and boasts a magnificent blue/red head and neck and pendulous snood. Every time the cockerel crows, Boyo replies with a resounding "gobble-gobble". To date, he seems entirely unaggressive, and has the look of an immensely wise, rather tired, old man. One of the females is called Marilyn, owing to her star quality. When being recorded on video her keenness to investigate resulted in the camera lens misting up with her breath. Sadly, the other female has a weak leg. Being wild and nervous, she flapped about when approached and clearly did herself some damage. Our vet is sure nothing is broken and we trust she will recover, in time. The immediate reaction of the two vets we consulted was to say that "modern" turkeys are too heavy to bear their own weight, and not intended to survive for long.'*

Already we were confirming, at first hand that turkeys' personalities are distinct – out of just three birds, we had Boyo, serious but unfailingly sociable, Marilyn, inquisitive and outgoing, the other female very timid. How many differing characters would be found in one of those units holding anything up to twenty five thousand birds?

*

After keeping the turkeys separate from the hens and their cockerel for a while, we decided to let them share the same straw yard and orchard. Sadly, one adaptation had to be made for Boyo. A strip of wood across the gateway into the orchard, no more than two inches (5cms) high, presented an insuperable obstacle to Boyo: he could barely lift his feet from the ground, let alone fly into a treetop like his wild counterpart. Poultry scientists' genetic selection for meatiness had done its worst.

There was another, even sadder, aspect of Boyo's condition. In common with all turkeys bred for the intensive industry he was, once mature, far too heavy and broad-breasted to mate naturally. Yet his instincts to procreate remained strong. Frequently he displayed all the signs of arousal, fluffing up his feathers, extending his snood, which would then change to a ruby red...yet he could never mount either of his female turkey companions.

One day our cameraman Bob was with us, filming for a forthcoming video. He'd all but run out of film but he did manage to capture the moment when Boyo did his very best to achieve his purpose but, as ever, failed dismally.

*

In spite of his physical problems, we felt confident that Boyo was enjoying life. In September 1990 we wrote to our supporters: *'Marilyn continues to be outgoing and friendly and has developed a passion for the loganberries that grow over part of the poultry enclosure...Clearly Boyo considers himself guardian of the hen/turkey run, gobbling loudly at any sudden noises, from tractors to laughter. He's becoming steadily more "outgoing" and is the least aggressive creature imaginable. Sadly, he's too slow in all his movements for his own good, and rarely wins in the loganberry stakes! We write at length about turkeys, because the turkey meat industry is all set to expand hugely, and we must prevent this from happening. The industry will be aiming at something approaching 40 million birds to be slaughtered in 1991, yet each one will be a Boyo, or a Marilyn, each one with its own individual character and desire to live a pain-free life.'*

Boyo lived peaceably with us for just over a year. Violet loved him, and never tired of crossing the lawn to the little orchard to pass the time of day with him. And he never failed to plod slowly towards her, serious as always yet clearly welcoming her presence.

*

Some might say Chickens' Lib displayed foolish optimism, with this talk of preventing the expansion of the turkey industry. But in a campaign one must aim high. So we produced dramatic posters and glossy leaflets by the tens of thousands, and lobbied the turkey industry relentlessly. When searching around for a leaflet format that just might make the horrible facts about turkeys' lives grab the public's attention, we decided to put the message in the turkey's own words, as a series of questions and answers. For example, *'Q: Don't you get ill? A: Yes, often. Without antibiotics, millions of us wouldn't survive at all. We suffer from things like turkey rhinotracheitis (TRT) which makes us cough and sneeze, and then we get swollen faces, and painful sinusitis. They give us drugs for that, all right, to get us fit for slaughter. Some of us die, though, and the rest of us are so bored, we peck at the dead bodies. Q: We've heard that over thirty million of you go for meat every year. Where do you all come from? A: Well, that's a horrible story actually. Because of all the selective breeding that's gone on, the chaps amongst us have become terribly heavy. Our breasts are so "meaty" we can hardly walk, and we certainly can't mate any longer. Couldn't do it...'* And so on. We were pleased when an education authority in the West Country included our leaflet in teaching material for secondary schools.

*

Despite all the campaigning, turkey meat production continued to escalate, its image as a healthy food doubtless boosted by the Health Education Authority, a body that should have educated *itself* before getting into bed with the turkey industry. It wasn't as if there had been no warnings. In the first three months of 1989, thirteen multiple drug-resistant strains of Salmonella typhimurium were isolated from turkeys on farms in Lincolnshire and North Yorkshire alone (2). We'd sent information about this to the HEA, informing them of conditions in the intensive turkey industry and stressing the dangers of antibiotic resistance in the human population.

However, nothing came of our interventions, and later Bernard Matthews' now infamous 'Turkey Twizzlers' were to infiltrate thousands of British schools.

*

May 1991: Our May newsletter that year included the news that in April Boyo had been found dead: *'He'd been on excellent form (by his standards) the previous day, so we believed he suffered a heart attack, due to his appalling built-in obesity. He was inscrutable (it would be presumptuous to form conclusions about what was going on in his mind, or what the wise expression in his eyes signified)... "Majestic" was the word that sprang to mind when he fluffed up his feathers to impress onlookers...However, Boyo was a travesty of what a turkey should be. In their wild state, turkeys can fly at 50 mph, yet Boyo was only able to plod along at snail's pace, barely able to lift his feet off the ground. Before burying him, we weighed him and he registered 50 lbs, around three and a half stone...When Boyo died, the two females huddled together, apparently in a state of shock, for several hours.'*

We reminded our supporters of how Bernard Matthews posed for promotional photographs before a backdrop of his magnificent headquarters at Great Witchingham Hall, a flock of free-range turkeys at his feet. *'We must change this image',* we said.

We ended our tribute to Boyo thus: *'We had him for a year, and have gained much from knowing him – a magnificent photograph which we are using to great effect, and an education in turkey behaviour, which is both strange and interesting. In welfare terms, Boyo's life has, we believe, been of great significance. The valley seems quiet now, and we shall miss his presence.'*

*

One year later, we re-visited Chelford market but found no turkeys on sale. Straw in the cages was testament to stricter regulations by then in force (3). Following our complaints, we'd been assured that auctioneers would now longer bring their hammers crashing down on the rows of cages. Hopefully these changes apply to this day.

Mr Gummer's having none of it

On February 20th 1990 we issued a Press Release to coincide with a letter to the then Minister of Agriculture, John Selwyn Gummer. In it we challenged him to spend twenty four hours in a battery shed containing a minimum of 20,000 battery hens, or a broiler or turkey shed housing a similar number of birds. For the benefit of the media (and the Minister?) we included some background information:

'Battery hens develop brittle bones, malignant tumours, fatty livers, deformed feet etc. and undergo severe deprivation and stress. Broiler chickens (meat-type birds) are slaughtered when only 6-7 weeks old, yet by then many are crippled, diseased and suffering from painful sores and ulcers. Turkeys are crowded together so that aggression is rife. Cannibalism is common, the birds pecking relentlessly at each other, often at the eyes. To counter this tendency, farmers de-beak some turkeys. Those not de-beaked are kept in conditions of deepest gloom. Slaughter of these heavy birds ("spent" breeding males can weigh as much as a child of 8-9 years) poses huge welfare problems, especially since most have diseased hip joints. By law, turkeys may be hung upside down on the slaughter line for up to six minutes.*

Chickens' Lib recognises that Mr Gummer (who is a member of the General Synod of the Church of England) would be exposed to stress, and even to grave doubts as to the morality of keeping living creatures in the conditions outlined above. It is therefore suggested that he takes a copy of the Bible with him, along with food and drink but no extra lighting except a torch. Communications with the outside world would be vital, since a power failure would result in the suffocation, within minutes, of any person or animal within the building.

Mr Gummer will receive his challenge, by Datapost, at the Ministry of Agriculture, Whitehall Place, London on Tuesday 20th February 1990.'

No reply was forthcoming from the Minister.

*

In that same year, 1990, John Selwyn Gummer was reported in *The Times* as declaring vegetarianism to be a wholly unnatural practice, at variance with the biblical teaching that we humans are masters of the fowl of the air and the beasts of the fields, making it, in Mr Gummer's reported words, very proper to eat them. In our May fact sheet we commented: *'Chickens' Lib considers mankind has proved himself to be a hard taskmaster, more akin to a slave driver, where the fowl of the air are concerned.'*

Later, Mr Gummer was to hit the headlines, feeding his small daughter Cordelia a beefburger, his intention being to stem the mood of rising panic over BSE, the terrible brain disease in cattle, transferable to humans. But far from calming the general public he shocked people, who saw the gesture as using his daughter to back up the Government's propaganda machine.

On May 15th 1990, *Farmers Guardian* covered John Gummer's May address to the British Poultry Federation, during which he was reported as stressing the importance of building public confidence in the quality of British produce, while not allowing that confidence to be undermined by what he called 'maverick groups'. If the cap fits, we thought...

*

June 14th 1990: Violet, Irene and I handed in a battery hen petition numbering 20,000 signatures to 10 Downing Street. Joanna Lumley lent her support by accompanying us, as did Liberal MP Charles Kennedy.

Having said our goodbyes, we Chickens' Libbers stood around in Whitehall for a few moments feeling a trifle flat, and reluctant to go straight home. Here we were, dressed in our most respectable clothes, having travelled down from Yorkshire...

Then an idea came to us. MAFF's headquarters were just a step away, in Whitehall Place. Maybe we should request an impromptu meeting with the minister? After all, being a thorn in MAFF's flesh just came naturally to us.

On autopilot now, and certainly not thinking sensibly, we crossed the road and entered the foyer full of apparent confidence, explaining to the person on reception that we'd come to see Mr Gummer. The words had hardly been spoken, when hot on our heels the man himself came bustling through the door.

Without a moment's hesitation, let alone rational forethought, I went up to him, hand extended. The scene that followed went like this:

"Mr Gummer!" (spoken in warm tones).

He takes my proffered hand, shakes it in friendly fashion.

"Clare Druce, Chickens' Lib." I say, pumping his hand up and down.

He drops my hand in horror.

"We just wondered if we could have a word?"

"Speak to my Secretary!" (gesturing wildly to the male Parliamentary Secretary, hovering anxiously behind him).

Exit Mr Gummer, at high speed.

On leaving the foyer we noticed a board listing the day's diary. It explained everything: Mr Gummer's next appointment, a few minutes hence, was with representatives from the Country Landowners' Association, and therein lay the misunderstanding.

*

Mid May, 1992: We'd booked space at the Food and Farming Exhibition in Hyde Park, an important event, with many thousands of visitors expected. Irene and I travelled down together to London, and made straight for a cheap hotel near to the venue. On being shown into one of our rooms we were dismayed to see a pile of crumpled clothes on the bed. Happily, it turned out that the hotelier had picked up the wrong key. Well, you get what you pay for, and at least the bed wasn't occupied.

Hot weather promised a perfect weekend for an open-air event. We set up our stand and it looked impressive. Our posters were second to none and we had an impressive array of leaflets, booklets, postcards, badges and petitions to sign. We even had a fact sheet –produced jointly with Compassion in World Farming– on the newest welfare threat, ostrich farming.

We were pleased to find our stand right next to CIWF's, and even more so later, when we realized the Minister of Agriculture, John Selwyn Gummer himself, was a few feet away, taking a polite interest in their material. Could this be a chance to mend fences? Surely he would realize our good intentions, if only he'd stop to look at our carefully researched literature!

Of course, we *had* offended Mr Gummer. Our challenge to him to spend twenty-four hours in an intensive unit was perhaps still fresh in his mind, but even so...

I approached Mr Gummer, suggesting he might like to look at our display. He refused, point blank. We thought this absurd (maverick groups notwithstanding): here we were with our splendid goods, a mere half dozen paces away. I pleaded. He gesticulated. I pleaded again, to no avail. As we argued, Philip Lymbery abandoned his duties on the CIWF stall, having decided to record the occasion on camera.

Ah yes, scrutinising one of the resulting photos with the help of a magnifying glass, I see I was wearing a Chickens' Lib badge beside my exhibitor's label. It depicts a battery hen, and the wording is BATTERY CAGES MUST GO. Maybe it stirred up bad memories, the spectre of those twenty-four hours he never did spend alone in a battery shed.

But at least he's smiling in the photos, most of the time. Passers-by may well have mistaken us for old friends.

*

December 3rd, 1992 *The Guardian's 'Pass Notes No. 39'* feature John Selwyn Gummer. By now he's resigned from the General Synod over women's ordination, saying (reportedly): *'The Synod has finally turned the Church of England into a sect.'*

I learn from *Pass Notes* that he was a student at Cambridge (Selwyn College, appropriately enough) at the time I was teaching the clarinet in the city – quite possibly we'd passed each other in the street.

*

Update: By the dawn of the new millennium John Gummer was sounding genuinely concerned about global warming, indeed all things environmental. Could he also have found it in his heart to forgive Chickens' Lib?

The paper represents the cage floor space for four hens.

This sheet of paper represents the living space allotted to four battery hens. A battery cage offers no comfort, no variety and effectively denies the fulfillment of most of the hen's basic instincts. 95% of British eggs are laid in batteries.

IS THIS CIVILIZATION 1978?

It is argued that batteries for hens are an economic necessity. The same was said of the slave trade.

Please give your support to Chicken's Lib's call for the restoration of chickens' rights.

Violet Spalding, Clare Druce, Vivienne Jenkins and Spike Milligan delivering petition
at 10 Downing Street.
© CIWF

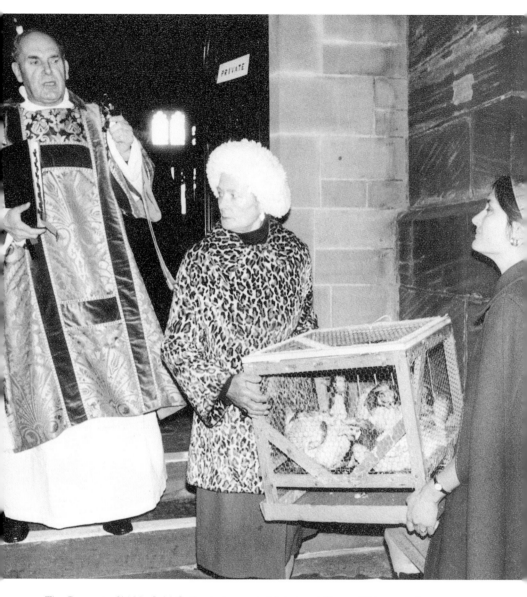

The Provost of Wakefield Cathedral escorts Violet and Clare off the premises.
© Yorkshire Post

A male breeder turkey from a Chickens' Lib leaflet.
© The Academic Press (Inc) London Ltd.

TURKEYS

THE HIDDEN SUFFERING

Battery hens, photographed from under the cages.
© Bob Allen

Irene – a busy day in the Chickens' Lib office.

Live plucked ostriches in South Africa.
© First published in Animal Voice (South Africa)
in August 1997

Postcard showing bits and specs.
© League Against Cruel Sports

VICTIMS OF 'SPORT'

Factory farmed ducks.
© Viva!

CHICKENS' LIB

Three of the 'Halifax Four'.

'Grey Girl' and recovered battery hens in Clare's garden.

Overleaf: Hens in snow.

ANTIBIOTICS – PROPPING UP A SICK INDUSTRY

To ensure the profitability of factory farming, antibiotics are administered to intensively farmed animals on a massive scale. These animals certainly produce cheap food, but many would now argue that factory-farmed produce is very expensive indeed, especially when it costs human lives.

For several years, our concern about the over-use of antibiotics down on the factory farm had been intensifying. We'd not been reassured by a letter from Leeds' Regional Poultry Husbandry Advisory Officer, dated March 12th 1980, in which he'd stated: *'Only in the case of broilers are certain growth promoters allowed to be used and an antibiotic does not fall into this group of products allowed to be used.'* This was wrong on two counts – the growth promoters used *were* antibiotics, and laying hens had these same antibiotics routinely in their feed, as they appeared to 'enhance performance', to use an industry term. It seemed that some MAFF officials were operating in the dark as far as antibiotics were concerned, as no doubt farmers were too.

In May 1991, not before time, Chickens' Lib issued a fact sheet (no. 29) which included a section on the dangers of antibiotic overuse in the veterinary field.

*

The discovery of antibiotics marked one of the greatest leaps forward in the history of medicine. No longer does a fever or an infected wound carry with it the danger of untimely death. Now we turn to antibiotics and feel safe. Or we did.

The tragedy is that many previously effective antibiotics have lost their life-saving qualities. Dangerous 'bugs' have worked out how to get the better of the drugs designed to kill them. No longer are antibiotics the silver bullet they once promised to be. By the 1980s antibiotic resistance had spread worldwide.

Now, several antibiotics must sometimes be tried before doctors find one that's effective; meanwhile, patients' lives may be endangered. For example, in the UK and in Australia the 'hospital infection' MRSA has developed resistance to trimethoprim. Trimethoprim, which is widely used to dose pigs, poultry and the human population, has joined the ranks of antimicrobials now useless in the face of a potentially fatal infection (1).

The root cause of the massive on-farm use of antibiotics is obvious: it's the way the animals are exploited. Poultry and pigs crammed into filthy windowless sheds in their hundreds or thousands, spending their lives on their own faeces, shut away from sunlight and fresh air, continuously under stress; dairy cows worked beyond their endurance – why ever should they be healthy?

*

As we all know, it's only fools who rush in where angels fear to tread, and what's more, a little knowledge is a dangerous thing. So I'll repeat that what follows is no more than a brief nod to a highly complicated subject.

We had no scientists on our staff (come to that no staff in the accepted sense) but we wanted to draw attention to our belief that, without the customary input of on-farm antibiotics, intensive systems would have failed from the very start. Factory farming has gone hand in hand with the discovery of antibiotics and, ever keen to cast its net wider, the intensive industry has failed to face up to the risks and dangers inherent in the misuse of our life-saving drugs.

So we studied the literature as best we could, produced a booklet and a video and, from then on, included relevant items in our fact sheets, to help keep our supporters informed. And we lobbied.

*

What follows is a rapid trawl through the years, starting with the Swann Committee. This was set up in the late 1960s to advise the UK government on the possible threat to human health arising from the use of antibiotics down on the farm.

Basically, there are three uses of veterinary antibiotics (antimicrobial and antibiotic mean the same thing): 1) those used as growth-promoters (banned now throughout the EU). 2) those used prophylactically, that is to ward off probable outbreaks of disease, and 3) those used therapeutically, when disease has already struck.

November 1969: The Swann Report was published, and it made clear the dangers: *'In systemic infections antibiotic therapy may be life-saving and the treatment may be made more difficult or the patient's life is threatened or even imperilled because of antibiotic resistance. We accept that this has already happened and we have no doubt that it could do so again...'* (2).

It seems that pressures from drug companies, the veterinary profession and government were too great: Swann was ignored.

In 1985 *Veterinary Record* stated that veterinary surgeons were *'under considerable pressure to prescribe antibiotics'*. The article also mentioned illicit supplies of drugs, and the fact that antibiotics were being used increasingly to counter *'unsatisfactory husbandry practices'* (3).

When, in January 2006, the remaining four antibiotic growth promoters still in legal use were banned throughout the EU, some of these same drugs continued to be used therapeutically on farmed animals. One such example is Salinomycin Sodium, which is recommended for broilers suffering from coccidiosis, an intestinal disease common among young chickens and characterised by diarrhoea.

*

We numbered two or three vets amongst our supporters, and one day an enlightening document arrived anonymously through the post. The Medicines Committee of the British Veterinary Association (BVA) had produced a Briefing Document dated May 1989, instructing how veterinarians should, at local level, counter *'uninformed, emotive and often incorrect statements about the use of antibiotics in animals.'* The author of the introduction to the document was the president of the BVA.

Its format was a series of suggested answers to frequently asked questions, all seemingly aimed at justifying the continued use of antibiotics, both to treat existing disease and as growth promoters. We learn that the US government *'...has in recent years rejected an "Imminent Hazard" Petition. It was argued* [in the Petition] *that the sub-therapeutic use of penicillin and tetracyclines as growth promoters was leading to a significant risk of transfer of multiple resistance from animal to human bacteria. It was claimed that typhoid fever in man might become difficult/impossible to treat. Rejection of the Petition was based on extensive studies which produced a totally opposite finding to the Swann Report. For the first time, a legislative body accepted that low sub-therapeutic concentrations of antibiotics in feed do*

not present hazard to man because they do not exert selection pressure.
Note that there are no references for these 'extensive studies'.

Then we read (though we in Chickens' Lib weren't meant to): '*At the Association of Veterinarians in Industry Symposium "Ten Years on from Swann" in 1981, medically qualified speakers* [wow! not just anybody!] *gave papers which cast doubt on the validity of some aspects of the Swann Report. Statements such as this were made – "...the concept that veterinary use of antibiotics is building up a reservoir of resistant Salmonella capable of producing dangerous sepsis in man is erroneous."* ' Given the title of this symposium – Veterinarians in Industry – its 'findings' were perhaps not surprising, in view of the entrenched nature of a highly lucrative trade in pharmaceuticals.

*

As recently as 1998 a spokeswoman for the National Farmers' Union (NFU) sounded as confident about the safety of antibiotics as the BVA had been: '*Antibiotics in this country have brought enormous benefits for animal health and welfare over many decades and we have not seen any scientific evidence of the transfer of resistance to humans*' (4).

However, in July of that very same year, MAFF published '*A Review of Antimicrobial Resistance in the Food Chain – A Technical Report*' which implied the exact opposite: '*Antimicrobials used for therapy in food animals are also used for human therapy. Only a few food animal therapeutics do not belong to a class used in human medicine.*'

*

Contrast the complacent lines of argument from the BVA and the NFU with comments from Professor Brian Spratt, made when addressing a meeting of international specialists in London the previous year, 1997: '*MRSA is an aggressive infection and can be life-threatening in hospitals. There is a real worry that if vancomycin (resistance) moves into MRSA there will be no way to treat those who are infected. If this happens, the consequence is likely to be that people will die from post-operative infections. If this organism becomes common in hospitals, many surgical advances will be halted. This is a major worry.*' (5)

Speakers at the conference warned that vancomycin-resistant strains of *Staphylococcus aureus* were already emerging in Japan. When Professor Spratt gave his warning, avoparcin (the veterinary equivalent to vancomycin) was freely available as a 'performance enhancer' (aka growth promoter) for broilers, turkeys, pigs, cattle, calves and lambs.

*

In June 1990, a letter to *The Lancet* from physicians working in two UK hospitals warned: *'There has lately been interest in the use of quinolones to treat patients with salmonella infections. One outstanding issue is the emergence of resistance.'* (6)

A month later, the same authors joined forces with MAFF's Central Veterinary Laboratory at Weybridge, once again conveying their doubts via the letters page of *The Lancet*, but now linking human and veterinary medicine: *'Thought needs to be given as to whether quinolones, such as enrofloxacin, should be given to animals.'* (7)

*

In our fact sheet 29 we'd reported on trials being conducted by the international drug company Bayer: *'...an animal test certificate (ATC) has recently been issued permitting enrofloxacin (Baytril 10 per cent oral solution; Bayer) to be used under controlled conditions in turkeys, chickens, pigeons and psittacine birds'* (8). Bayer, with its ATC for enrofloxacin, was permitted to conduct trials of the drug on a commercial basis. Any veterinarian suspecting a 'suitable' disease in his or her client's poultry flock could now put enrofloxacin to the test.

The active ingredient in Bayer's 'Baytril' is fluoroquinolone, identical to Ciprofloxacin and valuable in human medicine. For farmed animals it is typically prescribed to counteract primary and secondary bacterial infections.

Diseases associated with these pathogens include respiratory infections, arthritis and infectious sinovitis, all prone to run like wildfire through intensively stocked poultry sheds.

*

June 1991 had found the Government still complacent about antibiotic resistance. In our May newsletter we'd asked our supporters to write to their MPs expressing concerns about the wide use of antibiotics in the poultry industry. David Maclean, Parliamentary Secretary to MAFF, replied as follows to our supporter's MP so that the MP in turn could, probably unwittingly, pass on a load of misinformation to his constituent: *'Before any veterinary medicine can be placed on the market, it must first be licensed under the terms of the Medicines Act 1968. Licences are issued only after the Veterinary Products Committee (VPC) – an independent committee of eminent scientists – has satisfied itself that stringent standards on safety, quality and efficacy have been met. Scientists at the Veterinary Medicines Directorate (VMD) are responsible to Ministers, acting in their role as the licensing authority, for the initial assessment of application for product licences from pharmaceutical companies...On antibiotics the VPC has made a careful evaluation over the years of the question of their suitability for veterinary treatment and which ones can be used safely without posing any kind of threat to human health, whether by causing resistance to those antibiotics used in human medicine, or otherwise...Any approach from a company for an ATC would be turned down if it were considered that such a trial would pose a threat to human health.'*

Clearly, the Government, along with its associated 'safety' committees and the BVA, was, at least in public, willing to turn a blind eye on the mass of literature already pointing to the spread of dangerous resistance. However, storm clouds of doubt must already have been gathering over the Ministry of Agriculture, Fisheries and Food, for only seven years later MAFF's review highlighting antimicrobial resistance was issued. Within its pages appeared an astonishing list of antibiotics/antimicrobials routinely given to pigs, and written in the sure knowledge that humans were at the receiving end too: *' Antimicrobial treatment is more common in indoor pigs...Treatment must be given to the sow for puerperal disorders such as metritis, mastitis and for specific diseases such as erysipelas or leptospirosis. Piglets will receive treatment for enteritis and for respiratory disease. At weaning (usually 3 weeks) all piglets are gathered, mixed, and then reared to finishing weights. The first stage (weaners) are kept warm and usually develop post weaning diarrhoea. This is caused by E. coli and occurs on day 3 post weaning.'* Here follows a sad list (sad if one considers the degree of piglet suffering involved), detailing several other diseases, all presented as practically inevitable – for example *'At 8 weeks the pigs may be called growers and move to another house. Here they will develop Enzootic Pneumonia, streptococcal meningitis, and, possibly, swine dysentery. Respiratory disease may cause problems almost until slaughter... Antimicrobial [antibiotic] use varies dramatically from herd to herd. In a survey of pig farms in 1995 (Taylor unpublished data), farms were found which used only penicillin and streptomycin and perhaps topical tetracycline for wounds. These were high health herds and were free of most of the diseases requiring treatment. Other herds were infected with some or most of the diseases mentioned above and had been prescribed up to 10 antimicrobials. In a typical herd, there is use of neomycin, apramycin, amoxyclav, ampicillin, enrofloxacin or trimethoprim sulphonamide in the diarrhoeic piglets for E.coli enteritis.'* (9)

What price that bacon sandwich?

*

At around the time of David Maclean's letter about 'stringent standards' regarding antibiotic use (June 1991) Chickens' Lib took part in a television discussion on factory farming. Those of us likely to be invited to contribute in some way were arranged together, on the over-stocked benches you get in TV studios.

I found myself thigh-to-thigh with David Maclean and I swear I could literally *feel* his antagonism.

*

A decade later: In 2001 FAWN was in touch with the USA's Food and Drug Administration. A letter we received from the FDA explained that it: *'...proposed to withdraw approval of the new animal drug application (NADA) for use of the fluoroquinolone antimicrobial enrofloxacin in poultry* [because the drug] *causes the development of fluoroquinolone-resistant campylobacter, a pathogen to humans.'* (10)

By contrast, UK physicians could spell out their serious concerns in the pages of *The Lancet* yet nothing was done to protect human health.

*

The most recent statistics for antibiotic use are from 2007 and go like this:
- 54% sold for use in humans
- 40% sold for food producing animals
- 4% sold for companion animals
- 2% sold for combination of food and non-food producing animals

(11)

*

There's no question now that the UK's department of agriculture recognises the dangers of on-farm antibiotic use – and why shouldn't it? The issue has been understood for decades. In 1998 MAFF stated: *"The use of medicines is fundamental to the development of antimicrobial resistance. This was shown by Smith and Crabb (1956), and all medicines in use, whether in man or in animals can be expected to select for resistance."* (12) And no, 1956 is not a misprint.

*

So why are systems that promote ill-health in farmed animals, thereby necessitating the over-use of drugs, still permitted? The answer must be that governments past and present have weighed up the various pros and cons of the matter and the drugs have won. For it is the pharmaceutical industry that ensures that millions of 'food animals' stay alive until ready for slaughter, so keeping the wheels of British factory farming turning.

Consumers should remember that the drugs administered so freely to farmed animals are frequently related to, or identical with, the ones we give to our children in an emergency, or take ourselves – the names are familiar enough: trimethroprim, penicillin, amoxicillin, tetracycline, ciprofloxacin. Farmers reach for the medication, vets and the drug companies rub their hands – and to hell with the dangers.

*

In March 2012 Margaret Chan, Director General of the World Health Organisation, told an assembly of infectious disease experts in Copenhagen that the now widely predicted post-antibiotic era would mark an end to medicine as we know it. Many routine operations would become just too risky to carry out, she warned, and minor injuries would once again be potentially fatal.

I'll end this section with an extract from Chickens' Lib's May 1991 fact sheet:

'Chickens' Lib does not suggest that all veterinary drugs are dangerous or undesirable but believes that systems of animal husbandry that promote ill-health, because of overcrowding, lack of fresh air, etc, are to be condemned. No man is an island when it comes to drug-resistance. Lax standards in human or veterinary medicine in any part of the world can spread drug-resistant bacteria worldwide, through foreign travel. The use of antibiotics in all forms of medicine should be minimised.'

A police visit

Ever optimistic, at least in some respects, we were still hoping to see inside a typical intensive turkey unit. And now we'd noticed a turkey farm as intensive as they come. Faced with the sight of row upon row of windowless, factory-like buildings, and knowing there was little point in asking MAFF to check on the birds inside, what could we do?

The old saying 'nothing ventured, nothing gained' doesn't always pay off, but it was the best one we could come up with. We'd go along there, get as near to the sheds as we could, and try our luck.

Irene and I went together. We parked my car in the nearby village, and walked to the farm. Even at that stage we sensed the hopelessness of our quest. Yet, having come this far... The first building in the complex looked like a manager's bungalow, so we made for that. A man, probably the manager himself, came to the door, and we explained that we'd be interested to see inside a turkey farm. But no, there was no way we could look around, or indeed view a single turkey. And please would we leave the premises – now!

*

Thinking we'd maybe overhear something of interest, we stopped for a drink in a cold and dispiriting pub (Mrs Thatcher had recently ripped the heart out of the village, previously a coal-mining community). Workers from the turkey place must come in here, we reasoned. But no information reached our ears – today was proving fruitless.

Pale wintry sunshine showed up the tawdry shabbiness of the bar, adding to our depression and sense of helplessness. How could it be, we wondered, that British food production had sunk so low? Thousands of 'farmyard' poultry incarcerated in sheds, out of sight, out of most people's minds, maybe half-killing each other in their frustration, probably in pain, certainly living in misery...We finished our drinks and slowly made our way back to the car.

*

A couple of days later: on a wet and windy night, hours after darkness had fallen, our front doorbell rang. Hardly anyone used the front door; friends knew to come round to the back of the house. As I went to see who was there, I felt glad Duncan was at home.

Two policemen stood in the porch, and they lost no time in getting to the point. Did I drive a red Fiesta? Yes, I said. Was its registration such-and-such? Yes, again. And was I in the area of a certain turkey farm recently? Yes, I was. Then, as on the films, I may even have said "You'd better come in."

We went into the living room, where Duncan joined us. I explained Chickens' Lib's concerns about modern turkey farming and described our *modus operandi*. *Chicken and Egg*, my book on intensive poultry systems, had not long been published and I gave the police officers a copy. One chapter in the book covers our conviction that intensive methods for poultry keeping are not only cruel but illegal too. I pointed them to this chapter.

The upshot was that we all shook hands, they seemed genuinely pleased to take the book away with them, and that was the end of it.

*

But not for the turkeys: for them there would be no end, apart from cruel slaughter. How many millions have gone through the system on that farm alone since Irene and I were seen off some twenty years ago? Unimaginable numbers have been shut away in the seemingly endless range of sheds, denied sunlight and fresh air, forced to live on their own faeces and, I have no doubt at all, among corpses of those birds unable to survive the harshness of it all.

Ducks on dry land

1992. Worried about the factory farming of ducks, Violet, Irene and I visited the headquarters of Cherry Valley, the UK's major duck producer. We planned to study this escalating industry, starting with some very small samples of its raw material.

We'd noticed Cherry Valley's claim that it treated its ducks with care and respect, even with a degree of affection – an odd claim that stands today. Twenty years later, its 2012 website (www.cherryvalley.co.uk) presents a bizarre mix of the romantic and the harshly realistic. A proud mention of Cherry Valley's location in the leafy Lincolnshire Wolds is backed up by shots of cherry blossom, cheek by jowl with a grim row of intensive duck sheds, stretching away into the distance, the presence of all those leaves and flowers quite irrelevant to the thousands of incarcerated ducks. With a bold show of anthropomorphism, Cherry Valley ventures to suppose that their ducks lead happy and comfortable lives.

But to return to the year 1992: Cherry Valley had agreed to sell us half a dozen day-old ducklings. We needed these for educational purposes, we'd explained. On arrival, we waited for a few minutes in the company's impressive reception area, resplendent with maps of the world, testament to the company's global footprint.

An employee soon arrived to take us to the hatchery. There, towering metal cabinets lined a long corridor. We guessed each one contained hundreds, maybe thousands, of hatching eggs. The place felt like a laboratory or an eerily silent factory: certainly there was no hint of new life. Yet after a moment's wait six day-olds, their down already dry and fluffy, were brought to us. We must have looked a respectable trio (teachers, maybe?) for the management would accept no payment and fortunately didn't ask for details of our project.

Ducks were new to us, but we'd planned ahead. Penny, well used to re-homing ex-battery hens, had a large duck pond and already she'd offered swimming space on it, for when the ducklings were old enough.

Even so we came away a little anxious, wondering how well these tiny golden creatures, soft as thistledown, would thrive in our care.

*

I'd constructed a miniature living area for our ducklings, with a heat lamp suspended overhead, and for the first three weeks that was all they needed. Initially, their water container was a lid from an instant coffee jar – small ducklings could drown in anything much deeper, with no mother there to oil their easily-saturated down. But how they loved even this hint of water! Each time I renewed the supply they would 'chatter' with excitement. Or was it desperation? Certainly ancestral memory was telling them that water was vital to them: water was where they belonged.

We marvelled at their bills – disproportionately large, and shiny like pink plastic. The ducklings were altogether delightful, and many visitors were taken down to the basement to admire them.

*

Our six Cherry Valley ducklings grew apace, and soon we needed to enlarge their living quarters. When they reached a month old we passed three of them on to a good home, to avoid over-crowding. We told our supporters: *'Apparently, they have settled well, and will shortly be going outside to join various other ducks, with acres of land and two ponds. The three left behind demonstrated their sensitivity to change by becoming very suspicious and alarmed for two or three days. Soon they too will go to an excellent home and we hope to record them on video, experiencing a real duck pond for the very first time.'*

When Penny moved house a few years later she left the three Cherry Valley ducks with the new owner. Given that ducks can live for up to twenty years, I hope our six study samples enjoyed long lives on their various ponds, swimming around contentedly, having been spared slaughter at the customary age of eight or nine weeks.

*

MAFF's 1987 welfare code for ducks (still not updated) made for the usual grim reading. In view of MAFF's track record in double-talk, readers may not be surprised to learn that paragraph 1 in the introduction to this code contains the following inherent contradiction: *'The system employed should be appropriate to the health and behavioural and physiological needs of the ducks.'* (1) In the light of the recommendations to follow, one can only wonder at the mind-sets of those dreaming up such evident nonsense.

The advised stocking density for those kept on slatted, perforated or metal mesh floors remains at eight ducklings per square metre from week 3 to 8, or, when on solid (littered) floors (the most common system in the UK) it is seven ducklings per square metre. (2)

ADAS, in its *Reference Book 70*, was decisive if misguided, stating: '*... wire floor rearing and fattening has much to commend it.*' And: '*...water for swimming is not a necessity.*' In other words, ducks will grow fat and most will survive for a few weeks and prove profitable, even under conditions of severe deprivation.

*

From Cherry Valley's literature of the time, we discovered that in the early 1990s the company raised 6.5 million ducklings annually in the UK, while exporting a further 2 million day-olds to eighty countries, a proportion of which were Muscovy (aka Barbary) ducks.

The factory farming of Muscovies leads to severe welfare problems: Muscovies are nothing like the gentle Mallards, with their blunt bills and harmless feet. The Muscovy has a sharp beak and claws and, when under stress, uses both, to the severe detriment of fellow ducks. Consequently, partial beak amputation, dim lighting, and wire flooring were the order of the day. Often imported from France, Muscovy ducks were on sale in many UK stores, including Marks and Spencer, Sainsbury's and Harrods. Eventually, following sustained and effective campaigning by Viva!, these cruelly treated ducks were removed from most UK outlets (3).

In its early 1990s *Growing Manual*, Cherry Valley recommended a similar lighting regime to that of broilers – 23 hours of dim lighting, with an hour of total darkness to guard against panic in the event of a power cut. As with broilers, this ensured maximum eating time, leading to maximum growth. Troughs holding water were to be of a suggested depth of three inches (7.5cms).

As any child knows, ducks are designed to live in water. Equipped with waterproofed feathers, webbed feet for efficient swimming and diving, broad bills for straining out food from river or pond water, water is their medium. Under normal conditions, ducklings spend a lot of time on water from day one, their fluffy down water-proofed by contact with the mother's oiled feathers.

*

The internet is good for many things, but I miss the days when a telephone call to MAFF or ADAS would as likely as not tell you things you'd never find out from carefully edited websites, still less from a 'standard' letter. Now, you'll be lucky to speak to a real person, and ADAS will charge you for the simplest piece of information.

I remember having a valuable chat with an ADAS Poultry Adviser in the early days of our work on ducks. He referred to modern ducks as 'little monsters' and told me it was not unusual to find intensively-reared ducks stranded on their backs – knocked over by fellow birds in the congestion, and unable to right themselves.

Since then, we've several times seen footage of ducks stranded on their backs, as well as badly crippled ones using wings like crutches, as they struggle to move around the sheds: living proof of lack of proper inspection and of a complete disregard for their pain and suffering.

*

The slaughter of ducks also gave cause for concern. In our 1993 booklet *Hidden Suffering* we reported on 1990 research, conducted at Bristol. This found that not all birds were killed even when the electrical slaughter equipment was set as high as 250mA; ducks are apparently much less susceptible to cardiac arrest than other poultry (4). Worryingly, MAFF was advising 130mA for duck slaughter, raising our fear that millions of ducks may be inadequately stunned, returning to consciousness on entering the scalding tank. To make matters worse, ducks have a tendency to arch their necks at slaughter, preventing adequate immersion in the electrically-charged water bath (5).

Over a decade ago, killing ducks by gassing was found to be more humane, though even with this system ducks were found to require a longer exposure to the gas mixture than chickens or turkeys (6).

*

Water, as well as being necessary for ducks to swim in, keeps eyes healthy. If ducks can't submerge their eyes every day, they're likely to develop problems. From the producers' point of view ducks are messy, tending to splash water around, and they produce wet droppings too, leading to wet litter. Straw litter in duck units is supposedly topped up on a daily basis. To keep the straw as dry as possible, water, other than for drinking, is in most units kept to the minimum, increasing the general deprivation experienced by today's ducks.

*

1999: We decided to re-invigorate our duck campaign, and set about further fact-finding in the usual way – by writing to MAFF with a list of questions. Only this time we hit a snag. MAFF's reply was evasive, providing, we thought, a prime example of the cosy relationship between the Ministry and industrial farming: *'The duck industry is dominated by a single company and to supply some of the information which you request would result in a breach of confidentiality* (7), was the way MAFF put it. Since our concern was duck welfare and food production, we considered this lack of openness disgraceful. There was nothing for it – from now on we'd be on our own, gathering information from wherever we could.

However, during 1999 we discovered that the animal rights organisation Viva! was also planning to campaign against the factory farming of ducks.

It was decided we should join forces, and Viva!'s director asked me to write a report, the deal being that Chickens' Lib would receive a supply of free leaflets bearing both our organisations' contact details. I sent the report to Viva! and after additions and further editing at their end it was launched. *Ducks out of Water* was probably the first-ever comprehensive literature available on duck welfare. Since its publication Viva! has continued to lobby strongly against the factory farming of ducks, updating the report comprehensively in 2002 and again in 2006 (8).

*

May 2009: *Poultry World* reported the findings of a DEFRA-funded research programme prompted by increasing public concern for the welfare of intensively kept ducks (9). Over a period of three years, a series of ducklings of Cherry Valley stock were given various sources of water, ranging from so-called nipple drinkers (overhead devices involving ball bearings, designed to release droplets of water when nudged by beak or bill), through troughs and showers, to baths (to mimic proper ponds).

The conclusion was that the provision of troughs or showers would represent the best means by which commercial farmers could improve duck welfare. The problem of contamination of standing water was ironed out by the showers, which proved more hygienic, as well as economical of water.

Professor Marian Stamp Dawkins, one of the three researchers, told *PW*: '*Ducks made it very clear – they love to shower. They used the showers far more than any other source of water we provided. Now further research will have to be undertaken to study their behaviour more closely in terms of how often showering facilities are required. We have now acquired a commercial partner to look more fully at the impact of bathing resources on the birds' health and welfare.*'

Ominously, the *PW* article reported: '*...over half the birds moved into the treatment pens at 21 days after not having access to showers or head immersion facilities showed crusted eyes. All these affected birds had overcome their eye problems within 16 days of having access to showers or troughs.*'

Up to sixteen further days of eye problems, even with access to showers or troughs! With crusted eyes and nostrils, doubtless accompanied by unpleasant soreness, it's no surprise that the ducklings were found to prefer showers and troughs to the miserable nipple drinker. The same report noticed that when the ducks were faced with water for swimming they displayed initial reluctance to take to the water baths. But should that have surprised the researchers? The ducks in their experiments had never seen a mother figure, so why should they feel confident when faced with a relatively large expanse of water? When we took our full-size ducks to Penny's pond to launch them, so to speak, they were clearly suspicious and needed a few minutes' coaxing before deciding to take the plunge. Clearly showers are better than shallow troughs but they're not the same as open water, and they render redundant ducks' cleverly designed webbed feet, and purpose-built bills.

The British Poultry Council (BPC) had awarded the project a £1,000 scholarship to top up DEFRA funding which, according to an article by Steven Morris in *The Guardian* (May 20th 2009) amounted to around £300,000. This sum raised hackles in some quarters: Susie Squire of the Taxpayers' Alliance called the research a 'bonkers waste of money', while Devon chairman of the National Farmers' Union said the study proved that the government department overseeing farm animal welfare was 'quackers'.

However, in *Poultry World's* May 2009 article the BPC's Chief Executive, Peter Bradnock, expressed himself happy with the research, saying that it would lead to better welfare for commercially reared ducks, so *'removing the emotive issues associated with farmed ducks and water'.*

But Mr Bradnock, the picture is more complex! Water in shallow troughs or from nipple drinkers *has* to be the only water source for very young ducklings, to prevent sodden down and deaths by drowning. For their first three weeks of life, when orphan ducklings must not be drenched, their eyes and nostrils will be at risk of becoming increasingly encrusted, uncomfortable and even painful. So do troughs or showers, supplied by necessity at a later stage, even begin to 'remove the emotive issues'?

Not really, not if you do the maths. 21 days + 16 (remember, it took sixteen days for all the ducklings to overcome their eye 'problems') = 37, and 37 days is not so far off a commercially reared duck's entire lifespan (rather than the twenty years on offer to a normal, healthy duck).

Incidentally, I looked up 'emotive' in my dictionary, just to check. 'Arousing emotion' was the definition. Perhaps more emotion is called for, not less.

I was disturbed by Professor Dawkins' mention of further research to establish how infrequently shower facilities might be made available. In my mind it raised the spectre of rush hour situations at shower time, with thousands of ducks wanting the same thing, all at the same time.

*

In September 2009 *Poultry World* reported: '*Animal welfare bodies have in recent years piled the pressure on retailers and the UK duck industry to give indoor-reared birds access to open water.*' PW added that over the past five years Cherry Valley had been working on a design for an open sided veranda system, to include deep troughs in which birds can 'preen, paddle and wade', as well as enjoy daylight and fresh air. Professor Dawkins' research was conducted during a similar period.

In the same issue of *Poultry World*, ducks with access to water in a Cherry Valley veranda system are shown. No doubt they're much happier for not being totally enclosed in windowless sheds with shallow troughs or nipple drinkers for water, but it has to be said these ducks looked far from clean. In fact their feathers were badly soiled.

According to information in the article (nine rearing sheds housing 75,000 ducks) the farmer in question keeps his ducks in flocks of about eight thousand per shed. So it's factory farming all right, but with some improvements.

*

'*Cherry Valley is now in the process of getting Freedom Food accreditation for its system...Freedom Foods* [sic] *have been active advisers from the start of the development of the system*' (10). So says Cherry Valley's agricultural operations manager, Brian Kenyon.

While it cannot be denied that the Freedom Food scheme aims to alleviate some of the suffering of intensively reared farmed animals, the scheme will surely serve to validate those systems. The danger, as we in Chickens' Lib and many others see it, is that consumers may pick up a duck bearing a label displaying the hugely reassuring letters RSPCA coupled with the Freedom Food logo, believing that the bird they plan to eat has been truly free. Unless the label makes it clear that the large 'duck' they're wheeling over to the checkout is in fact a duckling, slaughtered at eight or nine weeks, who probably lived in a shed (with a veranda tacked on), forever jostling for space with anything up to ten thousand others, how will consumers know? Labels and logos are powerful things, yet they rarely tell anything like the whole story.

June 17th 2010: I phoned Cherry Valley, and left a message saying it related to the company's present slaughter methods. I wanted to know if Cherry Valley had advanced to using gas (so obviating the need to hang live birds in shackles) – or was the electrified water bath method still in operation?

Later that day a spokesman for Cherry Valley phoned me back, and it was bad news. The company doesn't use gas. I asked about the mA level employed in the electrified water bath, and the figure of 130mA was given. I expressed concern, and quoted the research at Bristol, going back some twenty years, that had assessed the need for 250 mA for ducks, while warning that even at that high level some might fail to receive a stun sufficient to ensure unconsciousness at the neck cutting stage. The same representative from Cherry Valley phoned back half an hour later to apologise. He had misinformed me – he'd now spoken to colleagues and the figures he'd given me were incorrect: a device at Cherry Valley to record the mAs passing through ducks on the slaughter line was checked regularly, and levels ranging from 199mA to 258mA were shown to have been those most recently in use.

I mentioned the matter of ducks raising their heads, so missing the water bath altogether, and my informant was at pains to emphasise how Cherry Valley takes great trouble to get the birds 'properly settled' while shackled, by means of dim lighting etc. He assured me there was always a veterinary officer present from the Meat Hygiene Service/ Food Standards Agency and that all officials on duty were 'very, very keen' to ensure that slaughter was carried out humanely.

Despite research indicating the extreme pain suffered by shackled poultry (11), the vast majority of ducks are still hung in shackles at slaughter. It's impossible to say how many ducks feel 'properly settled' when in such a painful and terrifying situation, but my guess is that those who do are few and far between.

The world's largest flightless bird

1990 saw an Oxfordshire couple about to turn their dream into reality. Linda and Francis Ayres, of Hangland Farm, near Banbury, had connections in Namibia. They'd seen ostrich farming there, and wanted to introduce it to the UK.

First, they purchased five young ostriches from a British wildlife park, then two more from a zoological collection. In 1991, sixty hatching eggs were imported from Namibia, probably making the first serious attempt to farm ostriches in Europe (1). Soon the Ayres were giving promotional seminars on ostrich farming, and would-be ostrich farmers flocked to hear them.

Ostriches have been farmed in Africa for well over a hundred years and more recently in other countries too – notably the USA, Canada, Israel and Australia – but the Ayres' ambition marked the first exploitation in Britain of a species that truly belongs in the wide-open spaces of the African plains.

The Ayres' promotional leaflet promised that by 1992 they'd be ready to supply 3-to-6-month-old chicks 'anywhere in the world.' Already they were importing chicks and operating the only quarantine station in the UK. They estimated the 1991 worth of an ostrich slaughtered at 14 months to be between £500 and £550, while a breeding hen, assuming 25 offspring reared annually, would bring in £10,000 per annum.

The Ayres were talking big money.

*

November 1991: Chickens' Lib and Compassion in World Farming joined forces, producing a fact sheet expressing their concerns for ostrich welfare. Our two organisations also issued a Press Release to coincide with the Ayres' first seminar at Hangland Farm. We stated our fear that ostriches could soon be subjected to the horrors of intensive farming, long-distance transport and cruel slaughter.

Francis Ayres remained sanguine however, telling *The Times*' agricultural correspondent that since ostriches have been domesticated for more than 100 years in Africa there should be no greater welfare problems involved than those encountered when rearing cattle, pigs and sheep, while MAFF informed *The Times*' journalist that it had not yet licensed ostrich meat but had it in mind to classify it as 'farmed game.'

By 1991 ostrich farming in Britain was in effect at the experimental stage, untried and untested, yet about to take off in a flurry of ill-founded optimism.

*

Ostriches don't only supply meat, leather and feathers. Every part of the bird can be turned into something: brooches and earrings from claws, ashtray stands from legs and feet... even those long necks have been hardened and turned into spaghetti jars.

Promises of fabulous profits were bandied about in this new industry, as virgin ostrich farmers jumped eagerly onto the bandwagon. When a booklet on ostrich farming was published by the Ostrich Farming Corporation Limited (OFC) based near Newark, £ signs floated in a clear blue sky above the ostriches pictured on the cover. And that said it all: ostriches promised rich pickings.

The OFC was soon in trouble, though. On April 14th 1996 *The Observer* reported its demise: '*As the Serious Fraud Office was called in to investigate the Ostrich Farming Corporation last week, it became clear the debacle has not deterred other companies offering investment in ostriches – or many potential investors. Last week, half a dozen firms continued to advertise ostrich schemes, some with similar claims to those made by OFC, which is being wound up by the Department of Trade and Industry.*'

Poultry World of January 1991 remained enthusiastic, informing its readers that ostriches can '*...reach a marketable live weight of 300 lbs of which 80lbs is prime breast meat...In the USA which is the source of most of the Ayres's commercial knowledge, breeding birds operate in threes, with one male serving two females – one mature bird and one youngster. But this cosy ménage à trois could be threatened by work on artificial insemination now getting underway in the USA.*'

In the same article, *PW* emphasised the dangers of dealing with these huge birds: '*It means that egg collection is very hazardous and we have heard of an American farmer who protects himself with a portable shed on his daily rounds.*'

Ostriches must be licensed under the Dangerous Wild Animals Act 1976; Dr Brian Bertram, Director of Slimbridge Wildfowl Trust warned that a kick from an ostrich could cause horrible, even fatal, injuries.

*

The ostrich, the world's largest flightless bird, has a lifespan and a reproductive time-scale not unlike that of humans; the females remain fertile till around forty, the males for much longer, and both sexes can live to be around eighty years old. The males perform elaborate mating dances, to attract the chosen female. Although not monogamous, the male will choose a 'major' hen as his wife. Ostriches are dedicated parents, sharing the task of incubating the eggs. The plumage of the male is black and he takes the night shift, the mid-brown feathers of the female providing better camouflage during the day.

Ostriches can grow to be eight feet tall, and run for long periods at speeds of 40 mph. They form extended family groups to care for their young, who remain dependent for around a year. Ostriches graze, mainly on seeds, buds, flowers and grasses. They have excellent vision, vital for detecting predators at a distance. Long eyelashes protect their large eyes from damage from dust and sandstorms.

*

And on UK farms? Ostriches are confined in barren paddocks. Hangland Farm's 1991 leaflet advised a half-acre paddock for a breeding pair, but explained that what they called 'the commercial offspring' (i.e. those reared to be killed for meat) could be more closely stocked. The British Domesticated Ostrich Association's suggested stocking density was slightly less generous than the Ayres', suggesting that one third to a half-acre per breeding pair would suffice.

*

The Farm Animal Welfare Council (FAWC) in its August 1993 'Guidelines on the Welfare of Farmed Ostriches' stated: 'Without an adult ostrich being present, young chicks will congregate and remain inactive so they need to move around, otherwise they can develop leg problems.' FAWC added that staff looking after the chicks should visit them 'several times a day' and encourage them to 'exercise and play'. This demanding regime rang hollow to us, and probably to ostrich farmers too.

High mortality among ostrich chicks was soon a worry at the Ayres' farm, despite it being the showpiece of the emerging UK industry. In 1993 a 33% mortality rate was recorded on a batch of 60 chicks under three months old, despite them being supervised for most of the day and even given baby-safe toys to play with (2).

Contrast this with a description taken from a South African publication describing ostriches farmed in a natural environment: *'On good veldt, which is not subject to overstocking and where the birds are left to fend for themselves, they are always healthy and vigorous, their eggs are practically all fertile and their chicks a picture of vitality.'*(3)

Orphaned ostrich chicks, as on the sort of farms being proposed for the UK, are vulnerable: *'Farmed chicks, for example, required exercising 10 times a day, and also needed a "mother figure". Those deprived of a surrogate mother might eat anything, leading to cases of stone or grass impaction.'*(4) With no parents to guide them, and barren paddocks or concrete-floored sheds for a home, it's no wonder that ostrich chicks are prone to stress-related behaviour.

In March 1996 an international conference was held in Manchester, England, entitled *Improving our Understanding of Ratites in a Farming Environment.* A grim picture emerged of the health problems suffered by ostriches (5).

Rebecca Pridaux, a vet attached to a practice specialising in ostriches, informed conference delegates that impaction, when food particles or 'foreign bodies' can't get past the gizzard and into the duodenum, was proving common in farmed ostriches, and especially in chicks. She went on to warn against leaving dangerous objects lying around in ostriches' living quarters (syringes was one example!) and ended on a depressing note, stating that some ostriches will impact on any type of bedding. One way around the problem, she advised, would be to keep the birds on concrete, or some other artificial flooring, and inside all winter long, especially in northern Europe (6).

According to one American 'expert', the recommended non-surgical method for removing life-threatening objects involved flushing out the impacted object/s with the help of a stomach tube, water and a garden hose, the bird meanwhile held upside down by the legs (7). Clearly, turkey pellets laced with antibiotics (the approved feed in the 1990s), along with an inadvertent sprinkling of non-food objects, was hardly providing the chicks with a substitute for the mixed vegetation suited to their digestive systems, and the presence of parents to teach them what to eat.

Delegates from the UK told of distorted legs, dislocations, gastro-intestinal tract disorders leading to 30% mortality, and more (8).

In the USA, adenovirus had struck ten farms in Oklahoma, killing 90-100% of ostriches under two months old. Impactions, secondary bacterial infections and pneumonia were among other conditions mentioned (9).

Australia's spokesman told of 'ostrich fading syndrome' (OFS) among imported ostriches on farms in four states. Symptoms included anorexia, malaise and an abnormal neck carriage (S shaped necks). Out of 2191chicks hatched on the Cocos Island Quarantine Station from eggs imported from Zimbabwe, 1096 died on the island, but no consistent cause of death was found. In late January 1995, surviving chicks were transported by air and road to mainland distribution farms, but many arrived weak, stunted and emaciated, some showing feather loss. On six Victorian farms mortality had averaged 75% (10).

At around this time, the German Federal Association of Veterinary Surgeons was calling for a ban on ostrich farming in their country. A survey had indicated that only 29% of German ostrich farms were operating to acceptable welfare standards.

Faults found included *'bad housing conditions, injuries amongst the birds, the wrong feeding programmes and careless management procedure'* (11). However, the above Association's views didn't prevail. A paper published in 2007 made it clear that ostrich farming still goes on in Germany, though it *'continues to be a controversial subject with regard to the aspect of animal protection'* (12).

We urged MAFF to follow Germany's call for a ban, but in a letter dated Feb 22nd 1996 MAFF admitted to having no records of the whereabouts of UK ostrich farms – such information, we were told, would be kept by County/District Councils. So no hope of a survey even, let alone condemnation of this new form of factory farming.

Our concern deepened when a leading ostrich vet told Chickens' Lib that some ostrich farmers were keeping their birds indoors for most or all of the year, despite FAWC's recommendation that ostriches older than three months should not be confined indoors for more than brief periods.

*

June 1995: Forty-two ostriches out of a group of 104 died. The plan had been to export these birds, each worth £5000, from the UK to North America. *Veterinary Record* reported that the birds had been kept permanently indoors, on a concentrate diet found to include *'a very heavy dose of the growth promoter monensin',* a drug highly toxic to ostriches (13).

This incident illustrates the lack of knowledge and care apparent in many entrepreneurs and further justified our fears that ostrich farming would intensify into true factory farming.

*

July 1995: Twenty ostriches (out of a consignment of 107) died *en route* from Devon to Manchester Airport, destination New Zealand. Craig Culley, spokesman for the British Domesticated Ostrich Association, expressed himself 'astonished' by the deaths.

A major article appeared in *Veterinary Record* in which the stresses imposed on adult ostriches during handling, loading, transportation and unloading were assessed. Care had been taken to accustom birds to handling, in order to minimise stresses on the day of the journey. (Birds *not* the subject of a survey, and therefore unaccustomed to pre-transport handling, may well have fared much worse.) Despite the pre-handling, approximately 60% of the ostriches slipped and 40% fell while being handled and loaded. The researchers concluded: '*The handling and loading of ostriches therefore constitute a serious problem involving hazard to the birds and to their handlers...The mortality and traumatic injuries sustained by the ostriches during all the procedures agreed with earlier reports, and confirmed that ostriches are very vulnerable to injuries, particularly in the neck and lower limbs (Foggin 1992, Wotton and Hewitt 1999, Minka 2003)... The fact that more injuries were sustained during handling than during the other procedures demonstrated that handling is the most stressful and risky procedure to the ostriches.*' (14)

During the thirteen years between the near-20% loss of ostrich life on the 1995 Devon to Manchester Airport journey and this 2008 survey, thousands of birds must have suffered at the hands of ostrich farmers, many of them complete amateurs. Picture the terrified birds, taller than the humans attempting to load them onto transport lorries, kicking out, slipping and falling in terror, their long legs and necks vulnerable to damage, pitting their considerable strength against that of the men struggling to control them.

*

We didn't have much scope for investigating the ostrich industry. Certainly there was no question of keeping a few, for study purposes. But we managed some good publicity, based on images obtained first-hand. Irene and I attended the Royal Show at Stoneleigh in Warwickshire and were able to take photos of delightful ostrich chicks, later to feature in our booklet *Today's Poultry Industry*. We also visited the Great Yorkshire Show in Harrogate, an annual event popular with farmers and public alike. There we took photos of a penned-up female adult ostrich, peering down at the crowds from her great height. That photo turned out well too, and we put it on a postcard bearing the caption *The Latest Victim*.

*

1994: Louise van der Merwe, our good friend in South Africa, publicised the scandal of live plucking of ostriches in her country. To the UK's credit, when MAFF's Dr David Mauat visited South Africa to negotiate the import of ostrich meat into the UK, he witnessed live plucking, deemed the process totally unacceptable and consequently put import plans on hold.

Dr Walter Lowe, Director of Public Veterinary Health in Pretoria, told *Animal Voice* (the mouthpiece of Louise's organisation): *'It was terrible. The ostriches went to the slaughter completely naked. We put an immediate stop to it and we try to monitor the situation now'*. He added that he hoped that before long live plucking in South Africa would stop. Dr Mauat hadn't been keen on importing meat on other scores too, including a recent outbreak of Newcastle Disease in SA, and possible residues of the drug Zerenol, a growth-promoter, in the meat (15).

*

Three years later, Louise sent us a photograph taken earlier that year in the Northern Cape. It showed two fully-grown ostriches completely denuded of feathers, oven-ready you might say, standing in their compound under a vividly blue sky. The scandal of live plucking was by no means over. Two years after the outright condemnation of the practice, scientific research, carried out at the University of the Orange Free State and sponsored by the SA Ostrich Producers Organisation and the Ostrich Breeders Association of SA, concluded that this ripping out of feathers did not stress the birds.

Mercifully, it does seem that compassion has prevailed, and live plucking is now no longer carried out in South Africa, so presumably the dubious findings of the above research were found wanting.

*

Ostrich News, Winter 1994 (16) included an article by Clive Madeiros, a specialist ostrich vet. In it he gave the following advice about the pre-slaughter treatment of ostriches: ostriches should be penned in a lairage on the evening before slaughter, and left there overnight, in complete darkness. Ideally, the birds should be hooded, the hood left on overnight in readiness to quieten the birds on their way to slaughter. It must be said that Mr Madeiros sounded doubtful about overnight hooding; he suggested that consideration should be given to the process. Clearly, hooding is convenient, but did he perhaps share Chickens' Lib's concerns about those luxuriant eyelashes? How painful would it be to have them pressed against the eyes by the hood, for many hours? And why hood ostriches overnight, when darkness itself would quieten the birds?

One can only assume the handlers want a difficult job over and done with, before the next day's trauma of on-farm killing, or the battle of loading the bird onto a vehicle bound for the slaughterhouse.

*

A telling report appeared in *Poultry World* on a seminar hosted by Roland Bardsley, a hotel owner and by then ostrich farmer too. Accompanying the article are three photographs. The first one shows Clive Madeiros demonstrating how to catch an ostrich. He's making a grab at its neck, while it flaps its wings wildly. The light-hearted caption reads: '*First catch your ostrich! Veterinary surgeon Clive Madeiros demonstrates how a bird is taken into custody, hooded (below) and led off to the processing plant.*' Below is a photo of the ostrich, face tightly hooded, being led away by two men, both of them considerably shorter than the ostrich, apparently the vet and owner Mr Bardsley. He is pictured separately too: '*Roland Bardsley smiles at the thought of the opportunities*' reads the caption. Opportunities, presumably, of making big money from ostriches forced to live out their grossly shortened lives far from home.

*

What did MAFF have to say about slaughter? In its August 1996 *Guidance on the Slaughter of Ostriches* the Ministry painted a picture of virtually unachievable conditions: '*No avoidable excitement, pain or suffering must be caused to any animal. Anyone involved in these operations must have the knowledge and skill to perform them humanely and efficiently in accordance with the regulations. Ostriches should always be moved in a calm and unhurried manner,* and so on....MAFF mentioned the hood, but didn't have anything to say about its overnight use.

Although ostriches were regarded as 'poultry', MAFF stated that, because of their size, they should be treated as a red meat species at slaughter and electrically stunned, so as to cause immediate unconsciousness lasting until death.

*

Fast forward several years: I emailed DEFRA with a few queries about the present state of ostrich farming in the UK, and a spokesperson for its Animal Welfare Team sent me the following information, in an emailed reply dated April 29th 2010:

DEFRA on slaughter: *'Killing ostriches by means other than electrical stunning is legal under present legislation.'* It was with relief that I later learned (though not from DEFRA) that from January 2013 EU law will prohibit ostriches from being slaughtered by neck dislocation or by decapitation, since these methods will be outlawed for any bird weighing more than 5 kg (17).

DEFRA on slaughterhouses: *'There is only one approved ostrich slaughterhouse in the UK.'* This means that either there's a lot of on-farm slaughter (and who knows how botched that might be?) or ostriches must travel long distances to the approved plant, despite the species' known vulnerability to injury during handling and transport.

DEFRA on the number of ostrich farms: *'According to the Great Britain Poultry Register (GBPR) there are thirty seven in the UK (excluding Northern Ireland) holding 954 ostriches though the GBPR does not differentiate between ostriches in zoos and wildlife parks from those on farms.'* In view of this lumping together of things, and as MAFF had no central record of ostrich farms when they were springing up all over the UK, it's impossible to judge quite to what extent the get-rich-quick bubble has burst. Happily, though, it appeared that entrepreneurs looking for quick and easy profits had, in the main, backed the wrong horse. Or so I thought...

*

Disturbingly, the front cover of the December 2011 issue of *Poultry World* featured a photo of several ostriches in the company of UK farmer Harold Paine, of Ostrichfayre. The article was headed *Ostrich Farming Poised for a Comeback?* Apparently, despite the boom and bust nature of the previous venture in Europe, *'there are still those who firmly believe the true commercial potential was overlooked as people focused on making rapid profits from the sale of breeding stock.'*

On Mr Paine's ostrich farm fifteen young ostriches to a half-acre paddock is the norm. Interestingly, he has tried allowing the parent birds to hatch out their young, recording a 90% success rate. However, he admitted that under artificial incubation: *'Out of 100 eggs incubated, we can be lucky to get 40 chicks...'* Mr Paine describes the downside of the 90% success rate thus: *'Nevertheless, retrieving the newly hatched chicks from the paddock and coping with the aggression of the adult birds highlights the care that needs to be taken when dealing with mature ostriches.'*

Mr Paine's findings only serve to highlight the dedication and fiercely protective feelings of the parent birds towards their chicks, emphasising the deprivation involved in the commercial farming of ostriches.

Turkeys again, and a cool reception

February 1992: Irene and I were booked in for a day at the turkey industry's national conference at the Hotel Majestic in Harrogate, North Yorkshire. As we crossed the hotel's grandiose Victorian threshold, delegates' tickets in hand, we were surprised to be intercepted by the conference organiser, Shirley Murdoch. Flustered and apologetic, she told us we were barred, explaining that many delegates had threatened to walk out if anyone from Chickens' Lib was allowed in.

Irene and I fumed. We'd paid on a Chickens' Lib cheque, there'd been no deception on our part; and (to her credit) Ms Murdoch hadn't objected. But once our names had been spotted on the conference programme, it seemed all hell had broken loose.

Under the heading *WELFARE PAIR SPARK THREAT OF WALKOUT* the next issue of *Poultry World* described the ensuing drama: *'The UK turkey industry came face to face last month at the national turkey conference with two of its bêtes noires – the French industry and the welfarists...The welfare movement was represented by two leading members of Chickens' Lib, Mrs Clare Druce and Mrs Irene Williams. They had not been invited, but their £80 registration fee had been accepted by conference organiser Shirley Murdoch and they were listed as delegates. The two women could not have caused more of a stir if they had applied for membership of the MCC and attempted to breach the threshold of the pavilion at Lords. On the evening before they were due to arrive at the Hotel Majestic it became apparent that as soon as they entered the conference hall a sizeable chunk of the audience would leave. "This left me with no choice,"* [Ms Murdoch] *said. "I explained the position to them and refunded their registration fees with something to cover their expenses. It was all very civilised." '*

But not entirely civilised. For quite a while Irene and I hung around on the other side of a barrier (hastily erected to keep us out?) refusing to leave, a target for scornful glances from passing turkey barons.

Sensing an opportunity not to be missed, we explained to a harassed Ms Murdoch that we'd intended to question the Chief Ministry Vet, Keith Meldrum, a speaker at the event. Partial beak amputation, artificial insemination and slaughter methods had all been on our list of welfare problems to be raised. These were urgent matters! Since we couldn't attend the conference, could Mr Meldrum perhaps come to us?

Not a good idea, according to David Joll, Managing Director of Bernard Matthews Ltd and chairman of the British Turkey Federation. *'It was not the time or place to enter into a lot of questioning of Keith Meldrum,'* he was to tell *Poultry World.*

However, to our considerable surprise, Mr Meldrum got wind of our request, left the assembly and led us to a comfortable little room at a safe distance from the seething delegates. There, in quiet seclusion, we talked at some length.

'In the event, however, they did get a chance to talk to Mr Meldrum,' [admitted a rueful *Poultry World*]. *'He agreed to speak to them privately and, as he told the conference later, "I spent an hour and a half with them and it was very valuable". The chief vet went on to warn delegates that they had to accept that there was a strong body of opinion that believed the industry should do more about welfare within existing legislative framework "It is a very important issue that will not go away. You are not getting your act together." '* (1)

Presumably an industry that was doing well saw no need to mend its ways, especially when contraventions of legislation were routinely ignored by the body best placed to mount prosecutions – MAFF itself. Research detailing the suffering of male breeding turkeys had been published *before* our talk with MAFF's Chief Veterinary Officer, and some was ongoing. Why had this unnecessary pain and unnecessary distress (UPUD in Ministry shorthand) been allowed to continue for years, unchallenged?

In the next chapter I'll give a few examples of relevant research.

Scientists prove suffering

1987: Dr S R Duff *et al.* had found antitrochanteric degeneration (disease of the hip joint) to be *'an extremely common cause of lameness in male breeding turkeys'.* (1)

Then in 1991, Dr Ian Duncan and colleagues at the Institute of Animal Physiology and Genetics Research, Roslin, conducted an experiment to assess not just the incidence of hip degeneration in male breeders, but the degree of pain felt by the crippled turkeys. (2) The birds used were of British United Turkeys' 'Big 6' breeding line (3). It's worth noting that the researchers selected only the best specimens for their project. Seventy birds were reared to the age of 52 weeks, after which twenty were chosen while *'...all birds in poor health, immobile or with unstable hock joints, together with birds which were very nervous and difficult to handle, were removed'.* These twenty of the best birds were divided randomly into two groups, one of which was treated with a steroid, to reduce pain. Those treated with the drug showed marked improvement in activity and started to display sexual arousal.

The experiment completed, all twenty turkeys were killed and *post mortem* examination showed that all had extensive hip degeneration. The most striking finding from the experiment had been the inactivity in birds *not* treated with painkillers: they had been observed to spend more than half of their time lying down.

Another investigation, *Leg Disorders in Male Breeding Turkeys* by Paul Hocking (a researcher also based at Roslin), was reported in the industry magazine *Turkeys* in June 1992, only a few months after our exclusion from the conference. The figure for mortality in male breeding turkeys was found to be high, ranging from 25-66% and the researchers described lameness in breeding males as a common cause of culling. By the time they go for slaughter, we learned, 75% of such birds are either lame or walk with 'an abnormal gait': *'The majority show marked limb angulation and virtually all males of the largest strains are reluctant to walk. In two separate studies over 90% of males showed degenerative hip disease on post-mortem examination.'* (4)

Why did these various proofs of routine suffering go unheeded? How has the turkey industry been allowed to get away with inflicting known and acute suffering?

And why, despite considerable publicity, have consumers failed to pick up on the fact that virtually any meal including turkey meat is based on the flesh of birds produced via the stressful sexual manipulation of sick and deformed male birds?

*

Soon after the Harrogate fiasco, the manager of a leading international breeding company claimed, during a phone conversation with me, not to be aware of the problem of hip degeneration in his birds. The Chief Executive of another such company told me (also on the phone) that in recent weeks a MAFF survey of the farms belonging to his well-known company had been carried out. And guess what? No trace of hip problems had been found!

Could this 'survey' have been the outcome of our time spent with Mr Meldrum, as outcasts in Harrogate? And could Mr Meldrum, or those concerned with processing the survey, have been fooled in some way?

It did appear that our publicity, in the shape of posters, leaflets and relentless letter writing campaigns, might be paying off. For at last the Farm Animal Welfare Council (FAWC) was all set to investigate the turkey industry.

FAWC, you will recall, is the independent body set up to advise government on matters relating to farmed animal welfare. Working parties for specific reports are generally made up from about one third of the Council's members. A point worth bearing in mind is that farm visits are made by appointment, the date often arranged months in advance.

FAWC looks at turkeys

1992: By invitation, thirty seven bodies, ranging from industry, through companies and veterinarians to animal welfare/rights organisations, submitted their views on the turkey industry to FAWC.

Two years later, FAWC invited six welfare organisations, including Chickens' Lib, to a meeting in advance of the report's publication. Such discussions with welfare organisations were always held in the afternoon, following consultation with the industry in the morning of the same day.

During the meeting I'd sat astounded and confounded, while extraordinarily complicated mathematical principles were bandied about, understood, I guessed, by few present. Gradually though, it had dawned on me what they were about. Two or three times I tried to get the matter in hand translated into plain English and finally forced an admission. Yes, turkeys grow upwards as well as in other directions, and luckily there's headroom in plenty in turkey units. Incredibly, the members of the turkey working party were saying that turkeys could get by with less floor space than their increase in weight might seem to warrant.

*

In 1995, six years after the start of the Chickens' Lib turkey campaign, the Farm Animal Welfare Council issued its 'Report on the Welfare of Turkeys', and a shocking light it threw on the industry.

The report was useful for the facts and figures it revealed. We'd already found out a good deal about the industry, but in some respects our worst fears were exceeded. For example:

- Flocks of up to twenty-five thousand turkeys, kept together in one controlled environment building, were considered standard, in the larger units. (1)
- Many farms were found to be exceeding the Government's Turkey Welfare Code's recommendation for space per bird 'by a substantial margin'. (2)
- Around 90% of UK turkeys were kept intensively (3).
- The food of the breeding stock was 'managed', via feed restriction, to minimise leg disorders and maximise fecundity. (4)
- Aggression was minimised in controlled environment buildings (windowless sheds, dependent on automation) by dimming the lights to 1- 4 lux (5).

*

1-4 lux confirmed our suspicion that turkeys lived in near darkness, in an industry bid to suppress aggression. But we weren't strong on the lux measurement front – we needed to find out more. We spotted an advertisement for a lux meter, a device for measuring light levels, which included a list of recommended 'illuminance values' in the work place. Here are some examples:

Corridors, stairs etc	100–150 lux
General office work	300–500 lux
Fine bench work	1000–1500 lux
Minute work	3000–5000 lux

Anything below 100 lux wasn't even mentioned. I remember questioning someone who understood these things, and he likened 5 lux to candlelight.

*

The anticipated ugly picture, already well publicised in Chickens' Lib's literature, was at least now set out in an official document. But many aspects of FAWC's report shocked us greatly. Take this glaring example: despite existing legislation stating that no more than one third of a bird's upper beak may be removed (6), FAWC, perhaps shocked by the degree of aggression in turkey sheds, had suggested the removal of one half, so making a more thorough job of the partial amputation. To its credit, the Tory government turned down this suggestion.

The Welfare Code for Turkeys stated: '*The size of a unit should not be increased, nor should a unit be set up unless it is reasonably certain that the stockman in charge will be able to safeguard the welfare of the individual bird*' (7), yet FAWC went along with the industry in these words: '*The Council accepts that it is not possible for the stockman to look at each bird individually during routine inspection but a good indication of flock health must be gained.*' (8) Again, the old, old story of bending the rules to suit factory farming – and this from the Farm Animal Welfare Council!

We were shocked by the meek acceptance of the *status quo* shown by FAWC. At no point did the Council question the legality, let alone the morality of subjecting turkeys to the conditions outlined in its report. With friends like those on the FAWC working party, we thought, what turkey needs enemies?

In a subsequent Chickens' Lib newsletter we sent our supporters the following puzzle, extracted from the FAWC Turkey Report:

The puzzle: 'Producers should plan to stock their houses at no more than the stocking density calculated from A= 0.0459 W2/3 where A is in M2 and W is liveweight in kg.'

'We're not too clear about it, but it's part of the 1995 FAWC Report on the Welfare of Turkeys,' we warned our supporters before giving them FAWC's 'solution'. It went as follows: "We believe that big turkeys require, weight for weight, less space than small ones, because as turkeys grow their size increases in three dimensions (length, width and height) whilst the floor area they occupy increases in only two dimensions."(8)

Our comment to supporters concluded: *'FAWC is recommending even less space for "big turkeys". This would represent yet another backward step in terms of turkey welfare. (End of puzzle.)'*

*

In 2010 I wrote to DEFRA. I wanted to know for certain whether FAWC's 1995 recommendations for turkey welfare had been acted upon. Here's what I was told:

On light levels: DEFRA's spokeswoman for its Customer Contact Unit (am I a *customer* of DEFRA?) told me that light levels in controlled environment housing (windowless buildings with extractor fans etc.) are now 'normally' higher than 5 lux, and that 'most' flocks receive at least eight hours of darkness out of the 24. These figures, she said, reflected four research projects carried out by DEFRA, between 1995 and 1998.

I'd also asked about hip problems in turkeys, but was assured that 'as far as we are aware' hip problems are not an issue. DEFRA admitted the problems had been 'previously identified' in breeding stags, but currently has no statistics on its 'current prevalence'.

Catching the birds

The catching and pre-slaughter treatment of poultry is wide open to abuse. Take so-called bagpiping.

Bagpiping is a slaughterhouse 'game' where employees squeeze live chickens until faeces squirt out, to be aimed at fellow workers. I can remember two such cases that came to court. How many similar 'games' are played behind the backs of the one or two vets on duty, who may or may not be vigilant? Chicken slaughtering is not a rewarding job, nor one that attracts workers who feel deeply, if at all, for the animals' welfare. But before slaughter must come the catching process.

In our booklet *Hidden Suffering* (April 1993) we stated: *'Turkeys are large, strong and easily frightened birds. Catchers are generally unfamiliar to them and cause great alarm when they enter the sheds to collect birds for slaughter. Violent treatment of turkeys at all stages of catching, loading, unloading and slaughter has been witnessed on numerous occasions. Unfortunately, people working in the poultry industry are often unwilling to report cruelty, for fear of reprisals.'*

Without the animal activists who trespassed and managed to film the catching process there would still be no progress. Thank goodness for those people brave enough to show the rest of us the true picture.

In 2006, an RSPCA inspector, giving evidence in court, described a catching-related incident as depicting some of the worst cruelty he had seen. Two catchers in a Bernard Matthews' unit had been filmed tormenting a live turkey with a baseball bat, the turkey serving as the 'ball' in their sick game. By huge good fortune, an undercover investigator from Hillside Animal Sanctuary had been hidden on the premises that night, video recorder at the ready to take footage of the inside of a turkey shed, little expecting to film the catching process, let alone this atrocity. In court the two catchers claimed 'peer pressure' and described a 'culture' of cruelty at the plant (1).

In 2007 Hillside caught another Bernard Matthews' employee on camera, this time kicking rather than throwing turkeys, as the catchers rounded a flock up for slaughter. (2) More recently, Hillside has filmed shocking cruelty on the part of catchers in an intensive duck unit.

The question must be asked – how often does this abuse go on, countrywide?

*

After all the adverse publicity about red meat, horse meat, pork and intensively farmed poultry, meat-eating consumers may well scan any restaurant menu with dismay – whatever should they chose? Even fish is suspect now, what with farmed salmon swimming about in overcrowded, contaminated cages, dosed with antibiotics...

But wait! There's pheasant! Now, *that's* about as far away from modern meat and fish production as you can possibly get. Game birds are all-natural, part of country life's rich tapestry, a reminder of times when people connected the living creature with the food on their plate. And they die happy, don't they? One moment they're flying free, the next plummeting to earth dead, to be retrieved by some trusty working dog.

Even if you can't shoot them yourself, at least you know they've enjoyed their freedom. Yes, you'll decide on the pheasant...

THE SPORTING LIFE

For years, *Veterinary Record* (VR), the weekly journal of the veterinary profession, had been required reading in our office. The Government's Veterinary Laboratories Agency (VLA) issues regular reports on investigations into animal disease, based on submissions to their centres throughout the UK.

To our surprise we began to notice game birds cropping up in these reports. Frequently the diseases listed sounded oddly like 'diseases of intensification', the term used for conditions linked to intensive farming. But how could this be? Surely, game birds were part of nature, virtually untouched by human hand – until shot, that is.

So what were these devices called bits, causing such problems? And debeaking? *Wild* birds debeaked? Impossible! Pheasants suffering from septicaemia, arthritis, brain diseases? Blindness even? And what about 'starve-outs'? Surely they were confined to gloomy factory farms? And '*specs*'?

Whatever did these terms mean?

*

We found that the Game Conservancy (GC), based at Fordingbridge in Hampshire, had published a series of books on game bird management. Since it was hard facts we were after we ordered several titles, and soon glossy hardbacks were landing in the pigeonhole of our PO Box. Without exception they turned out to be both confused and confusing (in short, badly written) but within their pages were stark facts in plenty, often accompanied by photographs of what looked like instruments of torture.

When we first concerned ourselves with gamebirds, an estimated 17 million pheasants were shot annually in the UK. Today, the figure has more than doubled (1). Gamebirds have become big business, with birds on some premises numbered in tens of thousands (2).

Pheasants have a natural lifespan of several years but may be shot from the age of twenty weeks. By then, millions of artificially reared pheasants will have been abused almost beyond belief, a fact that the shooting lobby is determined to hide.

*

We concentrated on pheasants, since they represent the greatest number of gamebirds reared for sport. We tracked down companies supplying gamebird equipment and sent off for catalogues (but not from our office address!). As far as specs, bits and brails went, one hundred constituted the minimum order, but we went ahead: there's nothing like holding the real thing in one's hands.

Soon, not only our supporters but MPs and civil servants too were receiving samples of these loathsome devices.

*

Here's a quick guide to the gamekeeper's arsenal. NB: 'Gamekeeper' may sound old-fashioned and in fact two distinct stages are now common in today's gamebird rearing process. Often, large commercial hatcheries rear the chicks for the first few weeks of life then deliver the desired number to the site of the commercial shoot. For pheasants, this transfer usually happens at around week seven.

Warning: the information you are about to read is harrowing.

Bits: Made from metal or plastic. Come in three sizes. Fed between top and bottom beak and clipped into birds' nostrils. **Purpose:** To prevent the beak from closing properly, so minimising outbreaks of feather pecking and cannibalism in crowded sheds and enclosures. **Result:** Bits prevent birds from breathing through nostrils, and cause dry mouths and pain. They frustrate birds' basic instincts to pick up small food particles, and prevent effective preening. They must be changed at least twice, as the birds grow: bits are cut through with pliers, when outgrown. (Chickens' Lib believes that sinusitis, now common in young pheasants, is caused by obstruction of and damage to nostrils.) (3) **And finally:** Bits removed at least one month before the shoot.

*

Specs: Blinker-like discs, usually of plastic, clipped into nostrils, to prevent adult breeding birds from seeing directly ahead. **Purpose:** To discourage breeding pheasants from damaging other birds or pecking at eggs. **Specs with pins:** Kept in place with a plastic pin pushed into one nostril and out of the other, *en route* piercing the delicate nasal septum. Intended to stay in place permanently, the pin has a projecting 'arrow', which, once pushed through the second nostril, springs back. **Purpose:** As above. **Result:** All specs block the nostrils, impeding normal breathing. Specs, especially those with pins, sentence birds to a life of pain. Specs with pins were readily available in the UK in the 1990s. We should know – we ordered hundreds of them, right up to the year 2000, despite them being described by the Game Conservancy as illegal (4). (More of this confused situation later.)

*

Brails: Circles, usually of tape, to twist around one wing. **Purpose:** To prevent birds flying out of open-topped enclosures, for example disused walled gardens. Most often used on breeding stock. **Result:** Brails can impede circulation.

*

Partial beak amputation (PBA): Described as beak trimming in GC literature, PBA, as with poultry, involves the removal of part of the upper beak. Systems vary, from a red-hot blade (soon to be outlawed) to the infra-red method. In its 1990 publication *Gamebird Rearing* the GC was applying the belt and braces approach to the problem of aggression, recommending the bitting *and* PBA of ten-day-old poults with a further 'trim' as re-growth takes place, generally at intervals of 10-14 days. Probably the 'little and often' approach was adopted so birds wouldn't appear mutilated on the day of the shoot. However, photographs of PBA in GC literature show a thorough enough cut; the expression in one bird's eye as an electrically heated cutting blade is poised over a substantial section of its beak all too clearly illustrates the victim's terror (5).

We'd hoped the total pointlessness of inflicting *both* these abuses had been recognised in recent years, in all likelihood leaving bitting as the favoured 'solution'. However, a 2007 report described nine-week-old pheasants with staphylococcal arthritis/synovitis as having recently been fitted with bits *and* beak trimmed. Bacteria had entered the wounds, thought to be *'due to procedures such as beak trimming'* (6).

*

Quickly, we built up a picture of the birds' short lives, as described in GC literature. One person can 'trim' two hundred and fifty birds' beaks in around half an hour (7). 'A' size bits must be changed for size 'B', as birds grow (8). Upper mandibles may become deformed, owing to lack of abrasion against the lower mandible (9). At 6 to 7 weeks bits are removed and birds transported to release pens (large enclosed areas with trees, shrubs etc.) to be 'hardened off' and habituated to freedom.

Challenging targets are wanted, so release pens are sited strategically – on elevated ground, for example – to encourage birds to fly high on the day of the shoot (10). Disease outbreaks are common at the time of transfer to the release pens (11), the result of stress caused by bit removal and by relocation, the latter possibly involving a journey from hatching farm to estate.

In 1991, when the GC published *Gamebird Releasing*, it recommended crating the young birds at 34 birds to a crate measuring 90cm long, 60cm wide and 20cm high (36 inches x 24 inches x 8 inches) (12). Crammed in by any standards, and possibly for a long journey.

Four weeks before the proposed shoot, birds are encouraged to leave the release pens in order to experience 'at least a month of liberty'. (13)

*

Piercing the nasal septum is illegal for poultry under the *Welfare of Livestock (Prohibited Operations) Regulations 1982 (Section 3)*. FAWN had mistakenly assumed gamebirds to be included in this legislation, a misapprehension apparently shared by the Game Conservancy (14). However, in 2003 a spokeswoman for DEFRA told us otherwise: *'These Regulations* (the 1982 Regs) *are made under the Agriculture (Miscellaneous Provisions) Act 1968, which defines livestock as "animals being kept for the production of food, wool, skin, or fur on agricultural land..." however pheasants reared for sporting purposes do not fall into the definition of livestock under this Act. However these animals* [gamebirds] *are covered by the Protection of Animals Act 1911. Under this Act it is an offence to ill treat or cause suffering to any captive or domestic animal.'*

Forcing a pin through the delicate nasal septum of a live bird, via his or her nostrils? In any normal person's mind this constitutes extreme cruelty, and it appears from the last sentence quoted above that DEFRA supports this view. Yet somehow game birds, despite being more 'agricultural' than an animal farmed for its fur, have continued to fall between two stools.

It seems the blood sports people have been getting away with an illegal mutilation for decades, all the while skating on thin legislative ice, though the 1911 Act alone should have sorted out this cruelty from the word go. But, as with other victims of factory farming, it's the will to challenge illegal practices in the courts that's in short supply.

Not long after Chickens' Lib had purchased the range of Game Conservancy books on pheasant production and publicised their contents, those glossy hardbacks, full of revealing photographs of cruelty, were replaced with extremely short and bland leaflets.

*

In May 1994 we issued a booklet, *Rearing Pheasants for Shoots – the Disturbing Facts*, following this up with a leaflet displaying a League Against Cruel Sports (LACS) photo of a pheasant fitted with nasal septum-piercing specs. Later, we produced a postcard showing the same photo, alongside one of a bitted pheasant. Looking at it now, I'm imagining once more the pain that bespectacled bird must have endured, perhaps for months, years even, and I'm shocked afresh by the degree to which the bitted bird's beak is forced open. In our leaflet, we asked: *'Would it be acceptable to inflict these mutilations and cruelties on a blackbird, or a robin?'*

At one point, we appealed to the Royal Society for the Protection of Birds (RSPB), only to be told that birds reared for sport fell outside the Society's remit. But should *all* of them be excluded from the RSPB's concern? A method for refreshing existing breeding stock, and approved by the Game Conservancy, is 'catching up from the wild' (15). This involves trapping unsuspecting wild pheasants.

How could it be legal to 'steal' wild birds then subject them to bird-torture, we wondered? An RSPB leaflet, *Birds and the Law, Some Questions answered*, included this apparently frequently asked question:

Q: I know a person who traps finches and keeps them in an aviary. Is this illegal?

A: Yes, not only is it an offence to take British wild birds, but keeping them is also illegal. You should contact the police or the RSPB with this information.

Surely a wild pheasant, hatched in the wild, is a wild bird? The practice of taking wild pheasants into captivity should be challenged, in a court of law.

Prince Charles is keen on country sports. Was it possible that he was unaware of the cruelty lurking behind those invigorating days out with the shoot? We'd appeal to him and describe what goes on *before* the shoot, leaving the question of the morality of blood sports to the League Against Cruel Sports. We drew up a petition pointing out the pre-shoot suffering of millions of pheasants and appealed to HRH for support in our campaign.

*

Summer 1994: Armed with an impressive number of signatures, we wondered how best to present our petition. Travelling to London simply to hand our parcel over to a bored official struck us as a waste of funds. No, we'd post it at our local Post Office, and hope for press interest nearer home. But first we needed a celebrity.

Now, Holmfirth is a small Pennine town, the setting for the BBC's long-running (but now finished) TV comedy *'Last of the Summer Wine'*. Centred around three retired local characters with time on their hands, their absurd escapades were for many years played out amid the beautiful scenery of the Holme Valley.

Actor Bill Owen played the disreputable Compo. Dressed in shabby trousers kept up with fraying baler twine, Compo was forever being hounded down Nora Batty's cottage steps as Nora, her hair in curlers and brandishing a broom, fended off his unwanted attentions. We'd write to Bill Owen.

Bill was pleased to help. We agreed on August 12th, the 'glorious twelfth' that marks the first day of the grouse shooting season.

*

The Huddersfield Examiner of August 13th reported the event: *'Comedy star Bill Owen (pictured) took on a more serious role in Holmfirth yesterday when he gave his support to an animal welfare petition. Bill, alias Compo in the BBC's Last of the Summer Wine, helped to post a 50,000 signature petition from the Farm Animal Welfare Network. Posted at Holmfirth Post Office on "the glorious twelfth" the petition calls on Prince Charles, a keen grouse and pheasant shooter, to recognise the cruel exploitation involved in rearing birds for sport.'*

A week later, the situation had turned acrimonious. The *Express and Chronicle* of August 19th featured a retrospective photograph of our two dedicated helpers, Penny Perkins and Margaret Skinner, flanking a determined-looking Bill Owen, all three armed with large parcels of signed petitions. Under a bold heading *BIRD REARING ROW HITS "WINE" SHOOT* came the news that a vital filming venue had been axed. *'Feathers are flying over Last of the Summer Wine star Bill Owen's outspoken views on bird shooting. Incensed by Mr Owen's views, a gamekeeper has blocked the BBC film crew from shooting scenes for the next series on valley moorland. Producer and director of the series Alan Bell said permission was withdrawn by Snailsden Moor's head gamekeeper John Hollingworth last week only a fortnight before filming was due to start...Yorkshire Water, who own the moorland but not the shooting rights, said they are helping the BBC find another location.'*

Despite the hullabaloo, Bill refused to moderate his views. According to the paper, he continued to describe game bird shooting as 'a devilish sport'. The producer added: *'Bill is very sorry about the whole thing but when he believes in something he is very passionate about it.'*

*

We'd known that Bill Owen was passionate about injustices towards his fellow humans and he'd told us that this 'photo opportunity' marked his first venture into the world of animal-related injustice. So we'd been doubly grateful for his support and we were very sad at his passing, in 1999. *'Last of the Summer Wine'* was never to be the same without 'Compo'.

*

Following the publicity, letters, both supportive and abusive, were published in the local paper. When a Mr W wrote in (more than once) calling us loonies and troublemakers, we decided we'd had enough. We knew our facts. We had proof of the cruelty. At our request, the Holme Valley Express agreed to host a meeting between Mr W and myself, with a view to publishing the proceedings. As the time drew near, I felt increasingly eager to meet with our angry letter-writer.

Sadly, it turned out he was bolder on paper than in the flesh and, with no apology, failed to turn up. As far as we were concerned, Mr W was never heard of again.

The Star too ran an article on the 'Glorious Twelfth', describing the foul devices employed to control game birds and featuring our petition to Prince Charles. The newspaper contacted the British Field Sports Society for its views, to be told by a spokesperson that the practices we objected to represented 'good basic husbandry', and that game was about as free range as food gets.

Sixteen years later, the Veterinary Laboratories Agency in Thirsk, North Yorkshire, found staphylococcal septicaemia in pheasants submitted to them. The cause was thought to be *'removal of hard plastic anti-pecking bits from pheasants by twisting them without cutting them first, with the resulting damage to the nasal mucosa.'* This practice was believed to be *'sometimes responsible for introducing staphylococcal infections such as septic arthritis and tenosynovitis and this may have been a predisposing factor in this case'* (16).

*

Prince Charles' response was disappointing. We felt we'd been moderate in our request, in limiting it to pheasant *rearing*. We'd not asked him to de-commission his guns. HRH's Private Secretary, Commander Richard Aylard, thanked us for our letter of August 12th and the enclosed petitions. Apparently His Royal Highness had noted our views.

We wrote to our supporters: *'We feel that our "views" are not what matters, but the suffering of the birds... "Specs" deemed illegal by the Game Conservancy are readily available from a firm in Hertfordshire which operates as suppliers of game rearing equipment to Her Majesty the Queen.'*

We ended this section of our newsletter with an offer to our supporters – specs with pins (50p each inc. p&p), suggesting that samples might be displayed on street stalls. We also asked them to send the postcard of the pheasant wearing these cruel specs to Prince Charles, respectfully suggesting that he 'looks into pheasant rearing practices'. To date, we have no reason to believe that he has.

*

Later that same year, specs with pins were found on pheasants on the Queen's Windsor estate. *The People* exposed the scandal, the outcome being that the Queen directed Quadtag, the game bird equipment firm in receipt of her Royal Warrant, to stop manufacturing this device (17).

Despite the publicity, specs with pins remained in the catalogues of other UK game supply firms for a further few years. Now, with increased bad publicity from Animal Aid as well as LACS and Chickens' Lib, these instruments of torture are no longer advertised. But that's not to say that gamekeepers can't still get their hands on them.

*

As long-term listeners to *The Archers*, that BBC Radio 4 story of country folk, Violet and I had noticed something missing in the village gamekeeper's routine in the woods of Ambridge. No mention ever of bits, specs or brails, let alone of PBA or of diseases necessitating antibiotic treatment. No, the birds are just fed and 'looked after'.

Perhaps the script is influenced by *BBC Books'* 1995 publication *'The Gamekeeper – a Year in the Glens.'* There's a telling little passage in the book where the author, Charlie Pirie, faces up to the fact that after months spent caring for the pheasants, feeding them and keeping them safe 'like children, basically', comes the day of the shoot.

Not too rosy an outlook, for a gamekeeper's children...

*

January 2000: We sent our supporters a pre-drafted letter for them to sign and post to the programme's senior producer. The letter questioned the lack of any mention of cruel devices, and pointed out that: *'Losses from the diseases so rife on modern estates seem not to trouble Ambridge pheasants or their keepers...in recent years the pages of Veterinary Record certainly tell a story of escalating disease patterns. Cannibalism causes heavy losses too...'* We ended with the hope that the gamekeepers of Ambridge might begin to reflect the real world. Onto each pre-drafted letter, we'd stuck a sample bit. We even lent the programme's production team our copies of the Game Conservancy books, to prove we didn't dream up atrocities. We received a polite postcard from one of the producers – the books had been passed around the office, and the contents noted with interest...

But none of our efforts made a scrap of difference to the scripts. A gamekeeper's job is still seen through rose-tinted specs. With or without pins.

*

In 2002 Chickens' Lib was invited to attend the Farm Animal Welfare Council's annual open meeting. While there, I suggested that the Council should report on the game bird industry. Though not regarded as *bona fide* 'food animals', game birds are supposed to be eaten so we'd decided they qualified for a FAWC Report.

A few years were to pass until, in 2006, comments from interested parties (ranging from Chickens' Lib to Tesco plc) were invited, to assist FAWC to make its assessment of the welfare of game birds.

*

In 2004 the League Against Cruel Sports (LACS) exposed an ominous and exceptionally cruel trend – barren and highly restrictive cages for housing breeding game birds. At Pye Hall Game Farm in Eye, Suffolk, they claimed to have found *'overcrowding, cannibalism and a cold indifference to animal suffering'* (18). The following year, during the 2005 pheasant and partridge breeding season, Animal Aid (AA) carried out undercover filming on the premises of four major game bird companies, *G&A Leisure*, in Bettws Cedewain, Wales, *Heart of England Farms* in Claverdon, Warwick, *Hy-Fly Game Hatcheries* in Poulton-le-Fylde, and *Pye Hall Game Farm* itself.

All four establishments were found to be keeping groups of pheasant breeders at a ratio similar to that seen in the wild – one male to around eight females. But there any similarity to nature ends.

Row upon row of cages stretch away into the distance, with little protection from the elements. When alarmed the trapped birds attempt to fly upwards, only to hit their heads on the cage roof, often causing severe injury (it's known as scalping, in the gamebird industry). AA investigators found many dead birds. Among the living, head damage and severe feather wear were common. At *Heart of England Farms* AA filmed a bird wearing a grotesque device, somewhere between specs and a beak guard, with pins through the nasal septum (19).

*

While holidaying in Shropshire a year or two later we strayed over the border into Wales and found ourselves driving past the sign to a village that sounded familiar: Bettws Cedewain.

'That's where one of those game bird breeding places is – where Animal Aid did secret filming of the cages,' I said (or yelled, possibly). 'Stop the car!'

We found a parking spot and wandered around the village, hoping to catch a glimpse of *G&A Leisure's* caged birds.

Soon we came upon a newly built hotel, both extensive and flashy, no doubt providing five star accommodation for the Guns (as those planning

230

to take pot shots at the birds are called). Apparently Guns descend on this picturesque village from far and wide: '*An American agency, Chris Batha of South Carolina, offers shooting jaunts on behalf of G&A to groups of eight guns. The cost is $11,840 per person, with 300 bird-targets provided on each of four days*' (20). Do these visitors to *G&A Leisure*, loaded in both senses, know of the squalor and cruelty hidden behind the scenes?

We investigated the village from all angles and walked among the surrounding gently undulating hills, bathed that afternoon in warm sunshine, hoping to see something of the one thousand, six hundred and sixty cages described by Animal Aid. But the lie of the land was against us. Whenever we seemed about to reach a vantage point, a hill would intervene. The thousands of incarcerated birds were well hidden; *G&A Leisure* knows what it's about.

We did see a good many beautiful pheasants wandering alongside the hedgerows and into the road. Apart from the hotel, the only hint of big business was a gleaming new metal five-bar farm gate, firmly closed, and a notice to Keep Out on the grounds of 'biosecurity'. How useful that term is for keeping the public at bay, and how ironic that it's frequently associated with particularly filthy establishments.

*

The adverse publicity that followed Animal Aid's investigations caused a split to develop in the shooting world. It seemed that the British Association for Shooting and Conservation became worried that the scandal of cages would further besmirch the image of 'country sports'. Then came some good news for the birds.

On March 15th 2010 DEFRA issued a new Code of Practice designed effectively to see an end to caged breeding pheasants. Animal Aid had done great work in highlighting the dreadful conditions outlined above. I'll quote from their Summer 2010 issue of 'Outrage': '*The new Code of Practice states that "all laying systems for pheasants should provide a minimum space of one square metre per bird". Typically, caged breeding pheasants have a ninth of this space. The new requirement effectively makes the cages economically and logistically impractical. Sadly, the new Code does nothing for partridges, since the new space allowance per bird for them is already met by the existing system.*'

Then in its January issue *Poultry World* reported: '*Readers should be aware that an outright ban on laying cages – barren and enriched – is being canvassed by DEFRA in a public consultation document. The consultation relates only to game birds, but the poultry industry may find the suggestion alarming nonetheless.'* (Obviously, enriched cages for laying hens had sprung to poultry keepers' minds.)

How wonderful, we thought, all those redundant game bird cages! But any celebration on behalf of breeding pheasants was to be short-lived. Soon after the 2010 general election, the Tory/Lib Dem coalition wiped out the new Code, in what Animal Aid called 'a shameful government U-turn'. The incoming government appointed a keen advocate of country sports, James (Jim) Paice, as DEFRA's Minister of State. According to Animal Aid, within a month of taking up his new role Mr Paice had withdrawn the new Code of Practice and chaired an emergency meeting in which he succeeded in pushing through a watered-down version. A so-called 'enriched' cage would be allowed in place of the barren cage.

And what does this mean in terms of the welfare of the breeding birds? It means the birds will have a perch and a plastic curtain to afford a little privacy for egg laying. In the words of AA's Kate Fowler: *'Animal Aid has filmed these "enriched" cages on several occasions and can confirm that they are just as bleak and oppressive as the non-enriched version.'*

*

Most of our knowledge about game birds has been based on practices in the UK, but while writing this chapter I've looked at various websites. One day I lit upon a hauntingly sad image from America. A sturdy leather harness encircles a live pheasant as she lies helpless on the grass, denied any hope of movement, let alone escape. The device comes in different sizes to suit different types of birds, including the tiny quail, and is an aid for training gun dogs (21).

*

Our comments to the FAWC inquiry into the game bird industry, dated May 2007, included a list of the many diseases we believed to be caused by stressful rearing methods. For example, ascites, a disease originally occurring in poultry kept at high altitudes but now common throughout the broiler industry and among factory-farmed pheasants (22). Ascites manifests itself by an accumulation of fluid in the abdominal cavity, often associated with liver disease, disturbances of the blood circulation and heart trouble. Factory farmed broilers, factory farmed pheasants – the similarities in lifestyle are striking, though the abuses endured by game birds are more extreme, and go on for longer.

We quoted five references from *Veterinary Record* to ataxia, a disease caused by lesions throughout the nervous system, including the brain. Ataxia has only recently been identified in pheasants. Affected birds stagger, as if drunk.

We drew attention to blindness in pheasants, a condition *'noted in pheasant since the 1980s but its aetiology is unknown'* (23).

We pointed out that tumours in pheasants, especially around the eyes, are frequently noted in *Veterinary Record* as being on the increase (24).

We stated that life-saving antibiotics vital to human medicine are squandered on game birds, needed only because of unacceptable conditions.

We observed that it is when previously bitted and confined birds are moved into 'release pens' that many diseases show up. We put this down to the stress of bit removal, plus the catching process, followed by transport (which may be long-distance). Salmonellas, infectious sinusitis, E Coli septicaemia, avian TB, rotavirus infections and a host of other problems emerge at this time in the birds' short lives, and it's then that gamekeepers turn to their arsenals of drugs.

Enrofloxacin (a fluoroquinolone) is used. The danger to the human population of over-use of this family of drugs is well documented (25). Then there is erythromycin, a broad-spectrum antibiotic used to treat a wide range of bacterial infections in the human population, marketed for animals as Tylosin (and previously used as a growth-promoter). This drug is now in receipt of full authorisation for use throughout the EU, and recommended by the British Association for Shooting and Conservation (BASC) for the treatment of mycoplasmosis, or 'bulgy eye'. For a graphic image of a pheasant suffering from this devastating condition, see BASC's website (26).

We concluded: *'It is shocking that the pheasant, a bird regarded by most as a "natural" food, is contributing to the threat of a return to the "pre-antibiotic era", the time when TB, a childish ailment, a chest infection, an infected insect bite, and countless other ailments, both major and minor, carried with them the threat of premature death.'*

Possible residues of antibiotics in the meat of game birds are perhaps of less concern than the increase in antibiotic-resistant bacteria in the environment.

Not all game birds are eaten: large numbers of them die for sport alone. *'Pheasants are eatable, but hardly anybody eats them...Landowners say they cannot even give them away, and huge numbers of them end up buried in mass graves.'* (27)

*

In 2007 DEFRA's two-year long project *The effects of the application of bits and spectacles in game birds (Code- AW1301)* made depressing reading. In some kind of denial, I suppose, DEFRA stated that *'Despite* [bits'] *widespread use, the effect of these anti-feather pecking devices on the welfare of pheasants has received little attention.'* Not true. Way back in 1985, Olaf Swarbrick, a vet specialising in poultry, had contributed a lengthy article to *Veterinary Record* (Vol 116: 610-617) entitled *Pheasant rearing: associated husbandry and disease problems.* Too bad that no attention was paid to these 'problems' highlighted more than a quarter of a century ago. And it seems DEFRA's in no hurry even now – page 37 of the Project states: *'Further studies are required to determine the behavioural needs and preferences of captive pheasants.'*

Five years on, and DEFRA had no hard figures to accompany their 'studies', which may by now be ongoing. On July 13th 2012 Jason McCartney asked the following Parliamentary Question, only to receive a disappointing reply:

Jason McCartney (Colne Valley): To ask the Secretary of State for Environment, Food and Rural Affairs, how many pheasants are reared for sport annually; and what proportion of them are (a) beak trimmed and (b) fitted with bits.{115661}

Mr Richard Benyon: DEFRA does not hold information relating to the number of pheasants reared for sport annually, or the proportion of them that are beak trimmed or fitted with bits.

*

In November 2008 FAWC published its *'Opinion on the Welfare of Farmed Gamebirds.'* FAWC describes its Opinions as *'...short reports to Government on contemporary topics relating to farm animal welfare. They are a new format of advice to government and were introduced in 2007...They may highlight particular concerns and indicate issues for further consideration.'*

The gamebirds considered in this Opinion are pheasants and partridges, representing, FAWC tells us, an industry with an estimated value to the

UK economy of £1.6 billion. According to FAWC's 2008 Opinion, approximately thirty five million pheasants and five to ten million partridges were at that time released annually in the UK for shoots.

It seems mortality figures were not 'readily available' but apparently stakeholders suggested a likely 5% to 20% up to the time of release, with another 'significant' number of lost birds, those shot and injured, or not shot at all.

*

In the course of its enquiries FAWC visited all kinds of rearing systems, including the infamous cages for breeders. Much of the information in the 2008 Opinion is useful and revealing.

For example, we learn that it's not only specs with pins that pierce the nasal septum: apparently those perfectly legal ones that clip into the nostrils can cause *'eventual perforation of the nasal septum'* (28). How distressing is the word 'eventual' in this context. Bits too are now suspected of damaging the nasal septum.

We're told that partial beak amputation combined with bitting is still carried out, though 'not commonly' (29). Who are these enthusiasts, we wondered, inflicting two tortures when just one would do the dirty work?

Cages for breeders *'in their present form'* are frowned upon, as not offering breeding pheasants *'an environment in which their basic needs to express normal behaviour can be or are being met'* (30). Surely a powerful understatement.

The *'small raised metal cage for breeding partridges in pairs'* also met with disapproval, for the same reasons. The newer models were found to measure approximately 90cm x 30cm and 40cm high (36ins x 12ins x 16ins), and here we learn that some partridges are kept in these miserable little prisons for *'up to three seasons'* (31).

Brails (described throughout the Opinion as 'brailles'), restraints we'd hitherto believed to be tied to a wing to stop birds escaping from open-topped pens, are, we now discover, sometimes used throughout the breeding season in *enclosed* pens too, merely to prevent *'loss by mismanagement'* – in other words, a brailed bird can more easily be caught if it makes a bid for freedom through a gate carelessly left open (32).

The Opinion mentioned a study (unspecified) that suggested a figure of between 25 and 30% of birds *'that die or are lost from the shoot following release and before the start of the shooting season'* (33), confirming our

235

observations that mortality is notably high when birds are transferred to the relative freedom of release pens.

Perhaps the pheasants we'd met wandering the lanes of Bettws Cedewain were 'lost'. We certainly hoped so.

*

February 2010: I noticed a copy of *The Countryman's Weekly* on sale in our local newsagent's. An almost life size colour photo of a pheasant on the cover had caught my eye, along with the wording *Game Rearing – TWO PAGE SPECIAL*.

I took a closer look and noted the signs of suffering: the botched partial beak amputation, the damaged nostrils (aka nares). How could this photo have got past the picture editor? The end of this bird's beak was blunted, with strange additions like stunted feathers growing from it. The nostrils were blocked, apparently completely, as if a protective skin had grown over them. I bought the magazine so I could at least lodge a complaint.

I wrote to Mrs Theresa Dent, Chief Executive of the Game and Wildlife Conservation Trust, expressing Chickens' Lib's disgust at the image. The GWCT is based at Fordingbridge in Hampshire, like the Game Conservancy, but the two are separate organisations (34).

I received a reply from Christopher Davis, a veterinarian attached to the GWCT. After letting me know of the Trust's firm belief in its instrumental role in encouraging the FAWC 'Opinion', he went on to refer to DEFRA's Draft Welfare Code for Gamebirds. This stressed the aspiration that alternatives to management systems that inhibit birds from fully expressing their range of normal behaviours should be 'worked towards'. The code would also recommend that only fully trained and experienced stockmen should fit or remove bits. Etcetera, etcetera.

Mr Davis left any mention of the *Countryman's Weekly* cover photograph until the very last. It transpired that he still hadn't seen it and felt unable to comment, as any such comment would be pure conjecture. Within the doubtless grand and well-staffed walls of Burgate Manor, it seems nobody had been instructed to get hold of a copy of the magazine, let alone asked to discover the source of this blatant representation of illegal abuse.

But there's more to come. Only a few weeks after I'd bought *The Countryman's Weekly*, an article appeared in *Veterinary Record* describing DEFRA-funded research carried out into the condition and behaviour of bitted pheasants, based on birds on eighteen game farms in England and

Wales. And who collated the information on the effects of these bits? None other than Christopher Davis himself! So why the 'pure conjecture' line, when he (and his colleague D.A. Butler) had already admitted that: *'During the present study, bits were found to cause damage to the nares and bills of some pheasants. Most injuries occurred in bitted birds five weeks after bitting, when the birds were more than seven weeks old and it is probable that the bills had outgrown the bits...* [which] *did, however cause inflammation of the nostrils and crossed mandibles in some birds...'* (35).

*

So the cruelty of intensive gamebird rearing goes on. Even before the dawn of that costly day out in the country, when shooting enthusiasts get together to enjoy the company of like-minded people, over one third of the birds specifically reared as gun fodder may have died from disease or fatal injuries.

The remaining targets, now free of bits and brails but probably not of the pain they inflicted when in place, unknowingly await their fate, victims of an industry that knows no mercy.

Chickens' Lib to Farm Animal Welfare Network

By September 1992 we'd changed our name. There were two reasons for this, one more valid than the other. First, the valid one:

Despite our 'poultry only' rule, distressing information about other farmed species did of course concern us. Not only were we in touch with leading organisations worldwide, but we were based in a rural area. We couldn't avoid hearing cows grieving for their lost calves, and knowing that those tiny calves could be exported for the white veal market. We'd witnessed pigs, filthy beyond belief, being forced onto transport wagons, perhaps in for long journeys, knowing that pigs suffer the miseries of travel sickness (1). On a regular basis, vehicles loaded with sheep passed us heading for local markets, some perhaps later to endure transport by sea, and slaughter in countries where the process might be even more haphazard and painful than in Britain. It was hard to turn our backs on all this and the name Chickens' Lib began to seem less appropriate. But in changing to the Farm Animal Welfare Network (FAWN) we'd discarded a clever name, though our new headed paper made it clear that we incorporated Chickens' Lib.

The other reason was perhaps feeble. In recent years, MAFF had come to accept that our pressure group was here to stay. We'd gained a reputation for dealing in facts, and disseminating them with some success. The result was that now we were routinely invited to meetings alongside veterinarians, academics, and those working for long established societies. Together we'd sit around the table and one by one announce the name of the organisation we represented. When it came to my turn, Chickens' Lib sounded a bit light-hearted, almost as if I'd come along to lower the tone.

On these occasions there were always two or three men, always the same ones, who simply refused to have any truck with me, steadfastly avoiding catching my eye. Apparently I was beneath contempt. (Changing our name didn't actually improve things...)

But back to an account of how Chickens' Lib transformed itself into FAWN, an acronym rather too similar to FAWC, we were soon to realize. I did once receive a misdirected invitation to speak at a conference. Had I been bolder, I could perhaps have taken advantage of the confusion.

Not wishing to confuse readers, I'll continue to call our pressure group by its original name – Chickens' Lib.

*

In 1992 we produced a leaflet on the dairy cow, that overworked and generally little understood animal. But surely dairy products are acceptable? The very word 'dairy' has a fresh, reassuring ring to it. But it's an inescapable fact that cows feel deeply for their calves; in order to produce milk a cow must calve annually and the practice is to take the calf from her, often only hours after birth.

In her book *The Secret Life of Cows* (2) Rosamund Young, an organic farmer, writes of cows' strong family bonds. Not only does the mother care for her calf, but the mother of the cow about to give birth, the grandmother if you like, has been seen to show concern and commitment. The author gives the example of Dolly, a cow whose first calving went terribly wrong – the calf died and Dolly's womb was displaced. After the vet had visited, Dolly was made comfortable, propped up and covered with a blanket. But when checked on only an hour later, there was no sign of her. The policy on this farm was to leave gates open for the animals to roam at will and finally, after much searching, Dolly was found three fields away, being licked and comforted by her mother. How the distressed cow had known where to find her mother remained a mystery.

*

We had luck with a photo for our dairy cow leaflet. One gloomy day of heavy rain I steeled myself to take a full bucket of vegetable peelings to the compost heap at the far end of the garden. And there, grazing just beyond the boundary fence, was a cow with the hugely distended udders typical of a productive dairy cow. I hurried indoors for my camera. To my amazement, and despite the relentless rain, the resulting photos were remarkably good.

Our leaflet's wording, accompanying the startling image, ran: *The Milk Machine – producing pintas even while heavily pregnant.* The text on the reverse read as follows:

The Dairy Cow's Work is Never Done!

Produce a calf (have it taken away after only 12-24 hours), give milk for almost a year, produce another calf, more milk... So it goes on, with the repeated distress of birth followed by separation. Traditionally, a cow's udder holds approximately two litres of milk at any one time. THE DAIRY COW'S? A STAGGERING TEN LITRES! Every year, over 50% of UK dairy cows suffer lameness due to deformations caused by huge udders, poor housing (especially in winter) and diseases such as laminitis. John Webster, Professor of Animal Husbandry at Bristol University, has written: "To understand the pain of laminitis it helps to imagine crushing all your fingertips in the door then standing on your fingertips." *Prematurely worn out by physical and mental stress, most dairy cows are slaughtered when around six or seven years old – a cow's natural life span is nearer twenty years.*

THE PINTA CERTAINLY COSTS A LOT
IN TERMS OF ANIMAL SUFFERING.

The leaflet demonstrated fine co-operation between organisations. In addition to our contact details, we suggested that people wanting further information should write to CIWF (they would have far more than we did) or Hillside Animal Sanctuary (where rescued dairy cows were cared for). NSAFF's name was there too, since that organisation had paid half of the leaflet's printing costs.

Early in 2010 Nocton Dairies consortium applied for planning permission for dairy units that would house 8,100 cows and produce 250,000 litres of milk daily on one single farm at Nocton, south east of Lincoln. The cows would be kept indoors and milked three times daily, under a system known as 'all year round' or 'continuous' housing . Milk yield would be higher than average and the cows only allowed out onto pasture in their dry period. Those whose dry period coincided with winter weather would in all likelihood not go out at all.

Compassion in World Farming, the World Society for the Protection of Animals and the RSPCA joined forces in opposing the plan, as did possibly every other animal protection organisation in the country. The problem with planning applications is that moral issues count for nothing, at least when it comes to the welfare and feelings of animals. Objections on the grounds of cruelty, the condemning of cows to boring lives, pushed ever further beyond their natural biological limits – these matters could not and would not be considered. (Chickens' Lib has frequently suggested to planning departments that objections based on morality should be given equal weight to concerns about traffic nuisance, noise, environmental pollution and so on.)

Many objections – on grounds acceptable to Planning – were put forward by local residents. The application was withdrawn following new environmental demands from North Kesteven District Council's Planning Department, only to be renewed a few months later. As might be expected, Nocton Dairies presented its plans as a 'state of the art' venture – only the best of everything for their cows! What they failed to recognise is that cows are intelligent, cows like to make their own choices, and cows' natural food is grass and herbs.

By chance, I heard a radio item mentioning the drying off process in dairy cows, to prepare for the few weeks in the year when milk production ceases. And it set me wondering how painful this process might be. Any woman who has breast-fed will know the acute discomfort of overfull breasts. How do cows cope with the distress of overfull udders, before lactation stops altogether? Hoping for information, I turned to Dairyco, an organisation funded by dairy farmers, only to find that it indulged in anthropomorphism in a big way. In an email dated September 18th 2012 a spokesperson for Dairyco told me that when its members explain the drying off period to children (in school parties visiting farms, I assume) they liken it to the time when an expectant mother goes on maternity leave. Farmers drawing on this comparison must live in hope that no bright child will point out that a cow's baby is snatched away a day or two after birth, leaving the cow to grieve over her loss.

*

On April 29th 2009 a symposium had been held in Copenhagen: *'Experts Unite to Discuss Ways to Improve Dairy Cow Health, Fertility and the Environment'.* Dairy cattle experts and 'management scientists' attended from several European countries, as well as America and Japan, all eager to share their knowledge of recent developments in dairy cow nutrition. USA's Randy Shaver Ph.D. of the University of Wisconsin-Madison's Dairy Science Department apparently took the view that the bodily condition of the cows was not the issue – it was the price paid to farmers for their milk that mattered. Shaver spoke of US dairy farmers' attempts to find cheap replacements to bulk out the diet of a dairy cow: by-products such as soya bean hulls were suggested. His dismissive attitude to welfare rang warning bells. Are British dairy cows to go the same way as America's – confined in vast feed lots, where the animals' food is of the meanest kind, calculated to keep the milk on coming while ignoring the physical and mental health of the cows?

It was depressing to note that Japan, a traditionally dairy-free country, was represented at the symposium. Japan has allowed itself to be seduced by the Western diet, high in dairy products, meat and junk food in general, so it's no surprise that clinical obesity is already in evidence there. Similarly, China's demand for a Western diet has meant a huge increase in suffering, especially for dairy cows. I've just watched footage of a vast circular Chinese milking parlour – a chilling image of animals reduced to the status of machines.

*

'We have seen that the senses and intuitions, the various emotions and faculties, such as love, memory, attention, curiosity, may be found in an incipient, or even sometimes in a well-developed condition, in the lower animals.' So wrote Henry Salt in his 1892 book *'Animals' Rights – Considered in Relation to Social Progress'.*

241

There's a persistent misconception that sheep are stupid, almost amusingly so – people who unthinkingly follow a trend do so 'like sheep'. An article in *Nature* tells a very different story, bringing the maltreatment of sheep into uncomfortably sharp focus (3). *'Sheep don't forget a face – the discovery of a remarkable memory shows that sheep are not so stupid after all,'* ran the heading.

According to the article, sheep, like humans and monkeys, have cells in the temporal and medial prefrontal cortices of the brain, which encode faces. Sheep, again like humans, have a *'remarkable ability to discriminate between, remember and think about many hundreds of individuals.'*

The researchers found that individual sheep could remember 50 other different sheep faces for over 2 years, as well as human faces, even after long periods of separation. Twenty sheep were trained, with the incentive of food rewards, to discriminate between frontal pictures of pairs of sheep. Eventually, the sheep achieved an 80% success rate.

The conclusion to these experiments was that a sheep's capability for long-term recognition of faces is similar to a human's, and that sheep may remember and feel emotion about other sheep even in their absence.

It's something to think about, when you see one of those double-decker vehicles thundering past on the motorway, loaded with sheep on their way to market, or perhaps just beginning a long and arduous journey to end their lives in two or three days' time in some foreign slaughterhouse.

*

In 2000 we produced a sheep leaflet, pointing out the serious welfare problems afflicting large numbers of UK sheep. Sheep are different from most farmed animals – many are not confined on farms but roam on deserted hillsides, basically looking after themselves for much of the time.

Before going to print with our leaflet we turned to Professor John Webster, to ensure that our information was correct. We'd sent him a copy of a photo we intended to use of a sheep in Wales, grazing on its knees. Professor Webster emphasised that sheep do sometimes naturally graze on their knees. It's when they *move forward* on their knees that foot rot and lameness must be suspected.

In the same year, 2002, the opening paragraph in *Veterinary Record* of an article about lameness in sheep drew attention to the problem thus: *'The issue of* [sheep] *welfare is becoming increasingly important in UK farming, particularly as the contemporary economic difficulties in the livestock industries have led to concerns that, owing to their marginal value, fewer diseased sheep may be receiving veterinary attention.* The results of a survey sent to sheep farmers seemed to suggest that the downturn in their economic fortunes made no difference to the amount of veterinary care received by their sheep. However, the authors of the VR article had their suspicions: *'This evidence must be considered in the light of the possibility that many farmers may have provided responses that they perceived to be acceptable or desirable to the administrators of the survey, or to the general public...it appears that, despite acknowledgement by farmers of the importance of welfare issues relating to ovine lameness and other locomotor disorders of sheep, there remains great potential for the occurrence of preventable or incorrectly treated cases among sheep in the study area.'*(4).

The study area had been the Scottish Borders and it so happened that Duncan and I had a holiday in that very region, shortly after Chickens' Lib's new sheep leaflet saw the light of day. While there, we noted several flocks of sheep exhibiting lameness and on return reported each one to the Scottish Executive's Environment and Rural Affairs Department. I received a rather chilly letter from a Divisional Veterinary Manager in response to mine: every location I'd reported had been tracked down and the owners identified, he said. He ended his letter by stating the obvious: that any advice given would be based on farm animal legislation, or recommendations in the codes. It all read like a put-down. However, a much more encouraging reaction came via a telephone conversation I had with a different vet from the same department. He'd received our leaflet and considered we were 'doing an excellent job'.

*

Bites from insects and infestation with mites can cause acute itching and distress to sheep and almost total wool loss, a condition illustrated on our leaflet. Now we were to read that, distressed by the suffering he witnessed, John Williamson, a farmer all his working life, had blown the whistle on the appalling conditions among sheep in his area. Consequently the *Highland News* published some of the photographs he'd taken showing emaciated sheep, their skin raw and almost devoid of fleece, left to die and rot in fields (5). Mr Williamson accused government vets and the Scottish Society for the Prevention of Cruelty to Animals of turning a blind eye to the suffering of sheep. His revelations lead to the conviction of a young farmer, who was jailed for three months.

But sheep don't only suffer in the uplands of Scotland or Wales. Hillside Animal Sanctuary in East Anglia – where it's largely flat and often dry – has found evidence of appalling examples of foot rot so advanced that animals' feet were virtually worn away (6).

*

One of the outings on offer during the 1993 Poultry Welfare Symposium in Edinburgh (described earlier) was a visit to a deer farm; Irene and I decided to join that trip, thinking we were bound to learn something useful.

We'd heard that deer are shot while grazing in their fields – surely infinitely preferable to death in a slaughterhouse – and that the other deer seem not to be alarmed and in fact they scarcely look up as their companions thud to the ground. This smacked of a general lack of sensitivity on the part of deer, a theory soon to be discounted.

Surprisingly, the owners of the farm had chosen this of all days, with a coach load of visitors expected, to separate the mothers from their young. The scene was harrowing, as the mother deer crashed against the doors of their pens, desperate to get to their young. Then we knew for certain that deer are as sensitive as other species, at least when it comes to having their offspring snatched from them.

*

It was at around this time, when Chickens' Lib had recently embraced other farmed animals, that we met Wendy Valentine, who went on to found Hillside Animal Sanctuary. At Hillside animals are allowed to live out their days in comfort, sheltered from the harsh conditions often meted out to 'food animals'.

But Hillside is a campaigning sanctuary too. It investigates and publicises abuses to animals as well as giving them shelter – and it came into being as a direct result of yet another taste of MAFF's all too familiar stance.

In fact, the story of how Hillside began is deeply disturbing.

Hillside Animal Sanctuary

In 1994 I received a phone call from Wendy Valentine. She introduced herself as the founder of Redwings Horse Sanctuary and explained she was ringing for advice about a shocking discovery she'd just made. She and a friend over from America had been out walking in the countryside near Norwich when they'd come upon six low, windowless buildings. The door at the end of the nearest one stood open and the two women had ventured nearer, curious to see what was inside.

The scene they came upon was to change Wendy's life. She described to me the cages jam-packed with hens, live birds standing on long-dead ones, forced to lay their 'farm fresh' eggs against decomposing bodies trodden almost flat, barely recognisable as hens.

In the belief that they were doing the right thing, indeed the obvious thing, the two friends hurried back to Wendy's house and quickly returned with cameras. Surely the authorities would want evidence of these appalling conditions? This 'farm' must be exposed and closed down without delay!

*

Now, armed with excellent images, Wendy was unsure just where to turn for help. It happened that her American friend knew about Chickens' Lib and suggested that Wendy get in touch.

We advised Wendy to phone the local Ministry of Agriculture (MAFF) offices, in Bury St Edmunds. This was the correct course of action: their vets had powers of entry and it was MAFF's job to deal with farmers acting illegally. I tried to sound positive but felt little optimism, more a sinking feeling that we were about to come up against that old brick wall.

I offered to phone MAFF too, hoping that Chickens' Lib's input just might strengthen Wendy's case. Though far from popular with MAFF we did have a reputation for knowing our facts, and the law. Although we'd not seen these premises, it was agreed Hillside and Chickens' Lib would try a two-pronged approach. Quite early in the morning I spoke to the duty vet, a woman, expressing our concern. She sounded genuinely shocked by what Wendy had told her, now reinforced by me, and promised that she would inspect the premises that same day.

*

This is where I should, by rights, be able to say 'Imagine my astonishment when...' but I wasn't astonished, for what happened next was to follow a familiar pattern. When I phoned in the afternoon, the same woman vet spoke to me but by then she seemed like a different person. Yes, she said, she'd been to the battery in question and found no welfare problems.

And yet, while insisting there was no evidence of suffering, she'd sounded upset. In fact, I was convinced she was fighting back tears; certainly she was nothing like the concerned, professional woman of only a few hours ago. I could only conclude she'd been silenced by her superiors, and that Wendy Valentine and Chickens' Lib were together witnessing a cover-up of a most serious kind.

Innocent at that stage of the ways of officialdom, Wendy had approached MAFF expecting help and support. She'd assumed farmed animals would be protected and that rapid action would be taken to prevent further cruelty. But within a day Wendy was to join the ranks of the bitterly disappointed – those who 'do the right thing' only to discover that farmers acting illegally are spared prosecution time and time again, shielded by the very department responsible for drawing up the animal protection laws. Once again, we were to confront officials caught in the trap of their government department's own making.

*

From this point I'll let Wendy take up the story, as she told it in her first newsletter about factory farmed animals, written a few months later: *'Then, following what I believed to be the correct procedure, I went, accompanied by our vet [Redwings' vet] to report the farm to the Norwich Ministry of Agriculture, Fisheries and Food (MAFF). Initially they seemed to be very concerned and promised to visit the site (of which they had not previously been aware) that morning. They telephoned me later in the day with a completely different attitude saying that they had found nothing at the site which contravened the Welfare of Battery Hens Regulations 1987. I just could not believe what I was hearing...I feel it is an extremely frightening situation if MAFF, the body who police the welfare of farm animals and also the food for human consumption, have covered up such a serious situation. What else is going on that the general public may never be aware of?'*

Wendy suggested that those receiving her newsletter should write to the then Minister of Agriculture, the Right Hon. William Waldegrave. The newsletter was illustrated with five colour photographs, showing dead hens, filthy cages, droppings-encrusted eggs and a heap of droppings, rotten eggs and decaying hens piled up beneath the lowest cages in one of the units. The reverse of the newsletter was taken up with a concentrated fact sheet that we'd provided, outlining the legal situation and key points about the battery system.

At that time some forty million hens, accounting for 85% of the national flock, were trapped in battery cages because the general public were buying their eggs. The fact sheet ended with the plea: *INSIST ON FREE RANGE!*

*

November 10th 1994: We wrote to the Minister about the farm Wendy had stumbled upon, expressing amazement that its owner would not be prosecuted for cruelty. The reply, from the Minister's Private Secretary, was predictable. Peppered with phrases about 'understanding your concern' we were told that *'...our Private Secretary was unable to disclose any further details of this individual case, but could confirm that the Veterinary Officer in question found no evidence of contravention of the law...'.* Sickeningly familiar, yet extraordinarily inappropriate in view of the photographic evidence of conditions that flouted MAFF's own legislation to a startling degree. It seemed that yet again MAFF could call black white, and simply get away with it.

By early in 1995, Wendy's tireless work to expose cruel exploitation of farmed animals had begun. Quite soon she had set up Hillside Animal Sanctuary, based in Frettenham, Norfolk, to be extended some thirteen years later by the addition of Hillside Shire Horse Sanctuary at nearby West Runton.

Since the founding of Hillside Animal Sanctuary, its investigators have uncovered conditions on numerous farms and in slaughterhouses (both legal and illegal) where laws have been broken. They've not only filmed conditions in factory farms but in units boasting free range eggs, even, on one occasion, 'organic' eggs being sold under the Freedom Food logo. (That farm's FF accreditation was subsequently withdrawn.)

In 2001 Hillside, in co-operation with Animal Defenders, investigated two Bernard Matthews turkey farms in Norfolk. Under the heading *'Matthews is probed over turkey horror – RSPCA may bring charges'* the *Daily Mirror* (January 11th) reported on the vile conditions in the sheds – birds lying dead, others with festering wounds and one bird with a growth covering one eye completely. Following the report in the Daily Mirror, a former worker came forward, stating: *'The video pictures are a completely accurate account of what life is like on a Matthews' turkey farm. These birds had terrible deformities because of growth promoters. Some birds were carrying live maggots in their wounds.'*

No prosecution resulted from the investigation. How very fortunate for Mr Matthews.

*

As a result of 2003 surveillance by Hillside, a duck farm owned by a well-known company was featured on the BBC television programme 'Inside Out'. The TV interviewer asked a DEFRA vet if it would represent a breach of legislation if sick, trapped, blind and ailing ducks were found in the sheds, to which the vet replied: *'Yes, Absolutely.'* Notwithstanding video evidence using Global Positioning System equipment (GPS records the time, date and location of filming) this company was found not guilty of cruelty. Footage of this duck farm is included in Hillside's DVD *'Ducks in Despair'.*

In 2003 a particularly dreadful example of abuse of turkeys was exposed by Hillside. Dead and dying birds were filmed, some deformed, others sightless, heads pecked raw. A dreadful smell pervaded the area, tracked down to a mass of dead turkeys, left to rot in a heaving sea of maggots. Almost unbelievably, part of this farm boasted well-trusted welfare accreditation. Yet despite all the evidence of suffering no prosecution resulted. Images of the turkey farm in question can still be seen on Hillside's website, but there's no way that viewers can experience the stink from the filthy birds or from the fly- and maggot-infested piles of 'deads'.

I've just been re-reading a copy of a letter I wrote to Norfolk's Trading Standards department, dated October 14th 2003, concerning this same farm. At Hillside's request (seconded by us) Trading Standards officers had visited the farm four days previously. In a telephone conversation with me, a TS officer claimed to have been 'appalled' by what he saw. However, he stressed it was DEFRA's view that must count in the end, whenever a welfare inspection is involved. And, as we know to our cost, veterinarians' opinions are paramount and often highly contentious.

In my letter I'd listed key points shown on Hillside's video: birds with bloodied heads (the injuries clearly of long-standing), birds with enlarged hock joints, indicating a painful and entrenched condition, birds with diseased feet, damaged eyes (some missing altogether, the result of aggressive pecking) feather loss on backs (from aggressive pecking), birds with faces so severely pecked as to be scarcely identifiable, birds unable to walk, so likely to die from starvation. And birds who were just plain filthy.

In view of this long list, I wrote: *'I fully understand that only DEFRA is in a position to pass judgement on veterinary matters, but am a little surprised that the health aspect of food production is apparently out of your hands. Clearly, rotting carcases, clouds of flies, millions of maggots and severely unhealthy birds (some perhaps destined for human consumption) do relate to standards required for food production.'*

My notes on a telephone conversation I had with a DEFRA vet at Bury St Edmunds about this same farm went as follows: This Ministry vet had, on October 10th, found the farm to be *'quite a nice turkey farm.'* He'd considered the owner, and a stock person to whom he'd spoken, both to be *'concerned about the birds.'* He had looked into all seven sheds, so was basing his opinions on twenty seven thousand turkeys. The owner had told the vet that he'd *'had the RSPCA round.'*

On October 16th I phoned DEFRA's Head of Animal Health and Welfare Strategy Unit in London and spoke to Ms Diana Linskey. I indicated my unwillingness to continue attending meetings at which DEFRA initiatives were discussed, if the department had a hidden agenda in the shape of a determination to continue with cover-ups such as we and Hillside had witnessed over many years.

*

October 20th 2003: Yet again, I phoned DEFRA's Divisional Veterinary Manager (DVM) at Bury St Edmunds. He admitted, when pressed, that some birds on the turkey farm were affected by *'some quite recent injuries,'* though *'not all were recent'*. Astonishingly, he claimed it wasn't easy to judge conditions on the farm from Hillside's video footage, though apparently it had been good enough to show to the owner, who was now aware that he *'had a problem.'* The DVM said the turkeys had been *'fairly close to slaughter'* and that things were *'a little unfortunate'*. He then suggested that he and I were *'coming from different directions'*. I said I was coming straight from the demands of current legislation and he admitted that I was *'quite right'* regarding the legal obligation on farmers to make daily inspections of intensively farmed turkeys and to ensure that any injured or sick bird is isolated or culled.

In the course of the conversation the matter of trespassing was raised. When I asked how he expected people to know about cruelty to factory farmed animals other than via trespass, since most abuse went on behind closed doors in windowless sheds, the DVM seemed to feel himself at even more of a disadvantage. Certainly he had no pat answer ready.

I also pointed out that DEFRA's vets numbered around two hundred, to cover many thousands of farms holding livestock. And I reminded him that DEFRA, on its own admission, didn't even know the location of many farms.

In 2009 yet another shocking example of a welfare-accredited farm was publicised on TV, this time on Channel 5's Five News report. A free copy of the broadcast is available from Hillside. An additional and disturbing find on this farm was a note to employees from the farm manager warning of an impending inspection by a representative of the welfare scheme in question. Details of this damning note can be seen on www.hillside.org.uk/about-investigations.htm and it seems that this practice was, and may still be, par for the course.

*

Not all the animals found by Hillside in dreadful conditions are intensively kept – severe foot rot in sheep, and pigs living outside in squalor have also featured on the sanctuary's list. Yet, despite ample evidence, few incidents of abuse uncovered by Hillside have ended in the courts.

Among those that have, are convictions for cruel slaughter. Take the farm in Ripon, North Yorkshire, where, in the year 2000, sheep and goats were filmed being ritually slaughtered in a filthy shed and left to die in agony. Michael Hawkswell, one of the two defendants, admitted that the meat butchered by Isap Lakha was sold to Indian restaurants and to butchers' shop all over the country. The pair were given custodial sentences, Hawkswell receiving four months and Lakha two. Both were banned from keeping animals for ten years.

There was more illegal Halal slaughter, this time on a farm in Norfolk. Hillside filmed goats being butchered with blunt knives and again left to die slow, painful deaths.

There's a vitally important point to make here. It is unusual for Hillside investigators to venture even as far as North Yorkshire: almost all the cases of cruelty and neglect uncovered by the sanctuary have been in or near Norfolk. And this suggests the scale of the problem: illegal conditions such as those revealed by Hillside, Animal Aid, Compassion in World Farming, Advocates for Animals (now OneKind) Viva!, PETA, Chickens' Lib/FAWN and many others are to be found all over the United Kingdom.

Some of the worst offenders cannot be classed as struggling small-time farmers but are 'leading lights' in the industry. In 2000, and again in 2007 Hillside exposed a battery farmer who was well respected in NFU circles, having served on its poultry committee for several years. Despite official inspections following welfare complaints by Hillside, with accompanying video proof of hens in shocking conditions spanning a period of seven years, no action was taken against this man.

*

In 2009 Hillside discovered illness and neglect in yet another welfare-accredited farm, this time a pig farm. And the question must be asked: where are the inspectors responsible for ensuring that much-trumpeted higher standards are in place?

Some startling figures appeared in *Meatinfo* of February 19th 2010, regarding the exponential growth of Freedom Food (FF). 'Freedom Food' pigs had seen a 23% increase, from nearly 1.6 million in 2008 to 1.9 million a year later, accounting for 20% of UK annual pig production, according to the RSPCA. Inclusion of ducks in the FF scheme had grown by 84%, FF ducks now accounting for 42% of all UK duck production, and turkeys increased by 17%, accounting for 7% of UK production.

Surely a vast number of inspectors would be required to check on that huge number of animals? Who knows how many farmers involved in Freedom Food and similar schemes might hold the premium that goes with the logo uppermost in their minds, rather than animal welfare? And how often, if ever, are these welfare-logo-bearing farms inspected without prior warning?

It is obvious that thousands of suitably qualified inspectors, working on a basis of unannounced visits, would be required to ensure the viability of such schemes.

*

The list of atrocities found by Hillside investigators seems unending. In February 2011 undercover filming taken in late January was shown on Channel Five news (the item delayed by the dramatic turn of events in Egypt). A flock of ducks, reared at the time for Waitrose, was filmed at catching time. As the team of three catchers waded among the terrified birds (some severely disabled) they were seen to toss live ducks into the main throng of birds to urge the others on, one catcher lobbing a live one

across the shed for no apparent reason. While on the farm, the investigators saw a letter announcing that Waitrose was to visit on a certain date
– how courteous of Waitrose, to give ample warning of its 'inspection'!

*

Much of the last part of the above section is more about Hillside Animal
Sanctuary than Chickens' Lib. My excuse for this detour is that Chickens'
Lib was closely involved with the incident leading to the setting up of
Hillside. We have followed Wendy's progress with great interest, often
supporting her in representations to officials and on occasions attending
meetings with Hillside, alongside representatives from Freedom Food and
the RSPCA's Farm Animals Department.

As a pick-me-up after the above descriptions of abuse and incompetence,
I suggest a visit to Hillside Animal Sanctuary's website: www.hillside.org.
uk. It's so good to see animals being given what they deserve – a life
worth living.

*

In 1997, just three years after our first contact with Wendy Valentine and
after many years of frustrations of our own, we came upon some riveting
information. Apparently our disgust with the ways of the Ministry of
Agriculture, Fisheries and Food had been shared, but not by 'activists'
this time.

On this occasion, the frustration came from within the very heart of
officialdom.

A telling obituary

It was with the greatest interest that we read an obituary for a leading
MAFF veterinarian. Following an initial tribute to Thomas Whyte Stobo,
Veterinary Record published a second one, dated April 12th 1997.

Mr P.A. Sweeney wrote of his late friend Tom Stobo: *'In 1938 he
embarked on his illustrious career with the Ministry. After a year in
Warwickshire he was promoted to deputy regional veterinary officer. This
position entailed a lot of travelling as he was also responsible for Cheshire,
Herefordshire, Shropshire, Staffordshire and Worcestershire...In 1965 he
became regional veterinary officer for Lancashire and Yorkshire...During*

252

the next four years he became increasingly disillusioned with the work he had enjoyed...When he saw instances of welfare being compromised and his reports of abuses being suppressed he had had enough. A year before he was due to retire he asked to be released.'

What did that penultimate sentence mean? To us, its significance was clear. It meant that complaints by Mr Stobo were just not getting dealt with. Reports of welfare abuses, possibly perpetrated by high profile individuals or companies, were being swept under the carpet.

We wrote to MAFF, we wrote to the Chief Veterinary Officer. Then we wrote (more than once) to Glenys Stacey, at that time Chief Executive of the State Veterinary Service (now re-named Animal Health). We gave our interpretation of the sentence and asked for an alternative explanation. None has yet been offered.

*

The significance of the above obituary can hardly be exaggerated, nor can the fact that our pleas for an alternative interpretation to our own have been systematically ignored. But the silence from officialdom is understandable.

Successive governments have had no wish to highlight the inevitable welfare problems that occur within systems that they themselves have painstakingly enshrined in legislation. Furthermore, keeping on good terms with farmers would seem to be a priority – why else would 'welfare inspections' so often be made by arrangement, and so seldom end in prosecutions?

By the way, DEFRA *et al.,* it's not too late for that alternative explanation for Mr Stobo's early retirement. Chickens' Lib would still love to hear from you.

McLIBEL – THE BEST FREE SHOW
IN TOWN

The McLibel trial is now world famous, iconic even. And so are Helen Steel and her co-defendant Dave Morris, who stood up to McDonalds and, in truth, saw Goliath off. With remarkable courage they both refused to be intimidated by the threat, and later by the actuality, of being sued for libel by that giant corporation.

As members of Greenpeace London (no relation to international Greenpeace) Helen and Dave had, in the 1980s, been engaged in giving out leaflets entitled *What's wrong with McDonald's*. The accusations had covered many grounds: the destruction of rainforests (to make room for beef cattle to graze), the luring of children into unhealthy diets, the littering of our streets with discarded packaging, the health risks from fatty and sugary foods, poor employment conditions...and the assertion that McDonald's food production involved cruelty to animals.

Assuming that these two 'ordinary' young people would prove a pushover, McDonald's issued its writ for libel. So began what, by December 1996, was to have become the longest trial of any kind in English history. And no doubt one that McDonald's dearly wished they'd never embarked on. Having their dirty washing hung out for such an awfully long time could never have been part of the company's plan.

*

One evening in 1994 my office phone rang. It was Helen Steel. She'd called to ask if I would be an expert witness in their case, on matters connected with poultry. We didn't know each other then, but she'd read my book *Chicken and Egg; Who Pays the Price?* and appeared to think me a suitable person. Which was more than I did at that moment, as I clutched the phone, trying to keep calm.

Me, an expert witness in London's High Court? The prospect was awesome, in the proper sense of the word. I had no idea what the possible implications might be. Would I compromise Chickens' Lib in some unforeseen way, if I agreed? Was I up to the task? I promised Helen I'd think about it.

Of course I wanted to support the two defendants. McDonald's was responsible for encouraging a relentless promotion of cruelly produced eggs and cheap chicken, worldwide. But I had been alarmed by the prospect of the High Court and the mysteries of legal matters, and by the huge responsibility involved.

The next morning I turned to the RSPCA's legal department for help, and it was explained to me that the role of the expert witness is neutral. He or she is simply there to help the Court to come to a proper, informed decision.

Now at least I understood my role. I phoned Helen back and it was agreed I'd help. My appearance as an expert witness turned out to be in the summer of 1995.

*

Much has been written about the case, and a DVD made (1). There's the McSpotlight website too (2), where the entire proceedings may be accessed, so there's no call for a detailed account of the case here. I'll just give a flavour of Chickens' Lib's input.

*

The intelligence and tenacity of the two defendants amazed me. They were able to absorb the necessary information as they went along, working astonishingly long hours while desperately keeping one step ahead of their next daily appearance, brushing up their knowledge on the Tube on the way to the High Court, pushing themselves way beyond normal exhaustion for what they believed in – free speech and, in this case, the right to criticise a multi-national.

In the early days, voluntary support from a young barrister, Keir Starmer (now Director of Public Prosecutions), had encouraged Helen and Dave, especially since others had pointed out the hopelessness of taking on McDonald's. Throughout the long trial, the defendants were able to drop into Mr Starmer's chambers for vital discussions on how best to proceed. As time went by he'd seen them developing into potentially *'very good lawyers'* (3).

*

For a while Helen and I were in frequent touch, as I sorted out relevant papers on slaughter, on the sordid living conditions endured by broilers, the cruelties of severe feed restriction for the parent stock, the deprivation of caged hens, their diseases and close confinement. I was lost in admiration, seeing how quickly Helen boned up on these subjects, many details of which were new to her.

*

Before I was due in court I sat in on a day's proceedings, to familiarise myself with the strange goings on of the legal system. Dr (now Professor) Neville Gregory, at that time a senior research fellow in the Department of Meat Animal Science at Bristol University's School of Veterinary Science, was acting as the expert witness on poultry and pig meat, for McDonalds.

Initially, this confused me. I'd known Dr Gregory for some time, through his valuable work on poultry welfare. He'd helped me in the past, checking the accuracy of a complicated Chickens' Lib's fact sheet on chicken slaughter. My gut reaction was to wonder what he was doing there, supporting McDonald's. Then I reminded myself of what I'd been told – that the role of expert witness was to help the court to come to a proper decision.

In the event, Dr Gregory was a brilliant expert witness, and presumably no comfort at all to McDonald's, as he consistently confirmed the grim conditions for poultry described to him by Helen Steel. During Helen's questioning of Dr Gregory he volunteered something about broiler breeders that I hadn't heard before – they can be so hungry, he said, that they resort to eating the litter from the shed floor. On a lighter note, it emerged that Sun Valley's broiler litter was, on occasions, composed of shredded bank notes.

*

Helen Steel's meticulous questioning of Dr Gregory, and of Sun Valley's Group Technical Manager Mark Pattison, laid bare many welfare problems inherent in modern chicken meat operation, from the breeding stock to the rearing stage, and ending on the slaughter line. During slaughter at SV, pre-stun shocks were occurring, and the system of neck cutting, especially important if the stun fails, as it sometimes did at the SV plant, was unsatisfactory, leading to the strong possibility of chickens remaining conscious even up to the last stage – the scalding tank.

In his February 1993 report on a visit to Sun Valley's slaughter line Dr Gregory had stated that the company had not been adhering to the Ministry of Agriculture's Code for the Welfare of Poultry at Slaughter. Neither was Sun Valley ensuring cardiac arrest at the water bath stage, nor was it severing both carotid arteries at the neck cutting stage. Taken together these omissions severely limited the chances of a humane death, chances further diminished by the company's habit of stunning birds at 60mA per bird, precisely half the strength generally regarded as acceptable.

*

Many of the claims made in a document issued by McDonald's *'Animal Welfare and Husbandry – McDonald's Position',* were revealed as false. For example:

- *'McDonald's insists that animals used in its products are reared in a clean, safe, hygienic, comfortable environment, and that humane methods of killing are used.'* My comment: The words used above to describe conditions in broiler units are totally inappropriate, and the slaughter line at Sun Valley was found to be in urgent need of improvements.
- *'Chickens used for McDonald's products are not reared in cages. They have the freedom to move around at will.'* My comment: Using the 'not caged' argument is a tired old red herring, since no meat-type chickens are caged. And, especially towards the end of the growing cycle, broilers' freedom of movement is severely restricted.
- *'Sun Valley complies with the strict EC legislation regarding poultry rearing.'* My comment: At that time there was no specific legislation for broiler chickens. The first such EU legislation would be introduced in 2010.
- *'This* (the battery cage system) *is the company's preferred system for egg production because it is hygienic and efficient, providing a clean, low-risk environment which enables eggs to be separated from the hens and their droppings.'* My comment: I had no first-hand experience of Oasters Eggs, sole provider of all McDonald's egg requirements, but 'low-risk environment' was deceptive – all caged hens are at very high risk of developing brittle bones and many other cage-related

ills. As to 'hygienic' – that's not a word that springs to mind, when describing the inside of a battery shed.

McDonald's list went on, shamelessly shot through with inaccuracies and misleading statements.

*

On my first day as an expert witness, I arrived at the High Court much too early. I wandered around the area, hoping to find somewhere for a reviving coffee, but London was still half-asleep. Only McDonald's was open. I'd never once been into a McDonald's, never wanted to, but with the doors of every café in sight closed, on that morning its brash interior looked hugely tempting. Even so, I went without my coffee. Just suppose I'd been spotted, relaxing in McDonald's ...

*

Richard Rampton, the QC acting for McDonald's, tried his hardest to discredit me. Sounding exquisitely bored, he warned Mr Justice Bell that I had *no* qualifications to back up my claim to be an expert witness, indeed was not worth listening to. The implication was that I was a fraud.

To some extent this was true, at least the first part. A diploma in clarinet teaching was hardly relevant. Earlier, Mr Justice Bell had expressed the fear that I would operate on 'instinctive judgement', in view of my campaigning record. I suppose he meant the *'well she would say that wouldn't she?'* syndrome. He was concerned too that I hadn't seen into any Sun Valley farms, or visited their slaughter plant (Sun Valley, its name a supreme irony, was the sole provider and slaughterer of McDonald's UK chicken meat). I think at that stage the judge assumed the broiler system could be perfectly acceptable; nor did he know that I had in fact asked Sun Valley's management if I could visit one of their farms, and even steeled myself to ask to observe their slaughter line. Not surprisingly, considering Chickens' Lib's reputation, both my requests had been refused.

But by the time I entered the witness box, Mr Justice Bell had decided he could listen to me. He explained that in his opinion there were two ways of arriving at expertise – one through the normal channels (appropriate qualifications), the other exemplified by my method: hands-on experience and meticulous information gathering (not quite his words, but that was their import). Maybe hearing that we'd received the RSPCA's *Lord Erskine Award* in recognition of our campaign to improve poultry welfare upped my status in his eyes. Whatever had brought about the change of heart, I was now a *bone fide* expert witness.

Despite that, Mr Rampton was soon up to his old tricks again. We'd recently produced two videos. The first one, *Chicken for Dinner?*, though made on a shoestring budget, contained some brilliantly emotive shots and the script comprehensively exposed the cruelly deprived lives led by broiler chickens. Our second video, *'Sentenced for Life'* described the battery hen's severe deprivations. The defendants wanted our videos shown in court. Mr Rampton did not. Sounding once again bored almost beyond endurance, he explained to the judge that he'd watched them both over the weekend, and M'Lord would gain nothing from seeing them!

Even at the time I thought this wasn't a very clever move. Might it not encourage the judge to view our videos? Did Mr Rampton fear their impact? In the event Mr Justice Bell announced that he *would* view them both.

Having Chickens' Lib's videos shown in the High Court was way beyond our expectations. Not many people were present, but that didn't matter. It was the judge whose opinion we wanted to influence, and he watched with attentive interest.

*

Helen, having by then absorbed a mass of information about battery hens and broiler chicken farming as well as the complicated anatomical and technical facts about slaughter, made the very most of her knowledge, frequently leading up to the entrapment of witnesses for McDonald's, as cleverly as any fully trained lawyer. Little by little she exposed the serious welfare problems at that time inherent in Sun Valley's and Oaster Eggs' husbandry systems, and the unsatisfactory state of SV's slaughter line.

I'd expected to appear in the witness box, on and off, for two whole days. The afternoon of the second day was the slot for my cross-examination by Mr Rampton, and I was looking forward to it.

But I was to be disappointed. Mr Rampton announced in his customary bored-to-tears voice that he 'had *no* questions for Mrs Druce'.

I like to think he was afraid he just might have ended up on the losing side.

*

June 19th 1997: I attended Mr Justice Bell's long-awaited verdict, a 45-page summary of his 800-page Judgement. The defendants won on some issues and lost on others. When it came to poultry matters I listened in delight, almost in disbelief. Here was outright condemnation of cruelty to poultry, mostly based on the systems *per se*. Below are some of the judge's comments, which we soon circulated widely:

On slaughter at Sun Valley: '*A proportion of the chickens that are used to produce the First and Second Plaintiffs' food are still fully conscious when they have their throats cut. This is a cruel practice for which the plaintiffs are culpably responsible...in my overall judgement those (charges) that are justified, relating to the restriction of movement of battery hens, broiler chickens and chickens which have their throats cut while still fully conscious are sufficient to justify the general charge that the First and Second Plaintiffs are culpably responsible for cruel practices in the rearing and slaughter of some of the animals which are used to produce their food.*'

Of the battery system: '*I conclude that the battery system as described to me is cruel in respect of the almost total restraint of the birds and the incidence of broken bones when they are taken for slaughter.*'

Of Sun Valley's broilers: '*Sun Valley's stocking density is what they think they can manage in order to make money without matching loss...I have already referred to the Second Plaintiff's Animal Welfare and Husbandry sheet on "Chicken – Sun Valley", which says that the chickens have freedom to move around at will. In my judgement that is palpably untrue of the last few days, at least, of their lives in Sun Valley houses...I can see no reason why at least 7% of broilers, and possibly more, should have to suffer the discomforting leg problems with which they live on. In my judgement it involves cruelty.*'

And of broiler breeders: '*My conclusion is that the practice of rearing breeders for appetite, that is to feel especially hungry, and then restricting their feed with the effect of keeping them hungry is cruel. It is a well-planned device for profit at the expense of suffering of the birds.*'

*

In the years following their libel action McDonald's took steps towards improving their image. Battery eggs were replaced by free range ones, conditions for these sounding well above average (the company insists on tree cover on the range, a significant benefit for the birds, and an encouragement for them to use all of the range). This has led to McDonald's winning the RSPCA's Good Business Award two years running. Another award for McDonald's has been CIWF's Good Egg Award.

McDonald's now supports Oxford University's Food Animal Initiative. One project of the FAI (www.faifarms.co.uk), jointly run with the World Society for the Protection of Animals, is to establish an international network of viable, humane and sustainable farms.

Much was made on the McDonald's website (4) about the company's pride in sponsoring the 2012 Olympics, and information about farm visits that would be on offer. I doubt whether any of their broiler chicken production facilities were opened to visitors. I imagine that 'biosecurity' might have come in useful, keeping the public at a safe distance from scenes which some may have found disturbing.

Meanwhile, the battles go on, worldwide. On June 23rd 2010 *Mailonline* reported that the Center for Science in the Public Interest (CSPI) was threatening to sue McDonald's for its *'creepy and predatory ploy'* of enticing children into their restaurants (via pester power) with the promise of presents of toys (5).

A new word has entered the language to sum up what has happened to those fast-food restaurants seeking to dominate the world's eating habits. And that word is McDonaldization.

*

To sum up : In 1997 a High Court Judge deemed three intensive poultry systems cruel – battery cages for laying hens, the broiler system, and broiler breeders' feed restriction. Not only were the systems indicted, but the specific companies responsible for inflicting suffering on the birds, too. In addition he condemned many aspects of poultry slaughter, some of which may yet apply in slaughterhouses today.

The UK's 'David and Goliath case' should surely encourage prosecutions of the perpetrators of intensive systems. Had the McDonald's libel case been a criminal one, its outcome could have changed the lives of millions of abused poultry.

I rest my case.

Nearly a controlled explosion

In Spring 1998 we wrote to our supporters: *'We're at the moment preparing a leaflet which will be suitable for display in churches...the leaflet's message will be endorsed by Church of England bishops (how many, we don't yet know...)'.*

It turned out that thirty-two bishops were willing to sign, and we were sincerely grateful to each and every one of them.

On the front of the leaflet we quoted the Bishop of Dover, the Rt. Revd. Richard Llewellyn: *'All animals, in their complexity and beauty, must surely concern Christians, since they are part of Creation. During this century farm animals have been exploited on an unprecedented scale. Many now experience little other than misery from birth to death as factory farming systems deprive them of any comfort and – as scientific research confirms – cruelly frustrate nearly all their needs. The battery cage system, which produces most of Britain's eggs, is a prime example of such systems. As Christians, we must surely do all in our power to bring an end to this lack of proper respect for God's creatures.'*

*

July 18th 1998 marked the beginning of the Lambeth Conference, an event that takes place every ten years or so, when Church of England bishops from all over the world gather to discuss burning moral issues of the day. This one, the thirteenth, was presided over by Britain's Archbishop George Carey, and we'd learned that 749 bishops would be present.

Perfect! Without prior planning, we had a leaflet tailor-made for the occasion and hot off the press. We made a parcel of the necessary number (plus a few spares) and posted it off to the conference venue in Canterbury, along with a polite covering letter: we'd be very grateful if each bishop could be given a leaflet, was its gist.

A day or two later I took a phone call from the Canterbury police. Our leaflets had caused 'a great deal of disturbance', an officer informed me, our parcel nearly becoming the subject of a controlled explosion. While I listened, I was picturing seven hundred and forty-nine bishops, resplendent in their finery, being hustled outside to somewhere reckoned to be a safe distance from our parcel bomb. Some dismal car park, maybe, earmarked as the gathering place in the event of fire.

Rather decently, all things considered, the Archbishop's Public Affairs Officer, Mr Louis Henderson, later replied to us on Dr Carey's behalf, thanking us for the leaflets and letting us know that copies of the leaflets had been made available to all the bishops attending the Lambeth Conference. It appeared no grudges were borne, despite the alarm and disruption caused. We were heartened!

But we heard nothing from any of the bishops. Not one word.

*

Later, we were to read that the most hotly debated issue at the conference had been homosexuality within the Anglican Communion. It was decided, by a vote of 526 to 70 that *'homosexual practice... is incompatible with Scripture.'*

How wonderful, Violet and I agreed, if, instead, the ghastly debasement of animals in the name of cheap food had been hotly debated; how heartening if *that* had been deemed incompatible with Scripture.

*

My father had died in 1991, and three years later Violet moved to a residential home in Harrogate, to be near my sister. From there, she continued to fire off campaigning letters. Early in 1998 she'd written to the Archbishop of Canterbury yet again, and received a reply, dated January 19th 1998, from the same Public Affairs Officer who'd written to us about our leaflets' narrowly avoided fate.

Once again, the fact that the Archbishop was the Vice Patron of the RSPCA was given as reassurance and proof that he had made his views clear on animal welfare. Mr Henderson then stressed that the Archbishop could not impose his views on the Church as a whole.

But why not, we wondered? After all, we're talking about the very people who claim to revere God's creation. Surely abused farmed animals should automatically come within reach of the church's compassion, and was not the Archbishop, of all people, in a position of influence?

The abomination of factory farming needed to be condemned from every pulpit, as once it was in York Minster by our dear Patron the Bishop of Salisbury.

Baby foods and school dinners – food for thought

We'd been looking into what goes into baby food and school dinners. In 1998 I'd written to H.J. Heinz Company Limited asking their Consumer Contact Manager, a Mr Brian Hooker, if 'spent' hens were still to be found in Heinz Baby Foods, and on May 15th I phoned him for a chat. During this conversation Mr Hooker stated that Heinz used spent broiler breeders, and it sounded as if this was the company's preferred source, perhaps its only one. In one way this came as a relief, for some highly disturbing information had come to us years earlier.

Alastair Mews, when Chief Veterinary Officer at the RSPCA, had told me that in some slaughterhouses for 'spent' hens the electrical current was set low, to minimise the shattering of the vulnerable birds' bones. Shards of bone in the meat would be highly undesirable in pastes and soups, even more so in baby foods! This practice ensured a dreadful end for battery hens; many were reaching the knife, and even the scalding tank, fully conscious. I have no way of knowing if this calculated cruelty has continued into the twenty-first century.

Mr Hooker's written reply, dated June 5th, was more guarded, and less specific. He referred to carefully selected suppliers and to safety and quality, to independent veterinary checks and exacting standards. However, it seemed that the company didn't actually specify any particular type of poultry. So maybe spent broiler breeders were not the only type of chicken on offer to babies. Spent battery hens too may have been in the mix.

*

It proved hard to find out much about the national scene and eventually we limited our fact finding to West Yorkshire. Kirklees' Catering Service informed us that the chicken 'chunks' used in West Yorkshire school meals were derived from battery hens, and that dehydrated or minced chicken (quite probably from battery hens too – at that time spent hens were just about worthless, so definitely a bargain) was used in 'Chicken Teddies'. What were Chicken Teddies? I queried. It seemed they consisted of re-hydrated chicken meat formed into Teddy Bear shapes.

The baby food scene continued far from reassuring. A lady speaking for Cow and Gate baby foods told me their producers operated in line with standards so their products are fit for human consumption. We were all too well aware that standards for human consumption of meat could be rock bottom, with millions of farmed animals reared amid filthy conditions. Not only the animals, but babies and schoolchildren too surely deserved better.

Feeling we had the beginnings of a good story, and one that urgently needed telling, I contacted one of the serious Sunday newspapers, and an arrangement was made to meet two journalists in London, over lunch. I explained that I was vegan, so it would be helpful to go somewhere with a suitable menu – Indian perhaps? Yes, yes, they agreed, a good idea. Then the message came to meet them at *Le Pont de la Tour*, a restaurant where, I am told, Tony Blair had wined and dined President Clinton (and doubtless Cherie and Hillary too).

Anxious not to be late, I arrived much too early and hung around. I told a hovering waiter that I was expecting friends, and sat people-watching as a stream of immaculate thirty-somethings poured in. Stockbrokers? Bankers? It was interesting to speculate (speculators too, in all likelihood). As the minutes ticked by I felt increasingly like a bag lady, and half expected to be thrown out.

Eventually, the two young men did arrive, and we sat down and consulted the menu. In the event, they chose what they wanted, two excellent lunches, while I made do with a huge heap of rocket and some dry bread (though a little dish of olive oil was rustled up, at my request). I chomped my way through as much of the chewy greenery as I could, my thoughts turning to rabbits, wondering why on earth this place had been chosen. The answer, I suppose, was obvious – my journalists desired only the best, on expenses. And to hell with vegan diets!

They seemed interested in what I had to tell them, and made noises about following the story up, but nothing happened. Had they used their wits, they could have beaten Jamie Oliver to it, and perhaps saved a generation of small children from the insult of those tragic Chicken Teddies.

The battery cage ban at last?

January 28th 1999: The European Parliament votes for a ban on battery cages throughout the European Union – a huge step forward for animal welfare, and recognition of all the hard work by activists throughout Europe. As long as egg quality, and above all morality, are set aside the battery system works brilliantly: without sustained campaigning over the years, there might have been no end to one of the cruellest animal husbandry systems ever invented.

With the necessary endorsement by all EU Farm Ministers achieved, on July 19th 1999 Council Directive 1999/74/EC was published (1), setting down minimum standards for the protection of laying hens, and including a date for the ban – January 1st, in the year 2012. In addition, various minimal improvements in cage space were set out, to be introduced during the years leading up to 2012, a date which gave farmers thirteen whole years in which to scrap their cages.

Yet the Directive contained a fatal flaw. The enriched cage system, with its empty gestures to better welfare, is not included in the ban. The ban only applies to what have become known as 'barren' battery cages – those containing no 'furniture' (of which more later).

Right up to 2010 some countries (Poland and France are two examples) were asking for the date to be pushed into the future. France, as a founder member of the EEC/EU, had no excuse for its inaction but many EU Member States had only recently joined, and their egg production was still largely dependent on barren battery cages. The sheer impossibility of all twenty-seven countries being able and willing to abide by the cage ban by the legally required date was obvious.

Looking beyond the ever-expanding EU, there are few signs of an impending ban on cages, barren or enriched. As things stand, billions of hens are destined to spend their days standing or crouching on sloping grid floors, unable even to spread their wings, debeaked, neglected and abused from day one until they meet a terrifying death.

VIOLET SPALDING 1908-1999

My mother's health deteriorated in 1998, and the following October she died.

For a long time, Violet had been unable to take part in active campaigning – I'd been the one attending meetings in London on Chickens' Lib's behalf. But the moral support had been there. Even now I find myself, just for a split second, thinking I must let her know about some interesting development on the campaign front.

Along with the big events I remember little things, like the two of us having a celebratory drink in a dingy pub in Wakefield (we must have had time to kill, while waiting for a train). The House of Commons Agriculture Committee's Report had just been published, with its recommendation for a ban on battery cages in their present form 'say, five years from now' (2). That was in 1981– a full thirty-one years before the scheduled EU-wide cage ban, with all its shakiness and imperfections. What a blessing that we couldn't foresee just how slowly and feebly the wheels of progress would turn.

In our Christmas newsletter we wrote to our supporters: *'Old established Friends of FAWN will be very sad to hear that Violet Spalding (Clare's mother) died in October...An intrepid campaigner, she saw the inside of many a horrific battery and market, demonstrating fearlessly outside (and inside!) the Ministry of Agriculture and challenging conditions on appalling "farms" and markets, before such activities were commonplace... Her contribution to the fight against factory farming was considerable, and will be remembered with gratitude.'*

Shortly after Violet's death, Mark, our daughter Alison's husband, wrote about Violet. His poem expressed so much about her life that I've included it here. The title reflects the fact that in her youth Violet had been a fine singer.

Exhalation for a Singer

The breaths she took were massive,
and the change she made was deep.
The air she trapped and then let go
by war then peace then war was shaped
and met this world's numb cold full on
to take offence and make defiant
sympathy with simple pain.
She was not going to stand for it.

In the darkness there would be flowers
and in the silence there would be song
for a tune is like a long, long life,
formed in the air, but born in the lungs.
The world she made was massive
and the breaths she took were deep.

Mark Robinson 1999

*

1999 was a difficult and sad year, not only for me but for Irene too. She signed her last Chickens' Lib newsletter that spring. Exhausted after nursing Eric through a long illness, she decided after his death that it was time to 'retire'. Of course I understood, but I greatly missed her invaluable help and excellent company. And I must add that in spirit Irene has never retired and still does everything she can, in a personal way, to carry on the fight.

*

Penny Perkins had by now worked with us for a long time, and she took over many of Irene's tasks, so enabling Chickens' Lib to continue. Together we discussed future campaign tactics and sent out leaflets, videos and newsletters, while Penny valiantly kept the office side of things in order.

ENRICHED CAGES – A GAPING LOOPHOLE

Despite years of sustained campaigning against *any* form of cage by all serious animal protection organisations, the 'enriched' version of the battery cage for laying hens is, as stated earlier, not included in the 2012 ban on the barren battery cage.

In 2012 the RSPCA launched its new campaign opposing the enriched cage. February 2012's issue of *Poultry World* quotes the Society's senior scientific officer as saying: *'The message we want to drive home is that, despite the new welfare law, hens will still be kept in cruel cages.'*

But what exactly is an enriched cage?

Basically it's still a battery cage, the birds living behind bars on metal or plastic grid flooring, the cages stacked up in tiers, many thousands of hens to a building. Compared to the old-style cage, there's mandatory additional floor space per hen measuring roughly the size of a postcard (CIWF's graphic comparison), bringing the entire minimum space per hen to 750 sq. cm (116 sq. inches), little more than the area of a sheet of A4 paper.

According to the EU Directive, enriched cages must include a perch, a nesting box and a claw shortening device, plus precise provisions for food and water supplies – all necessary to a hen, but wildly inadequate as supplied in an enriched cage, especially in the case of the nesting box. The very term 'nesting box' sounds comforting – cosy almost. But in the enriched cage context it's simply a curtained area, behind which the hen finds the same sloping cage floor, the grid now covered in matting of some kind. Not a wisp of straw, no soft material with which to arrange her nest.

Back in April 2001 *Poultry World* published an article entitled *Practical Experience of Furnished Cages* (for 'furnished' read enriched). Accompanying it was a photo of ADAS international poultry consultant Arnold Elson crouching in a back-breaking stance, peering into the bottom tier of enriched cages at ADAS's experimental farm, Gleadthorpe. As in the barren battery cage, effective inspection of hens in the bottom cages is unlikely to happen. To make matters worse, in the enriched cage the very presence of nesting boxes must render thorough inspections, as demanded by law, virtually impossible. Even if a poultry worker does attempt to carry out his work properly, engaging in the painful feat of kneeling, crouching etc. for substantial stretches of time, how are effective inspections to be achieved where nesting areas exist? How will the worker judge what the hen behind the plastic curtain (which he or she may or may not pull aside, in order to get a proper view) is up to? Might that hen *not* in fact be laying an egg, but instead seeking refuge from the stress of cage life? On the other hand she may be severely injured, or simply dying of Cage Layer Fatigue, having finally given up the struggle. With built-in obscured areas, admittedly of vital importance to the laying hen, the prospect of thorough daily inspections of the individual birds is virtually nil, rendering the whole system illegal *per se.*

*

Now take a moment to imagine a free-ranging hen's day: she'll be walking, running, perhaps indulging in a little low flying, laying an egg, hopefully with straw available so she can construct her nest, searching around for herbs, worms and insects. Under natural conditions, a large proportion of a hen's day is spent foraging and research has proved that she definitely prefers to work for her food rather than eating from a 'given' supply (1).

She'll be feeling the grass under her feet, maybe sunbathing, certainly dustbathing, freely spreading her wings, grooming with space around her, choosing her companions, planning her next activity, and deciding when it's time to roost for the night. It is no wonder the welfare movement is in general agreement that the enriched cage fails utterly to provide a suitable environment for creatures capable of such a wide range of activities.

Back in February 1994, Keith Pullman, then editor of the United Kingdom Egg Producers' Retail Association, foresaw this scenario: *'Any thoughts that... the enriched cage will satisfy the anti-intensive farming brigade is really clutching at straws. I am told that the Farm Animal Welfare Network (incorporating Chickens' Lib) now employs 13 full time staff between their various groupings and, on top of that, add the RSPCA's vast wealth, and you can see that the welfare issue is going to run and run.'* Well, Mr Pullman was seriously wrong about our thirteen-strong staff, but certainly right on the first point – that enriched cages will never satisfy the 'anti-intensive farming brigade'.

In 2010, in its *Opinion on Osteoporosis and Bone Fractures in Laying Hens* FAWC stated that bone fractures are common in hens in enriched cages, pointing out that the suffering incurred will *'severely compromise at least four of the Five Freedoms, i.e. freedom from discomfort; freedom from pain, injury and disease; freedom to perform normal behaviour and freedom from fear and distress.'*(2) This same *Opinion* also states that catching birds in enriched cages is difficult and new fractures can be caused at this time (3), thus confirming our fear that when hens are grabbed and pulled from 'enriched' cages, the obstructions caused by perches and curtained 'nesting boxes' will compound their suffering.

*

I've seen the enriched cages at ADAS's Experimental Husbandry Farm at Gleadthorpe in Nottinghamshire, legal as far as the EU Directive goes but grossly inadequate for hens' needs. Designed to hold four or five hens, these looked much like the barren battery cage, while including the minimum statutory additions – the nest boxes, perches etc.

Perches were 5cms (two inches) or so off the floor, in effect taking up precious ground space. For hens stuck in what is in fact a battery cage, perches do offer a vast improvement on permanently gripping a harsh sloping grid floor, and it's been observed that in enriched cages they spend much of their time perching. In view of this, I'd not be surprised to see *'The adverse effects on the laying hen caused by excessive perching'* as a future research project, grasped at by some poultry scientist casting around for funding.

Perhaps the most glaringly unattainable provision in the EU Directive, and one I've not yet touched on, is for *'litter such that pecking and scratching are possible'* (4). Interestingly, true dustbathing, that vital activity if a hen's feathers and skin are to be kept clean and healthy, is not mentioned. That is surely because all those involved in drawing up the 'provisions' recognised the impossibility of supplying dustbathing material within the confines of cages. At Gleadthorpe, a small square of artificial grass purported to fulfil the Directive's demand for somewhere to peck and scratch. I deemed the medium both futile and unhygienic, since droppings would surely get lodged in the plastic 'grass'.

As mentioned earlier, hens in battery cages perform mock or 'vacuum' dustbathing, so compelling is the instinct to keep feathers and skin in good condition. Knowing the vigour with which hens go about this activity, it is obvious that in a unit holding thousands of birds, a large proportion of them in elevated cages, the air would become thick with particles of dust, sand or whatever material was provided, plus feathers, skin, and much else. Since hens and workers alike would suffer, it's no wonder that the EU directive simply ignores this vital need.

*

I've also been able to see colony-style enriched battery cages, this time on a working farm. Colony cages can hold any number of hens, as long as the required 750 sq. cm (116 sq. inches) of floor space is allowed for each bird, plus the 'extras' demanded in the Directive. Cage manufacturers may multiply this space per hen as many times as the industry wants. Some of the colony cages I saw held up to sixty hens.

This farmer also kept hens in conventional battery cages, still legal at the time of my visit. I'd asked beforehand if I could see these too, but he'd refused, doubtless fearing I'd be looking for trouble (and he could have been right).

Therefore I was surprised when he showed me into what seemed at first glance to be a huge, very modern conventional battery unit. He'd had a change of heart! Gleaming metal cages stretched away into the distance, and there was that familiar unending clamour of hens' voices. It took me a few seconds to realize that this was the colony house. There were of course many fewer divisions between the elongated cages. At least the hens could make their way from one end of the cage to the other for a bit of exercise, but not with ease, on the sloping grid floor. And they'd forever be jostling for space with their fellow inmates.

In this unit, the set-up boasted an ingenious idea for providing 'litter for scratching and pecking', as demanded in the Directive. Once or twice a day a small quantity of chicken food was automatically distributed in one corner of each cage, onto, I seem to remember, a little area of plastic 'grass'. And no doubt the hens did attempt to scratch and peck in it, simply for something to do.

Next, we climbed a metal staircase to an upper level of cages, to view a re-run of downstairs. Now I was even more aware of the magnitude of the operation. Here were thousands more caged hens, their lives devoid of true meaning.

*

Under the heading 'Colony system gets thumbs up' *Poultry World* (September 2009) describes the Hy-Line/Griffiths/TECNO system installed at Oaklands Farm Eggs (director Gareth Griffiths), where each cage houses eighty birds. Studying *Poultry World's* accompanying photo of Hy-Line's TECNO system, it seems to me that those hens in the lowest tier of cages must live in deep gloom. Though superior to the non-colony cages on show at Gleadthorpe, colony-style cages nevertheless suggest nothing more than a new and chilling version of factory farming.

For further information about Oaklands Farm Eggs' massive operation in Shropshire, visit www.oaklandsfarmeggs.co.uk where you can read how their 'girls', responsible for producing around 500 million eggs a year, 'have moved house' and are 'sitting pretty', in their new cages. Oddly, it doesn't seem possible to view these new homes, in amongst the razzmatazz about good welfare and superior eggs.

On December 8th 2011 a spokesman for Oaklands Farm told listeners to Radio 4's 'Farming Today' how the hens queue up in 'regimental' fashion, awaiting their turn in the nesting area, suggesting to me that the provision for laying in colony cages is totally inadequate to meet the hens' needs.

*

February 2010: *Poultry World* informed readers that: '...*orders are in the pipeline for 10m enriched cage places in the UK over the next two years.*' This figure implies a significant proportion of hens (around 20% of the probable national flock) are, theoretically, destined to spend their lives trapped in cages. The photo accompanying the article clearly showed that the hens had been debeaked. From their state of the art cages they peer out, craning their necks, just like any old-style battery hen.

However, the enriched cage may prove not to be the best of investments. *Poultry World* (February 2012) reported the following downturn in Oaklands Farm Eggs' profits: '*A massive investment in enriched colonies by Oaklands Eggs has not yet seen the expected returns from the market. According to financial results presented to Companies House, pre-tax profits for the year to April 2011 came to just £2.23m on a turnover of £44.78m, compared with a profit of £3.05m in the six months to April 2010.*'

*

Research in The Netherlands found that in colony cages housing twenty or more hens, feather-pecking leading to mortality all but reached a horrendous 22% in birds with intact beaks. FAWC, when investigating enriched cages, quoted research indicating that in enriched cages holding larger numbers of birds mortality in general was high, and 'medium' when caused by feather pecking 'and/or cannibalism' (5). Given these statistics, 100% partial beak amputation looks likely to be the order of the day. Little wonder that DEFRA has so often stepped back from naming a date for the abolition of this mutilation.

Another serious welfare problem exists when birds are permanently caged. Fed finely ground food unsuited to their physical and mental needs, and with no opportunity to search out alternatives, they develop oral lesions (mouth ulcers). 1986 research by Dr Michael Gentle showed that lesions start to develop at six weeks of age in chickens given such a diet. By week thirty, all the chickens he was observing displayed lesions. Oral lesions are caused when particles of food stick to the inside of the birds' mouths, attracting bacteria and possibly blocking salivary ducts (6). In a letter to me dated May 30th 1988, Dr Gentle offered his opinion that birds with oral lesions suffer extreme discomfort or pain.

*

As long ago as 1982 we'd contacted Desmond Morris about the plight of the battery hen. Without delay he helped the cause by writing a memorable article for the *Sunday Telegraph's* 'Opinion' column. Here's an extract from it: *'Anyone who has studied the social life of birds carefully will know that theirs is a subtle and complex world, where food and water are only a small part of their behavioural needs. The brain of each bird is programmed with a complicated set of drives and responses which set it on a path to a life full of special territorial, nesting, roosting, grooming, parental, aggressive and sexual activities, in addition to the simple feeding behaviour. All these other behaviours are totally denied the battery hens.'* (7)

Any form of cage fails utterly to fulfil the needs of laying hens. It's a tragedy that the poultry industry refuses to shake off the factory farming mindset, but continues to encourage the fabrication of the next generation of hen prison cells.

*

Compassion in World Farming has instigated a scheme whereby Good Egg Awards are given to bodies that pledge to source eggs from barn or free ranging hens only. Companies already signed up include Cadbury's

Crème Eggs, McDonald's Europe, Subway and many others, including supermarkets. Local authorities are taking the pledge throughout the UK too, meaning non-cage eggs are now used widely in schools, prisons etc. The hens' best hope is that CIWF's awards will squeeze out a good number of cage-obsessed farmers.

I'm glad to say CIWF gives a Rotten Egg Award too. A recent one went to Tesco, a company apparently wedded to the stocking of (then still legal) eggs from hens in barren battery cages. In 2010, 1.3 million hens could have been spared the misery of cage life annually, if Tesco had pledged to ban these eggs (8).

Since 'battery cage-free' surely must include 'enriched-battery-cage-free', it's just possible that the boast for those orders in the pipeline for 10 million enriched-cage hen places may backfire, the cage enthusiasts finding themselves the proud owners of thousands of empty cages.

*

In the spring of 2012 Hillside Animal Sanctuary carried out an investigation of an enriched cage unit. *The People* subsequently published a photo of the trapped hens, an image that told the whole squalid story of suffering. Apparently almost as closely stocked as in the old 'barren' battery cages, feathers in poor condition, some perching on uncomfortable, badly designed perches, a glimpse of that ludicrous patch of imitation grass...(9).

As a result of the EU's token cage ban, the outlook for millions of laying hens in Europe remains grim.

*

Equally tragic for the hens is the enriched cage scene in the USA. In United Poultry Concerns' Spring-Summer 2012 issue of *Poultry Press*, its president Dr Karen Davis explains that legislation entitled *Egg Products Inspection Act Amendments of 2012* will assure the future of the 'enriched' cage, while giving the barren cage an unspecified but, in the words of the Humane Society of the United States, *'ample phase-in period'* before any ban is put in place (10). I'm not qualified to explain the complexities of US legislation, but here are some facts:

On their website, United Egg Producers describe themselves as a co-operative of egg farmers from across the United States, owning approximately 95% of all the nation's egg-laying hens. In 2011 the Humane Society of the United States (HSUS) and United Egg Producers (UEP), formerly bitter opponents over the caged hen issue, agreed to work together for federal legislation to ban the barren battery cage at some unspecified future date. (Karen Davis tells me that originally the date of January 2030 was proposed.) But, as in the EU, the so-called enriched or colony cage would not be included in any ban.

Presumably HSUS saw this as an overall improvement to a shocking scene, but Karen Davis disagrees strongly with HSUS's capitulation, quite rightly I believe. In Karen's words:

'Until 2011, the HSUS campaign for cage-free egg production had the U.S. egg industry scared. Fear of HSUS led UEP to "reach out to HSUS in March 2011," Gregory told Feedstuffs. *Would HSUS president Wayne Pacelle be receptive to "a transition to enriched colony cages as an option to ending our conflict?"*

The rest is "history". HSUS and UEP now both say that abandonment of cage-free ballot campaigns is the only solution. Both sides stress that their pact is a financial solution.

Under the new dispensation, battery cages, albeit "enriched" with new plastic furniture that will soon be filthy, will be enshrined. Once the U.S. egg industry invests $4 billion-plus dollars into converting to "enriched" cages with their zillions of "welfare" devices, the system will be in place. Ditto in the European Union.' (11).

The dilemma as to whether it's better to fight on for significant improvements or to accept something that's only marginally better, while hoping to push things further at some future date, is familiar to everyone concerned with animal welfare. After all, it is the animals who are suffering. Is not a small slice of the cake better than the spectre of none at all?

In the case of 'enriched' cages, I think the picture is crystal clear. Allowing battery cage units (euphemistically called 'colony barns' in the States) to seal the fates of countless millions of hens for the foreseeable future is as useless, in terms of welfare, as it is wrong.

United Egg Producers has a website (12). It shows hens in barren battery cages. To the untutored eye, the hens, though crowded, look pretty good, heads down, enjoying their food, food they don't even have to search around for! But look closer.

To anyone familiar with the 'cycle' of the battery hen it appears these hens have not been long in their cages, perhaps a mere week or two, for their feathers are still in good condition. And the feed troughs have just been filled, so at the moment of filming the hens are busy.

And now look at their savagely mutilated beaks. That's something that no film, however keen to promote a cruel system, could hide.

Outlawed in Europe

Violet and I first met Peter Singer in the 1970s and we'd kept in touch over the years. A young Australian, he'd been studying at Oxford and campaigning with a group of friends against factory farming.

Now dividing his time between the posts of part-time Professor of Bioethics at the University for Human Values at Princeton and part-time Laureate Professor at the University of Melbourne's Centre for Applied Philosophy and Public Ethics, Peter is now known throughout the world for his writing, much of it on philosophy and animal rights.

Following a meeting with Bill Hawks, Under-secretary for Marketing and Regulatory Programs at the United States Department of Agriculture (USDA), Professor Singer, who describes himself as having a 'strong but strictly amateur interest in the field of farm animal welfare', came to realise that *he* knew more about what was happening in European agriculture than did Mr Hawks, and probably, as he put it, 'the entire United States Department of Agriculture' (1).

Around the year 2000, Chickens' Lib's funds were dangerously low and we'd sent out an urgent appeal to all our supporters. Professor Singer came back with the suggestion that we might write an account of the progress achieved in animal protection legislation in the EU. This would be published in book form and Chickens' Lib would be paid for the work involved, so easing our financial situation.

Grateful for the promise of help, I agreed to this interesting plan but soon realized the enormity of the task before me. Daunted, I turned to Compassion in World Farming's campaigns manager Philip Lymbery and asked him if he'd be interested in co-authoring the book. Mercifully, Philip agreed to find the time, and in the end both Chickens' Lib and CIWF benefited when *Outlawed in Europe* saw the light of day two years later.

In Peter Singer's words: '*If the people responsible for animal welfare in the United States Department of Agriculture know nothing of the most significant improvements in animal welfare for decades, it is fair to guess that most people in the United States, and even some members of animal rights or animal welfare organizations, will be equally unaware of what is happening across the Atlantic. This book is intended to provide the information that is needed, in the hope that greater awareness will lead to a desire among Americans to do something about the shocking cruelty to farm animals that is being addressed in Europe, but is continuing to occur on American farms.'* (2)

There were many significant legislative improvements to record, some already in place, others with a future date set for enactment: for example, the abolition of crates for calves and the practice of depriving the young animals of iron and roughage to promote 'white' veal (outlawed in Britain since 1990 thanks to CIWF founder Peter Roberts' inspired efforts) would be banned throughout Europe by 2007.

Sadly, the picture remains far from rosy for some calves reared for veal – it's still legal to keep them confined for rearing and fattening in individual crates for the first eight weeks of their lives. The main improvement, apart from the shorter time-scale for isolation, is that the stalls/pens *'must have perforated walls which allow calves to have visual and tactile contact,'* and, most importantly, the calf must be able to turn around (3). For a virtually newly born and utterly dependent calf, life must seem harsh and lonely, but better than in the old days of total isolation, living in near-darkness, unable to see neighbouring animals, forever unable to turn around. Having said that, many British farmers have totally abandoned the crate concept, keeping calves in small groups from the start. But thousands a year are unwanted for any purpose, and are shot shortly after birth.

A similar pattern existed for sow stalls, in that they were already banned in the UK and Sweden, the prohibition to be extended to all EU member states by 2012. I well remember an intensive pig farm Irene and I came upon, one hot afternoon. There'd seemed to be nobody about on the farm, and we'd peered into a long shed. Inside, crammed into individual stalls, were the sows, perhaps a hundred of them. Our unexpected appearance took them by surprise, and they all started to their feet in alarm, struggling to get upright within the close confines of the surrounding bars. Thankfully, that cruel way of keeping highly sensitive and intelligent animals is now outlawed throughout Europe.

In 2002, an estimated 99% of US laying hens were kept in battery cages with no hint of a future cage ban, while the EU already had a forthcoming ban in place, albeit a highly unsatisfactory one.

Listing the improvements in Europe had been satisfying. There were areas of progress for activists to be proud of. And yet my sense of satisfaction on seeing the finished book was limited. Despite improvements, so many of our farmed animals continued to suffer! Depressed, I raised this with Louise van de Merwe. Wisely, she commented that legislation marked the first and vital stage in the fight – without legislation in place stating what *should* happen, the battle to abolish cruelty to farmed animals would be even harder to win.

MAFF to DEFRA

In 2001 the Ministry of Agriculture, Fisheries and Food (MAFF) transformed itself into the Department of Environment, Food and Rural Affairs (DEFRA). An article in *The Independent* questioned the effectiveness of the new look: *'Dreams do sometimes come true. The dearly held wish by campaigners for a change in agricultural policy, most recently about how foot and mouth disease is being tackled, and for the culling of MAFF itself, has been raised at least in name. But with the departure of Nick Brown as minister of agriculture, and Margaret Beckett's arrival as minister in charge of the Department of Environment, Food and Rural Affairs, is it a case of MAFF is dead, long live DEFRA, or plus ça change?'* (1)

From this point onwards in the book, the erstwhile MAFF becomes DEFRA.

The risks we take

BIRD FLU – FACTORY FARMING'S LITTLE PRESENT

'Treat chickens, turkeys and ducks like dirt. Cram them by the thousand into dimly-lit, windowless sheds. Deprive them of fresh air and sunshine. Be 100% sure they're vulnerable to infectious diseases. Force them to live 24/7 on a build-up of their own faeces. Once they've gone to slaughter, stockpile

their manure (often contaminated with body parts) on farmland. Finally, if the deadly H5N1 bird flu virus is present, ensure it's accessible to rats, foxes and wild birds. And humans.

AND THERE YOU HAVE IT – A RECIPE FOR DISASTER! '

So ran the wording on our postcard sent to supporters with our February 2007 newsletter, following the confirmation of an outbreak of bird flu on a Bernard Matthews turkey farm. Actually, we provided everyone with several cards, with a dozen or so suggestions as to possible recipients – the usual suspects, ranging from the Chair of the British Medical Association to the Archbishop of Canterbury.

The hosts of the Highly Pathogenic Avian Flu virus H5NI are poultry and wild birds, and the danger of the virus mutating into a form highly contagious among humans is real. Were this to happen the consequences worldwide would be serious, potentially catastrophic. Some scientists believe that the deadly 1918 pandemic of "Spanish" flu, which killed many millions worldwide, occurred when avian flu crossed the species to humans.

The H5NI virus can survive outside the bird, in its faeces or carcass, for around five days in warm weather, but for up to thirty days or more in cold temperatures (1). During an outbreak of avian flu in Britain, farmers still persisted in spreading used poultry litter (and all it may contain) on fields (2). Amongst all the talk in the media from experts in *their* fields (bacteriologists for example) I heard no mention of this dangerous practice. Why is the link between lazy, unhygienic behaviour and the spread of deadly diseases not being shouted from the roof tops?

What does the World Health Organisation have to say about avian flu? *'There is a constant risk that the H5N1 will combine with another strain of influenza,' said Dr Takeshi Kasai, Regional Advisor for Communicable Disease Surveillance and Response. 'The influenza virus is unpredictable; in areas where H5N1 is endemic, WHO and its partners are working to build surveillance systems to identify changes in the behaviour of the virus, raising awareness about the risks and protective measures, and building skills and capacity to respond to outbreaks quickly.'* (3)

It's amazing how many risks we humans take in the name of cheap poultry. Dr Aysha Akhtar (US Food and Drug Administration and the Oxford Centre for Animal Ethics) has pointed out that havoc can be wreaked without the horrors of terrorist attacks. Society can achieve a similar effect simply by cramming billions of birds into factory farms, creating a worldwide laboratory for infectious diseases.

Police visit number three

We'd not long been in our latest house when I had another visit from the CID, on this occasion by appointment. The time, eleven o'clock in the morning, had been arranged several days in advance and the purpose of the visit made clear. By association I had been involved in a theft of battery hens, somewhere in the south of England.

Several months previously, I'd received a letter requesting help from a young man who'd been part of a team rescuing battery hens from their cages – a night raid, I presumed. Our letter writer had been the one to drive the van to the scene of the 'crime', and he'd been the one caught. He was about to be prosecuted while the others, those who'd gone into the sheds, had slipped through the net. I'd been more than pleased to help, and sent the defendant anything I thought relevant: items connected with the law, and the suffering of battery hens. Perhaps the police had found our literature when searching his house, hence their trip to Yorkshire.

At the time of their visit we were having a conservatory built onto the back of the house. The garden was a sea of mud, cement mixers grinding away, men at work – never mind, I thought, my visitors would come to the other door, the proper front door.

I was vacuuming the living room at around nine o'clock (more displacement activity than necessity) when the two detectives appeared, having used the wrong entrance, picking their way through squelching clay and over treacherous trenches, and arriving two hours early. I did wonder if it was a ploy to catch me unawares, up to some unspecified but illegal behaviour. Rather put out by their premature appearance, I showed them up to the 'office', telling them they could look at anything they wanted to, while I went downstairs to make coffee.

By now, the campaign had shrunk dramatically from its former grand size. We'd moved to a smaller house, partly because we no longer needed space for storing stacks of posters and leaflets; now, much of the archival stuff could be put up in the loft. The present office doubled up as a spare bedroom for two of our granddaughters, who often stayed overnight. There was enough space in the room for one single bed, and we'd bought a new metal cabin bed, so office things could be kept under it, at floor level. The purchase was soon regretted, since the space below became something of a no-go area to anyone but the most highly motivated. Penny's desk was squashed into one corner of the room, mine into another, and shelves of files lined the walls. The set-up did serve its purpose, just about, but to trained eyes may well have looked like a cover for suspicious activities.

I brought the coffee up and the three of us had a friendly discussion that got the two detectives precisely nowhere, since I knew nothing that could help them with their enquiries. One of them had smallish children and he happily took a copy of *Minny's Dream* away with him.

It transpired that both officers had been inside the battery from which the hens had been rescued, and been appalled by what they'd seen. So, on the basics we were in complete agreement.

*

Who knows, the police may still be looking for those activists who took a few hens away from the living nightmare of a battery shed.

In Chickens' Lib's opinion, and as Violet had often said, the true criminals were those perpetrating the animal torture. And we didn't just mean the farmers. Much of the blame must lie with government officials, those sitting at their desks with nothing to lose and doing none of the dirty work, while failing utterly to ensure that the country's animal protection laws, penned and endorsed by their own department, are upheld.

Pâté de foie gras

Many organisations have done much more than we ever did to draw attention to that cruel 'delicacy' – *foie gras*. But now we felt we should at least support the general campaign. *Foie gras* is obtained by force-feeding huge quantities of food to helpless ducks or geese a few weeks prior to slaughter, until their livers grow to many times their normal size. The procedure, when food is rammed down the birds' throats via a metal funnel, is known in France as *gavage*.

DEFRA assures us that there's virtually no chance of anyone being allowed to set up in *foie gras* production in the UK, yet there is no prohibition against its import or sale. Consequently, it's available in 'high class' stores and regularly served in restaurants in the UK. One such restaurant was in Raymond Blanc's beautiful hotel in the Cotswolds, Le Manoir aux Quat' Saisons.

It was Mr Blanc's much trumpeted enthusiasm for all things organic and wholesome that especially took our attention – all those luscious vegetables and herbs, whenever possible gathered fresh from his hotel gardens, as seen on TV! How could Mr Blanc claim to serve wholesome food while *foie gras* featured routinely on his menus? If Mr Blanc were to ban *foie gras*, those chefs still determined to keep this disgusting product on their menus just might take note and follow his lead.

In 2007 we produced postcards, scores of which must have made their unwelcome arrival at Le Manoir. In addition, we copied the wording from our first *foie gras* post card onto a pre-drafted letter to the Minister of Animal Welfare, Ben Bradshaw, so our supporters could let him see that it wasn't just 'animal lovers' who objected to *foie gras* – scientists saw it our way too. The post card to Mr Blanc read like this:

FOIE GRAS – what the scientists say about force feeding:

'*When ducks or geese were in a pen during the force feeding procedure, they kept away from the person who would force feed them, even though that person normally supplied them with food. At the end of the force feeding procedure, the birds were less well able to move and were usually panting but they still moved away or tried to move away from the person who had force fed them.*' Member of the EU's Scientific Animal Health and Animal Welfare Committee, reporting on farm visits to observe *foie gras* production.

'*The production of fatty liver for foie gras raises serious animal welfare issues and it is not a practice that is condoned by FAO.*' Food and Agriculture Organisation of the United Nations.

'*This practice causes unacceptable suffering to these animals.*' Dr Christine Nichol, Professor of Animal Welfare, School of Veterinary Science, University of Bristol, UK.

'*Force feeding quickly results in birds that are obese and in a pathological state, called hepatic lipidosis, or fatty liver disease. There is no doubt that in this pathological state the birds will feel very ill.*' Dr Ian Duncan, Professor of Applied Ethology, University of Guelph, Canada.

*

Having seemingly achieved nothing via our first post card, and after trying repeatedly and unsuccessfully to elicit information from Mr Blanc's personal assistant, we produced a second postcard. This time its heading was in French:

FOIE GRAS?

CE N'EST PAS CHIC, MONSIEUR BLANC!

Chickens' Lib reminded him, adding:

'In fact, this "delicacy" is the grim end-product of appalling cruelty. Imprisoned, then force-fed, ducks and geese suffer untold miseries before their diseased livers reach your tables.'

Please, M Blanc, take foie gras (fatty liver) off your menu!

*

Following emails and searches on the website, we found that *foie gras* had suddenly been removed from menus in all Raymond Blanc's dozen or so bistros, located in major cities throughout Britain. But Le Manoir aux Quat' Saisons was standing firm.

Could it be that Mr Blanc's privileged guests simply couldn't contemplate starting a meal without a portion of diseased liver on their plates? It was to be a while before we could rest easy, on that score.

Legislation for broilers

2010 saw the long-awaited EU Broiler Directive, representing the first ever legislation to include specific standards for meat-type chickens. And it proved deeply disappointing.

Though previously no more than a recommendation in a Code, the maximum stocking density suggested for UK broiler chickens had stood at 34 kg of chicken per square metre (75 pounds of chicken in 10¾ square feet), perhaps better explained as one nearly full-term chicken allotted floor space equivalent to a sheet of A4 typing paper. However it's been readily admitted that many British broiler farmers exceed this stocking density, especially near the end of the birds' lives (1).

The EU maximum stocking density is now set at different levels, allowing 39kg (86lbs) of chicken per square metre, a figure which could be increased to 42kg/sq.m (92½ pounds) *'if stricter welfare standards are met'*(2). Presumably this shocking example of over-stocking has been arrived at to accommodate Member States (presently numbering twenty seven) where existing conditions could be even worse than in the UK.

By way of a low-grade form of 'gold plating' the UK is to limit stocking densities to 39 kg/sq m – already the UK norm – stipulating that producers will be obliged to inform DEFRA of this high level. (In this context the term 'gold plating' applies to a Member State choosing to demand higher standards than those set out in a Directive.)

For the rest of the EU, the highest stocking densities are officially allowed only where ventilation and various environmental aspects are 'state of the art'. But given the huge numbers of farms and the totally inadequate number of inspectors, who is likely to check after the initial approval is given?

A good aspect of the new Directive is that a period of six hours of darkness out of the 24, at least four of which must be uninterrupted, is now mandatory so birds can rest properly. Though one should question whether crouching down on potentially filthy litter, perhaps on sore and painful legs, can pass for rest.

*

Worldwide, the intensive broiler chicken industry remains as ruthless as it is squalid, and will surely continue so for as long as consumers buy cheap chicken, or until the system is outlawed. In our 1995 booklet *Today's Poultry Industry, The Inside Story* we quoted Professor John Webster of Bristol University: 'a cruel mess' was how he described the broiler system.

Meanwhile, and all too often forgotten, there's the cruel suffering of the breeding stock, those birds strategically 'slimmed down' so they are fit enough to produce clinically obese offspring.

THE SPANISH CONNECTION

In September 2009 I received a letter from Manuel Cases, Deputy-Chairman of ADDA, the Spanish organisation *Asociación Defensa Derechos Animal* (Association Defending Animal Rights). He'd remembered past co-operation with Chickens' Lib over our booklet *Today's Poultry Industry* and wondered if there was scope for another such venture.

At first, my reaction was negative – Chickens' Lib's voice was now insignificant, compared with larger and more active organisations. Opportunities for distribution of material were limited. And yet...I was reluctant to turn my back on the idea. We could afford a new leaflet and existing funds must be put to good use. Surely we still had a voice? But without a plan in place for distribution there was no question of a joint venture with ADDA.

Then Hillside Animal Sanctuary sprang to mind. Every year thousands of visitors come to see Hillside's rescued animals, and all are offered information packs to take away with them. Hillside has an impressive mailing list too.

I put the idea of a three-way shared leaflet to Wendy Valentine and we came to an agreement: if Chickens' Lib organised and paid for its production, Hillside would take care of the bulk of the distribution of the English version. I promised to come back to Wendy once I'd had time to think of the best subject matter, which must then be approved by both Hillside and ADDA.

Suddenly, the world was my oyster. Here was a great opportunity to highlight an important issue, preferably one that in our view no other organisation had touched on in sufficient detail.

*

My thoughts returned to the NFU-hosted tour of a North Yorkshire battery, all those years ago. I remembered an individual hen, the one pecking at a button on my coat, and recalled how concerned I'd been that my children shouldn't breathe in the foul air. I thought about how conditions there had sparked off the conviction that keeping animals intensively, crammed together in vast numbers, is not only cruel but inherently illegal. Legislation has been updated since then, but not substantially changed. Still the suffering goes on, while the scandal of a ratio of staff to birds, guaranteed to result in poor 'welfare', has not been addressed.

This new leaflet would draw attention to the sheer impossibility of fulfilling EU legislation. The presence of sufficient staff could not change the cruel nature of the systems, but adhering to the law would render most forms of factory farming unprofitable. Our shared leaflet would limit its scope to this one argument.

I put the idea to Manuel and he liked it, as did Wendy. I promised to get to work on the wording, which ADDA would translate and adapt, as necessary, for Spain.

*

This was to be the wording at the head of the leaflet, dated January 2010:

FACTORY FARMED POULTRY AND THE LAW

• *Statutory regulations intended to protect intensively reared poultry are flouted on a massive scale.*
• *For daily inspections of factory-farmed birds to be effective, a significant increase in the current typical workforce is required.*
• *If enough workers were employed to enable effective inspection, intensive systems as presently practised would prove instantly uneconomic.*

Under the heading *Inspection*, the *Welfare of Farmed Animals (England) Regulations 2007* state: *Animals kept in husbandry systems in which their welfare depends on frequent human attention must be thoroughly inspected at least once a day to check that they are in a state of well-being.*

Surely, any reasonable person would assume that a 'thorough' inspection must involve paying careful attention to each and every one of such animals. Indeed, this had been the interpretation of similar wording in much earlier legislation. In that court case back in 1982 when a Surrey battery farmer was found guilty of neglect, the concept of the individual bird had been central to the outcome of the case. The EU has now banned the barren battery cage. But I have argued that enriched cages present as many if not more problems of thorough daily inspection.

When it comes to legislation for broiler chickens, the picture is no better. Paragraph 8, Annex 1 in Council Directive 2007/43/EC states: *'All chickens kept on the holding must be inspected at least twice a day. Special attention should be paid to signs indicating a reduced level of animal welfare and/or animal health.'* The health of broilers or of ducks, turkeys, quail or any other species of animal crammed together *en masse*, can never be safeguarded.

Nowhere in animal welfare legislation is neglect of sick, injured or dying farmed animals regarded as acceptable. Rather, it is deemed illegal.

A question of survival?

Never once in its early days did Chickens' Lib aspire to address global issues. The slogan on our headed paper was *Chickens' Lib – fighting cruelty* and in those long ago days we simply meant the cruelty of the battery cage system.

With our trademark cage, we'd shown Londoners and officialdom the truth – the pitiful live victims. But, as time went by, the campaign developed and of necessity changed. Along the way we were to see the bigger picture, discovering just how disastrous are the side-effects of factory farming for animals and humans alike and how widely its destructive net has been cast.

The prosperous among the world's exploding population now eat more and more meat, while dairy products are fast becoming popular in previously non-dairy countries. To take just one example: New Zealand is rapidly increasing its stock of dairy cows to supply cheese to the Japanese. Multinationals exploit the assumption that meat equals the good life, while junk food outlets continue to spread like an ugly stain throughout the world, worsening global warming while accounting for an increase in obesity, Type 2 diabetes, certain cancers and heart disease.

Ironically, it's possible that global warming, coupled with more enlightened views on health, will benefit 'food animals' faster than all the campaigning for better animal welfare, let alone the principles of animals' rights. Now, eminent thinkers and scientists are opening their minds to the possibility of a new way of eating, often for essentially practical reasons.

*

In March 2010 Sir Liam Donaldson, the UK Government's Chief Medical Officer warned: *'Our diet is warming the planet. It is also damaging our health'* and his words echoed the conclusions of many eminent scientists (1). He went on to estimate that reducing meat consumption by 30% could save 18,000 human lives from premature disease every year in the UK alone.

But a mere 30% reduction is unlikely to go far in solving the problem of a world where millions routinely go hungry. Take animal feed: According to United Nations' Food and Agriculture Organisation (FAO) figures, 60% of the world's crop of maize and 97% of the world's soya are grown for animal feed (2). Maize is a staple in the diet of some societies, and contains most of the eight essential amino acids found in meat, fish and eggs, while soya goes one better, being comparable in food value to beef. In the UK, half of all wheat and barley goes to feed farmed animals (3).

The grain:meat conversion ratio is complicated, since many factors must be considered. For instance, cattle reared on grass or goats on scrubland are eating what humans could not (but could protein-rich nuts grow there?). On the other hand, intensively reared pigs and poultry are fed on the high protein foods listed in the above paragraph, all of which are suitable for direct consumption by humans. Millions of cattle, notably in the USA, are confined on concrete in feedlots; they never graze, but must have every scrap of food brought to them.

The facts behind the 97% of soya that's grown for animal food are especially shocking. Vast areas of forest have been destroyed and continue to be destroyed to provide land for the crop, a fact highlighted in Friends of the Earth's press release of October 19th 2010. In addition to worsening the rate of global warming, research for a FOE report, carried out at Oxford University, analysed the health implications of a range of dietary options. The conclusion was that diets lower in meat could cut UK deaths from heart disease by around 31,000, deaths from cancer by 9,000 and deaths from strokes by 5,000 each year: *'Switching to diets that contain no more than three meat meals each week could prevent around 45,000 early deaths and save the NHS around £1.2 billion each year – as well as helping to tackle climate change and curb deforestation.'*

On June 6th 2012, under the heading *Tesco fends off accusation over Amazon beef,* the *Guardian's* environmental correspondent described a Greenpeace report. It claimed that JBS, the Brazilian supplier of meat and cattle by-products, has over recent years violated its own ethical sourcing code and sold meat, leather and other by-products to leading UK companies, including Tesco, Sainsbury's, Asda, Ikea, footwear company Clarks and food firm Prince's. *'...this latest study alleges that in the past three years JBS has failed to live up to its pledges. According to evidence amassed by Greenpeace, the company bought animals from at least five farms accused by the Brazilian government of illegal deforestation, between June and December 2011.'*

Ironically perhaps, JBS's motto is 'In God we trust. Nature we respect.'

*

The global scarcity of water is now foreseen as an impending reason for unrest and even for wars.

Surprisingly, an article in *The Ecologist* (4), which described lack of sufficient water as the greatest barrier to increasing food production, failed to mention the vast water use by animals, especially those confined in factory farms where the atmosphere is typically dry and warm, encouraging maximum water consumption.

In the same article, Lloyds Insurance Group was quoted as listing water problems in South Asia as being due to high population densities, climate variability, hydropower requirements, poor water governance and widespread ecological collapse of freshwater systems. No mention of the elephant in the room: the massive expansion of factory farming, especially of poultry, in that part of the world.

Consider this example of the water needed for beef production: to produce one kilogram of beef, approximately fifteen thousand litres of water are needed. Or, put another way, one 250g (a half pound) portion of beef on the dinner plate will have used the same amount of water that one human needs for thirty-four years of life, assuming a meagre one litre a day (that's just over two pints) (5). Professor Martin Rees, in his second 2010 Reith Lecture, *Surviving the Century*, advocated a vegetarian diet as a way to save the earth's resources. The figures he chose to illustrate the point were as follows: to produce a kilogram (2.2 pounds) of vegetables takes two thousand litres of water, in contrast to the fifteen thousand required for the same amount of beef.

In our 1993 booklet, *Hidden Suffering*, we included information about the gulf between human nutrition in the West and in Asia: *'Asian adults consume between 300 and 400 pounds of grain a year: three fourths or more of the diet of the average Asian is composed of grain. A middle-class American, by contrast, consumes over a ton of grain each year, 80% of it through eating cattle and other grain-fed livestock'*(6). There are 2,240 pounds in a ton, or just over 1,000 kilos. The information quoted was dated 1977, and the trend since has been for Asians to move towards the diet of a middle-class American, with all its dire consequences for human health, the environment and, last but certainly not least, the inevitable victims of it all, the animals.

Any agriculture system uses water, but intensive animal farming, often promoted as the solution to feeding a hungry world, involves an unnatural and unsustainable amount of it.

*

One solution to hunger could be cultured, or in-vitro, meat. In-vitro meat is grown in a laboratory – its source is animal-derived, but no animal's death is needed to start the process. To date, the resulting meat is of the sort that might be found inside a beef burger – there's nothing yet resembling a lamb chop or a chicken, but this may well be developed if consumers hold fast to the idea that their protein food must look like an animal, or a part thereof.

Hanna Tuomisto of Oxford University, where she studies the environmental effect of food production, is quoted as saying that switching to lab-produced meat could theoretically lower livestock greenhouse emissions by up to 95%, since both land and water use would also drop by 95% (7). The Dutch government is supporting research into in-vitro meat at Maastricht University and similar work is under way in the USA, Scandinavia and Japan (8).

'Quorn' (9) is grown from a naturally occurring mycoprotein organism, first found in the soil of a field in Buckinghamshire, England, and now widely available as the protein ingredient in ready meals. I gather it is good to eat. (While being suitable for vegetarians, it does contain egg white, so is not acceptable to vegans.) Like soya products (tofu for example) Quorn contains all eight essential amino acids and is therefore comparable to the protein obtained from beef, but is low in saturated fat, with zero cholesterol.

Straight talking

December 2010 saw the publication of the Farm Animal Welfare Council's *Opinion on Osteoporosis and Bone Fractures in Laying Hens.*

On reading it, I remembered Mr Easterbrook's words about the battery hen, written in 1948 when the cage system was in its infancy: *'...often with their bones so brittle they will snap like dry twigs...'*, and reflected on the extraordinary length of time it takes for progress to be achieved. Progress? For me, this Opinion *is* progress in that it highlights the stark truth that osteoporosis is not only associated with the barren battery cage but with those alternative systems generally heralded as 'improvements'.

FAWC harks back to the 1989 work on battery hens at Bristol, which revealed 29% of new fractures (those incurred during the catching and transport of 'old' hens) (1) and describes the collapse of spinal bone and paralysis from bone weakness, once commonly called Cage Layer Fatigue (2).

The Opinion points out that the keel bone (sternum) may be damaged during collisions, when birds land awkwardly, perhaps when jumping down from perches (3), and states that bone fractures associated with osteoporosis are believed to be rare in wild birds, or in domestic fowl in times gone by (4). Years ago, I complained to MAFF about the lack of dimmer switches in free range and barn-type units – almost unbelievably, some farmers were simply turning off the lights in the evening, leaving birds who hadn't yet settled down for the night suddenly plunged into darkness. Many fractures must have occurred due to this stupid practice, let alone to the overcrowding which continues to this day.

FAWC states that when bones first break 'acute pain' is probably felt (5), followed by chronic pain due to nerve sensitivity and inflammation (6), and that the barren battery cage scored worst in mortality figures from osteoporosis (7).

Crucially, the unequivocal need to adhere to the *2007 Welfare of Farmed Animals Regulations (England, Scotland and Wales)* which *'gives legal force for the need to exercise and avoidance of trauma'* is spelled out (8).

The British poultry industry is said to be keen to assist with research into ways of improving the state of laying hens' bones, and FAWC comments that any improvement would *'also have commercial benefits by reducing bone splinters in meat.'* (9) Better, I thought on reading this, than the method, hopefully now abandoned, of turning down the electric current at slaughter.

The Opinion draws attention to the suffering of birds already in pain from broken bones, when they're shackled, awaiting slaughter (10).

Project AWO231, a Scottish Agricultural College/DEFRA initiative, compared the figures for bone fractures in both intensive and extensive systems, describing their prevalence, in all bones, as 'disturbingly high (11).

System	Old fractures %	New fractures %
Conventional cage	23	24
Enriched cage	27	6
Barn	42	10
Free range	44	10

The above table makes for uncomfortable reading for anyone who'd hoped for a clear conscience when buying eggs from 'alternative' systems. Free range birds can be severely overcrowded, suffering especially in badly designed houses (too few pop-holes to the outside, for example) or during those times when flocks of thousands must shelter inside in bad weather.

Similar research, a Bristol/DEFRA project this time, revealed the very high extent of damage to keel bones (36%) in hens kept in enriched cages, while the average prevalence of such injury in other non-cage systems was 86%, with 95% recorded in 'the worst flocks'. A contributing factor was perches, 'many of which were not well-designed' (12).

With these grim statistics before us, we now read that the prevalence of bone fractures has not declined over the last twenty years and 'may be rising'(13). In view of this deeply depressing scenario, it's encouraging to see FAWC questioning whether hens suffering from bone fractures should be transported at all, citing the demands of the Welfare of Animals (Transport) (England) Order 2006 (with similar regulations for Scotland and Wales) which require birds to be fit for any proposed journey (14).

Predictable suffering is now specifically against the law and yet the FAWC *Opinion* confirms that such suffering is par for the course for millions of laying hens.

*

Research over the years has concluded that flocks of between 50 and 60 hens are ideal, since that number can readily recognise each other. Traditionally, flocks of up to 500 were regarded as workable – both figures far cries from today's commercial excesses. It's to be regretted that FAWC was not able to study a selection of small free-range units, let's say where birds were divided into uncaged flocks of no more than five hundred hens, in housing designed to suit their needs.

It's my guess that under such conditions almost no injuries or bone degeneration would be found.

So where's the progress, after all these years?

That there has been progress is beyond dispute. A major example is the 2012 EU-wide ban on the worst system of all for laying hens, the barren battery cage. In this chapter I've drawn together a miscellaneous, and no doubt far from comprehensive, list of improvements. Some are more significant than others but all indicate the importance of public pressure, without which little would have changed.

As always, it's necessary to look beyond window dressing by the poultry industry and into the hard facts, for pretty pictures and encouraging terms may still deceive. The figure for free range eggs has soared from only 4% of all British eggs in the 1980s, to just over 50% for shell eggs (that's those sold as whole eggs, not incorporated into pasta, mayonnaise etc). Yet, as shown in the previous chapter, the label 'free range' can mislead, for the hens may still suffer stress, disease and injury.

The term 'Barn Eggs' evokes a rustic, almost cosy picture, much at variance with reality. In this indoor system the hens usually move around via perches, ladders and platforms at different levels and may (legally) be so densely stocked that floor, platforms and perches are virtually obscured by the mass of birds – and that's certainly not the image presented to the consumer. In fact, in terms of congestion, today's 'barns' for laying hens could be likened to battery sheds minus the cages.

The fact is, serious welfare problems can exist within any system for poultry keeping.

*

Some progress: From April 1st 1995, legislation has demanded that the length of time permitted for a turkey to be suspended in shackles must be reduced from six minutes to three (1). Better still, in 2010 Defra estimated that around 90% of turkeys are no longer shackled for slaughter, but gassed – a significant welfare improvement, meaning that some nine out of ten turkeys can remain in their transport crates until overcome by the gas, and so may be saved much stress and pain. Ironically, the exception to this is in the run up to Christmas, the season of goodwill. Then, much on-farm slaughter goes on – from November, the figure for turkeys killed by gassing could drop to around 65% (2).

*

Thanks largely to CIWF's campaigning, animals' sentience is now acknowledged. Previously, animals had been officially regarded as 'goods', no different from cabbages or cement. Since 1997 the concept of animal sentiency has been written into EU law, as a legally binding Protocol annexed to the Treaty of Amsterdam. Now, Member States are required to pay full regard to the welfare requirements of animals. As so often happens, reality may fall far short of the aspiration, but the above represents a valuable start.

*

A battle won: finally, the desired breakthrough with the Co-op occurred, though recent pressure on supermarkets from CIWF, plus the example of other companies, must have played a large part in completing the work we'd begun all those years ago. In the autumn of 2006, the Co-op declared its 'own brand' eggs to be free range. Then two years later came even better news: from February 2008 no shell eggs from caged hens, own–brand or otherwise, would be sold in its stores.

And there was more: all Co-op fresh chickens and fresh chicken portions were to be from birds sourced from within the UK, and reared in 'naturally ventilated and sunlit barns' (presumably weather permitting, for the latter), given 30% more space than 'standard' chickens and provided with environmental stimulation, such as straw bales to perch on. Their diets would be calculated to encourage slower growth, and they'd be allowed six hours of darkness out of the 24, to allow for rest, this last feature anticipating the EU Directive by two years (3). And, according to *Poultry World's* September

2012 issue, Morrisons supermarket now specifies similar conditions for all their 'standard' chickens.

*

Legislation, that valuable commodity that looks so good on paper, has continued to be upgraded; especially important is the 2006 Animal Welfare Act (of which more later).

*

Far more meat-type chickens are free range than was the case when Chickens' Lib first campaigned for them. The downside of this is that most continue to be the offspring of half-starved parent stock.

Broilers marketed under Freedom Food standards are said to be in better bodily condition than their 'standard' counterparts, and I'm told by Dr Marc Cooper, the RSPCA's senior chicken welfare scientist, that the females of the parent stock of the Hubbard birds chosen for FF's slower growing birds are not feed restricted. Only the males are rationed. Since breeders are kept at approximately nine hens to one cockerel, Dr Cooper pointed out that the Hubbard breeding line (4) chosen by FF represents a 90% improvement, and it would be churlish not to celebrate this obvious welfare improvement. But here's the rub: by various means the hens' food must be kept separate from that destined for the cockerels, forcing the desperately hungry males to watch while the hens eat their unrestricted rations. And this is especially ironic. For under natural conditions a cockerel will stand back courteously, having drawn the attention of a favourite hen to a tasty morsel. Factory farming destroys so much...

In the past, grids often caused severe damage to breeders, resulting in swollen head syndrome (5). To what extent this still happens I cannot say. In 2010 I noticed an advertisement for a 'brand-new males-only pan' on the back cover of *World Poultry*. The makers, Roxell (5), boasted that the pans made for comfortable eating for the male breeders, offering 'fast and uniform feed distribution'. I looked at Roxell's website and the pan's design looked reasonable. But all the better design in the world won't lessen the misery of hunger still endured by the vast majority of broiler breeders, worldwide.

*

I emailed a query to Bernard Matthews Farms Limited, asking whether the company's free range birds could be the offspring of females artificially inseminated with the semen from, in all likelihood, disabled male parents (6). No response was forthcoming, so it's only sensible to assume that there's no progress to report on that front.

A tiny proportion of ducks are truly free range, with access to water for swimming, and the Soil Association's standards may currently be the best but, as with all commercially reared poultry, the ducklings will be killed years before their time.

*

Some twenty-first century free range eggs are as good as they get, given the strictures of commercial egg production.

The chickens whose eggs are sold in Sainsbury's under the Woodland Eggs brand name spend their days amongst trees, ideal for descendents of the Jungle Fowl. Even the species of trees are specified. Woodland Eggs (7) operates in co-operation with the Woodland Trust (8), the charity that works to ensure the protection and regeneration of British woodland. The Trust receives a small percentage on every dozen Woodland Eggs sold and, since 2004, has planted more than a quarter of a million trees on over a hundred farms where Woodland Eggs' hens roam.

And there's more to come. Woodland Eggs is associated with Noble Foods which in turn is associated with Goldenlay. And I was told in an email that all Goldenlay Eggs are now free range (9). Now *that's* progress! Images on Woodland Eggs' website of hens wandering among trees, in dappled sunlight, could hardly be further from the stark image on our old black and white postcard, its caption *The Taste of the Country?*.

By email, I tried to sort out the precise connection between the three companies, but Noble Foods wanted to know more about me, and once they did, there were no more incoming emails. Surely, after all these years, memories of our demos have faded ... or perhaps not.

I looked on Goldenlay's website (10) and discovered that its eggs are advertised as being rich in Omega 3. And there's a little jingle to emphasise the fact, inspired by an old playground rhyme:

Chick, chick, chick, chick, chicken,

Lay a healthy egg for me...

Only the playground version goes ...*Lay a little egg for me.* I suppose you can't really blame Goldenlay for changing the words a bit. After all, Chickens' Lib did plenty of that, and on Goldenlay's very doorstep.

*

In 2009 the Farm Animal Welfare Council issued its report *The Welfare of Poultry at Slaughter* (11). One of FAWC's recommendations is that pre-slaughter inversion and shackling should be phased out, a view shared by the EU. So there is hope on the horizon, though that horizon may be a far distant one. Already, effective gas killing systems exist but, once again, hard economics will dictate the speed of change.

*

2010: Guests at Raymond' Blanc's *Manoir* may still lust for *foie gras*, but they're now doomed to disappointment.

As mentioned earlier, this product of extreme cruelty had been withdrawn from Mr Blanc's range of bistros, and in 2009 I made a few phone calls, to find out why. An obliging chef at one of these bistros explained that since Mr Blanc supported Freedom Food, *foie gras* was no longer an option. This triggered a memory – I'd spotted a little item in *Poultry World* about Freedom Food's '*Simply Ask*' campaign. And guess who was mentioned as one of the initiative's prestigious champions? Raymond Blanc, none other!

I immediately phoned Freedom Food, pointing out that it wouldn't be too good if guests 'simply asked' about *foie gras* while dining at Le Manoir, only to have Chef obligingly describe the cruel force feeding, the terror shown by the birds, the diseased livers. Doubtless Freedom Food took my observations up with Mr Blanc, who, rather than withdrawing his support for the *Simply Ask* scheme, finally gave in.

If you key in Oxfordshire on FF's *Simply Ask* website, Le Manoir still comes up as an approved place to eat, but now there's no mention on the menus of *foie gras*. (www.simplyaskrestaurantfinder.org.uk)

*

The opening paragraph in our 2008 report *Today's Intensive Turkey Industry* reads: '*The Farm Animal Welfare Network (aka Chickens' Lib) is calling for the introduction of CCTV cameras in all intensive turkey sheds, to help reduce the appalling abuses known to take place behind closed doors on Britain's "hidden" turkey farms. Though no such progress has yet been made, there's now a powerful move towards CCTV in all slaughterhouses, spurred on by undercover filming.'*

In January 2009 Animal Aid began its programme of secret filming in 'red meat' (non-poultry) slaughterhouses, gathering material from seven different establishments and revealing instances of appalling treatment of animals. At Tom Lang Ltd., in Ashburton, Devon, forty hours of activities were recorded over a period of two weeks. The evidence was shocking, made even more so by the fact that Mr Lang's establishment was on the Soil Association's list of approved slaughterhouses.

As a result of Animal Aid's filming, three slaughtermen were suspended, and a spokesperson for the Meat Hygiene Service stated there was *'clear evidence of breaches of animal welfare legislation'*. CCTV cameras have now been installed at Tom Lang Ltd., but who knows for how long the appalling treatment of animals had been going on, or for how long it would have continued but for Animal Aid's work? (12)

The Daily Mail took up the story and the publicity generated led to support from Compassion in World Farming, the Food Standards Agency, the Soil Association and the RSPCA for Animal Aid's call for CCTV cameras to be in continuous use in *all* UK slaughterhouses.

In February 2010, the RSPCA issued another press release: the Society wants to ensure that cameras are up and working in all FF-approved slaughterhouses as a preventative measure or, at worst, to provide evidence in cases of suspected bad treatment of animals awaiting slaughter.

On June 11th 2010 *Online Meat Trades Journal* reported Halal meat supplier Naved Syed of Janan Meat MD as calling on other processors to follow his lead, by installing CCTV cameras in all Halal abattoirs. Killing for Halal-approved meat is on the increase. Since the Halal method involves no pre-stunning of the animals, it is vital that the procedure is monitored on camera.

*

Welcome though the above signs of progress are, they cannot compare with what was to happen in 2012.

For then, thanks to bold and tenacious work by Animal Aid, DEFRA, that old brick wall that Chickens' Lib had so often come up against, was to be substantially weakened.

The Crown Prosecution Service

March-April 2011: Hidden cameras placed by Animal Aid's investigators within the premises of Cheale Meats' slaughterhouse record examples of terrible abuse. Almost unbearable to watch, the footage shows two Cheale Meat employees cruelly abusing pigs awaiting slaughter.

Kelly Smith (40) is seen repeatedly beating pigs, using the sharp side of a 'slap stick' (an implement used in slaughterhouses, to urge animals on). One animal is struck thirty times in 62 seconds, including around the head. In Animal Aid's words; *'...an attack that forced the animal to sit down like a dog, and pant heavily as the blows rained down.'* (1) One of the offenders drags a seriously lame pig by the ears, towards the slaughter area.

Piotr Andrzej Wasiuta (29) tortures pigs by pressing lighted cigarettes to the animals' snouts. You hear one cry out in shock and pain.

*

The prison sentences these two criminals received may seem inadequate for intentionally causing such suffering – for Smith it was seven weeks reduced to four (he appealed his sentence, but bail was refused) and for Wasiuta nine-weeks, reduced to six. But at least some degree of justice was done.

But there would have been no such outcome had DEFRA had its way.

*

In Kate Fowler's words: *'Getting anyone to court has proved a long and difficult task. Initially, DEFRA refused to prosecute and gave a series of excuses as to why it could not do so. And because of DEFRA's decision, the Food Standards Agency (FSA) said it would not even investigate. Animal Aid's appointed legal team had to remind the FSA that it had a statutory duty to do so, no matter what it thought the outcome would be. Sure enough, it then undertook an investigation. The next step was to try to get DEFRA stripped of its powers to prosecute.'* (2)

No easy feat, you might say, considering DEFRA's track record of holding all the cards. The expertise of Ministry vets has hitherto been held vital to back up prosecutions. But Ministry vets have often been found wanting, proving themselves experts only in ignoring evidence of cruelty or in their willingness to obey dubious advice from on high.

And true to form, instead of leaving no stone unturned in a quest to prosecute Cheale Meats' particularly callous offenders, the Coalition's farming Minister Jim Paice refused to accept Animal Aid's evidence, expressing his opinion that such evidence, obtained illegally, would fail to stand up in court.

To take up Animal Aid's story again: *'Our only chance was to lobby hard for a historic reduction in DEFRA's powers. After a year of campaigning and reminding the world that DEFRA had a serious conflict of interest, the news that the Crown Prosecution Service (CPS) would take over decisions on whether to prosecute was quietly announced on the CPS website. We were another step closer and, equally importantly, we had weakened DEFRA's ability to shield all farmed animal abusers from the law in future.'*

Inevitably, I thought back to the times we'd presented first MAFF then DEFRA with firm evidence of cruelty. Those countless occasions when we'd been assured that all was well in this or that particular hell-hole. And I thought back to Mr Stobo's obituary in *Veterinary Record*. Remembered how he, a MAFF vet, had experienced the same suppression of his welfare concerns and, unable to stomach the frustrations any longer, had taken early retirement.

The British Veterinary Association (BVA) supported Animal Aid in its campaign. Its president, Harvey Locke, stated: *'The method by which the issue was highlighted should not, in our opinion, preclude further investigation by the Food Standards Agency and DEFRA into these incidents with a view to lawfully obtaining evidence to either support or refute the accusations arising from the Animal Aid footage.'* (3)

On March 3rd 2012 Simon Clements, Head of the Welfare, Rural and Health Prosecutions Division of the Crown Prosecution Service said: *'This decision* [to prosecute Wasiuta and Smith] *was taken in accordance with the Code Prosecutions. After careful consideration of all the evidence, I am satisfied there is sufficient evidence for a realistic prospect of conviction and it is in the public interest to prosecute this case.'* (4)

And so came about a truly historic reduction in DEFRA's powers.

*

For a full run-down of the shameful story of cruelty at Cheale Meats and of DEFRA's determination not to prosecute, visit Animal Aid's website. There, for a complete picture of AA's persistence, you'll find its *'Timeline for the case against Cheale Meats Employees'*. Disturbingly, AA discovered that Cheale Meats is a Freedom Food approved slaughterhouse. This status was temporarily withdrawn after Animal Aid's secret filming was revealed, but reinstated in November 2011. (5)

Significant progress in legislation

The 2006 *Animal Welfare Act, England and Wales* (with similar legislation in Scotland) specifically requires that an animal's needs must be provided for and that legal action can now be taken *before* the worst consequences of neglect are manifested. In the introductory section, under the heading *Unnecessary Suffering*, this is the crucial sentence: *'A person commits an offence if he knew, or ought reasonably to have known, that the act, or failure to act, would have that effect* [that is, to cause unnecessary suffering] *or be likely to do so.'* (1)

I find myself thinking back to Angela, our hen with the mass of rotting eggs inside her body. Because the MAFF veterinary certificate we obtained described her as being 'in a bright condition' her suffering was dismissed in court (though the farmer was indicted on other charges). Surely, under the 2006 Act this should not happen, since the failure of the farmer to act to alleviate Angela's suffering had been glaringly obvious.

Oddly perhaps, those 'needs' specified in the 2006 Act (2) are still based on the original 'Five Freedoms' (see my chapter *Five Freedoms and a Convention*), none of which can realistically be expected to be fulfilled within intensive systems. To take just one example: *'For the purpose of this Act, an animals' needs shall be taken to include its need to be able to exhibit normal behaviour patterns.'* (3). This may seem more of the usual meaningless language – but it is only meaningless if no action is taken when suffering is found.

The 2006 Act represents progress. Already the RSPCA is prosecuting far more cases of cruelty, especially to domestic pets, thanks to the wording of the new Act.

*

In 2009 the Farm Animal Welfare Council (FAWC) issued a Report entitled *Farm Animal Welfare in Great Britain: Past, Present and Future* in which it revealed a philosophy aiming far higher than the expectation of a mere absence of suffering, whether present or potential. FAWC considers the need for such things as play and contentment, and asks whether the individual animal has a life worth living, from his or her own point of view.

*

In March 22nd 2010 FAWC circulated its *Strategic Plan for 2011-2015* to Council members, Ministers, veterinarians, advisory groups and stakeholders of all colours, seeking their comments. Those consulted were asked to rate general topics on farm animal welfare in order of perceived priority, and invited to say which specific issues should next be considered. Nearly two hundred bodies were listed, including Chickens' Lib.

For me, two sentences leapt off the page: under *'Farm animal legislation, regulation, enforcement and surveillance'* this question was posed: *'How appropriate are current legislation and regulations, and are changes needed to ensure that each and every farm animal has a life worth living? How effective and efficient are current methods of enforcement and welfare surveillance?'* I read the passage several times. This was straightforward language, and it related to the very nub of our campaign.

'Each and every farm animal' – let's take that first. Remember the editor of *Poultry World's* fury over the case of the Surrey farmer fined for failing to inspect his flock?: *'...So I am wondering'* he wrote *'what* [the farmer] *did wrong in a mass management system that depends on catering for flocks, not individual birds. Quite rightly he was concerned about flock health and maintaining the best environment for the flock. When we fail to do that we deserve all the RSPCA can throw at us, but not for failing to look every bird in the eye every day.'* This was written some thirty years ago, but over the intervening decades we've detected no significant changes for the better. Rather, the trend has been for groups of livestock to get bigger, with no indication that the ratio of staff to animals has improved.

'A life worth living' – this delves even deeper. Consider broiler chickens – destined to five or six weeks of mere struggle for survival, often endured with pain, always terminated in terror, the parent stock living for a year or so in chronic and at times severe hunger. The list is long of farmed animals whose lives could not, at the wildest stretch of the imagination, be described as worth living.

In the next sentence came FAWC's request for comments on the effectiveness and efficiency of current methods of enforcement of legislation and of welfare surveillance. It's been a major purpose of my

303

book to highlight the lack of enforcement of legislation and the dire lack of surveillance.

This latest communication from FAWC must have raised the spirits of many, while causing alarm bells to clang throughout the intensive farming industries. For at last the question has been asked from a government-appointed body: are changes needed to ensure that *'each and every farm animal has a life worth living'*?

FAWC's communication, signed by its chairman Professor Christopher Wathes, gives real cause for optimism.

*

On April 10ᵗʰ 2010 Professor Wathes contributed *Veterinary Record's* *'Viewpoint'* column. In it, he elaborated on the concept of celebrating the good things in an animal's life, rather than merely stopping short at avoidance of the bad. He talks of enabling the fulfilment of animals' 'environmental choices and harmless wants', and of the need to provide for an animal's 'comfort, pleasure, interest and confidence, and the highest standards of veterinary care'. So, the need is now seen for something infinitely better than a life merely devoid of downright suffering.

*

A letter I received back in 1990 from Roy Moss, MAFF's by then retired Chief Vet (he who had disposed of the putrid broiler feet) serves to emphasise today's progress, contrasting as it does with Professor Wathes' words. I'd sent Mr Moss a Chickens' Lib fact sheet and booklet, which he was kind enough to comment on. *Inter alia*, he questioned whether it was possible to know what leads to pleasure or contentment in a hen (states of well-being we'd claimed on the hen's behalf) and suggested that this passage might be better deleted.

Interestingly, Professor Wathes warns that moves to improve the lives of animals may be compromised by what he describes as 'powerful economic and other forces'. Chickens' Lib came up against those as long ago as the late 1960s, and it's only rational to believe that they will always exist.

Professor Wathes *Viewpoint* suggested a sea change in attitudes and, as such, a potential forerunner of genuine progress.

Why 'necessary' suffering?

When Helen Steel and Dave Morris refused to be intimidated by McDonald's, the suffering endured by millions of factory-farmed animals was condemned in London's High Court.

For example, when summing up Mr Justice Bell had this to say on the subject of keeping chicken breeding stock desperately hungry: *My conclusion is that the practice of rearing breeders for appetite, that is to feel especially hungry, and then restricting their feed with the effect of keeping them hungry, is cruel. It is a well-planned device for profit at the expense of the suffering of the birds.*

In areas related to poultry welfare the case represented a triumph for justice but failed to herald significant changes for the better, for the case was a civil action for defamation, and not based on criminal offences. The question remains: what hope is there that a broadly–based criminal charge might prove successful, that is to say one that will strike at the heart of intensive farming, in essence destroying the concept of 'necessary suffering'?

Writing in the *Journal of Animal Welfare Law* in June 2007 Debbie Rook, Principal Lecturer in Northumbria University's School of Law, drew attention to court action in April 1985. Then, in the case of *Roberts v Ruggiero*, the Court concluded that existing legislation could not be used to challenge the practice in question (in this case cruelly restrictive veal crates) (1).

By contrast, the author then described a case in which the outcome had been very different. Much earlier (in 1889) a case, *Ford v Riley*, had concerned the painful dehorning of cattle on a Norfolk farm. In that instance: *'...the Court agreed to decide the broad question of whether the practice of dehorning was illegal rather than look at the narrower issue of the particular actions of the defendant...using this broad approach the Court held that the practice of dehorning was illegal.'* (2) The Court's finding had been based on its decision that there were better, far less painful methods of achieving the desired results.

Of course things were different then. The multinationals had not yet imposed their iron grip upon world 'food animal' production. Maximum profits for the companies concerned and the interests of shareholders were not involved. But this difference should be no disincentive in the fight for justice for animals. Governments must be challenged, for it is they who have issued legislation demanding comfort and well-being under systems that preclude both. And it is patently obvious that for every farming system that imposes predictable and often sustained suffering for the animals, there exists a substantially better one.

Debbie Rook went on to give reasons to be optimistic: '...*the case of Roberts v Ruggiero seemed to close the door on any prospect of using the offence of cruelty to challenge the suffering of farm animals caused by intensive farming practices. It is submitted here that, relying on Ford v Riley, the courts are able to take alternative methods, which cause less suffering, into consideration when assessing proportionality. This...is a significant factor and should not be excluded outright. To ignore it would effectively give the farmers freedom to define what constitutes cruelty since only suffering above and beyond the farming practices they choose to use would be relevant. Such an approach would, in the words of Bell J, "hand the decision as to what is cruel to the food industry completely, moved as it must be by economic as well as animal welfare conditions." ' (3)*

The author concluded her article thus: '*Bell J found this unacceptable in a civil case* [the McDonald's libel case] *and it is hoped that the criminal courts would find it equally unacceptable in any case of alleged cruelty to farm animals.*' (4)

*

In January 2012 Peter Stevenson, an English lawyer who works for Compassion in World Farming, published an important document entitled *European Union Legislation on the Welfare of Farm Animals.* The document spells out the reasons for optimism that court action, challenging the legality of various intensive farming practices, would stand an excellent chance of succeeding.

The author points to the high level of importance attached to animal protection laid down in *The Treaty on the Functioning of the European Union.* (5) This Treaty not only recognises animals as sentient beings, but stresses that the EU and its Member States shall, when formulating and implementing their policies in certain key areas, pay '*full regard to the welfare requirements of animals.*' (6)

Furthermore, the European Commission had this to say: '*This* [the above-mentioned Treaty] *puts animal welfare on equal footing with other key principles mentioned in the same title, i.e. promotion of gender equality, guarantee of social protection, protection of human health, combating discrimination, promotion of sustainable development, ensuring consumer protection and the protection of personal data.'* (7)

Peter Stevenson addresses the contentious subject of 'unnecessary suffering' (a term that surely leaves room for some suffering to be deemed 'necessary') quoting from *The General Farm Animals Directive* of 1998 (8). Article 3 of this EU Directive states that EU member countries shall *'make provision to ensure that the owners or keepers take all reasonable steps to ensure the welfare of animals under their care and to ensure that those animals are not caused any unnecessary pain, suffering or injury* (9). He concludes that: *'This provision could arguably be used to challenge the legality of industrial rearing systems. It should not be difficult to establish that such systems cause pain, suffering and/or injury. The challenge would principally turn around what is meant by "unnecessary". It could be argued that the pain, suffering or injury involved in industrial animal production is not necessary as in each case viable non-industrial alternatives are available.'*

Drawing attention to another provision in the same Directive, this one headed *'Freedom of movement,'* Peter Stevenson shows that the following wording gives further cause for optimism: *'The freedom of movement of an animal, having regard to its species and in accordance with established experience and scientific knowledge, must not be restricted in such a way as to cause it unnecessary suffering or injury. Where an animal is continuously or regularly tethered or confined, it must be given space appropriate to its physiological and ethological needs in accordance with established experience and scientific knowledge.'* (10)

Surely a cursory glance at just one form of industrial farming – the confining of laying hens in 'enriched' cages – should raise well-founded doubts as to that system's legality.

*

Most intensive farming takes place behind closed doors, in windowless buildings, often behind high barbed wire fencing and well-protected by electronic security devices. But despite these measures much evidence continues to be obtained, often unofficially, to prove that suffering is widely caused to, and endured by, farmed animals.

So what can be done? Are we to meekly accept the fact that the legislation which should be protecting farmed animals from extreme suffering is failing utterly to do so? To look at the problem another way: should those living in the eighteenth and nineteenth centuries have viewed the shameful slave trade as acceptable because it was widespread and considered a good thing in economic terms? And is the task of exposing the true extent of the cruelty to 'factory farmed' animals to be left to those willing to take considerable personal risks while obtaining evidence, risks that all too often achieve no lasting positive impact?

Many of us already sign petitions, while others may join organisations and march with like-minded people. And these are excellent things to do. But there is more that we can all do, and to good effect, as long as we persevere.

Since the problem concerns the law of the land, our MPs are the appropriate people to approach. Not once, not twice, but until we feel that he or she understands the scale of the cruelty involved, and moreover is willing to put pressure on government. And since UK legislation covers intensive systems in place throughout the EU, we must also approach our MEPs, with the same persistence.

*

Court action is essential. What is urgently needed is a successful case that would contradict the assumption that animals must continue to suffer because the suffering they endure is 'necessary'. Mr Justice Bell considered the information before him and concluded that many areas of factory farming were inhumane and therefore unacceptable.

Now it is up to informed members of the public to insist on change. Given the evidence, the rational conclusion must be that the widespread suffering of intensively reared animals is not 'necessary' but merely convenient to trade and to sections of the farming industry.

*

So who might promote a prosecution in a criminal court, taken against a company (or companies) involved in husbandry systems likely to cause 'necessary suffering'? Surely the RSPCA is the body to take on the task. This highly-respected organisation has the necessary expertise, and doubtless their many thousands of members would be generous in their support of such a move.

Conclusion – to a journey without end

In 2010 we wrote to our supporters: *'We feel the time has come to wind up Chickens' Lib...and perhaps after 40 years that's a good thing! Thank goodness many organisations are out there, all over the world, working incredibly hard, fighting the evils of animal abuse, in whatever form.'* And so our campaign has ended.

*

In the early days of Chickens' Lib Violet and I were able to face the harrowing East End butchers' shops, and later the battery sheds, because we needed first-hand knowledge – plus the hens. We tried not to dwell on their misery – constantly thinking about it could become destructive. I did develop a personal technique for bad moments, though. If I felt nervous, for example before giving a talk, I'd imagine myself inside a battery shed. *That's* why I'm doing this, I'd tell myself. Think about the hens. Go for it.

But sometimes pictures come into my mind unbidden, unwanted even. A battery hen is waking up after yet another night spent crouching on the grid of the cage floor or, if in a so-called enriched cage, perched on a plastic rod. It's about 3am in the shed, and the rows of dim, cobweb-festooned lights have just come on, to ensure that most eggs will be laid early, to fit in with the farmer's schedule. Once again, she must face another seventeen-hour 'day' of boredom and frustration, pain and misery.

I find that image intolerably sad, the more so because the exclusion of the enriched cage from the 2012 barren battery cage ban illustrates the grim fact that, despite all the campaigning by activists, the EU hasn't moved on very far at all.

*

We had a strawyard constructed to accommodate our little flock of rescued hens and turkeys. About the size of a small living room, its roof was covered, keeping the deep layer of straw on the earth floor perfectly dry. A traditional chicken hut, with nest box and a perch for roosting, stood between the strawyard and a small orchard. The birds sheltered in the hut at night, but had constant access to the fox-proof strawyard.

The strawyard was spacious and full of interest, with food and water available, but when I opened the door from the hut to the orchard each morning the hens would rush down the ladder, whatever the weather, eager for grass under their feet and the chance to peck around for insects in the earth. They'd even venture out when snow lay on the ground. Complicated scientific research wasn't called for. Simple observation supplied more than enough material for conclusions to be drawn about their needs, their 'harmless wants'.

*

Within the European Union, and elsewhere too, legislation is in place to protect farmed animals. Now the pressing need is to ensure that those laws are enacted. But that step, though highly significant, should represent nothing more than a beginning

Unless radical changes are made in the way we think, the world's escalating human population seems hell-bent on stumbling blindly down the road of industrial-style farming, recklessly feeding protein-rich crops to incarcerated animals. Superficially this system may appear to supply our needs, yet in reality it is not only immoral – furthering as it does cruelty to animals and starvation in an already hungry world – but it is doomed to failure. As illustrated earlier it can be argued, and increasingly it *is* argued, that our species must find a new agenda, a more compassionate and less wasteful way of feeding itself.

Many now believe that learning to survive peacefully with our fellow travellers on Planet Earth, while protecting them from exploitation, is a project of the greatest importance and urgency.

REFERENCES

Them Ministers is a cunning lot (page 17)
1   Email from Karen Davis to the author, September 15th 2012
2   Gregory, N.J. and Wilkins L.J., (1989) 'Broken bones in domestic fowl: Handling and processing damage in end-of-lay battery hens' *British Poultry Science*, 30, pp.555-562

A visual aid for Parliament (page 28)
1   Central Television April 25th 1988
2   From William Wilberforce's 1789 Report, put before Parliament to support the fight to abolish the slave trade.

The nuns' story (page 29)
1   The Agriculture (Miscellaneous Provisions) Act 1968
2   *The Lancet* September 24th 1988
3   *The Independent* January 14th 1989

The Halifax four (page 39)
1   Marian Stamp Dawkins, *Though Our Eyes Only – the Search for Animal Consciousness* (New York 1993)

Brainy birds (page 43)
1   Personal communication to the author from Professor Joy Mench, Department of Animal Science and Center for Animal Welfare, University of California, Davis, USA
2   Rogers, L.J., *The development of brain and behaviour in the chicken* (Wallingford, Oxon UK, CABI Publishing 1995, p 217
3   Communication with the author, August 16th 2012
4   Professor John Webster, speaking on March 17th 2005 at Compassion in World Farming's conference *From Darwin to Dawkins*, convened to discuss animal sentience.

The church (page 45)
1   www.hillside.org.uk
2   www.ciwf.org.uk

Who is Mr Big? (page 59)
1   *Poultry World* November 8th 1979

Illegal systems (page 65)
1   www.hse.gov.uk/agriculture/poultry
2   www.hse.gov.uk/pubns/web39.pdf
3   www.hse.gov.uk/research/rrhtm/rr655.htm

The RSPCA and the scapegoat (page 68)
1   *Poultry World* January 28th 1982

Police support for battery system (page 80)
1   Information in letter from West Yorkshire Police's Freedom of Information Project Officer, dated July 5th 2010
2   *The Guardian*, November 12th 2007

Five freedoms and a convention (page 83)
1   www.coe.int
2   *Standing Committee of the European Convention for the Protection of Animals Kept for Farming Purposes*, Strasbourg 1994 General Provisions, Article 2 a,c,d
3   Ibid, Enclosures, Buildings and Equipment, Article 10, 1

Inside Information (page 86)
1   Information in a letter dated January 1st 1989 to Chickens' Lib from Professor John Webster, Dept. of Animal Husbandry, University of Bristol. Also *World Poultry* Misset Vol 11 No 4, 1995

Bitten but unbowed (page 100)
1   *Huddersfield Examiner*, March 21st 1991
2   Ibid

A cruel 'solution' (page 106)

1 House of Commons *First Report from the Agriculture Committee Session 1980-81* Volume 1, Appendix 1, p 79

2 DEFRA 2002 *Code of recommendation for the welfare of laying hens*

3 Breward, Gentle, *et al.*, (1990) 'Behavioural evidence for persistent pain following partial beak amputation in chickens', *Applied Animal Behaviour Science*, 27 149-157, Elsevier Science Publisher, B.V., Amsterdam

4 MAFF Leaflet 480, *Cannibalism and feather pecking in poultry*

5 FAWC *Report on the welfare of laying hens in colony systems*, December 1991, part V, para 12

6 Ibid, Part VI, *Summary* of *Dissenting Views* of: Mr G Berry, Mrs Ruth Harrison, Mrs F Hodgson, Mr C Hollands and Miss Cindy Milburn.

7 Grigor *et al;* 'An experimental investigation of the costs and benefit of beak trimming in turkeys' *Veterinary Record*, 1995 136: issue 11, 257-265

8 Marchant-Forde *et al.*, *Comparative effects of infrared and one-third hot-blade trimming on beak topography, behaviour and growth* 2008 Poultry Science Association Inc. USDA Agricultural Research Service.

9 Guidance on the Mutilations (Permitted Procedures) (England) (Amendment) Regulations 2010: Beak trimming of Laying Hens.

10 Dr Karen Davis *Prisoned Chickens Poisoned Eggs* Revised edition The Book Publishing Company 2009 pp.62-64

A can of worms (page 113)

1 House of Commons *First Report from the Agriculture Committee*, Session 1980-81, vol. 1

2 Ruth Harrison *Animal Machines* Chapter 2, London 1964

3 MAFF Report of the Committee of Inquiry into Fowl Pest (the Plant Committee) (Cmnd 1664, 1962)

Bungled slaughter (page 115)

1 Gentle, M.J. and Tilston, V.L., (2000) 'Nociceptors in the legs of poultry: implications for potential pain in pre-slaughter shackling'. *Animals Welfare* 9:3 227-236

2   Bryan Heath, 'Slaughter of Broilers', *Veterinary Record*, Vol. 115, Issue 5, 98-100

3   www.animalaid.org.uk

An ugly picture (page 119)

1   *A field investigation of leg weakness in broilers*, 1986 Booklet 2520 MAFF (Publications) 3

2   Ibid, 10

3   'Bed re-use, yes or no?' *World Poultry* No 1, Vol. 26 2010

Down in the quarry (page 122)

1   Frans Fransen 'How green are broilers in cages?' *World Poultry* No 10 Vol. 26 2010

2   Council Directive 2007/43/EC laying down minimum rules for the protection of chickens kept for meat production.

Factory farming's smallest victim (page 125)

1-3   *Quail production* MAFF/ADAS M.P.S. Haywood, 1985

4-8   M Gerken and A.D. Mills *Welfare of domestic quail* Fourth European Symposium on Poultry Welfare, Edinburgh September 1993

9   Hall, Jeremy, 'Small bird that's packing a punch' *Poultry World* November 2012

Sleuthing with Irene (page 136)

1   Danbury, T.C., 'Self-selection of the analgesic drug carprofen by lame broiler chickens'. *Veterinary Record* Volume 146, Issue 2, 45-49

2   Wieneke, A.A., Roberts, D., Gilbert, R.J., 'Staphylococcal food poisoning in the United Kingdom, 1969-90 (Document)' *Epidemiology and Infection* 110(3) 519-531

3   Ed. F.T.W. Jordan, *Poultry Diseases*, Bailliere Tindall 1990, p61, 70, 265

4   Knowles, Toby G. *et al.*, *Leg disorders in broiler chickens: prevalence, risk factors and prevention*, February 6th 2008

5   *Poultry World* February 2010

Poultry litter claims victims (page 139)

1 McLoughlin, McIlroy and Neil 'A Major outbreak of botulism in cattle being fed ensiled poultry litter', *Veterinary Record* Vol 122, Issue 24, 579-581

2 *Veterinary Record* 2005 Vol 117; 22

3 VLA website: www.defra.gov.uk/vla

4 www.worldpoultry.net/news/antibiotic-resistant-bacteria-persist-in-chicken-manure 10.08.2009

Chickens and food-borne ills (page 146)

1 *British Medical Journal* July 7th 1988

2 'Poultry-Borne salmonellosis in Scotland'; *Epidem.Inf* (11988), 101

3 www.foodstandards.gov.uk

4 'Control programme helps kerb [sic] salmonella in turkeys'. *Poultry World* February 2010

5 Skirrow, M.B., 'Campylobacterenteritis – the first five years'. *J. Hyg., Camb* 1982

6 Healing, T.D., Greenwood, M.H., Pearson, A.D., 'Campylobacters and enteritis', *Reviews in Medical Microbiology* (1992) **3**, 159-167

7 Michael P. Doyle *Food-borne pathogens of recent concern* The Food Research Institute , University of Winconsin, Madison, Winconsin 1985

8 Ibid

A word of warning (page 149)

1 Lawrence, Felicity, 'Farmer jailed for selling rotten meat' *The Guardian* November 30th 2002

2 www.meatinfo.co.uk December 16th 2010

3 www.meatinfo.co.uk/news/fullstory.php/12068/ Rotting_meathiddden_with_...
www.thisishullandeastriding.co.uk/news/Farmers-market-traders-animal-cruelty... 26/02/10

Half-starved (by design) (page 151)

1 *House of Commons First Report from the Agriculture Committee on Animal Welfare in Poultry, Pig and Veal Calf Production.* Vol 11, Minutes of Evidence, 104

2   J.A.Mench, *Problems Associated with broiler breeder management* Dept. of Poultry Science, University of Maryland, College park, MD 20742, USA

3   *4th European Syposium on Poultry Welfare,* 1993, Working Group IX of the European Federation of the World's Poultry Science Association.

4   Paul Hocking and John Savory *Welfare implications of food restriction in broiler breeders,* Roslin Institute Annual Report 1994/5 p 42

5   Coutts, GS, BVMS, MRCVS, *Poultry Diseases Under Modern Management,* p 53, Nimrod Press Ltd, 1987

6   Duff, S.R.I., *et al.,* 'Head swelling of traumatic origin in broiler breeding fowl', *Veterinary Record* 1989; 125: 133-134

7   The 1998 EU Council Directive 98/58/EC, Annex, para 10

The shortest of lives (page 160)

1   *The Welfare of Animals (Slaughter or Killing) Regulations 1995* Schedule 11 **1**, a-c

2   FAWC *Report on the Welfare of Farmed Animals at Slaughter or Killing, Part 2: White Meat Animals* May 2009, paragraphs 256 and 257

3   Ibid

Clinically obese humans (page 162)

1   www.diabetes.org.uk

2   Letter from Professor Crawford to Chickens' Lib, dated January 8th 1987

3   *Poultry World* August 14th 1987

4   Crawford, N.A., *et al., The food chain for n-6 and n-3 fatty acids with special reference to animal products,* Nuffield Laboratory of Comparative Medicine and The Institute of Zoology.

5   Jenny A Cresswell, Prof Oona MR Campbell, Mary J De Silba, Veronique Filippi, 'Effect of maternal obesity on neonatal death in sub-Saharan Africa: multivariable analysis of 27 national data sets'. *The Lancet* Vol 380, Issue 9850 pages 1325-1330, October 13th 2012.

6   *Modern organic and broiler chickens sold for human consumption provide more energy from fat than protein.* Wang Y, Lehane C, Ghebrenskel K, Crawford MA. Public Health Nutrition 4: 1- 2009

Overseas links (page 166)

1 www.animal-voice.org and www.humane-education.org.za
2 www.upc-online.org
3 Dr Karen Davis *Prisoned Chickens Poisoned Eggs* Revised edition 2009, Book Publishing Company, Summertown TN
4 Ibid pp 197,127,128
5 Ibid p 108
6 Association of Colleges and Research Libraries of the American Library Association, August 2009 Vol 46, No.11
7 www.alv.org.au
8 Letter to Chickens' Lib from MAFF, from the Minister's Private Secretary, July 15th 1969

Enter turkeys (page 172)

1 www.farmsanctuary.org
2 British United Turkeys Ltd Technical Advice Sheet Issue 2006 *Artificial insemination for female turkeys*

Introducing Boyo (page 175)

1 Letter to Chickens' Lib supporter from the Health Education Authority, dated September 27th 1990
2 Threlfall, E.J., *et al.*, 'Multiple drug-resistant strains of Salmonella typhimurium in poultry' *Veterinary Record* 1989 124(20): 538
3 The Welfare of Animals at Markets Order, 1990

Antibiotics – propping up a sick industry (page 185)

1 Maple, Hamilton-Miller, Brumfitt, 'World-wide antibiotic resistance in methicillin-resistant Staphylococcus aureus' Department of Medical Microbiology, Royal Free Hospital School of Medicine, London. *The Lancet* Vol 1 March 11th 1989
2 The Swann Report, chapter V, 8.9
3 'Antibiotic resistance in Salmonella' *Veterinary Record* Vol 117 No. 14 October 5th 1985
4 *The Guardian* November 13th 1998
5 *The Guardian* May 24th 1997

6   Letter to *The Lancet*, Vol 335, p 1459 from the departments of Medical Microbiology and Microbiology in Birmingham and Manchester's Monsall hospital.

7   The Lancet, Vol 336, p125 July 14th 1990

8   J.M. Rutter, Veterinary Medicines Directive, Weybridge, Surrey. Letter to Veterinary Record dated March 30th 1991

9   *A Review of Antimicrobial Resistance in the Food Chain, 5.1.2.3.Pigs* MAFF July 1998

10   Letter to Chickens' Lib dated March 15th 2001 from Public Information Specialist, FDA, Center for Veterinary Medicine, USA

11   www.vmd.gov.uk/Publications/Antibiotics/salesanti09.pdf

12   A Review of Antimicrobial Resistance in the Food Chain, July 1998 – A Technical Report for MAFF p. 52, 4.4

Ducks on dry land (page 194)

1   Codes of Recommendations for the Welfare of Ducks, MAFF 1987. Introduction, 1.

2   Ibid para. 36 a

3   FAWN/Viva! *Ducks out of Water* pp 9-10 www.viva.org.uk

4   Gregory, N.G. & Wilkins, L.J., 'Effect of stunning current on downgrading in ducks', *British Poultry Science* 31: 429-431 1990

5   Raj, A.B., Richardson, R.I., Wilkins, L.J., Wotton, S.B., 'Carcase and meat quality in ducks killed with either gas mixture or an electric current under commercial processing conditions', Division of Food Animal Science, University of Bristol, England. *British Poultry Science* 1998, 404-407

6   *Ibid*

7   Letter to FAWN from MAFF, September 23rd 1999

8   As 3

9   Jones, T.A., Waitt, C.D., Dawkins, M.S., (2009) Water off a duck's back *Applied Animal Behaviour Science* 116 (1), 52-57

10   'Access to water – without all the mess' *Poultry World* September 2009

11   Gentle, M.J., Tilston, V.L., (2000) 'Nociceptors in the legs of poultry: implications for potential pain in pre-slaughter shackling', *Animal Welfare*, 9: 3, 227-236

The world's largest flightless bird (page 203)

1   *State Veterinary Journal* April 1992 Vol. 2, No. 1
2   DJvZ Smit, 'Ostrich Farming in the Little Karoo' Bulletin no. 358 *Die Staatsdrukker*, Pretoria
3   Clive Madeiros, reported in *Veterinary Record*, October 15th 1994
4   *Improving Our Understanding of Ratites in a Farming Environment.* Proceedings of an international conference held in Manchester 27th-29th March 1996 ISBN 0 952758 0 7 p 50
5   Ibid
6   Ibid
7   Ibid
8   Ibid
9   Ibid
10 *World Poultry* – Misset Vol 12, no 1, 96 p9
11 www.worldpoultry.net//ostrich-farming-in-germany–an-animal-welfare-issue-id6676.html
12 Baird, G.J., et al., 'Monensin toxicity in a flock of ostriches', *Veterinary Record* 1997, 140: 624-626
13 Minka and Ayo, 'Assessment of the stresses imposed on adult ostriches (struthio camelus) during handling, loading, transportation and unloading', *Veterinary Record* Vol 162 pp. 846-851
14 *Animal Voice* Compassion in World Farming (SA) Summer/Autumn 1994 No 115
15 *Ostrich News*, winter 1994, vol.111 No.4 pp 11-12
16 Council Regulations 1099/2009

Turkeys again, and a cool reception (page 212)

1   *Poultry World* March 1992

Scientists prove suffering (page 214)

1   Dr S R Duff *et al.*, 'The Gross Morphology of Skeletal Disease in Adult Male Breeding Turkeys' (1987) *Avian Pathology* 16: 635-651
2   Duncan, I.J.H. *et al.*, (1991) 'Assessment of Pain Associated with Degenerative Hip Disorders in Adult Male Turkeys', *Research in Veterinary Science*, 50:200-203)
3   www.but.co.uk
4   *Turkeys* June 1992, p 16

FAWC looks at turkeys (page 215)

1   FAWC 1995 Report on the Welfare of Turkeys para. 1
2   Ibid
3   Ibid para 16 (v)
4   Ibid para 16 (ii)
5   Ibid para 39
6   The Veterinary Surgery (Exemptions) Order 1962 No. 2557 4c
7   MAFF Code of Recommendations for the Welfare of Turkeys 1.3
8   See (1) para 129

Catching the birds (page 218)

1   www.hillside.org.uk/documents/Turkeypages.pdf
2   Ibid
See also www.hillside.org.uk/about-investigations.htm

The sporting life (page 221)

1   *FAWC Opinion on the Welfare of Farmed Game birds*, November 2008
2   *Veterinary Record*, 2007, Vol. 161, 5, 152
3   FAWN's submission to FAWC
4   *Egg Production and Incubation,* chapter 3, Game Conservancy 1993
5   *Gamebird Rearing*, chapter 8, Game Conservancy 1990
6   SAC Monthly Report September 2007 Game birds
7   *Gamebird Rearing*, chapter 4, Game Conservancy 1990
8   *Gamebird Rearing*, chapter 8, Game Conservancy 1990
9   Ibid
10 *Gamebird Releasing*, chapter 4, Game Conservancy 1991
11 *Veterinary Record*, 2001 vol. 149: 10, 287
12 *Gamebird Releasing*, chapter 4, Game Conservancy 1991
13 *Gamebird Releasing*, chapter 8, Game Conservancy 1991
14 As (4)
15 Ibid, chapter 2
16 VLA Surveillance Report *Veterinary Record* 2009;165: 585-588
17 *The People* November 20th 1994
18 *Assault and Battery* Animal Aid September 2005 p24
19 Ibid p 22 See also www.animalaid.org.uk
20 See 18 (Part 3)

21 www.gundogsupply.com

22 *Veterinary Record* 2003 vol. 153, Number 15 p452

23 *Veterinary Record* 2001, Vol 149, Number 10 , p 287

24 *Veterinary Record* June 6th 1998

25 *The Lancet* 1990, Vol 336, 125

26 www.basc.org.uk

27 *The Guardian* February 10th 2005

28 FAWC *Opinion on the Welfare of Farmed Game birds* November 2008

29 Ibid para 55

30 Ibid para 50

31 Ibid para 51

32 Ibid para 42

33 Ibid para 47

34 www.gwct.org.uk

35 Butler, D.A. and Davis, C., 'Effects of Plastic Bits on the Condition and Behaviour of Captive-reared pheasants', *Veterinary Record* 2010 Vol 166, 398-401

Chickens' Lib to Farm Animal Welfare Network (page 237)

1 R.H. Bradshaw *et al.*, 'Travel Sickness and Meat Quality in Pigs' *Animal Welfare* Vol 8 No 1, February 1999 pp 3-14, Universities Federation of Animal Welfare

2 Rosamund Young, *The Secret Life Of Cows*, Farming Books and Videos Ltd, 2003

3 Keith M. Kendrick *et al.*, *Nature* Vol 414 November 2001, Laboratory of Cognitive and Developmental Neuroscience, Babraham Institute, Cambridge, CB2 4AT UK

4 A.C.A.Clements *et al.*, 'Reporting on Sheep Lameness Conditions to Veterinarians in the Scottish Borders', *Veterinary Record* June 29th 2002 150, 815-817

5 *Highland News* March 30th 2002

6 www.hillside.org.uk also see www.onekind.org

McLibel – the best free show in town (page 255)
1   *McLibel – Burger Culture on Trial.* John Vidal , Macmillan 1997 and the DVD *McLibel: The postman and the gardener who took on McDonald's* Spanner Films
2   www.mcspotlight.org
3   As (1) p 175
4   www.mcdonalds.co.uk
5   www.dailymail.co.uk/news/article-1288903/McDonalds-faces-Happy-Meals June 24th 2010

The battery cage ban at last? (page 265)
Council Directive 1999/74/EC Article 5, 2

Violet Spalding (page 267)
House of Commons First Report from the Agriculture Committee Session 1980-81 para 150

Enriched cages – a gaping loophole (page 269)
1   Duncan and Hughes, 1972
2   FAWC *Opinion on Osteoporosis and Bone Fractures in Laying Hens* December 2010 para 60
3   Ibid para 45
4   Council Directive 1999/74/EC Chapter 111, 1c
5   FAWC information adapted from Workpackage 7.1, Laywel, 2006
6   Gentle, M., 'Aetiology of food-related oral lesions in chickens' Research in *Veterinary Science* March 1986, 40 (2) 219-224
7   Morris, Desmond, 'Opinion´ *Sunday Telegraph* May 23rd 1982
8   www.ciwf.org.uk
9   *The People* May 27th 2012
10 Press Release from The Humane society of the United States, May 24th 2012 *Senate Bill Introduced to Improve Housing for Egg-Laying Hens and Provide Stable Future for Egg Farmers*
11 Davis, Karen, 'Agreement Raises Flags for Egg-Laying Hens' *Poultry Press* 22.1 (Spring-Summer 2012)
12 www.unitedegg.org

Outlawed in Europe (page 277)

1   Peter Singer's Preface to *Outlawed in Europe – How America is Falling Behind Europe in Farm Animal Welfare* Clare Druce and Philip Lymbery Archimedian Press, New York 2002. A project of Animal Rights International

2   Ibid back cover

3   *The Welfare of Farmed Animals (England) Regulations 2007* Schedule 6, 1 (3)

MAFF to DEFRA (page 279)

1   The Truffler: 'MAFF is dead, long live DEFRA' *The Independent*, June 16th 2001

The risks we take (page 279)

1   Dr Mohammad Yousaf, Department of Animal Husbandry, University of Agriculture, Faisalabad, Pakistan. 'Avian Influenza hits the industry again', *World Poultry*, Vol 20, No 3, 2004

2   www.animalaid.org.uk

3   www.worldpoultry.net/news/avian-influenza-still-a-threat-says-who-7254.html 24th March 2010

Legislation for broilers (page 284)

1   *Report on the Welfare of Broiler Chickens* Farm Animal Welfare Council, para 19, April 1992

2   http://ec.europa.eu/food/animal/welfare/farm

A question of survival (page 288)

1   www.TheLancet.com/series/health-and-climate-change

2   United Nations' Food and Agriculture Organisation (FAO) Rome, 2006

3   DEFRA statistic 2006

4   *The Ecologist* April 28th 2010

5   www.waterfootprint.org

6   Ehrlich, Paul, *et al., Ecoscience: Population, Resources, Environment,* San Francisco: Freeman, 1977, 315; Pimental *et al.,* 'Energy and Land Constraints in Food Protein Production' *Science,* Issue 190

7 *Scientists turn pig stem cells into test-tube pork* Maria Ching www.statesman.com/news/world/scientists-turn-pig-cells-into-test-tubes-196959.html March 15th 2011
8 Ibid
9 www.quorn.co.uk

Straight talking (page 292)
1 Farm Animal Welfare Council's 2010 *Opinion on Osteoporosis and Bone Fractures in Laying Hens* para 3
2 Ibid para 4
3 Ibid para 5
4 Ibid para 7
5 Ibid para 11
6 Ibid
7 Ibid para 15
8 Ibid para 19
9 Ibid para 27
10 Ibid para 29
11 Ibid para 33
12 Ibid para 34
13 Ibid para 35
14 Ibid para 20

So where's the progress, after all these years? (294)
1 The Welfare of Animals (Slaughter and killing) Regulations 1995 No. 731
2 Letter to CL/FAWN from DEFRA's Customer contact Unit, dated June 18th 2010
3 The Co-operative's Animal Welfare Policy on Chickens and Eggs statement, in a letter to FAWN dated Novemer 12th 2000
4 www.hubbardbreeders.com
5 Duff, R.I. *et al.,* 'Head Swelling of Traumatic Origin in Broiler Breeding Fowl', *Veterinary Record*, August 5th 1989
6 Email to Jeremy Hall of Bernard Matthews from FAWN, dated December 6th 2010.
7 www.woodlandeggs.co.uk
8 www.woodlandtrust.org.uk

9   Email to CL/FAWN from Noble Foods dated November 1st 2010
10   www.goldenlay.co.uk
11   FAWC *Report on the Welfare of Farmed Animals at Slaughter or Killing Part 2: White Meat Animals*, 2009, para 118
12   www.animalaid.org.uk/h/n/CAMPAIGNS/slaughter/ALL

The Crown Prosecution Service (page 300)

1   Animal Aid, *Outrage* Issue 167, Summer 2012
2   Ibid
3   *Farmers Guardian* August 9th 2011
4   *CPS News Brief* March 30th 2012
5   See Animal Aid www.animalaid.org.uk Timeline, 30th November 2011

Significant progress in legislation (page 302)

1   Animal Welfare Act 2006, Chapter 45, **4,** a-d
2   Ibid, **9,** (2) a-e
3   Ibid (c)

Why necessary suffering? (page 305)

1   QBD, 3 April 1985 (Stephen Brown LJ, Stocker J) (unreported). Source: Rook, Debbie, 'The Legality of factory farming under UK law', *Journal of Animal Welfare Law* June 2007
2   (1889) 23 QBD 203 Source as (1)
3   Source as (1)
4   Source as (1)
5   Treaty on the Functioning of the European Union,. http://eur-lex.europa.eu/LexUriServ/LexUriServ.do?uri=OJ:C:2010:083:0047:0200:en:PDF
6   Article 13, Treaty on the Functioning of the European Union
7   http://ec.europa.eu/food/animal/welfare/policy/index en.htm
8   Council Directive 98/58/EC of 20 July 1998 concerning the protection of animals kept for farming purposes. Official Journal L221, 08.08.1998 p. 0023-0027. http://eur-lex.europa.eu/LexUriServ/LexUriServ.do?uri=CONSLEG:1998L0058:20030605:EN:PDF
9   Article 3 of Council Directive 98/58/EC (see 8)
10   Paragraph 7 of the Annex to Council Directive 98/58/EC (see 8)

INDEX

BROILER (MEAT TYPE) CHICKENS
  baby birds 122
  baby foods 264-5
  bacteria in stored litter 144
  battery cages for broilers 124
  botulism in cattle, from chicken
    litter 139-143
  breeders 151-7
  British Poultry Meat Federation 153
  Bristol School of Veterinary Science
    138-9, 256
  deformed birds 122
  hock burns 136
  leg disorders 119, 138
  lifestyle 120-121
  litter contamination 140-143
  Ibid, in the US 144
  litter contamination in the US 144
  MAFF booklet 115
  ulcerated feet 136
BROILER CHICKEN BREEDING
  STOCK
  breeding birds 6, 154
  elite stock 154
  export of, 6
  'healthy lives' claimed Peel Holroyd
    153
  High Court judgement 305
  hunger 'dilemma' 151-5
  swollen head syndrome 153-4
Blanc, Raymond 283-4
Bower, Joanne 5
Boyo 175
Bradnock, Peter 200
Brambell Inquiry 83
British Domesticated Ostrich
  Association 205
British Fields Sports Society 227-8
British Poultry Council, duck research
  200

Brown, Henry 159-160
BSE 37, 181
Bryant, John 62
Bury St Edmunds MAFF/DEFRA 245

C
Campylobacter 147-9
Catching the birds 219, 251-2,
  in enriched cages 271
CCTV cameras 298-9
Chan, Margaret WHO 192
Cheale Meats 300-302
Chelford market 175-6, 180
Cherry Valley 194-6, 200-202
Chesterfield A&E 101
'Chicken Teddies' 264-5
Chickens' feet, export trade 139
Chickens' Lib membership 55
Chickens intelligence 43-5
Chicks (male) destroyed at day one
  160-161
Church of England 45-51
CJD 37
Clegg, Dave 103
Cobb Breeders 152
Co-op supermarket 58, 295
Compassion in World Farming 51,
  136, 203, 295
Condemned meat on sale 149
Convent of Our Lady of the Passion
  29-31, 33-8
Council of Europe Convention for
  farmed animals 84
Council of Europe convention 84-5
Countryman's Weekly 236
Cow and Gate 264
Crown Prosecution Service 300
Cultured meat 291
Currie, Edwina 34

Partial beak amputation (PBA)
106-112
of game birds 223-4
hot blade method 108
infra-red method 110-111
of turkeys 109
Patrons 99
Pattison, Mark 256
Perkins, Penny 57, 268
PIGS
filming of 51, 251
'intelligent and lovely' 50
living in squalor 51
Runcie, Lord re pig welfare Bill 49
Police 32, 56, 80-82, 85-6, 193-4, 281-2
Post mortem certificates 7, 123-4
Poultry Science Association 110
Prince Charles 226-8
Prosecutions 64, 98, 250, 305, 308
Punch 32, 75

Q
QUAIL
ADAS *Quail Production* document
125
injuries 127
major producer Fayre Game 127-131
Queen, the
and Goldenlay 76-78, 88-89
Royal Household 88
Royal nursery 88
Silver Jubilee and Chickens' Lib 1
Queensland Animal Liberation
Movement 43
Quorn 291

R
Rampton, Richard QC 258-9
Raymond, Ernest 4
Rees, Martin on vegetarian diet 290
Roberts, Peter (CIWF) 40, 62, 278, 305

Roberts *v* Ruggiero 305
Robinson, Mark 268
Rogers, Lesley 44
Rook, Debbie 305-6
Roslin Institute re Chickens' Lib's fact
sheets 57
Ross Breeders 152
on broiler breeders 151
Royal Society for the Protection of
Birds 225
RSPCA 21, 41, 68-71, 85, 90, 94-5, 98,
102-3, 105, 308
Ryder, Richard D, 90

S
Salmonella 34, 146-7
in turkeys 147
Schumacher, Fritz 20
Scottish Egg Producer Retailers
Association 59, 90
Secret filming in abattoir 299
Filming in EU and UK pig units
51
Selection for fast growth 120
Sentamu, Archbishop of York 50
Shackling, pain at 293, 295, 298
SHEEP
intelligence 242
welfare problems 242-4
Shippam, Ernest 5
Singer, Peter 277-8
Slaughter
broiler chickens 115-9
electrified water bath method 115
emergency 37
ducks 198
male chicks 160-161
pre-stun shocks 256
scalding tank
spent hens 40, 264
Slave ships 29

Slave trade 308
Smith, K-Lynn, on chicken intelligence 44
Soil Association 297, 299
South Africa 166-8, 211
Spratt, Brian 188
Spencer, Colin 95
Spent hens 40
Stacey, Glenys 253
St Andrew's Fund 93
Starmer, Keir 255
'Starry supporters' 99-100
State Veterinary Service (see also Animal Health) 253
Steel, Helen 254, 305
Stevenson, Peter, document on legislation 306-7
Stobo, Thomas Whyte 252, 301
Strang, Gavin 18
Stress in game birds 224
Sun Valley, rè McDonalds 256-7
Swann Committee and Report 186-8
'Swastika' feet 122-3

T
'Throwaway hen' 24-5
Thrush, Tony 92-3
Trading Standards song 79
Treaty of Amsterdam 295
Tree cover for chickens 297
Tumours 96
Tuomisto, Hanna 291
TURKEYS
  facts 172, 295
  heavy turkey competition 173-4
  hip degeneration 214-5
  insemination of females 174-5
  lifespan 172
  males' sexual frustration 178
  personalities 177

salmonella in, 147
thirteen strains of drug-resistant Salmonella typhimurium 179
turkeys 'enjoy' artificial insemination 174
turkey conference 212-14
'Turkey Twizzlers' 179

U
Unigate broiler farms 141-2
United Nations' Food and Agriculture Organisation 289
US enriched cages legislation 275-7

V
'Vacuum' dust bathing 41-2
Valentine, Wendy, first contact with 244
Veterinary Laboratory Agencies (VLA) 142-3, 221
Veterinary Record re game birds 221
Vets, not helpful 105
Viva! 198-9

W
Waitrose pork 51
Wall Street Journal 65
Water
  global scarcity of, 290
  more used in meat-based diet 290-291
Wathes, Christopher 304
Webster, John 66, 242, 285
Williams, Irene 55-6, 268
Workforce, reduced 20
World Health Organisation 192

Y
York Minster 263
Young, Rosamund 238-9

ACKNOWLEDGEMENTS

With warm thanks to Bluemoose Books for offering to publish my book; for understanding that it's about issues we ignore at our peril.

Thanks to my editor Lin Webb for her eagle-eyed work on the ms, and for her good company. Thanks to Kathryn Harrison too for her enthusiasm and careful proofing.

With thanks to Duncan who never once complained about Chickens' Lib taking over family life. And to Alison and Emily, who as children willingly helped with the campaign and still live by its beliefs.

With thanks to Chickens' Lib's innumerable helpers, who ranged from students who spent a day in our office at mail-out time, to 'regulars' who helped us over the years. And to the hundreds of activists who so often spared time to make our demonstrations a success. We were hugely grateful to them all.

With thanks for the invaluable help of Irene Williams and Penny Perkins.

And thanks to Jüri Gabriel, whose good advice helped me greatly.

With thanks to Joyce D'Silva, Mark Gold, Philip Lymbery, Richard Ryder, Peter Singer, Peter Stevenson and Andrew Tyler: all of whom have been ready to offer encouragement to, and share information with, Chickens' Lib. And to Richard Young for advice and for his tireless work within the Soil Association, exposing the dangers from the over-use of antibiotics. And many sincere apologies to all the great people I've somehow failed to list.

Thanks too to those honest scientists who willingly advised Chickens' Lib. And to the Church of England bishops, the MPs, the MEPs and all the VIPs who supported our campaigns.

In fact a huge 'thank you' to everyone who supported Chickens' Lib, here in the UK and worldwide. Without you, our campaign would have been nothing.

And finally a loving tribute to all the cruelly-treated farmed animals, observed or rescued by Chickens' Lib, from whom we learned so much.